D0992136

Management Philosophy

Springer
Berlin
Heidelberg
New York
Barcelona
Hong Kong
London
Milan
Paris
Singapore
Tokyo

Ole Fogh Kirkeby

Management Philosophy

A Radical-Normative Perspective

With 2 Figures

 Springer

658
K 59 m

Prof. Dr. Phil. Ole Fogh Kirkeby
Thorvaldsensvej 27, II
1871 Frederiksberg, C
Copenhagen
Denmark

Originally published by Samfundslitteratur, Frederiksberg,
Denmark, 1998, ISBN 87-593-0682-3
The Danish title is: Ledelsesfilosofi – et radikalt normativt perspektiv

ISBN 3-540-66892-6 Springer-Verlag Berlin Heidelberg New York

Library of Congress Cataloging-in-Publication Data
Die Deutsche Bibliothek – CIP-Einheitsaufnahme
Kirkeby, Ole Fogh: Management philosophy: a radical-normative perspective /
Ole Fogh Kirkeby. – Berlin; Heidelberg; New York; Barcelona; Hong Kong;
London; Milan; Paris; Singapore; Tokyo: Springer, 2000
    ISBN 3-540-66892-6

This work is subject to copyright. All rights are reserved, whether the whole
or part of the material is concerned, specifically the rights of translation, re-
printing, reuse of illustrations, recitation, broadcasting, reproduction on mi-
crofilm or in any other way, and storage in data banks. Duplication of this
publication or parts thereof is permitted only under the provisions of the
German Copyright Law of September 9, 1965 in its current version, and per-
mission for use must always be obtained from Springer-Verlag. Violations are
liable for prosecution under the German Copyright Law.

Springer-Verlag is a company in the specialist publishing group
BertelsmannSpringer
© Springer-Verlag Berlin · Heidelberg 2000
Printed in Germany

The use of general descriptive names, registered names, trademarks, etc. in
this publication does not imply, even in the absence of a specific statement,
that such names are exempt from the relevant protective laws and regulations
and therefore free for general use.

Hardcover-Design: Erich Kirchner, Heidelberg

SPIN 10724787   42/2202-5 4 3 2 1 0 – Printed on acid-free paper

call

> *"Whosoever can be taught to be a man of honour,*
> *to him a word is as a blow."*

Walter von der Vogelweide (c.1200)

> *"ou gar pou egōge technēs tinos tou legein metochos"*
> *(at any rate, I possess no art of speaking)*

Socrates: Phaedrus, 262D

University Libraries
Carnegie Mellon University
Pittsburgh, PA 15213-3890

Preface

This book is a philosophical treatise on management. It is not an attempt at constructing an intermediary world between the two areas. On the contrary, its aim is to show that only philosophy can transform management so as to reveal its inner core: Leadership. Hence, it does not present a "philosophy of management", but it is management turned in upon itself as the genuine human practice which it is, in order to liberate itself.

Thus, if anything, it has to be a philosophy of Leadership. From this perspective the book is an attempt at drawing the contours of a leadership committed uncompromisingly to the absolute. I have almost no sympathy for all the recent attempts at making management "spiritual", of transforming it into a project of all the mixtures of "self-": self-management, self-realization, self-worship ... Towards the new area of "value-based" management, or "business ethics", I have many reservations as well. We cannot dispense with postmodern experience in any other way than through the attempt to overcome it on its own premisses: the rule of contingency, the problematic of any notion of an ego and a "self", the construction of experience through language games, or as Michel Foucault named it, following Friedrich Nietzsche, "jeux de verité", "games of truth", games of certainty. But postmodernism has to be defeated, because no matter how right its diagnosis of our predicament might be, its conceptualization through the many metaphors of "constructionism", when all is said and done, is wrong.

No doubt, the extensive use of Greek terminology in this book might put off readers not well acquainted with philosophical terminology, however, the use is very well motivated:

Firstly most of the Greek concepts have been translated into Latin during the Roman era (many by Cicero, actually), and are in this form a common part of our European linguistic heritage. Words like "official" and "habit" are based on translations from the Greek "kathēkon", and "hexis", to the Latin "officium" and "habitus", but their common significance is rather misleading. Wrong connotations, even "wrong" paradigms, are invoked. Returning to the Greek terms almost makes a fresh start possible, by escaping these undesirable implications.

Secondly, the Greek social and mental reality is able to furnish us with knowledge of another and hitherto still unreflected experience, already emphasized by the hermeneutic-phenomenologial tradition identified with the names of Martin Heidegger and Hans-Georg Gadamer. Behind the social bond among the free Greek citizens and behind their fabulous ability of conceptualization, experiences of acting, thinking and feeling lay waiting for us. This is especially important with regard to Plato, Aristotle, and the Stoic tradition. These experiences relate to a knowledge of how the good life, the life led by a claim to authenticity, has to be lived. A life always centrered around the community, not the individual.

Thirdly, Greek culture had an interrelationship with nature characterized by reverence, an attitude very far from the one nurtured by modern science and technology; but this attitude needs to be more and more cultivated during an era of devotion to sustainability and ecological passion.

Thus, the virtues of management and leadership so important to this book have to be rendered in their Greek garments too. In this way a careful and protective attitude towards humanity could be preserved, safely distant from the negligent obsessions of strategy and pragmaticism. However, the hermeneutical challenge to philosophy is immense in interpreting these Greek concepts, because they themselves are the originators of the concepts or figures of thought through which they are now, once more, blown into life. So, as mirrors to our reality, it is difficult not to blur them by our own breath.

The key concepts of the book are Aristotle's: **pragma, hexis**, and **event**. These constitute the way of acting and the human character from which, when shaped in the right way, the virtues of leadership follow almost automatically. But praxis and personality only make sense as phenomena realized in the event. The identity of the event forms the arena in which the content of the right actions and of the right attitudes is created.

However, this book does not deal with ethics in a way common within philosophy. It sketches out another way of conceiving values, opposed to the cognitive tradition, and also the reverse of utilitarianism, and even deontology.

The book refers extensively to recent literature on management and organizations, but it does not collect its critique in separate sections or sum it up. Rather it lets it be an implication of its own discourse. So, it is left to the reader to accomplish this severe criticism of modern theories of management.

Important to the project of which this book is a manifestation is the attempt at conceptualizing a radical concept of normativity, a concept through which any – no matter how subtle – strategic intentionality can be detected and rejected. This means that values can be approached only as virtues, as the unity of thought and desire within the pattern of human action, and in the reflections thereof.

This is expressed through the distinction between management and leadership, and though the suggestion of the virtues of management and leadership. The leader's ability to be an example is of immense importance here.

The book draws heavily of the phenomenological philosophy which I have developed during the last ten years, and which eventually has come to be known as a "Radical phenomenology". This means that it has the conditions in common with critical theory that it has to use the concept in order to lead it to its limit. However, in this it also has something in common with poetry. It evokes the unsaid from an awareness of the limits of language, and hence, of cognition, and it nurtures the metaphor consciously, finally abandoning it in the face of Otherness.

Philosophical inspirations have been, besides Plato, Aristotle and the Stoics, Immanuel Kant, Søren Kierkegaard, Martin Heidegger, Maurice Merleau-Ponty, Ludwig Wittgenstein, and Gilles Deleuze.

The starting point of this whole venture was to create a discourse on Management and Leadership that takes philosophy seriously. So, this book should be seen as an attempt to draw business science into the world of philosophy, not to make a popular treatment of strategic management and organizational theory by way of philosophy. This, of course, shall make special demands upon the style. My choice has been to use a style that attempts to juxtapose an almost poetic prose with a more prosaic, analytical style. Both are needed by the overall normative perspective where the concept is drawn to its limit, transforming itself into its original fulcrum, the metaphor. Thus, the style is nurtured deliberately as a hybrid, combining genuine philosophical passages with a prosaic treatment of the ways of business life, mixing abstract philosophical argument with historical knowledge and current example. As such, the book might still be seen stylistically as a work of postmodernism, even if, due to its philosophical content, it tries to shake off this very legacy.

A Short Introduction to Some Key Concepts

The core idea of this book is that values can only be approached as virtues. This implies that values can only be exemplified, they can never be defined analytically. The person is the essence of virtue. Thus, the borderline of talking about values shall always be a person's ability to legitimize his own actions. Often this is done by a reference to universal, "ethical" values. However, in a concrete case it is very difficult to prove that an act is the necessary consequence of the implication of such a value or norm. Life consists of events, and events are complicated and hard to identify when one finds oneself within them. Every event presents a limit to our knowledge of it, just as a person's knowledge of himself reaches a limit. Invoking values as the guiding principles of one's action often comes up to referring to one's way of living, to one's character, to one's upbringing, and here it becomes obvious that there is an important momentum of chance at play. Of course, virtue is the result of our own conscious effort, but it demands more than that. A borderline presents itself here that is connected to the secret of personal identity.

But from another angle too, we encounter a borderline, because it is impossible to state when a universal virtue is fulfilled.

The meaning of values are bound to the event, to time and place. The complexities embedded within the event might reveal a deeper content of even canonical, universal values, than we have hitherto believed to be the case..

The concept of "virtue" reveals that: we agree on the difficulty of deciding which person is the most virtuos, but we seem to try to compare values in a much more firm way.

This notion of a borderline, concerning values, virtues and personal identity, points to the transcendence of these concepts. They cannot be fixed. I shall try to illustrate this through the concept of "The Fourth".

Communication can be illustrated as a relation between two persons. However, a third person can be thought of as the silent wittness to their conversation, and hence, symbolically as their consciousness. Traditionally, we place our sense of values and norms inside this "Third", even if we might project this being into the heaven. The Fourth, on the other hand, is a horizon of knowledge, emotion and action that cannot be identified with our values or norms, not even the universal ones. The Fourth can never be transgressed by thought, but presents itself as the absolute to which we tacitly appeal when we relate to these dimensions of life. The absolute as a bordeline of knowledge, action and emotion, toward which virtue aspire, is called **Radical Normativity** in this book. As far as virtue is important to a Leadership that differs from Management, Radical Normativity is important to Leadership too.

Real Leadership then, is a way to act that must be understood as a genuine and general human phenomenon before it is filtrated through the perspectives of managerial functioning. This implies very strong demands upon the leader, demands upon his personal integrity and to his sense of virtue. He must be aware of his duty towards individuals and society; for him there can be no easy road to compromise.

This point is emphasized by a distinction between the ideal types of Management and Leadership. The ideal type of the manager is characterized by an asymmetrical relation. Being the subject the manager is only confronted with an object, the employee. It is impossible for the employee to become a subject (the manager) and for the subject to become an object.

The ideal type of the leader can be made conceptually manifest through a model where subject confronts subject. This relation is symmetrical, because insofar as the subject, functioning as a leader, might have a surplus within the fields of power, knowledge, or information, then this can be said to be "granted" to him by the employee. In this symmetrical relation the employee can be named "the co-lead", or the "co-directed". The prefix "co-" emphasizes the reciprocal concept of duty lying behind the subject-subject relation. The genuine image of the subject-subject relation would be friendship, and hence the ideal of real leadership.

The problem faced by this book is not least the fact that the manager is the unhappy victim of capitalism's long and enduring war against labour. Now the warrior needs his enemy. The manager has come to know this, and as a leader he has to admit to it. He must acknowledge the irrationality of capitalism in relation to the optimum utilization of the potentials of labour. But he must not pretend. As a leader he must not feign humanism when the real question is about the optimum evaluation of "human capital". He must refuse the rhetorical temptation to make cost-benefit analysis appear as the considerations of ethical endeavors.

Social competencies in a normative setting have often been called "virtues" in Western Culture, at least when individual, ethical autonomy, and self-assurance, were emphasized. The alternative is "duties". But this concept, originating in Stoic philosophy, must be understood on the basis of the fundamental analysis of "virtue" from an epistemological and ontological point of view. In this book we must, little by little, close the ring around this concept of "leader-virtue", trying to be fair in giving equal influence to the general human aspect of virtues, and to its specific connection to managerial functions. The sad fact is that there are circumstances under which even a leader is forced to act in a way inconsistent with the code settled upon by communities based on trust and mutual knowledge.

It is the burden of the leader to be split between the considerations of human rationality and capitalist rationality; to be split between the considerations of stakeholder rationality and the considerations of the needs of the individual and of the public, between the realms of God and the emperor.

In this book I shall present six virtues. I have tried to anticipate their necessity at the analytical level. They combine the functional demands to management and absolute normativity. They bring these two different worlds into contact, but they do not pretend that their inherent opposition can be cancelled except on very rare occasions. These six virtues must be seen as a grand hypothesis of leadership, and as a suggestion of how to read one's own experience within the perspective that managerial and leadership practice are subject to the right of human integrity.

A short remark about the greek quotations: I use no accentuation marks, but only emphasize "eta" and "omega". I copy the short diphthongs directly from the greek spelling: "oi", "ou", ..., e.g., "haplous", "simple".

Acknowledgements

I want to thank especially two people, although I ought to thank quite a few. I want to thank professor Per Oluf Berg, Copenhagen Business School, for encouraging me to write this book and for inspiring me in relation to its conceptual framework. And I want to thank Gustav Peebles for an excellent revision which helped to widen the field of possible readers of this book.

Table of Contents

Part I

Management or Leadership   *1*

Chapter 1. Management and Radical Normativity   *3*
    1.1. Management and Philosophy   *4*
    1.2. The Paradigmatic Connection   *9*

Chapter 2. The Radical, Methodological and Normative   *17*
    Perspectives
    2.1. The Radical, Methodological Perspective: *17*
    What Words Cannot Do
    2.2. The Radical, Normative Perspective   *25*

Chapter 3. Leader or Manager   *31*
    3.1. The Ideal Type of Management   *39*
    3.2. The Ideal Type of Leadership   *44*

Chapter 4. To Make the Stakeholder-model Radical: *57*
    Leadership as Communication, or The Fourth

Chapter 5. Of the Concept of Leading   *71*

Chapter 6. Management, Innovation and Cooperation   *79*
    6.1. The Origin of the Capitalist Production Process   *79*
    6.2. Cooperation and Innovation   *87*
    6.3. Innovation: The Dilemma of Management   *93*
    6.4. Some Aspects of an Idea of Ideal Cooperation   *96*
    6.5. "Technology of Knowledge": Knowledge from the   *106*
    Point of View of Management Philosophy
    6.6. To Re-create Cooperation: Subcontracting as   *110*
    a Necessity

Part II

Dialogue or Metalogue   *121*

Chapter 7. The Machine of Dialogue versus the Organic,   *123*
           Inner Monologue

     7.1. Of Bodies and Voices   *127*
     7.2. The Principle of Translocutionarity   *134*
     7.3. The Illusion of Representation   *141*
     7.4. Further Epistemological Consequences   *142*
     7.5. But What about Dialogue, Then?   *145*
           And Management via It?
     7.6. Will and Desire: To Get in and out   *149*
           of the Dialogue, Safely
     7.7. Irony and Dialogue   *150*
     7.8. The High Hopes of Dialogue   *156*

Part III

The Virtues of Leadership   *161*

Chapter 8. Praxis and Hexis   *163*

     8.1. The Concept of Praxis   *164*
     8.2. Learning   *169*
     8.3. Hexis   *172*
     8.4. Universal versus Professional Virtues   *177*

Chapter 9. The Virtues of Management and Leadership   *181*

9.1. Katorthōma and Kathēkon   *198*

Part IV

Space and Time in Management   *201*

Chapter 10. The Space of Management and Leadership   *203*

　　　　　　10.1. Chōra   *205*

Chapter 11. The Time of Management and Leadership   *215*

　　　　　　11.1. The Concept of Influence   *217*
　　　　　　11.2. What It Means to Be Inside or Outside an Event   *220*
　　　　　　11.3. The Problem of the Ontology of the Event   *223*
　　　　　　11.4. Kairos   *227*
　　　　　　11.5. Kairology   *232*

Chapter 12. The Drama of Decisions. The Theatre as a Metaphor   *239*
　　　　　　of the Union of Time and Place: The Play of Fate

Chapter 13. The Myth and the Saga   *247*

Chapter 14. The Narrative: The Theatre of Memory and   *251*
　　　　　　the Aesthetic Energy of Management and Leadership

Bibliography   *261*

Index   *271*

Part I

Management or Leadership

CHAPTER 1

Management and Radical Normativity

The idea of this book is to contribute an array of perspectives on what management and leadership might possibly be to the running debates within business economics. The light cast by these perspectives emanates from the conception of management as first and foremost a common human phenomenon. Management and hence leadership are roles peculiar to social interrelations prior to their existence as phenomena studied by business economics. They can only be fully studied, interpreted, and understood through the optics posed by the concept of **radical normativity**. By **Radical Normativity** is meant the ability of a person to relate, in thought, emotion and action, to the "absolute". Until the next chapter where this concept is analyzed thoroughly we must be content with a definition of "the absolute" as something that cannot be fully comprehended by experience, that cannot be put sufficiently into words, and that, hence, cannot be conceptualized or made into universal values or maxisms.

From this stance the book is an expression of the sensation of a general lack of this radical normativity as a platform within business economics when management versus leadership are discussed. Radical normativity is too often absent when managerial roles and the phenomenon of management generally are dealt with.

This does not mean that normative problems are shunned in business economics today. Quite the opposite is the case. The research program "value-based management", and the different strategies of "business ethics", "ethical accounting", "responsibility" and "trust" as codes of firm behaviour, and at the macro-level the concept of "normativity", all testify to the fact that business economics is more than aware of normativity. Yet **radical** normativity is hardly ever taken into consideration.

This means that although normativity as a phenomenon is taken for granted, its possible conceptual content is not discussed. Instead one analyses the possibility of normativity from an operational or strategic perspective. Normativity is seen as composed of firm values which could be "managed", i.e., "handled" due to this firmness. A firmness interpreted as unambiguous in content is demonstrated by the clear and motivated consent by different stakeholders. This allows it to be presented as an obvious fact that "normativities" can be compared, and perhaps even "added" to each other. Accordingly, value is a measurable entity, and hence, a possible parameter of a decision system, too. Moral value can be translated so as to be compatible with the three "big" values setting the horizon of managerial strategies and their inherent theories: survival, profit/revenue and development. Further, it is acceptable to differentiate values into notions of "corporate values", thereby transgressing the moral and ethical area.

When writhing a book on Management Philosophy it is also of no small importance to reflect on the fact that management theory has itself been a business – as demonstrated by John Micklethwait and Adrian Wooldridge in their bestseller from 1996 "The Witch Doctors: What the management gurus are saying, why it matters and how to make sense of it" – and hence a business to write books on management as a business, too:

> "The management consultancy business generated 11,4 billions dollars worth of fees in 1994; it is on course to bring in 21 billion dollars in 1999. At McKinsey, the biggest strategic consultancy, each partner accounted for 468.000 dollars of revenues. More than half of today's leading consulting firms did not exist five years ago." (Micklethwait, Wooldridge: 1997, p.3)

On the other hand, what I am trying here, is to insist on the perspective of **radical normativity**, and hence to stick to the fact that the good leader is a rabid person not prone to compromise, a rare figure in the vortex of this (post?-)post-modern world. In the last instance her/his project is a revolutionary one: it must anticipate a future that might come to exist, but only through the certainty of "the power of old" residing in tradition.

To make this project real, philosophy is demanded.

Philosophy does not just have to define the frame wherein the project of the manager is described, but the manager himself must be some kind of a philosopher.

Just as there exist many opinions concerning what makes a good leader, there are also many different philosophies. Hence, it is very important to present that kind of philosophy that can constitute the frame of reference from which the project of the good leader is able to be articulated.

1.1. Management and Philosophy

The choice to write a book on two areas as different as Management and Philosophy seems a risky venture. It is a belief shared by many people that management has to do with forms which the practical relation between ends and means might assume. To manage, and even to lead, always seems to have had power and the ability to keep it as its subject. It is about ruling, governing, and the competence to decide within a space where sufficient knowledge and information are rarely present; it is about managing with the will to risk, but all too often at the expense of somebody else. The subject of management has always been the goal of making a group, an institution, an organization, a nation, into the strongest one. To manage and also to lead has always been about victory, conquest, about strengthening and about survival. The subject of management has always been strategic thought and action. To manage has nearly always been about gaining prestige. To manage has most often been about making money.

Philosophy seems to deal with almost all the opposite attitudes.

It is not necessarily directed towards praxis; so-called "theoretical philosophy" gains more and more influence during Modernity. As different personalities as Ludwig Wittgenstein and Henry Miller could both say that philosophy has got nothing to do with living.

If philosophy deals with power, it is the power of thought, and from this you seldom get rich. Philosophy seems to presuppose that it is possible to acquire a sufficient amount of knowledge before you act – and also that it is possible to take the consequences of this knowledge seriously, when it points at the renouncement of acting at all.

Philosophy believes in an un- or a-strategic relation to reality. A philosopher would seldom want to lead his fellow men directly, not to speak of the managing of them, although great philosophers since Plato and Aristotle did present their visions about the good society and the good human being. But here the precondition seems to have been dominating ever since Socrates that the only thing you can do safely as a philosopher, is to stimulate others to help themselves (the only philosopher that to my knowledge has contributed directly to the elaboration of a constitution was Jeremy Bentham). It is even the ideal of the real philosopher to slough any prestige like a used snakeskin. And after all, most philosophers did not show very much sense of business or money-making – whether they should want it or not.

How on earth can one combine such different fields of thought and practice, and even hierarchize between them? Both items are inherent in the concept of "Management Philosophy". These difficulties arise because the point is not just simply "philosophy of management", if by that is meant the use of philosophical ideas in managerial theory and practice. Of course, such a practice has been going on for very long: It is a common expression still that a manager "has got his philosophy", one even speaks of "the philosophy of making money". It is definitely not a question of simply reflecting philosophically on management. The issue is even not to establish philosophy as a meta-science in relation to management – a role philosophy has partly fulfilled in relation to the Humanities, the Social Sciences and, not that seldom, to the Natural Sciences.

Rather, what is at stake here is the conceptual **fusion** of *Philosophy* and Management, where this means that thinking and acting as a manager would entail thinking and acting philosophically. That this does not count the other way around should be obvious.

From this perspective both management and leadership might seem to be put under tutelage as autonomic fields of theory and practice by being subjected to a radical normative imperative. And this is exactly the way in which one can create this new field.

On the other hand we are today facing a rather vast field of "philosophies": philosophy of music, of art, of aesthetics generally; philosophy of science, of history, and social philosophy; philosophy of economics, and of technology; philosophy of language ... one could go on. You can hardly find a field of science that has not got its "philosophy".

But this simply means that every scientific field needs, or is even forced, to legitimize its existence through reflecting its own basis of reflection through a so-called "meta-discourse". It seems as if every phenomenon becomes more and more facetted, and that it is legitimate to view it from more and more perspectives. But as cross-scientific activity grows, the fields will overlap; and the more perspectives compete via the ambiguity of phenomena, the stronger shall the demand grow for the ability to identify the phenomenology of any given field of research. This goes for the field of management too.

Thus, it is of extreme importance to which kind of philosophy management shall be the subject.

Now, as a scientific field, management must be understood as most precarious, due to four causes:

a. management cannot be analyzed through observation alone, and hence, not exclusively through hypothetical-deductive procedures. This phenomenon is closely related to the manager's own understanding of his praxis. Hence, the distance between researcher and research-field demanded by canonical criteria of scientific behaviour seems hard to accomplish here.
b. managerial behaviour has to be defined and hence studied as a species of the genus "general human behaviour". Thus, no technical excuses are able to release this behaviour from general normative codices.
c. managerial behaviour seems to express general traits of social behaviour well-described in psychology, sociology, the science of history and practical philosophy. Yet no unified theory exists that embraces these fields in relation to application.
d. these classical fields are supplemented by many rather new disciplines claiming to have created an apparatus capable of analyzing managerial behaviour, or at most, the most crucial aspects of it. These are not only broad, classical disciplines like sociology or political science, social psychology and psychoanalytical schools, but more narrow disciplines inside the field of business economics like "strategic management", "symbolic management", "organizational theories of management", and "logistics". These scattered disciplines often overlap in relation to their "paradigmatic basis", and to their theoretical and methodological practises, almost enforcing the arbitrariness of analysis.

Given the background of this overall picture it seems necessary, and even urgent, to reflect upon the very phenomenon of management in order to develop Management as a **genuine, autonomous field**.

Management-theory does not have to feel isolated in this situation. These problems are common to many of the disciplines of the Humanities and the Social

Sciences, concurrent with – what so many experience and apparently agree upon as – the speedy and spectacular change in every aspect of "reality". But in relation to one dimension of reality, management theory appears rather unique: within its field the problem haunting all of the Social Sciences, since Max Weber made a diagnosis of it nearly one hundred years ago, is put into focus. The problem of the opposition between normativity and "descriptivity". Of course this cannot be seen without reflecting upon the raising importance of managerial skills to the development of social and cultural values.

This book takes a unambiguous position here: any reflection in relation to the phenomenon of management, any meta-discourse on the subject of management, **has to be radically normative**.

The precondition to this position is that every legitimized social practice continues a conception of reality, and perpetuates it, if it is allowed to exist, and thereby creates the foundations of the future. Practice causes and practice binds. Through practice the old is spun into the new. But the normative optics consist first and foremost of two items:

a. There only exist **normative** criteria of management, no others. What is objective must be considered as an untenable construction. Any economical perspective, technical perspective, or social perspective, is also able to be reduced to values. Just like the philosophical perspectives centred around the diminishing of the suffering of other people, or around the ability of empathy beyond personal costs.

    There is a **hidden normativity**, including both good and evil, in the actions of the manager, whether he is conscious of it or not.
b. That primarily a manager or leader is a human being, a person, and hence a member of the community of human beings that encompasses all his decisions and all his professional activities. Every particular action of a manager will create – and permanently continues this creation – the managed and the manager himself within a relation of communication of a specific character. Either its face value is power, or it is not.

But management consists of many things. And managers, even leaders, are of many kinds. You shall find the politician, the general, the sergeant, the coach. You shall find the dean, the director, the senior manager, the CEO. There is the too often underestimated upper-midlevel manager, not to speak of the supervisor. And at the beginning, and at the end, of everything there is the perpetual "I did it my way": our happy/unhappy relation to/with ourselves, that since the days of Greek philosophy and tragedy has been described as the combat of reason ("nous") and desire ("epithymos"); as the attempt to manage passion, aggression, cowardice, and hence, fate – or is it – contingency?

This book deals mostly with management inside the fields of business, and within the public sector, i.e., the traditional fields of business economics. From management and leadership within the political fields, the military, the educational and the research systems, within the NGO's, and within the world of sport, it only fetches a few examples. But its aim is to relate to managerial functions and to leadership in most fields, because the idea of radical normativity is anybody's business.

There is a reasonable amount of philosophical discourse in this book, as has probably already been noticed. And to some degree, a certain amount of philosophical terminology is in it, as mentioned in the Preface, but mostly Greek philosophical concepts which are a part of our cultural heritage. The paradigmatic starting point is phenomenological philosophy, and this is of a nature that favours everyday language rather than scientific terminology – we shall discuss this issue in a moment.

Confronted with the choice between reproducing thoughts in the most common linguistic clothing, and rendering them in a professional terminology, I have chosen the happy medium: to try to create an apt terminology with the resources of everyday language, but with the tools of phenomenological experience and a knowledge of phenomenology.

This is important on the one hand because some professional terminology is needed to qualify a field of research scientifically, i.e., to construct the distance between the consciousness of the actors inside the studied field, and the gaze of the philosophical observer. On the other hand, philosophy alone can produce the terminology capable of releasing a theory of management from the bonds of competing scientific fields and their canonical theories within the wide world of the social sciences, not least within the smaller world of business economics. This should also mean a liberation from the world of the gurus, of the charlatans and the preachers, and of the pseudo-scientific pretenders as well.

The necessity to extricate Management Philosophy as an autonomous discourse from the other sciences derives from its claim to a unique scientific profile. This does not necessarily mean that this very profile must fit the one established with so much authority through the universe of natural science.

It was never my intention to become involved in a critical confrontation with the extensive literature within the field of management theory. I do not even want to set myself up as a judge of existing contributions to "the philosophy of management" and related subjects with a bias on existential or psychological aspects. In some parts of the book, especially Part II, I do not speak much about managerial problems, but I prepare the possibility to conceive of management as a practice. However, I did choose to focus on classical and canonical problems of management theory where this was essential as a means to emphasizing my discourse. And I did choose to refer to literature of significance from management theory, when this could deepen or widen a perspective.

I also choose not to integrate sociology, political science, psychology and social psychology, first and foremost because I do not find that Management Philosophy should have anything to do with any aspect of the domain of behavioral science. Quite the opposite is the case. It is of great importance to free, for its own sake,

Management Philosophy from the relation to these scientific projects and to their methodological and (hidden) normative ideals.

What I did want, was to create a sculpture – and let it be a mobile – of a point of view, the form of which is radical normativity. This overall frame demands dimensions, movements, and surfaces that cross the usual design within business economics generally and within management theory more specifically.

This throws an ideal of discourse, of textual reality, into the world, from which the image of the good leader should emerge. When the reader walks in and out of this textual sculpture, or even around it, coaxed by its movement, it should be possible to hear his voice, see his gestures, and perhaps even his face.

1.2. The Paradigmatic Connection

Today one could almost find an obsession with so-called "paradigms" – a word originally used by Plato about the eternal ideas behind all existing phenomena. Everybody feels obliged to search for paradigms, even to track them down behind every theory and behind any book, behind every thought and almost every word and action. People wish to confront them with each other, as if the ideal was to produce an infinitesimal arithmetics of ideas, of visible paradigms. So it seems wise to anticipate this operation by somebody else, and to present the paradigmatic settings of this book now.

Perhaps you are able to "wear" a paradigm like a tie, or to be uncertain whether you did carry it with you, and anxiously touch the place on your coat where it usually is, like a wallet. Like clothes and wallets then, it is something you might forget. Here a paradigm seems – if not improper or assumed – to be an optics subject to change in relation to the changing contexts. But, let us hope, paradigms should normally be phenomena belonging to the physiognomy of the eye, and hence to the personality (the mind's eye/I). Hence, they should express the same obviousness and necessity proper to the act of seeing. A man not only coexists with his paradigm, he identifies with it – or it appropriates him, developing its fragrant filigree-logic by way of him.

The point of view of this book, and the foundation of all of its perspectives, emerge from the **phenomenological** paradigm.

But phenomenology consists in a spectrum of differentiated and sometimes not quite reconciled frames of reference, starting with its exegesis by Edmund Husserl, via Max Scheler, Hans Lipps, through Martin Heidegger, to Jean-Paul Sartre, to Maurice Merleau-Ponty and the Danish philosopher Knud Ejler Løgstrup.

Whereas the phenomenology of Edmund Husserl (1859-1938) was still able to claim that genuine knowledge of the essences of things could be founded upon human experience, and language still seen as a humble servant to cognition, phenomenology after the Second World War was wellaware of the Janus-Face nature of concepts. This arch-experience of phenomenology emphasized the creative and destructive forces of language in relation to cognition. Common language as both a spring of real knowledge and as a barrier to it was to become the horizon of Martin Heidegger, and later on the principle lesson to Jacques Derrida, Gilles Deleuze and J. Lyotard, hence, to post-modernism. It did focus on the vortexes and the safety belts of texts, on their abysses as well as on their firm Babylonian gardens.

The so-called experience of **contingency** has set the agenda of doing philosophy since the Sixties. This concept refers to the latin word "contingere", "to touch", like one link in a chain touches the other. And the concept is actually carrying this metaphor inside it, because it was created by the Latin philosopher and politician, Boëthius, as a translation of two concepts from Aristotle, **symbanein** and **endechomenon**.[1] The former means "the fact that something happened". The latter means "a necessity in the world of events that does not exclude the possible (the possibility of not-coming-to-be), i.e., a necessity without determinism". So **contingency** refers to the unique fact of the event, that which cannot be undone. And to the consequences which originate within this singular event – consequences which in them bear a hidden necessity. A necessity which we make real as if we were free.

Contingency reflects the theoretical and empirical impossibility of giving an explanation of the emerging of the event, and hence reflects the lack of ability to predict it and to predict the framework of its consequences. The double fact of History, on the one hand, the "working aporia" that history is the chaos that invades and inhabits us, destroying any scientific enterprise and any Prima Philosophia; on the other hand that history, the big and the small one, is experienced as meaningful nonetheless. Contingency is the paradox of history. This phenomenon of contingency, of which Gilles Deleuze spoke with the voice of the great stoic philosopher, Chrysippos, as "fate without necessity", catches every philosopher in the event from which he speaks about events. He is appropriated by the event, and hence by the words, that "it uses" with him as a media. He "is spoken", when he speaks – (Heidegger: 1959; Deleuze: 1969).

Thus, it would be a great mistake if that which could be understood as contingency would then be restricted to mean "what is not necessary, but only possible". Contingency reflects, as a concept of experience and of conception, the feeling of a double necessity: the necessity of the event, and here the arch-event of being born, and born into a time, a place, a body, which was never chosen by you – Sartre made this experience a subject in "L'Être et le néant" – which we so often baptize "fate". "Fate", from the Latin word "fatum", a translation in itself of the Greek concept of **heimarmenē**. Within this concept, which the Stoic philosophers were the first ones to develop in its full content, lays a doubleness too: it refers both to the "heirmos

---

1. Vries, Josef de (1983): Grundbegriffe der Scholastik. Wissenschaftliche Buchgesellschaft, Darmstadt. Looked-up: "Sein", "Seiendes", "esse", "ens". "Endechomenon" originates from "endechetai".

aition", the ironhard causality, and to the freedom of choosing the right life in spite of anything that might happen – and to such a degree that accidents, misfortunes, are seen just as opportunities to give the wise man the real possibility to prove himself. And here we meet the second necessity involved in the concept of contingency: that you yourself create a necessity in your pattern of reactions towards the events. Then you yourself might be the principle of contingency: you yourself are the secret necessity of the things you do, and hence what happens to you. Contingency here consists in the fact that this secret can never be revealed, can never be prone to any explanation. Through it the pertinent question can be posed afresh: what does it actually mean to be an "I"?

Perhaps it ought to be noticed here already that the experience of contingency, and not least the knowledge of it as a condition for thinking and action, is extremely important to the manager.

This experience of contingency, the logo of post-modernism, destructs the enterprise of any rational philosophy, and hence of any attempt to establish a social science on the principles of a "scientia generalis". Thus the following conditions of scientific thinking are all impossible to adhere to:

a. that thought is fully transparent to itself: the ideal of the "strong reflection", of a "ratio sufficientis" which I am myself through my ability to think.
b. the ideal of a certainty which it is totally possible to substitute, a certainty founded on a universal reason.
c. hence, the ideal of argumentation, i.e., of dialogue, as a path to truth.
d. the principle of modest induction: that a reasonably general knowledge can be constructed from a certain number of events, because sets of events are very rarely complete: sometimes from a few events, and even from one event only.
e. the idea that thoughts are able to be presented in a consistent and perhaps even simple system (like the one of Sraffa for example (Sraffa: 1960) which presented a system without contradictions.
f. the belief in a hidden language of experience behind everyday language which philosophy and science are able to reach.
g. hence, the belief in a concept of thinking where thought is something beyond the application of syntax, semantics and pragmatics of speech.
h. the ideal of representation and hence the correspondence criterion of truth: that a world exists "out there" that is different from thoughts and words and to which they can be compared.
i. the belief in History as an objective, autonomous media and hence the confidence in explanation and prediction.
j. the confidence in "axiology", in the principle that the basis of human action is able to be established as a set of unambiguous (and even ultimative) values.
k. the belief in the acting and planning subject invested with a balanced, strategic foresight, and with sufficient power and knowledge to realize his goals.

Phenomenology and post-modernism intermingle through one person, the German philosopher Martin Heidegger (1889-1976). He is the link between Friedrich Nietzsche's (1844-1900) distrust of rational thought, meaningful history, of science, of Humanism and of Western culture all in all, and the negative theology of Jacques Derrida, the essence of "deconstructionism", as well as the philosophical novels of Gilles Deleuze and the last short post-modern fables of Jean-Francois Lyotard.

In several essays during the fifties Heidegger abandons the afore mentioned beliefs, ideas, and ideals of thinking, thereby opening a space of possibilities where the philosopher is set free – both positively and negatively – to follow a new way.

The lived, chaotic life pierces the bulletproof glass of rational thought pervading the world of concepts. The philosopher cannot escape his own life. There is no bird's eye view of the world, but only a thought that is always already the world itself. Thinking can no longer fly, but is caught in the body in which it is thought and in the event wherein it is spoken or written.

But this does not have to mean that the philosopher must surrender to his prejudices. On the contrary, he is confronted with a new kind of freedom, the freedom to create the propositions through which he thinks. He is able to anticipate his own thinking. In other words, he has become a new kind of poet.

He can create fables, narratives, and even plays, novels, where the persons are concepts, and the plot is the logic. He is able to draw on experiences lost by the academic, philosophical tradition, where thought itself has been devoured by its own gluttony.

The poetic way of thinking might express the fact that thought is transgressed by language without missing the experience of the lived life.

What we get here is a clear cut, but perhaps sometimes disillusioned, "Lebenswissenschaft", a science of the lived life, relying on the poetical stamina of the narrative, and on its ability to let thought last through the winter in the warm lands of rhetoric and poetics.

I think it is important to realize that "postmodern phenomenology" constitutes a peculiar paradigm, but this paradigm must not be confused with a "radical humanism" such as Burrell and Morgan present it in their rather influential book "Sociological Paradigms and Organisational Analysis" from 1979.[2] Heidegger already taught us that in 1946 in his "Letter on Humanism". We must speak of a "transhumanism" instead: what "human" means can only be sought by transgressing any existing concept of man.

---

2. G. Burrel and G. Morgan have tried to set up paradigms within sociology with a special aim at business economics. They distinguish four, two by two, antagonistic paradigms, namely: functionalism versus hermeneutics, radical structuralism versus radical humanism. Those distinctions might be circumscribed by the canonical opposition between "objectivism" and "phenomenology" or "critical theory" already used during the sixties (Burrell, Morgan: 1979).

Perhaps this "postmodern phenomenology" deserves a better name. It is definitely "post-postmodern", but that sounds clumsy, and "phenomenological postmodernism" sounds ridiculous. Phenomenology has passed through the movement, "post-modernism", of which it itself was an important origin, trying to reconcile itself with contingency, not fighting it any longer. What shall we call it? "Hyper-modernism"? No, for it definitely contains a conservative element. It turns against the world of information, of texts, knowing that it itself is bound to texts, and even that mind itself might be a textual structure. I think we shall call this paradigm just plainly **radical phenomenology**. We thus evade the "-isms", and escape all hints to homogeneous or even uniform periods of frames of reference, such as "postmodernism".

A Management Philosophy in which the voice and face of the manager/leader is sought after, must also seek in this zone; it must try to probe for a man that shall come to be, rather than being an empirical eulogy of successful managers and their illustrious accomplishments.

Thus Management Philosophy, like philosophy, must seek man in his fables, in his narratives, in his myths, but without an authoritative reading. Fable and story, comedy and tragedy, are only territories upon which a trace has been left. A trace from the future. If man is a goal, we can only investigate his physiognomy between the lines in those texts, in their pauses, in the unsaid. After all, the metaphor might be fitting that it is the fables and the stories, not us, that effectuate the interpretational labour; we are interpreted and understood to a higher degree than just simply being the users of the narrative forms as instruments at our discretion.

Whereas not so many years ago the scientific illusion of facing an objective reality – perhaps even through a window glass – was still possible, the picture now seems to have placed us inside a room, and under the spell of a revenge of time. Here the fables and the stories, the epic and the drama, constitute the only forms in which temporality can be caught without being victimized by it – they appear as gentle fortresses against the army of time.

Radical phenomenology, then, focuses on contingency as the pivot of experience. If Management Philosophy wants to understand itself as the legacy of this paradigm it must take contingency seriously. This posits some important restrictions to managerial thinking:

a. that it is impossible to program social reality, including one's own.
b. that reflection shall only help a little in creating one's own identity: concepts like "formalization", "model", "plan", "communication", "role", "dialogue" and "argument", and even "deliberate decision", shall be of little help.
c. that contingency makes operation-analysis impossible and that anticipation has nothing to do with calculation or with scientific prediction.
d. that contingency makes an accurate, thorough and a secure analysis of the situation impossible, because such an accomplishment would presuppose that the analyzer did not belong to it.

But contingency has got a positive side as well:

a. it restores the confidence in the unseen, unknown, and unanalysed.
b. it brings back magic as the horizon of knowledge.
c. but first and foremost it focuses on the will as the most important instrument of cognition and of action.

Contingency underlines the fact that there does not exist any objective reality, but that it is we who create the world which we perceive as real, through a language which only makes this experience possible, because it can refer to a reality which neither belongs to it nor to us.[3]

Here the metaphor will play a decisive role in making perception precise and deep, yet without sustaining the illusion that we are able to escape the individual fascination to which it binds us (Lipps: 1938/1976; Lipps: 1958). Contingency gives to the unique a hitherto unknown significance, because the general and the abstract fail: the concept has lost its transparency, the criteria of relevance has become irrelevant. Contingency emphasizes the confidence of the individual in his intuitive competence, not in rational reflection. Contingency emphasizes the "ease" peculiar to the action of the good person of which Plato speaks in the dialogue "Cratylus", as opposed to the almost always brooding and strained way through which the good action is implemented when grounded upon "values", upon a conceptually manifest knowledge of the good.[4] Contingency seems to create difficulties to any casuistic, any fine-meshed net of moral rules, to any moral manual.

But first and foremost the experience of contingency opens up towards the knowledge of the significance of the event.

"The event" is that which any situation is transformed into when it is christened "the battle of x", "a wedding", "a sales promotion", "a layoff". The event makes that

---

3. Plato already phrased the "postmodern" arch-insight that language creates experience in his dialogue "Cratylus": "ho logos to pan sēmainei kai kyklei kai polei aie ...": "speech makes all things (pan) known and always makes them circulate and move about, and is twofold, true and false" (Plato: 1926/1996, 408C).
4. The good, virtue, **aretē**, is characterized first by the "ease of motion, and secondly that the flow of the good soul is always unimpeded ..." as Socrates phrases it, when he investigates the etymology of the good (Cratylus, op.cit. 415D). Virtue then is bound up with that naturalness that to us is the quintessence of the good character, or the good mind. Primarily virtue is not realized through the rational, voluntary choice, but important choices and insight, wisdom, combine gradually into a "habitus", into a **hexis**, as Aristotle names it, that let the good action emerge from our – hard-won – "nature". This perspective is the direct opposite to the conception of values as "mental objects", or even maxims, subject of "translations" into rules of action. We shall return to the important concept of **hexis** later on.

which happened clear and tangible, but at the same time blurred and concealed, because the meaning of the event comes into existence in an event of meaning. The two dimensions cross each other, they can never unite. Once you give the event a name, you are already in another event. Hence, the event might be called the spot where the manifest meets the infinite, where presence confronts absence, i.e., nothingness, the quintessence of the impotence of thought towards its own conditions, to paraphrase the Danish philosopher, Søren Kierkegaard.

The arch-metaphor of the experience with contingency consists in the longing for, and the powerlessness of rational thought against, **kairos**, "the right moment". The moment where it might be revealed who you are through the meaning of the things you do. We shall return to this Greek concept, in Part IV.

CHAPTER 2

The Radical, Methodological and Normative Perspectives

In the following chapter I shall try at first to sketch the methodological deliberations that have guided the way in which I use concepts. Then I shall explain the concept of "radical normativity" through the concept of "The Fourth".

2.1. The Radical, Methodological Perspective: What Words Cannot Do

In this world at the edge of the millennium there can hardly be found no **inscription** anymore. The flesh of the world cannot be branded any longer, because the world is no longer flesh. The words cannot recognize the bodies of objects and relations through the stamp of their own image, through their unique brand. The stigma is melted on the skin by the heat cast by bodies burning with an insipid and bitter insolence. The old cure of Nietzsche and the new one of Deleuze and Guattari[5] does not work anymore: the cure of cleaning the bodies from the brands, and hence to cancel the guilt that kept the icons like neon-casting between the outer and the inner skin.

Perhaps the truth is that there is no flesh any longer, no real bodies. There are not even machines of desire and repression. Only words remain.

So the magic does not work any longer. The word cannot conjure anything up. There are no faces, no hands, no genitals, no conversation, no touch, no satisfaction, not even non-satisfaction, only invocation of words by words. Hence, there is **out-scription**. An enlisting of an army of anonymous individualities (yes, a paradox) preparing for a war that does not exist. Where words command endless columns of words in unidentifiable places, having already lost any feeling of time, seeking soil and blood, death and dung, in vain.

Words in the ear, words in the mouth, words on the hands, words in the hair, words on the bench, where you wanted to put your tired words to rest ... words in your eyes.

Out-scription, the world is called upon, and it answers all too soon, from all too many places.

---

5. F. Nietzsche depicts the early, tragic history of mankind as an invention of guilt by power, in "Zur Genealogie der Moral" (Nietzsche: 1955), and G. Deleuze and F. Guattari follow him in "L'Anti-Oedipé" (Deleuze & Guattari: 1997)

All the world is taken to a census every five minutes, and for each name mentioned, a thousand people will turn up. Not driven by guilt or fear, not even from anger or ressentiment, but from a conditioned reflex called "thought", from deliberation, from reflectivity.

How are you able to do philosophy in a reality where there is no struggle between the concept and the world, but where any tiny word functions like an automaton? How do you cast a critical glance upon a world where the word and the world are not satisfied with peaceful co-existence, but dissolve into each other like the young chemist's dream of a synergy only found in Tristan and Isolde.

Everything is everything. Nothing, except the concept of "nothing", is banished from our world, like its old aunt, evil.

How is it possible to think in a world where everything consists in thinking? (And the philosopher has to think, has he not? Or even more precisely, in a world where everything is thought, even emotion?)

Thinking and "wording" unite. Words are thoughts and thoughts are words. Reality is **out-scription**, reality is written in our minds. Our minds are written in reality. There is a Dance Macabre where words and thoughts now only skeletons are holding each other by the hand, along with any verdict always already written. It is the ghost of the evident.

But within the process of **out-scription,** the word means almost nothing. Hence the thought inside it (or outside it) means just as little. The word is written in water. The thought is blown up into the air. Anything goes, because anything is true. In this kaleidoscope the world is that which starts afresh. Shake it, and you shall always find almost the same. It shall convince you, again and again. Truth will never disappoint you, because it is meant to please everybody.

How on earth could one imagine to conceptualize in a world like that? **Out-scription** seems to mock any conceptual framework. The real problem is not that truth has become rhetoric, but that rhetoric has become truth.

Should we "go Matisse", and create a mini-monument of minimizing? This had to be post-innocent anyhow, because childishness too has been **out-scribed.** But it seems hard to believe in a new originality, even in an ab-originality, although this last inclination seems to be rather common.

Or should we "go Joyce" or even "go Deleuze", and create a philosophical novel with all the conceptual layers mingled and mixed in a profound junction on the surface? Render to multitude, to "poikilia", and create a sort of folded, compressed program of the possible thoughts of an average philosophical gentleman and manager, during one day, in the year of 1999?

Or should we pretend that nothing has happened, and try to "inscribe" our concepts on the skin of this vulnerable millennial reality, and hope (The (post-)postmodern hope) that they shall inscribe us too?

What can a philosopher do with words? Not to speak of the question: What can a management-philosopher do with words?

But alas, where there are no words, there is no action. Today's enterprise might be said to look like a theatre, but there is no pantomime on the repertoire. Pierrot and harlequin are absent at the moment, they visit the clinic of the deaf-and-dumb.

But there might be something that we can do.

It would not be "inscription", and certainly not "out-scription", and not "ascription",[6] nor – I guess – "circumscription". "On-scription" sounds futile, as do "re-scription", "up-scription" and "down-scription". But "off-scription" appeals to me. It invokes the image of letting go of precisely that which you are trying to encircle, trap, catch with your very words. It recalls a gesture of – what in German is called "Gelassenheit" – of the attitude of he who does not care in the same way as everybody else. But this does not mean that he does not care at all – quite the opposite – yet, his attitude is very far from affable. Anyhow, it also conjures up a slight touch of magic: The thing you are talking about proves immune towards inscription and even towards out-scription; it just curls into itself, spinning around its own axis exuberantly, like a (white) whale, leaving for those unknown depths from whence it chose to rise to the (our) surface and cause us to wonder.

Let us take this concept then, **off-scription**, and see what it might disclose to us about the condition of using concepts.

To "scribe something off" might just simply mean to stop worrying about it, to leave it to its own devices. Hence, it expresses a gesture of letting go. But in "off-scription" there could also be a sort of disappointment about the thing (or person), that was "off-scribed". In this attitude you might sense repressed anger, but something else could be in it too: a feeling of reverence, i.e., that this thing was just too big for you, so you had better cut the line, before the boat is drawn out upon the deep sea, and perhaps even down into the abyss.

It might still have something to do with sounding the depth. And the metaphors of fishing are not at all inapt, because when using concepts you also choose the strength of the rod, the type of wheel, the size of the hooks, the kind of bait, and the width of the meshes in your net.

So all too often one catches the fish that one deserves. However, it does not seem totally impossible to fish in another way, using instruments and baits that do not anticipate the take. Used figuratively, this implies a certain kind of carefulness, when using words.

First of all you have to abandon the figure of **denotation**, or **representation**. You have to do this in two ways:

a. to abandon the illusion of "the two worlds", a world of words and a world of things. Hence, one must abandon the figure of "inscription".

In the late fifties Martin Heidegger destroyed this figure by stating that words

---

6. This is a word used by the French philosopher Paul Ricoeur in his attempt at an ethics (Ricoeur: 1990). The word designates the all-important role of moral consciousness in identifying our obligations towards ourselves and others.

do not describe any objective world; that words do not describe thoughts, or mental significances that are different from words; that there does not exist any "transcendental ego" that – as a neutral referee – commands the struggle and the union between sounds (the voice outside and inside your head) and that picture of the world which is given through the other senses (Heidegger: 1959).

It is also in this connection important to note, that this reality of a trans-linguistic world cannot be saved by referring to "forces" of any kind. The price is always functionalism.[7]

b. to abandon the belief in – what you may call – "the possibility of translation", i.e., that it should always be possible to render a concept in another wording. You have to get rid of the illusion of paraphrasing. A word can never be substituted with a safe and sound meaning. This means that a word can never be removed from one framework or context into another without at least a slight loss of meaning. A word is also **seen,** be it through the reference to examples or to figurative content, or through the invocation of the written word by the reference to spelling – as means to evade ambiguity (as with "fair" and "fare"). Where this claim might have its reservations and exceptions in relation to common words (one can neither see the word "and", nor the word "hence", nor the word "to see"), it relates in an unlimited way to concepts.

These considerations imply quite a lot in relation to the role of metaphor. And since it is metaphor that every methodological thinking in the world of the Humanities and the Social Sciences has to deal with, let us face it.

A metaphor most often implies the other senses (than sound). It is not sound transformed to sound that gives a metaphor its power. But of course it is possible to say, "his voice sounded like a damaged pick-up!" When the metaphor relates to the other senses, it transgresses the wall between these senses by combining them. Or better, it makes them compatible (computer-metaphor, because programmes are called "compatible" or "non-compatible") or exchangeable (money-metaphor). "Logic is the money of thinking", Karl Marx said. Such a logic is inherent in the homonym: smell and sight, touch and sound, taste and the chilliness of the skin, are suddenly at the same level. We are dealing with a so-called "synaesthesia", a co-operation of the senses. And a "kinaesthesia", the primordial function of touch. Combined, they will render the concept of "synkinaesthesia", the co-operation of the senses towards the world trough movement, i.e. **praxis,** (Kirkeby: 1994).

Many of the most powerful metaphors are synkinaesthetic:
"Shall I compare thee to a summer's day?"
In "The Timaeus", (Plato: 1926/1966) Socrates compares his feeling for the Utopian State with the feeling for a beautiful living creature or a statue: "to recognize

---

7. A price paid heavily by Deleuze and Guattari in "L'Anti-Oedipé". But Heidegger himself denounces the concept of an ontological concept of force or more specifically the socalled "will to power" in his book on Nietzsche (Heidegger: 1961).

them truly is to see them move" (19B-C). It is only living picture that shows all the facets of the body's surfaces, contours, its colours and shades, because it places it inside time, in the vivid scenarios of public places.

But the very best metaphors do not even create such a clear designation. On the contrary, they postpone the reference, they keep the significance floating.

Aristotle expresses this in his "Art of Rhetoric" in the following way:

> "It is metaphor above all that gives perspicuity, pleasure, and a foreign air (xenikon), and it cannot be learnt from anyone else"[8]

What does it mean, that a word is first and foremost **seen**, what Aristotle calls "the perspicuity"?

It means the following:

a. that it relates to a visual image, be it something that can be ascertained by the other senses (and often by other people) too, and which we use to call "real" or "actual" (phantasia or eidōlon). Aristotle says, that such words "set things before the eyes" (pro ommatōn poiein), "by words that signify actuality" (1411b, III, xi, 2).

b. that – as a sound – it is reproduced to memory through its letters. This shall often be the case with concepts, particularly when they have a foreign origin, and hence might be difficult to remember.

However, could there not be another way in which the sound is **seen**?

One way could be as beauty. This is what Plato suggests in the dialogue "Phaedrus":

> "But beauty (kallous), as I said before, shone in brilliance among those visions; and since we came to earth we have found it shining most clearly through the clearest of our senses; for sight (opsis) is the sharpest of the physical senses, though wisdom (phronēsis) is not seen by it, for wisdom would arouse terrible love, if such a clear image of it were granted as would come through sight, and the same is true of the other lovely realities; but beauty alone has this privilege, and therefore it is most clearly seen and loveliest."[9]

Now Heidegger's famous words "Das Denken ist ein Hören, das sieht" (Thinking is a listening that sees) (Heidegger: 1957), suddenly might be easier to interpret, because we could imagine what it is that thinking/thought actually **sees**. It is Beauty.

But what is the place of this inside a book on Management Philosophy? What has Beauty to do with the philosophy of the Social Sciences, and with their metho-

---

8. (Aristotle: 1939/1994a, 1405a, III, ii, 8-9).
9. (Plato: 1917/1995, 250D-E).

dology? And what can we learn from a dialogue where the person, the name of whom it bears, says to Socrates:

"and you know yourself that the most influential and important men in our cities are ashamed to write speeches (logous te grafein) and leave writings behind them, through fear of being called sophists by posterity." (Phaedrus, 257D)

And where the central person, Socrates, says the famous words on the negative consequences of the invention of the letters through the mouth of the Egyptian, Thamus:

"For this invention will produce forgetfulness in the minds of those who learn to use it, because they will not practice their memory. Their trust in writing, produced by external characters which are no part of themselves, will discourage the use of their own memory within them. You have invented an elixir not of memory, but of reminding; and you offer your people the appearance of wisdom, not true wisdom, for they will read many things without instruction (aneu didachēs) and will therefore seem to know many things, when they are for the most part ignorant and hard to get along with, since they are not wise, but only appear wise." (275A-B)

The young will become easy prey to the sophists through the written word. For the sophists have one technique for influencing people, **persuasion** (peithein), while the real philosophers teach.[10] And the written word seems even better to persuade because of its seeming objectivity.

So the sophist, in the universe of Plato, influences through images, through phantasms, and he uses the written word. Hence, if we shall follow Plato, "to see the sound" cannot be identical to the visualizing of any image (that comes from the senses), nor to the visualizing of the image of the written word. True philosophers have to do one of two things, or even both. They have to concentrate on beauty and to stick to the invisible inside that which can be seen.

We then have to try to answer the following two questions:

a. How do we "see the sound?" How do we find the invisible within the visible.

b. How does Beauty relate to the task of conceptualizing? Is there a method here?

---

10. Timaeus, 51E: "Now these two Kinds (Reason versus True Opinion. OFK) must be declared to be two, because they have come into existence separately and are unlike in condition. For the one of them arises in us by teaching (dia didachēs), the other by persuasion (hypo peithous); and the one is always in company with true reasoning (alethous logou), whereas the other is irrational (alogon)" (Plato: 1929/1966).

To answer the first question it is important to explain, at least very shortly, why the words from Greek philosophy are of such great importance.

If we speak of a "Greek experience", this experience might reflect both another social reality and another "distribution" of cognitive capacities. We might speak about another concept of knowledge. But we have got a hermeneutical problem here, because the conceptional glasses through which we perceive the Greeks now, were made once, in Athens. Something is returning to itself through us, and there are countless of reasons to think that this fact has changed our mode of approach, releasing us from the suspicion of being forced to practice within a (vicious) circle.

To **see** the sound means to touch the place where it reaches the world, to feel the point where the sounding of a depth might begin. To be **in** the sound of your own voice is not identical to visualization, but closer to a reflection of an echo on your skin: the experience of the bat. The impression does not place something before your eyes, but it takes your sight with it.

So, to see the sound is to seek the places where there is an echo. Such places might be words themselves, having sounded, echoed, through so many years. The Greek had got these words. **Chōra**, the place, and **hexis**, the right mood, and hence, the way to approach it; **ēthos**, the identity of the one who may approach, and **pragma/ergon**, the event of approaching, the right moment, **kairos**. At this place you are let by **philia**, friendship, and by **kathēkon**, duty ...

I shall name **chōra** in the first place, because **chōra** is the word of "place". It shows us that in order to see a sound, we have to let it sound in a particular place. We have to do it in a special way. We have to exist in a certain mode. We have to be there, at the right moment. We have to act towards others in this place appropriately. We have to change this world into a place where virtue is as spontaneous an act as breathing.

These concepts point to invisible places. Places that are invisible, because we are already occupying them.

When we try to conquer them through a name, they shall repel us – although it is their prerogative always to bear the same name.

Hence, these concepts also point to a time that cannot be made tangible, a time that cannot have its own concept.

These concepts always flee from us into places and times where we cannot go. But we pursue them with all our might, not knowing that they dwell in our shadows. Moving gently with us, resting invisible when the sun is in its zenith, and standing out, clear cut, behind our backs, seeking themselves out through our very act of searching for them.

Thus, to conceptualize demands a sense of the invisible – as Maurice Merleau-Ponty said. A sense of the limits of sense. In those concepts the secrets of our actions and thoughts are hidden. How then, should we be able to reach them through thinking and acting?

We have to approach them gently, always being aware of the **horizon** that they open to us.

We shall not reach their place through drawing distinctions, or through invoking laws of identity, or of non-contradiction. Formalisms and analytical sound grids of concepts shall not serve us either; and theories only, if we remember, what "theoria" really meant: a report to Athens from an observer who had visited the Olympic Games of a neighboring city-state. "Theoria epistēmē": the knowledge that belongs to him who has called on Otherness with the right mind. In acknowledging this the worn-out concept of "theory" can serve us in a new way.

Then, to see the sound means to have developed the right feeling for Otherness, for the way in which the world throws the voice back. Can this be conceived of as a "reflection" or even an "answering"?

But what about the second question: Beauty as a way of approaching truth that does not make you blind, or perhaps, makes you blind to the right things. A beauty that sets your mind right ("orthos logos", the right thought).

But Beauty seems to be that which is seen in the place of something else. However, "in place of" does not mean "instead", ("anti-", "stellvertretend") invoking an unreal world of shadows that we must be content with. Beauty is the way to perceive that matches sight. Seeing answers to Beauty, as if it had a voice. Or perhaps: The sound of seeing is Beauty.

But how can we identify Beauty, when we are not allowed to translate one word into others?

It seems practicable, no matter how strenuous, to point to choreographies in which the right actions usually moved themselves. So, Beauty opens a horizon[11] to the observer, or investigator, where peoples' ways are staged like silhouettes. However, through the concept of Beauty we cannot be invested with a deduced framework of more and more minute concepts getting us closer and closer to a concrete phenomenon, called "the beautiful". There is no grid, no network, only a dynamics of intangible emotions leading to an overwhelming, or it is perhaps just an "accurate"? question. And do not ask: "What is it?" Nobody should know what it is, actually. It has no reality, only an actuality, that instantiates itself as an overwhelming question.

We can only visit the place.

So it is the task of the philosopher to seek honestly for the significance of a concept, the meaning of which so many seem to know. To seek for a logic of intension and extension that fails, to seek for a concept that is abolished in the very process of its application. Beauty, then, might seem to hide itself behind the surface of what the fashionable, conceptual designers used to call "aesthetics", but it is certainly not found there. More probable it shall seek refuge among the unimpressive, find a

---

11. I shall remind: "horizon" comes from the Greek word "horizō": to limit, to delimit, to part, to decide, to fix, to define. Hence, as a metaphor it draws on the dimensions of place and time, as well as on the dimensions of words and thoughts. It even refers to interaction between people.

shelter in the very small things, or hide among the herringbone patterns of everything, grey, anonymous, but with a soft, hardly perceptible radiance, like jade inside velvet. But it can be seen by the alert eye. An immanent brilliance hardly traceable as anything else but a soft smouldering, a spark blown off from the worldfire.

Not Vermeer, not LeCourbusier, not Karl Lagerfeld, nor Benetton, not in those forms, but behind them. Not even Phaidias or Michelangelo, nor Botticelli or Hundertwasser, not even Moore or Giacometti, but behind them. Ceci (la beauté), n'est pas la beauté. Not even Goya, Picasso, nor even "New Brutalism", with its mask of the hideous.

So Beauty summons the philosopher. To invent her.

And concepts summon the philosopher too, to invent the world to which they might refer.

To the Management-Philosopher, to the Philosopher and Manager, this might also appeal: the challenge to co-create, to join us all in creating, the world that is. The true, the beautiful and the right/straight (alēthēs, kalos, orthos).

So the methodological principles searched for in the beginning of this chapter would be closer to poetics than to rhetoric.

But from the stance of methodology – "meta-hodos", "after-the-way-gone", looking back to see (not in anger), where you really did walk, on what you actually did – there is, at the moment, nothing more to say.

2.2. The Radical, Normative Perspective

The concept of methodology presented in the first chapter of this book comes so close to the canon of phenomenological anti-method that it is difficult to distinguish from the deliberations on the **normativity** of social action. But this is only valid, of course, when normativity itself is prone to a conception which posits it in opposition to any "technique", any "quantification", any possibility of the "operational". It is only valid when it is placed outside the possibilities of any translation through analytical instruments like "principles", "maxims", or even "values".

In this way **normativity** becomes what philosophers recently used to call a "transcendent immanence;" thus playing with the famous epistemological apparatus invented by Immanuel Kant.

What this strange hybrid, "transcendent immanence", might mean in relation to our topic can be illustrated in the following way:

In an interview in the magazine, "Fortune", from Sept. 28, 1998, the old, influential "guru" of management, Peter F. Drucker, comments on modern management. He says

"Medium-sized companies are where 'American management has done really sensationally', and it is here the growth in the economy is too. They attract the able young people, because they are able to get much more space of activity and more job security than in the big companies.

The management at big companies, however, is very uneven. The worst trend in management is those enormous millions paid to people at the top when they lay off 12.000 people. You have no idea how contemptuous upper-midlevel managers are of those people. They are the ones who do all the work, the ones who tell the people they are fired."

And now he presents the point that is of special value in this context:

"That bitterness is a very high price to pay. I once read a book about Marco Polo in which he asked Genghis Kahn what he expect of his officers. And he said: 'Of an officer I expect that he takes care of the men before he takes care of himself. Of a general I expect that he takes care of the horse before he takes care of the men.' Polo asked why, and he said: 'An officer leads by doing; a general leads by example.'"

There is a movement in this narrative about Mr. Polo, an inertia, that shows us that something is lacking. And this is exactly why this narrative is so impressive. It leads you towards a border, and this border is retiring every time in such a way that you think you shall now be able to touch it. As "Otherness" it keeps its secret.

There is an example here: that the real general cares most for his horse. But it might have said, that he should care for lice on his body, or for the grain(s) of sand on which his horse should come to tread one fine day before the battle.

Of course, the example with the lice only counts if they actually disturb his acting. This narrative is also about functionality. The general could never care for the soles on a poor farmers shoes in the neighborhood of the army's quarters.

The example with the horse is such a good one because it is balanced. And as being in balance, it constitutes a middle, the point of balancing of scales. But the measure used points to a border.

This border could be exemplified by the narrow neck of the hourglass, or even by the lens-opening/closing of the camera. Both metaphors show a passage, a shifting of worlds – like the arch-metaphor here, the tunnel of the uterus. There is a "rite de passage" at work that unites time and place.

This example establishes a border-experience of a special kind. It is not centrifugal, but it is centripetal. It draws attention into its circle and leads it through itself out into the other world: the world of possibilities, of the necessary and the contingent, i.e., the future.

By saying only one thing, it presents a border, a limit, onto experience. A border, the meaning of which is to be transgressed.

That is the significance of the construct "transcendent immanence". To place a border ready-to-hand, to posit a limit immediately at your face, and in your hands, which you cannot transcend, but have to carry with you, wherever you walk, this is the function of the example. An old vademecum of possibilities and of the very limitations of experience handed over to you.

At one and at the same time, we are met here with the phenomenon of **contingency**. This fact that you only have got this one example in a world of possible worlds, where almost infinitely many other examples might have been the one, enforces you to generalize from this place only. Accidence presents itself as necessity. This is the jail of perspective; you carry the cell, the peephole and the bars around with you, like a convicted snail. You have to know the world from the bottom of a well, i.e., from your memory only – where a world of worlds of other memories would have been possible. And this is both the fact of contingency and of the "transcendent immanence": you carry your jail around with you, and the very limitation of your own view will emerge as the peepholes – composed mostly of words. The circular field above you at the opening of the well shall become the empirical fact that the very state of your imprisonment in darkness is the foundation of seeing the light. This is the content of the most famous metaphor of all philosophy, the so-called "cave metaphor" of Plato's dialogue "The Republic".

The concept of **normativity** circles around two regions of metaphors: the metaphor just mentioned, the one that as a characterization of the work of Plato was called "the chorism" by Aristotle. The "chorism" – from the word "chōra" – means the existing of an absolute schism, of a fissure, even a crack, between the world of eternal ideas, Being ("ontōs on"), and the world of timely and transient and false phenomena, Becoming ("ginesin"). We shall relate to chōra, "the place of places", in a later chapter.

Normativity presupposes the figure of "the chorism" and its metaphors. This means that no phenomenon would ever in itself be sufficient as an object of experience. But it also fastens an experience of the border, so beautifully expressed by Leonard Cohen in singing "There is a crack in everything, that is where the light comes in."

This experience of the insufficiency of experience is of great importance to any discussion of ethics, and hence to the terrible hybrid word "Business Ethics". But it is also vital to any attempt at establishing a platform on which to found the discussion of an ethics of management.

First and foremost this raises two issues:

a. you can never through analysis, i.e., give any definite content to a value. The Münchhausen-procedure[12] seems to work here.

---

12. The so called "Münchhausen trilemma" was invented by the German philosopher, Fries, around 1800. It asserted that no proposition could ever be demonstrated to be absolutely true, because it could either be reduced to 1. a circulus vitiosus, 2. an infinite regress, 3. an axiom resting on a mere postulate. The Belgian artist, Escher, has most ingeniously visualized those three predicaments of thought in his etchings and woodcuts. By the way, you often find his pictures on the walls of more or less bewildered (I hope) physicists.

b. you shall never be able to decide the intension or the extension of the concept of a value through consensus.[13]

Values can only be lived. They are inextricably bound up with the person, as the Aristotlean concept of **hexis** shows. A value can only exist as a **virtue**.

That means, that a value is just as secret a phenomenon as personal identity. A value is precisely a "transcendent immanence".

Values emerge as virtues, and hence they are just as floating, as intuitive, as imaginative, as demanding, as intangible, as promising, as evocative, as trans-conceptional, as non-analytical and as deep, as persons and words.

That values can only be approached as virtues is an important thesis of this book, and I shall return to it.

The other metaphor of **normativity** also belongs to Plato.

It appears around the play with number **four**.

Through Christian culture we are habituated to the holiness of the number "three". The Trinity is an untouchable unity. In Greek culture, and in the eastern religions as well, the number "five" would often be carrying this content of the sanctuary.

But what is outside the Trinity? This thought is very difficult, and to ask it implies profanity – which Karl Marx used to practice in speaking of "the holy family", and in identifying The Father, The Holy Spirit and The Son with the rent from land, from capital and wages in the famous "trinitarian formula" from the Third Volume of "Das Kapital". In any events, in Christian thinking there are often four: God, the Holy Spirit, the Holy Virgin and the Son.

Plato proceeds in his own way concerning the number "four". In the dialogue "Timaeus", probably from the later part of his life, he makes the following narrative trick:

In the very first lines of the dialogue Socrates asks the three other characters (Timaeus, Hermocratēs and Critias):

"One, two, three, – but where, my dear Timaeus, is the fourth of our guests of yesterday, our hosts of today?" (17A)

This question shall never find an answer. The fourth person stays unknown, even if it is he who creates the link to the dialogue of yesterday, which might have been "the Republic". However, the person missing could have been Plato himself – as the

---

13. I shall not elaborate here on the consequences of this claim to the so-called "formal pragmatics" of Jürgen Habermas, and hence to the "ethics of discourse" built with apparent stability on this fundament.

translator of The Loeb Edition, R.G. Bury, suggests, – so, in that case, he would both be missing and present.

Then Socrates states:

"the task of filling the place ("anaplēroun") of the absent one (apontos) falls upon you and your friends here, does it not?" (ibid.)

This is genuine Platonic. Because now you get a whole dialogue, which should have been told by a person who is absent ("apontos"), i.e., the dialogue is spoken in his place, a dialogue about place.

A few pages inside the dialogue Socrates touches the subject that might have been spoken on by the absent one, namely the creation of the perfect state. From this we might imagine that this dissertation of place should have been on the proper place of place, i.e., the social place, the community, the new ēthos – because one of the senses of ēthos is "home-place".

In the earlier dialogue, the "Phaedrus", Socrates speaks like that:

"All my discourse so far has been on the fourth kind of madness (tēs tetartēs manias), which causes him to be regarded as mad, who, when he sees the beauty on earth, remembering the true beauty, feels his wings growing and longs to stretch them for an upward flight, but cannot do so, and, like a bird, gazes upward and neglects the things below." (Plato: 1914/1995, 249D)

The fourth madness belongs to the one who believes in "the chorism", to the real philosopher, in other words. Is this the person, the fourth one, who left the party of Timaeus?

Radical normativity can be illustrated through these examples, and hence, through the concept of "The Fourth". Because the radial normativity refers to an absence, and because it refers to "the upward gaze".

Thus the structure and content of the ideal state can only be told by an absent one, i.e., it can never be told as anything else but a sketch, a shadow. The utopia from "The Republic" was never meant to be implemented on earth.

But why the number "four"?

Because in Plato the dialogue is so important. The "logon didonai", the game of asking and answering, is a game between two persons, the number "two" dominates here. But as a game between two (prototypically, there might often be more persons, as in the dialogues) a third person is always needed as a referee.

Socrates would most often play this role. And figuratively this role is the role of moral consciousness. It is what Freud called "the superego". Hence, as a common moral sense, it is very dogmatic. It is, to interchange the two words of our conceptual hybrid, not a "transcendent immanence", but an "immanent transcendence". Socrates used to state that "he knows nothing", so he does not impersonate the dogma, the command, even if he impersonate the number "three".

But to make this attitude absolutely clear, it might be important to make the figure of the "transcendent immanence" stand out metaphorically. This could be made by introducing a fourth "person", or better perhaps, a fourth "instance", a referee of the referee, but certainly not a judge. Merely an absent one (apontos), but the one that might have told us the true story. The absent fourth is the quintessence of **normativity**. We shall name him "The Fourth". Nobody can fixate "him" onto any opinion, nobody can make "him" responsible of definite values, of the mores, of common sense (doxa). "He" sticks to "the chorism;" "he" shall never be satisfied with phenomena, with objects and thoughts and feelings. He presents us with the possibility of the Other (heteros), of the "otherwise", of the other way, the only mask of the absolute: the invisible.

CHAPTER 3

Leader or Manager

Let us begin this chapter by making a short diagnosis of the circumstances that make the very question inherent in the heading of this chapter possible: Why this recent obsession with leadership versus management?

Management theory may have had a long, and often hidden tradition through modernism. What impresses one far more than secret states' bureaucracies in Prussia and Russia is the Catholic Church with its hierarchical structure and marvellous organization, which one is able to deduce from the baffling results alone: christening the wilderness, making cosmos out of chaos, disasters of management and leadership notwithstanding, such as the popes' exile in Avignon. The strong influence of Plato's "Republic" could, until the Baroque, only be due to the amazing way in which it matched the managerial practices of the Church, giving support to its intellectual élitism and visions of the millennium.

Church-legitimation of managerial structures would come very close to philosophy, because theology is. And thoughts about management would, far into the 18th century, be philosophical by nature, not just because of the rhetorical tradition, but because of the domination of the political perspective through which management and leadership were approached. Voltaire, Montesquieu, and Rousseau were French philosophers aiming to delimit power and hence, domination, by analyzing the structures of leadership. To them the manager was the aristocrat, and the leader the one chosen by the "people" (still a small percentage of the population, after all).

However, the legacy of Machiavelli's study in cynicism from 1513, "The Prince", did suggest the outline of another reality, a reality manifested by Protestantism in its demand of sincerity and propagated as a utopian society in Thomas More's contemporaneous "Utopia". The ideal Protestant prince was hard but just. He did not weigh his words, but spoke from the heart. In his reign people acted out of duty to the state or the nation. Little by little they also acted out of duty to democratic values, but this still concerned only politics. In the business enterprise, despotism was the rule far into the twentieth century.

The political metaphor of the strong man still dominated every thought of leadership and management, and with all the paradox of history, more than a few of the "strong men" in our century were produced through socialist ideologies. Politics and the army furnished management theory with most of its content until the Second World War.

New technologies, new markets and the arms race changed this picture from the sixties onwards. Information technology, interventionism, new educational structures and new durable consumer goods transformed firms and organizational structures through the eighties. Now management had to lead processes, not people.[14] Leadership merges with the creation of innovations and knowledge, and like these it becomes, little by little, a commodity. Managers are raised like blood-stock in the emerging business schools, or put on the couch of the therapist.

During the eighties management becomes wedded to social responsibility, and the manager is forced into the role of a priest who must create and protect the core rites, symbols, and icons of corporate culture. He must be able to master meaning. He has to please his parishioners, the shareholders, every day, under pressure from his cardinals, the board members, and the standing clerical conference, the stake-holders. At the same time he must calm the potential rebels and renegades, the workers.

The manager finds himself swamped in difficulties. He has too many mouths to feed.

The top manager must secure economies of scale, give the product the right im-age, release the creativity of workers, inject commitment; he must guarantee that the firm protects the environment, that it is devoted to considerations of sustain-ability; he must make the subcontractors feel safe, and make every customer feel important; he must engage the clever applicant, and dismiss the useless; he must prefer female employees, but evade the pregnant ones; he must observe the stock-exchange; he must delegate his responsibilities, but not lose his power; he must ...

However, it is important to emphasize the fact that more and more candidates to the position of "managers" pop up, in business as well as in public enterprise, in entertainment and consultancy, in The National Health Service, in the education system, in sporting life ... Is the device actually: if he cannot do his job properly then why not make him a manager? A world consisting of one-man companies where everybody manages himself comes to mind. Or, following the prognoses of Charles Handy, who in books like "The Future of Work" from 1984, "The Age of Unreason" from 1989, and "Beyond Certainty: The Changing World of Organisations" from 1995, identifies the "portfolio worker": Firms greatly reduced in scale will mainly consist of élitist entrepreneurs and administrators of a generalist type.

Micklethwait and Wooldridge quote a 1995 survey done by the University of Warwick in England, stating that 1.35 more millions of managerial positions were created during the period 1981-94. With the same rate of increase, 630,000 new managerial positions at the year 2001 would imply that 18.5% of the work force would be managers (Op.cit. p.217). However, mid-level managers are being re-duced at the same time, reinforcing pressures on top-management.

No wonder managers today feel a rather great need of relating to their own prac-tice, be it of no other reason than to keep their job. In Denmark it is not unusual that top managers change position every year.

---

14. Cooper and Burrell observe the importance of recognizing "the production of organiz-ing rather than the organizing of production" (Cooper, Burrell: 1988) p.106.

It appears as did economic growth, bureaucratic success, the results of projects, sustainability, and even "quality of life", to a raising degree depend on the form of management. This dependence of the economy on the manager's style, on his personality, on his consequence and, not least, on his moral integrity, approaches the limit of the idealtype of management, pointing, rather shyly still, to both the necessity and to the possibility of leadership. It is as if technical problems and hence, differences of production processes, of trades and sectors, could be played down in relation to the social aspect of management – a fulfilling at a new level of the old statement of Peter Drucker in his book, "The Concept of the Corporation" from 1946 that an enterprise must be conceived of as a social system. However, the firm has for quite a long time been viewed as a place where psychological and hence, social forces and social patterns were at play: desires, powers, personal ambitions, crimes, punishments, victories, failures, guilt and forgiveness, hatred and reconcilement – not the sunshine of reason and enlightenment, but the dark reality of the prison and the penitentiary made familiar to us by Michel Foucault (Foucault: 1975). But in the corporate rooms we also shall find discourses almost speaking of themselves without any subject or autonomous author – postmodern man as an automaton – realizing nearly absurd, but deep-rooted patterns of behaviour and cognition. The firm is a crucial unit, a chessboard for the game of meaning.[15] Something points to the fact that management is simply forced into philosophy. As Peters and Watermann observes about the most excellent companies, it is most important to them that "if they know any one thing, they know how to manage paradox." (Op.cit. p.91).

The manager is a person who knows how to manage paradox – if paradoxes and aporias are something that can be managed, and ought to be managed, at all.

The manager is a spectacular person. He can, and he must be seen by everybody. He has been thrown out of the secure tower in the middle of his panopticon, of which Foucault, using Bentham, speaks. He is no longer the privileged observer, the silent well-bred yet vicious bureaucrat. He is an observer observed by everybody. He is back on the stage of the Greek amphitheatre. The manager and the politician become more and more similar. And managerial profiles and methods are transferred these days from private enterprise into the public sector, supported by privatization. However, this does not mean that any leading theorist of management

---

15. This terrible pseudo-existentialism, in its making strategic use of even the fear of death, a sad spin-off from the Corporate Culture Movement, is advocated by Peters and Watermann: "The excellent companies seem to understand that every man seeks meaning (not just the top fifty who are 'in the bonus pool') ... So strong is the need for meaning, in fact, that most people will yield a fair degree of latitude or freedom to institutions that give it to them" (Peters, Watermann: 1982, p.76-77). Unfortunately Peters and Watermann are not alone with this functionalism of the human condition. This critique does not mean, however, that "In Search of Excellence" is not an important book.

and organization shall find this a possible strategy, or even an ideal. Henry Mintzberg for example conceives of this trend as doomed to failure (Mintzberg: 1989, 1994).

Now, let us approach the promised analysis of the distinction between the concepts of management and leadership.

The very first question posed by a philosophy dedicated to management must be: "What is a good manager?"

But this "What" not only relates to a multitude of managerial relations and functions, it also questions the very concept of "Manager" itself.

The phenomenon of management covers a wealth of functions from the spontaneously constituted leader to the formally and carefully chosen one; it covers the managing of transient processes as well as institutionally well established and long lasting ones. It covers unimportant and trivial tasks, involving only a few, as well as assignments and missions of importance to the fate of nations, and even to the survival of the international community.

It is evident that the criteria pertaining to good management cannot be identical everywhere in this space.

In the first place management covers tasks consisting of almost undetermined goals without laid-down procedures, and almost without any organizational frame to structure the managerial functioning. The whole setting comes very close to the interpersonal relations and the communication of the "Lebenswelt" (the space of our ordinary and personal life; the spiritual atmosphere wherein we live).

And it covers tasks of operational precision with means and ends strictly marked out. These means are found in the form of thoroughly rehearsed procedures and well defined organizational structures developed down into the finest detail, resembling an infinitesimal choreography of movements and moments. The criteria of the good manager cannot be the same in this space either.

In the second place, management is formed by the content of the tasks which it has to fulfill. The structures of management or leadership of an army during a war must diverge from the ways of managing a theatre. The managing of a secret police force must differ from the managing of a bakery.

The managing of the production in an automated oil refinery with a workforce mainly consisting of mid-level and upper-midlevel employees has to differ from the managing of unskilled textile workers in a traditional low-pay area.

In the third place, other strategies are demanded from the management of high-technology firms producing durable consumer goods which continually demand innovation, like the walk-man, for example, and which are liable to being copied, than the management of consultancy firms or investment companies.

In the fourth place management of firms consisting of many different unities, combining different cultures and ethnic groups – like chain stores – demands other strategies than the management of relatively homogeneous firms bound to national markets – as is often the case with those producing foodstuffs, seeds and fertilizers.

In the fifth place, firms integrated into comprehensive network structures covering many fields of production demand other types of management than do firms specialized in relation to products and processes, like power stations.

In the sixth place, it is a rather different managerial situation to lead processes of production, the know-how of which you hardly understand, and thus to confront a staff which you are only able to guide at a symbolic level; compared to the managing of production processes, created by oneself from scratch.

In the seventh place, companies under pressure from shareholders, and rather conservative boards watching the slightest change in returns, demand other managerial tactics, other managerial talents, than do public enterprises or pensions funds, the resources of which are results of political decisions. The concept of manager is complicated by the fact that a manager in most cases is managed by somebody himself. The colonel leads the regiment, but the general leads the army corps. The chief of production manages production, but he himself is managed by the CEO. And the CEO is often managed by the board.

We are able to proceed almost infinitely. To wit, 60% of the eight million new jobs in the USA during the period from 1991 to 1995 belonged to the category "Managers and other professionals". This is the biggest group within the workforce.

But a further complication is created concerning the clarification of the concept of manager, because history has shown, supported by what seems logically possible, that a manager can be more than one person. I shall not take this fact into account, because our discussion of the identity of the manager counts for every one of a group of managers on an equal footing. But of course a group of managers or even leaders with a hierarchial structure poses special problems, also related to another aspect of management and leadership: who is the person to whom the real power belongs?

On the preceding pages I have already used the two concepts of "management" and "leadership" quite naturally. The concept of "management" is obviously connected to a **technē**, to specific tasks bound to the content of production, of marketing, of money and technology. The concept of "leadership" is connected to the "Lebenswelt", to non-technical interrelations and forms of communication, to non-profit activities, but first and foremost to the political and martial spheres. Hence, "Leadership" seems already to contain a normative element in relation to "management". No doubt these two concepts are concepts that refer to "reality" via "family likeness", to use the well-known concept of Ludwig Wittgenstein. Thus, we know very well when we are speaking of "leadership" versus "management", but it is extremely difficult to explain this ability to distinguish through formal criteria. The problem is that "leader" and "manager" have distinctly different traits, but also a field of intersection in relation to signification, where the transition between them flows. In practice, a leader often functions as a manager, and a manager as a leader. A manager could be a coach, an executive in a multinational company, a stevedore, the Secretary General of UN, or a tenant of a stall in a fair. But the coach and the Secretary General are able to, and ought to, be leaders as well.

Perhaps the point might be that "manager" and "leader" refer to properties seldom totally identical to the identity of one person. Could you not find a bit of the manager in Martin Luther King, as well as a bit of the leader in John D. Rockefeller?

However different the tasks of management seem to be, and even if the respective places of "management" and "leadership" already seem to be settled, these two concepts are able to serve as the core concepts of the totality of managerial and leading activity. As labels of two fundamentally different ways of approaching functional hierarchies, they can furnish Management Philosophy with a line of demarcation.

The concept of "the good leader" appears to be able to yield a more general meaning dependent on the applied criterion of "good", a meaning that seems to be able to escape deliberate definition. Indeed, in everyday use of this concept an unreconciled and overt opposition can be found:

For example, it would be hard to compare the managerial competence of a chief consultant under the English plan hired to restructure the National Health Service who will get grants through a point system based on the amount of cured patients, with that of the chief of production measured by the amount of cars produced in a factory. The comparison fails even if the industrial concept of "flow" might be found rational as a way to look at the time saved that sick people spend in the hospital beds and cars on the assembly line.

The concept of "good" is of course different here, and must be. Not only because the concept of "cured" is far more complex than the concept of "a well-functioning car", but also because a good doctor is able to create a good time in the hospital – the car, I presume, does not care about the stay on the assembly line, even if the workers do.

It seems, then, that the concept of "the good leader" is just as complicated and comprehensive as the concept of "leader" itself.

Both concepts have to be pinned down and marked out, but more through a creative gesture, than through mapping, recording and summing up.

The second indispensable question must resound: "Who is the good leader?"

This "Who" seems to point to definite properties in definite types of persons, or even to point to one personality only.

It is tempting to establish a catalogue of properties here, and it has been done very often in management theory. It is possible to claim their inborn character or to emphasize the element of acquisition through learning, be it experience or education, or both. Yet, if the properties of the leader are genetic, the very institution of education in management seems rather superfluous, not to speak of most of the profitable production of literature on management.

The more we search for the real leader in the properties of the individual, in the personality, the more Management Philosophy will evaporate on the hot frying pan of psychology. But this surrender to psychology and to a more or less "empirical science" will destroy the essence of Management Philosophy: Radical Normativity.

But perhaps we did not follow the path which appeared behind the question?

Perhaps this "Who" in the quest for the good leader was not meant to refer to any individual person, to a subject, to an ego, to a self, in the traditional meaning of those words.

Perhaps the distinction between **leader** and **manager** that seems obvious enough, might have quite another content than its almost trivial connotations?[16]

Well, I hope that it is now clear that the concepts of leader and manager can serve to establish two totally different ideal types of the relation between people, where labour and power have to be combined. Their little language game[17] creates, so to speak, a golden section, giving the possibility to place them in an autonomous area, where their inherent content can be fully developed. This content can be caught through a rather simple, conceptual framework confronting two fundamentally different human relations:

16. In his book from 1989, "On Becoming a Leader", Warren Bennis distinguishes between "leader" and "manager" by way of a rather comprehensive list marking the differences between the two types. For example, the manager uses control while the leader creates trust. Such oppositions, and hence similar issues treated in related works on management theory, must of course also be touched on in the analytical framework that I am going to develop. It is obvious that the mentioned distinction between "manager" and "leader", as an essential distinction within natural language, for many years must have been the subject of management theory, see, for example (Zaleznik: 1992). But the justification of my analysis is that in this comprehensive litterature the point of view of Radical Normativity is missing.

17. To whom, may I ask, shall this irony be ascribed that probably the most important concept of serious as well as of popular philosophy, also hunting the Social Sciences and the Humanities since The Second World War, was said to have been coined by Ludwig Wittgenstein, but was actually suggested to him by the economist Pierro Sraffa? The core concept of modern linguistic philosophy originates from economic theory!

Management

subject – object

asymmetric

- the means-end-relation is immanent and possible to set out explicitly

- basic metaphors: strategy, domination, control, guidance, instructions, requests, orders, commands, or threats, obeyance, adaptation, acceptance of authority, inequality,
- few possibilities to question legitimacy
- a closed, "formatted" space
- a projected, anticipated time (authoritative logistics)
- a strong organizational centre
- science

Leadership

subject – subject

symmetric

- the means-end-relation is transcendent and not possible to set out explicitly

- basic metaphors: dialogue, teaching, request, appeal, commitment, empathy, identify oneself with, understanding, reciprocity, solidarity,
- absolute demands to legitimacy
- a free space
- an open, poetic, an adventurous time (organic logistics)
- no formal, organizational centre
- magic

Figure 1

The ideal type of "leadership" was developed by Plato as the framework of interrelation between the philosopher and his pupils, in his dialogues (we shall return to this issue in Part II). The distinction between the two types was first and foremost developed in the modern era by G.W.F. Hegel in his "Phänomenologie des Geistes" (Phenomenology of Spirit) from 1807, in the famous chapter dealing with the relation between the master and the slave, where he develops the concept of "Anerkennung" (recognition) as the communicative core of the second ideal type.

3.1. The Ideal Type of Management

The ideal type of the manager is characterized by an asymmetrical relation: a subject is always confronted with an object. It is impossible for the object, within the given context, to become a subject, and for the subject to become an object. Their positions might come close to each other, like the captain might come close to the major, and at an almost equal footing take part in the final choice in the decisive emergency situation, but they are never able to be identical.

Thus the subject should ideally be characterized by a surplus in relation to the object within the following fields: experience, competence, information (also concerning what is specific to the firm), knowledge (both general and bound to the life of the firm). This subject is not under any obligation to state the reasons for his decisions, commands or actions. His right to authority is most often based on functional criteria, but he is able to legitimize his position beyond functional criteria as well. He is expected to know what he is doing, and to know best. Nobody can question him when he plays the game of "what he takes for granted", or the game of the "eloquent silence".

It is obvious that this idealtype in practice often will be built on a formalized difference between subject and object. It is simply built on power legitimized in the last instance by private ownership, at least in the field of business. But of course this does not prevent the existence of informal managerial positions (even if an informal manager often will be called "a leader").

The manager relates to his "object", primarily the employee, through the recognition that "it" offers him. He, on his side, answers through his acceptance of this recognition from the employee that shows due reverence to his power.

We are within Hegel's "master-slave relation". The play of power taking place within the setting of this relation finds its legitimacy in the permanent possibility of the manager to refer to established relations of means to ends. But it is presupposed that he has a privileged knowledge about those relations, both through his position, his competence, and his access to information.

The manager possesses the power of definition. He is authorized to lay down a language that makes manipulation of the agenda legitimate, first and foremost because it makes it invisible.

The sometimes offensive demands from the "object", to get an answer relating to the concrete content of the managerial functioning can always be met through a grandiose gesture referring to given patterns of means and ends, e.g., where the omnipotent and omniscient retorts "And did you really not know that?" The end could here be both economical in a broader or more specific sense: taking the pay-offs into account, the technical problems, the image of the firm, the need of financing, etc. And the means are justified through a "scientific discourse" often delimited in relation to the more or less fragile rationale of the different fields of business economics.

Questions about the possibility of giving reasons for the very form of the managerial process can be refuted by the manager by "arguments" like: "Are you able to imagine a production process without some kind of management?" The vague "some kind of management" here could easily be identified with precisely that kind of management which justifies the existence of exactly this manager.

The manager can in extreme cases force himself through in his authority, without bothering to refer to any rationale, through a silence, that presents any demand of an explanation as a question about the lack of knowledge of norms and values.

But normally the ideal type of the manager contains a certain limit to the way power is used: any exercise of authority must be acceptable to the "object", either through the referring to legitimate means-ends-relations, to norms peculiar to professional forms of life, or to the structure of the organization. The position of the employee, his identity within the organization in relation to the success and survival of the firm, forms a just reason of managerial behaviour. The more the employee feels uncertain about the consequences of his position, the easier it is to legitimize strong sanctions from the side of management. But those sanctions are, of course, in the modern firm, contractually determined and regulated by law at a rather abstract level. Investigations of military psychology gives some evidence to the fact, rather evident to careful observers of modern business life, that success on the battlefield is inversely proportional to the obstinate type of authority (Dixon: 1976). Authoritative senior commanders are prone to repeat mistakes, slow to admit failures, inclined to underestimate the enemy; they have a tendency to ignore warning signals, and to inhibit change. Hence, the functional argument in favour of hierarchical management might be challenged, at least by this canonical analogy, insofar as history allows us to identify hierarchy, conservatism and authoritative personalities. The contract as an instrument of this subject-object relation, and as a metaphor of modern business relations too, is conceptualized and analyzed by Oliver Williamson in his "transaction-cost theory" (Williamson: 1985). But the exposition of this theory often hides the fundamental contradictions between subject and object, symbolically expressed by the term "manager", behind the apparent symmetry of contractual relations. Williamson's ability to formalize and, hence, to make operational, the contradictions behind central, modern economical phenomena like trust, mistrust, bounded rationality, differences in relation to resources, range of ownership, and knowledge, seems also to be an ability to make these contradictions and asymmetries invisible. In other words, he seems not to be suspicious towards the power of the contractual-relation-figure that can cause superficial harmony to be mistaken for real symmetry. Besides, by stressing negotiated agreements between what might be conceived of as a "contractor" and a "client", the whole setting of transaction analysis implies that tasks are able to be unambiguously described (Fikes: 1982). As soon as this premises cannot be adhered to and the informal and tacit aspects of tasks are emphasized, the framework of contracting makes an almost infinite spiral of renegotiations necessary until the point is reached where contracting seems to contradict functionalist arguments, if not to block any functionalism at all.

Metaphors of the subject-object relation inherent in the concept of management are guidance and control. They are characterized by the notion that one part of the relation is not able to know what serves his own good. Hence guidance, and an ideal of education dominated by the concept of guiding, might often follow the path that the guided, the pupil, ought not to possess this knowledge. This competence belongs to the manager. He shall determine the goals which education shall serve, and this is not personal development, not the fundamental Greek ideal of **paideia**, but the ability to serve a narrow **technē**. From the manager's perspective the firm is a mobilized community. Hence, any individual is under the pressure of serving communal survival. The employee must obey, or commit treason.

These kind of metaphors must obviously exhibit the vague ideas of the proponents of functionalist justifications of hierarchical management (and leadership), because their conceptual gestures invoke tasks of coordination, often huge construction projects (roads, tunnels, bridges) or the demands of emergency situations such as natural disasters (history is often invoked here). But the core metaphor of (hierarchical) management has always been, and will probably always be, that of war. As has already been noticed, these metaphors of war are able to furnish sets of value beyond discussion: to obey your superior, to attend to your work, to sacrifice yourself to the community, to do even more than your best, to die for the case. The slogans and successes of Japanese management from the seventies and onwards can easily be recognized here. But one secret of Japanese managerial success is no doubt a far more pronounced trait of reciprocity on the side of management here, even if it was never symmetrical in our sense of the word.

The metaphors of war, of course, also furnish functionalist justifications of management at a more technical scale: the concept of "task force" originating in the joint effort of the three military services, is a fashion word to almost any managerial universe. The military origin of behavioural codices of conservative management, such as instructions, requests, orders, commands, or even threats and punishment, is rather obvious. But also the early school-systems borrow most of their codes of conduct from the military or the penal institution and the reformatory – as Michel Foucault has demonstrated so masterly (Foucault: 1975).

Perhaps yet another common metaphor of the functional necessity of hierarchical management ought to be mentioned here: the one of the orchestra. Even Karl Marx himself falls victim to this one in his praise of technology and its liberating forces. The point is that the cooperation between the musicians demands coordination from a technical perspective. Spontaneous symmetry is seen as impossible here among musicians without the conductor: "If the bassoon plays portato here, but the bass staccato, how on earth could any kind of music emerge from that?"

But the transference of such a kind of metaphor, and many others as well – the manager being the "brain" of the firm's "body", and so on – is truly problematic. Among the best conductors, like Sergiu Celibedache, one finds a transference of musical ideas almost "telepathically;" he makes the musicians euphoric. One also find an application of techniques, where anarchy sometimes seems to be used to directly create the utmost organic results.

The quintessence of management's relation to space and time is, of course, Taylorism. This program was revived with renewed force and laid down in the recent program of "Total Quality Management":

Place is closed and "formatted" (this computer-metaphor is more than a metaphor, because the computer is the ideal of control here, of the relation between power and knowledge).

Even the aesthetics of the work place is subjected to functional and hierarchical aims.

Time is projected and anticipated. Also a strict, formalized logistics, and a strategic, if not cynical, interpretation of the principle of "just-in-time" set the agenda.

The situation is anticipated through operations analysis and decision-systems, and transformed into an event under the conditions of maximum control and in relation to the very "brute" criteria of business economics, such as pay-offs and the conquering of markets. This is the "lean production" of the predator.

We shall return however to the role of place/space in management and leadership, in Part IV.

There is a strong, organizational centre in the world of management. The centrifugal movement is favoured, not the centripetal. This conceptual figure is the main connection between managerial theory and organizational theory. The notion dominating epistemologically here is that there exists one and only one true discourse of the reality and operations of the firm, into which all other discourses can be translated.[18] Its physiognomy was examined by Drucker and Mintzberg, but its real problems in the modern firm was attempted to be eliminated by "Symbolic Management" through fashionable, but by now rather aged, concepts like "Culture of the firm", "the mission" and "the vision" of the firm. The quiet historical fact that

---

18. Hence, managerial literature did not seem to take W.van O.Quine's famous "Principle of the indeterminacy of translation" seriously until Derrida and Foucault invaded the American Academic world in the late eighties, and gradually began to challenge the established worldview – well supported by the increasing knowledge of the works of Ludwig Wittgenstein.

the only two things that cannot be invented are religion and culture bit back with epistemological vigour and even irony on this supposed master plan.

It is a last, important trait of management that the manager rely totally on a conservative concept of science. The prototype here is "rule-based action" – action based on general laws and models applied to data. The concept of "data" also involves "everything relating to the employee", and hence this strategy naturally reinforces his position as an object. The manager is predisposed to use the handy metaphor of the computer on the organizational setting. And the computer is a product, among other important conditions of course, of **cybernetics**, which hails from the Greek word, meaning "The science of steering, of control". The huge influence from Computer Science and Cognitive Science on management theories from the seventies and onwards, reflects the search for formal and hence hierarchical procedures of mobilizing and coordinating the efforts of subgroups, and of levels as well as fields of competence, into an organic unity in the pursuit of joint, but authoritative, objectives. Organic differentiation is a function of mechanical analysis (operations analysis).

A short reminder: the ideal type of management is limited both in relation to historical development, in relation to the sector, industry, and trade to which the firm belongs, hence in relation to type of production, and it is limited in relation the regional location of the firm. It is also limited by the size of the firm – managerial problems is by now really complicated in the middle-size firm. It is limited by the educational level of its work force, and by its average age – managerial problems are serious in high-technology enterprises employing academics and others groups with high-level resources of knowledge, who often possess rather inscrutable competencies. It is limited in relation to ethnic and religious groups, and in relation to sex; it is limited in relation to organizational structure as well as to its peculiar managerial tradition (Edwards: 1979). A firm that employs mostly younger computer scientists and information-workers cannot permit itself to apply authoritative managerial strategy. Neither can consultancy firms. A recent example from Norway reveals that the staff simply left a consultancy firm with a management unwilling to negotiate managerial strategies, and founded a new one themselves.

Employees conscious of their existence as "human capital" and "knowledge capital" are not that easy to order around. Even sky-high salaries will not help here. The more than 20.000 Ph.D's that Andersen Consulting employ shall probably want the most important freedom for the modern, highly educated employee: free space. Free space means liberty of action in relation to both the inner and outer reality of the firm, but it also means the right to partake in management, and in profits. Management is often forced to give shares to this kind of employee in order to keep him. The claim of Scandinavian trade unions from the seventies for economical democracy, i.e., a participation in private ownership, has now become a reality through the initiative and strategy of management. The irony of history? Or is it the irony of technology?

3.2. The Ideal Type of Leadership

Leadership can be made conceptually manifest through an ideal type where subject confronts subject. This relation is symmetrical. This means that insofar as the subject functioning as a leader might have a surplus within the mentioned fields (power, knowledge, information ...), then it is only through real (not just formal) acceptance from the side of the other subject, the employee. In this symmetrical relation the employee can be named "the co-lead", or perhaps less clumsy, the "co-directed". The prefix "co-" emphasizes the community lying behind the subject-subject relation, and even the solidarity.

The demand of legitimacy is an absolute one; it is not able to be paid off through a gesture referring to the thumbscrews of market forces, stockholders or technology. But it is an important point that the acceptance of this surplus in the leader only can be legitimate as far as the "co-directed" actually possess the "psychic" resources to make this acceptance real.

This might of course open up a vicious circle, because which of the two parties must have this surplus as the first? But we must remember that we are here in a landscape of the ideal type, where peculiar "democratic" situations of decisions, of education, and of acting, or perhaps only the serious conversation between equal and involved persons, shall fix the pattern.

Decisive here will often be the idea that all human beings have the same preconditions through their human nature, not only with regard to cognition and emotion, but also in relation to the conative faculty, to the will: it is not only a fact that everybody is able to join the task force and to cope with the technical jobs, and that they are able to feel the solidarity and passion needed, but it is supposed that they have the urge to do so as well. However, exactly the faculty of will is problematic here, from an epistemological and empirical point of view, if it is claimed to be an equally distributed faculty.

The position of the leader becomes paradoxical here, and to a certain degree it is contingent as to his person. He is the one who happens to possess the insight and knowledge that authorizes him to be the promoter of essential processes. He is the product, the child of the event, as we shall explain it in Part IV. But he is also the product of his own will, and here, he is a secret not just to others, but to himself. On the other hand, the fact that it is him and nobody else who must lead, seems to point towards a sort of process of selection, a process with a secret optimum – and the will must certainly be involved in that optimum. In this case one might be reminded of the strange destinies of Garibaldi, or of Winston Churchill.

This decisive factor here is the will. The will cannot, empirically, be conceived of as an equally distributed faculty like the cognitive and the emotional ones.

The will, the "conative" aspect of man's mental capacities, is a capacity that is especially convincing in the extreme, where we witness its ability to enforce in spite of all odds. The will seems to be the concept through which the **contextual** dependence circumscribing the subject-subject relation is capable of being reflected.

If it is not through a personal quality that the leader distinguishes himself compared to the other, "the co-conducted", subject of the relation of leadership, then the will alone is able to be the unknown quantity which places him as the solution to the equation of the firm's fields of problems. Or put another way: "the will" is an abstraction to a peculiar sense of action identical to the fact that he, the leader, actually is the vital centre of the process of conducting. "The will" here does not necessarily have to be conceived of as a "talent", but could be regarded as a conglomeration of circumstances, a sensitivity to the inertia of the event that grants one person only a certain force. Thus the concept of "the will" correlates neither to concepts like "experience", "knowledge", nor "competence".

One must be very careful here. The concept of "the will" has often been related, if not to fascist ideologies alone, then at least to ideologies that focus on the right to dominance proper to the excellent individual. I shall come to speak much about the will in this book, but I will do it under one condition: that the will is conceived of as a faculty, and as a quality, that does not express the "ego", the autonomous, epistemological pivot of thinking and acting, but something quite different. In my works on phenomenological philosophy I used to define the will as the following: " "the will" is that which through/by me permanently happens to the body of reality."

This definition displaces the centre of signification from the individual to the event. The leader, then, is both the conqueror and the victim of "his" will. The philosophical emphasis is removed from Nietzsche back to Schopenhauer, and actually, back to the Aesthetics of Immanuel Kant and his delineation of the pathos of the faculties of knowledge. This "pathos" designates the emotional basis of certainty, that constitute even logic. For Kant the ability to convince is the work of the will[19] (a thesis which we shall examine further in Part IV). Like the biography of Cesare Borgia by W.H. Woodward illustrates, there are no heroes, no one that master destiny, but only children of the event (Woodward: 1913).

To emphasize these circumstances is necessary for at least one reason: if the will is posited as a peculiar faculty/quality of some single individual, then the ideal type of leadership, the subject-subject figure, would be destroyed.

The will which any sound explanation must ascribe to the action-pattern of a certain individual under certain circumstances does not need to mean more than an extraordinary "sensitivity to realities and possibilities" provoked by a certain event and its certain settings (that this peculiar sensitivity constitutes a managerial virtue, shall be demonstrated in Part III). When we focus on the event, then it no longer seems totally strange that "will" might relate to several individuals at the same time, and that the concept of "will" not only transgresses the person as an isolated individual, but the concept of "person" itself. The will might then be thought

---

19. Kant, I. (1793/1974): Kritik der Urteilskraft. Herausgeg. von Wilhelm Weischedel. Suhrkamp Verlag, Frankf.a.M., Paragraph 21.

of as a force which is itself the subject. But it is important to notice that such a kind of wording must be understood, not so much in a metaphorical sense, but as a function of the limitations inherent in the explanatory power of language, and, hence, in thinking.[20]

There arises an aporia here. As an ideal type, leadership must look like one of two alternatives: either it is contingent in relation to the concept of the individual, or deeply rooted there.

In the first case the necessity of leadership is equivalent to the necessity of a leader, not of that leader. Technical demands necessitate a leader, but they do not give him any rights towards the employee as an object. The "co-directed" himself submits to what his personal insight tells him to be "technical necessities" demanding leadership. Carried through to its logical extreme this perspective would imply that anybody was capable of taking the leader's place. In principle it should be possible to choose him through drawing lots – which often seems to be a superior alternative to the activities of head-hunter firms! But something else must be at work here. Contingency as the frame of reference must not be confused with chance. As mentioned earlier, there is much necessity within contingency. So the aporia might not be that hard after all.

This can already be seen, if one reflects upon the fact that it is almost impossible to discuss the content of the concept of "technical causes" to managerial changes without involving other types of causes as well. Even the theoretical isolation of this factor seems very delicate. The field of the "technical" might often cover far more "social" reasons and causes, due to its embeddedness in patterns of interrelation. The introduction of a new machine on the shop floor is very seldom motivated by technical parameters alone, like raising the quantity of output, improving quality, reducing waste of raw material, or obeying public demands for the protection of environment. The considerations of the effects of this machine on the increase in control of the work force will almost always be present. Also considerations about discipline are evident, i.e., relating to the implied, new recruiting strategies: which types of employees, with which education, social background, age (and even colour and ethnic origin) are now able to be relevant. It is hard to exclude an organizational dimension in any "technical" change of the production process. Similarly, when it relates to the change in other types of processes in the firm, like information-processes, it is even more obvious. Thus, strategies of decentralization, paradoxically enough, are favoured because of the need to cope with the problems of solving

---

20. I think it important to evade giving reasons for the emergence of the right leader, at the right time, which shall evoke functionalist theories of society and institutions where the firm is conceived of as a kind of "organic" "mega-consciousness" – a field today often named "cognitive organization-theory". The concept of the will presented here is not meant to underrate the importance of the individual, quite the contrary, because it would make the concept of "virtue" impossible.

the information problems on the basis of computer systems. Their success might be due to the fact that they simultaneously solve technical and social problems.[21]

In the second case the necessity of leadership cannot be realized without taking the person of precisely that leader into account. This is probably the most usual way of perceiving the concept of leadership: identifying the person and the function. But this does not have to be a normative identification, by any means; one could just mention Morgan or Bill Gates.

These two ideal types of leadership (not of leadership versus management) both demand that the necessity of the leader arises from the recognition on behalf of the "co-directed" of the inevitable need for this very function. This goes both for mere functionalism, as a mutual reflection of the fact that processes in the firm demand the decisions of one person only; and in relation to the setting, where the leader is a historical fact. But the content of the recognition is rather different in the two cases. In the first case, the necessity of the leader refers to demands from techniques, cooperation, coordination, or administration, and most often the type of legitimacy will be conservative and hard to challenge. The firm and trustworthy bureaucrat that (re-)creates the manageability of the credit and debit of a once renowned firm rich in tradition, but overridden by bad management and shareholders' greed, would be an example here. In the second case, we confront a necessity less tangible, more spontaneous, and to a higher degree reflected in relation to situation and context. Powerful political leaders, the products of violent historical processes, are found under this ideal type. But this type of leadership could also be more settled, more anticipated and fixed through sedimentary patterns like organizational structures, customs and rule-governed action. The event of leadership will here always be the final reason of the claims to legitimacy.

To both types of leadership it is vital that the "co-directed" encounters his leader through a "You". This "You" must of course be understood figuratively, and not as a way of simply addressing the leader. The "I" that encounters this "You" is more than just a reciprocal "You" to the "I" of the leader. They form a unity.[22] This implies that their roles should always be interchangeable – which of course, has never been a historical fact until now, quite the opposite. Not only is it possible for the "co-directed" to identify with his leader, i.e., assume an authority which precisely does not belong to him; but he is able to identify with him in actuality. The "co-directed", then, is not alone able to assume an identity and hence, an authority which he could never be able to possess in reality. But by identifying with the dic-

---

21. This was already noticed by Börje Langefors in 1986. See (Langefors: 1986, p.72): "As we pointed out, the datalogical attempts at solving the information problems are very poor solutions. Instead the managerial means, decentralization and delegation in a way which eliminates all unneccessary data standardization, appear as very effective."

22. Of this peculiar unity much insight is found in the book "Ich und Du" ("I and You") written by the hassidist philosopher, Martin Buber (Buber: 1923).

tator everybody can be a symbolic leader himself, a great "co-directed". This character combines the qualities of the super human, the socially domonating daydream, and the human all too human, the almost comically fragile side of man, no matter how demonic, like Hitler. But psychology and sociology which so often have made this identification into a subject of investigation in order to understand totalitarianism, sometimes seem to forget that "co-directedness" often implies "co-responsibility", "complicity", and perhaps even "co-criminality" too. To obey an "I" which transforms you into a genuine "You", and hence, into an new kind of "I", shall never be able to escape the criteria of normativity. It must make itself worthy of Radical Normativity. Leadership must never be an excuse, not for the leader himself, nor for his subordinate and followers.

The "co-directed" then, should not just be given the right to understand the way his leader acts, but he is obliged to scrutinize it as well. To understand, really understand, is his duty. He is obliged to destroy any trait of symbiosis, however tempting and however soothing; he must question the very effect of identification. If this ideal type of leadership should be totally realized, then "the leader" must not function as an alien inside the mind of the "co-directed" himself. The understanding of the leader demands an effort of transparency on the side of the "co-directed" that summons yet an aporia up. "Charisma" is no excuse here:

To understand the leader, to meet him as a "You", demands that the "co-directed" himself becomes a real "You", contrary to an "I" hiding behind its right to demand from the leader all that which "it" will not demand from itself. Or alternatively, he renounces his demand for the last and most important from the leader, because he, through subordination, thinks that he ought to demand it from himself.

In other words, leadership as an ideal type cannot be fully comprehended through reference to the symmetrical relation between subject and subject in behavioral terms alone, it also demands a conception of an organization of the "inner space" of the employee. It is of utmost importance that the "co-directed" himself endeavours to delve into his own self. He must accept the duty of being a **co-conducter**.

But the fact of co-conducting presupposes a knowledge in both parties about their total dependence on each other. This was Hegel's point concerning relations of power. Each of them can only be an "I" insofar as they permanently create the "You" that legitimizes their being who they are. Leadership is of no value without the co-conducted's "co-".

It should be obvious that the leader never could enforce co-conduction among his employees. This would imply that it was his aim to make himself the absolute master of the subject-subject-relation – a project that would destroy symmetry immediately.

On the contrary, what characterizes the leader, and ultimately extinguishes him within the subject-subject-relation, is his will and ability to make the very unity of the subject-subject-relation a topic of intra-organizational communication. It is his cleverness when it comes to starting processes of reflection in relation to the very phenomenon of "co-conducting". It is not until he has acquired this ability that he is a real leader. Formal position and rule-based authority will not help him here. The first articulation of this will and of this ability is sincerity. To it answers **trust**. But neither sincerity nor trust are simple phenomena.

In Greek "sincere" is called "haplous" or "alēthēs". "Haplous" means "the simple", "that of which only one exemplar exists", hence "the unique". But sincerity might also be named "alētheia". This concept is the one which usually signifies "the truth" in Greek philosophy. In modern philosophy it is tied to the name of Martin Heidegger who uses it to denote a kind of truth that conceals itself, that neither presents itself immediately as a brute fact, nor juxtaposes world and words. Instead it dwells near us as a promise, leaving a trace. The presence of truth is absence – to phrase its paradoxical form (Heidegger: 1954).

Insofar as sincerity should depend on the unique, and on truth as a promise that cannot be challenged, and which conceals itself from any conception of it, sincerity is not something that can be learned nor "mise en scène". Sincerity is then inextricably tied to the attitude forming a person's life. From this perspective it might even seem wrong to say: "I want to be sincere!" Because through this very effort, the originality is often lost, the individuality of that which cannot be repeated nor reproduced disappears.

In leadership the instrument of the leader is not – as in management – instructions, requests, orders, commands, or threats. Nor does the leader expect obedience, adaptation, acceptance of authority. Rather he depends upon dialogue, teaching, request, appeal, commitment, empathy, the possibility of identifying oneself with, understanding, reciprocity, and solidarity.

True leadership does not execute control.

The leader suggests and recommends. He assigns, and asks for.

He encourages and he calls for.

His instruments of sanction can never be punishment, degradation or suspension, but must be admonition, instruction, warning and – if inevitable – reproach.

Leadership cannot imply domination, because it must understand itself within the fundamental relation of **recognition**. Thus the behaviour expected from the co-conducted will come very close to a set of general, social virtues, like the ones mentioned by Fukuyama: "honesty, reliability, cooperativeness and a sense of duty to others"[23] (We shall return to the phenomenon of "duty" later on).

In leadership it is decisive that the leader will not usually be able to refer to a

---

23. The phenomenon of "recognition" has justly been emphasized by Francis Fukuyama in his book "Trust" (Fukuyama: 1995, p.6ff and p.358ff). He also defines a set of "social virtues", cf. Chapter 5.

given catalogue of means and ends – that is, means and ends that are able to be directly presented, even if they often are just implied – but that he is forced to refer to a common foundation of values that seldom can be made explicit. The point here is that the normativity practiced by the leader might be called "transcendent", meaning "intangible", or at least not simply able of being subsumed under existing maxisms. This is the prerogative of real virtue: the actions speak for themselves alone.

One can sense a paradox here. An important aporia: namely that values are able to keep the symmetry of the subject-subject-relation only in so far as we can **not** put them sufficiently into words. The rock-bottom of this relation must be the feeling of the holiness of the other person. To be convinced of, or consent upon, the universality of the involved maxisms or values do not suffice.

When it is not possible to explicate the basic values founding symmetry, then consensus is excluded because you are not able to know the identity of the issue on which you in the last instance did agree. Symmetry, therefore, must be kept floating through an active attitude towards the other person. It must be a reciprocal attitude. The claims to reciprocity implied in such an attitude must be stronger than the ones constituting the communicative framework of consensus. Otherwise the consequences of "evil rhetoric" – manipulation, strategy and even totalitarianism – lay close at hand.

This attitude must be carried by emotions, by **passion**, not by rational references to positions accessible to reflection. This attitude could be **respect** which is, fundamentally, a care for the dignity of the other person. Here we move into a quite different ideal type than the one known from the institutionalized model of consensus among, by and large, all type of actors and stakeholders.

We move into the field of friendship.

The genuine image of the subject-subject relation would be friendship, and hence the ideal of real leadership.

It characterizes friendship whose quality is inversely proportional to the ability of the friends to give reflective reasons for their relation. At the same time friendship shows, set up as the foundation of leadership, exactly that convergence towards the transgression of the whole complex of "rationalities" proper to macro- and micro-economics, and to business economics especially, implied by the ideal type of leadership.[24]

We are therefore forced to confront, in all its nakedness, the problem of whether

---

24. Aristotle transforms friendship into an important subject in his Nicomachean Ethics. The French philosopher, Maurice Blanchot (Blanchot: 1997), has made a monograph about it, and another French philosopher, Paul Ricoeur (Ricoeur: 1990), has used it to deduce the phenomenon of politics from a normative perspective. The Danish lawyer and philosopher, Alexander Carnera Ljungstrøm, has used the concept of friendship to create an alternative perspective on law (Ljungstrøm: 1997).

the subject-subject-relation is at all capable of being realized inside the frame marked out by the well-known tasks of management and leadership? Must it stay a utopia, or at best a "regulative idea" in the Kantian sense?

On the other hand, one must take into consideration that if it should be impossible to explicate the basic values of thinking and acting in the shape of well-defined universal maxims, then the contextual dependence of every interaction, and hence, its character of being an event, would come to dominate the central approach to ethics. This does not necessarily exclude the orienting towards universal values, but it means that these values always must be seen as "magnitudes" that at one and the same time must be filtered through contingent concepts which will both reveal and conceal them.

Conceived of as genuine ideal types, real leadership relates to the place/space, and to the time, of the firm's "mini-reality" in a very different way from that of management.

Leadership does not structure place through hierarchies. The Danish firm Oticon attetsts to this by its removal of office walls and by constructing a total system of information accessible to every employee.

Leadership leaves it to the employee to establish the range and content of relations to costumers. Consultancy firms are especially able to apply this strategy.

The core concept of leadership in relation to place and space is "the free space". This freedom relates to the co-workers on the shop-floor, to management and to the costumers. Organizationally it is concentrated on the creation of "natural groups" with a high grade of autonomy – a development also enforced, of course, by high demands of technical competence and knowledge on behalf of the employee, and hence of the availability of an intense, personal initiative.

Leadership does not try to force the time of the employee into a time-schedule. It leaves it to the employee to plan his working-hours, only the amount of time is fixed.

Leadership leaves it to the employees, most often on a group-basis, to create an organic logistics, however difficult this may be. This is true even if bonuses, i.e., money, have to be the primary instrument to realize this concept, and commitment alone does not yet suffice.

Leadership relies on a guiding metaphor of "decentration". This means far more than "de-centralization", – a concept connected to the formation of levels of autonomy and of autonomous groups in the late sixties, especially in Italy and in Sweden.[25] "Decentration" is an epistemological, if not an ontological concept, that refers to the fact that the firm and its organizational setting does not constitute one single reality, but consists of many discourses. This post-modern predicament –

---

25. In Italy the workers demanded this organizational change. In Sweden it was an instrument of management to control workers without proper factory experience.

an example perhaps that the important role of philosophy in catalyzing empirical experience, manifesting itself in Foucault's so-called "discourse-analysis" and in Derrida's "de-constructivism", is taken for granted by the real leader. He does not try to master it, nor to control it. He tries to use it as an incomparable resource, as an inventive force. He does not try to overcome this Babylonian multi-discursiveness through the favouring of a "culture", nor through any gestures involving the mutual commitment to "missions" or "visions" of the firm. In other words, he does not try to structure it through any strategies of "symbolic management". He simply lets it grow. He supports this anarchy, trying to explore its fruitful momentum.

At last it is vital that modern leadership devote itself to what – a bit provocatively – might be called **magic**.

Peculiar to magic is the fact that the magician masters the means to an end, but that he does not feign the ability to transform this mastership into analytical manuals nor into a calculus of decisional steps. **Magic** refers to the utmost importance of an intangible "social" force inherent as an empirical, rather than a theoretical, fact, in real leadership.

In connection with the purpose of deciding what good leadership is, and who the good leader is, the question must be: how are we able to strengthen the subject-subject relation? How can it be realized? Where can it be realized? How can the average manager develop a sense of its importance?

How is the average employee able to become a co-directed, become a person that not only focuses on his rights, but on his duties? How is it possible to transform the subject-object relation into its counterpart, the symmetrical relation, in any context of production, and in any organizational setting?

To solve this question might not involve such difficulties as could be expected because there seems to be a movement from management to leadership these days. This movement is deeply integrated with the change in the firm brought about by information technology.

The picture of the managerial predicament at the end of the millennium resembles the following:

a. a common complex of problems arises to both business and the public, which is also common across industries, sectors and trades.

The peculiarities of products, production processes, i.e., of techniques, are no longer the factors that set the agenda through the differentiation of managerial situations. Even theatres are looked upon as firms today.

The technical rationales for management, the functional stance, seem to give way to leadership.

b. the reality of work is characterized by "empowerment": delegating of authorities, not least through joint ownership, and hence, a democratization of the work place. The employee is given a co-responsibility of growth and failure, and a partnership in gains and losses.

c. perhaps one could say that a well-functioning firm is characterized by the following parameters: successful communication inside the factory walls, as well as in relation to the stakeholders, a readiness to use and create knowledge, a high degree of independence among the employees, and passion. The high-technology firm shall be judged by its will and ability to realize these parameters which appear to overshadow the usually dominating ones: technically determined competence, cooperativeness, expertise, the faculty of enterprising, and ambition.

Leadership is needed to transform ambition into commitment, enthusiasm, and solidarity.

d. managerial strategies based on rule-governing must give way to a governing aimed at ends, scopes, and settings. In this manner, managerial practices and organizational structures based on codes, fixed procedures, and hierarchical figures will disappear, because it is too difficult to finish creating fixed procedures and hierarchical figures before a new type of task arises. Both tasks and customer attitudes are changing rapidly. Leadership might better cope with these kinds of patterns pointing towards change as a permanent condition.

e. all firms are subject to more and more equal conditions of marketing in a global setting with violent technological development, the possibility of nearly perfect information through the internet, and a saturation of the demand for traditional goods. Here the same ethical, social and environmental demands can be made by different groups in different surroundings. The only variable here is the resources and the commitment of the employees. Human resources will increasingly be the parameter of competition.

Leadership is better armed than management to meet the challenges of knowledge and "mental" capital.

f. the purely technical element in the processes of the enterprise is no longer the sufficient basis for competition. Now the commodity must be followed by consultant services and the construction of a capacity in the customer, because he buys processes and knowledge, not "things". The communicative competencies are here put into the centre, and thus, become what we call "the human factor". It is the same everywhere: from the sales of "sensing" pipe-systems for transporting crude oil to the marketing of cakes to people suffering from allergy, from the promotion of production modules in cement works in Hungary to the implementing of IT-systems in the factories of Bombay, from consultancy relating to the constructing of networks to the sales of futures. Even the National Health Sector, as well as the revenue department, seem to have difficulties in letting their products and services go: prevention is better than cure.

Leadership seems far more apt to take care of communication than management. Sincerity and trust makes the difference.

g. the differentiation noted by Jürgen Habermas between a technical-economical reality – "the system", as he called it – on the one hand, and a soft, green, reddening, human and humanistic reality, on the other – the so-called "world-lived-in" (Habermas: 1981) – is slowly becoming meaningless. Management and employees are forced into an irreversible process, in which everybody must be able to make an account of his individual aims of learning and strategies, of his personal value-basis, and of the inner consistency of his actions.

Leadership and its canons, in still leaving a world outside the corporate rooms, are far closer to humanism and to human affairs than management.

h. the firm presents itself as involved in the process of acquiring a character close to the "program" of communitarianism: a dialogue in progress between the whole of the enterprise and its parts seems to be the **sine qua non** to modern management. The perfect firm consists of employees that believe in its mission and its vision, in theory and practice, not because they have no convictions of their own, but because they have realized their responsibility to the whole, a whole which they themselves have been the principal authors of.

Communitarianism and leadership are two sides of the same coin, whatsoever its value.

i. the workplace is characterized by a right to freedom and autonomy. The employee exists for the sake of work, but work also exists for the sake of the employee. A work space is a starting point, not something settled.

The employee not only has rights, he also has duties. Now, the employee can make demands to the style of management: no manager can exist for even a short period of time, as long as he is not able to unite speech and action. He must be able to answer for his promises. Rhetoric, dominating marketing, has got straitened circumstances behind the walls of the enterprise.

Rhetoric, to which management is often prone, does not match leadership.

j. at least as important as intellectual competence, professional qualifications, and manual skills, is emotion. Knowledge and passion are deeply connected. The watchword is enthusiasm. The relevant knowledge does not appear until it is sought by the light of passion.

The leader alone speaks the language of the heart.

k. inside the world of mass production, of replicas, and average quality, behind the short life of objects, carefully designed wear, and fast money, a new ideal seems to grow: the ideal of the unique. The unique specimen is the ideal of the relation between production process and product. The keywords are quality, minute specification of product, dedicated services, and the expectation of a careful consumption. The criterion of success then, becomes aesthetic. The flawless, the elegant, the expensive, the rare, but new and beautiful beyond any functionalism is what matters. The enjoyment, the well-being, the adventure, the absence of even the smallest trace of guilt is what is promised.

But here it does not seem so easy to distinguish between management and leadership. Like the manager, the leader wants quality, but to him flawlessness and beauty cannot justify any product in spite of its usefulness. He must prefer the production of pace-makers to the production of diamond watches.

l. and perhaps the most decisive of these new(-er) phenomena in business life: that business itself, in the sense of "gains", of "profit", can be played down now, and has to give way to a more traditional commitment to a "sound business practice", to a new decency that does not look away from any negative effect of business. Such a new decency will not make profit prior to propriety. And "propriety" means a careful handling of humane and material resources, a social responsibility in the broadest sense, i.e., not being satisfied with the minimal criteria of sustainability.

The new criteria of success to the modern firm might easily be:

> a. Satisfied employees, i.e., employees that have attained a personal development, who feel safe, who trust their colleagues and management.
> b. Satisfied costumers and an unspoiled environment.
> c. Economical autonomy, i.e., risks are oriented towards development and financed by the firm itself.
> d. A balance between gains in money and in responsibility.

Leadership answers to this program.

What Management Philosophy can do in this context is not just support any suspicion of rhetoric, but also scrutinize the possible content of the following concepts: "Costumer-satisfaction", "autonomy", "responsibility" … and, insofar as they have any stamina at all, to force them into the borderland of Radical Normativity.

CHAPTER 4

To Make the Stakeholder-model Radical: Leadership as Communication or The Fourth

Now we shall return to the concept of Radical Normativity once more, to the concept of The Fourth, in order to relate this conception to business economics.

In business science the socalled "stakeholder-model" has eventually become commonly accepted. Its essence can be grasped by the following – which is also to be understood as a critique of classical Operations Research:

> "Those who serve, and all professionals serve, should keep their focus on those they serve, not on the service they rendered nor the instruments used. Professionals should change with the changing needs of their users. User-oriented professionals should go where the users go."[26]

And Ackoff presented the stakeholder-model's program with the following theses:

> "1. Toward more participative management ...
> 2. Toward less bureaucracy and fewer internal service monopolies ...
> 3. Toward less supervision of subordinates, less management of their actions, and more management of the interactions of the unit managed with other units ...
> 4. Toward more effective planning ...
> 5. Toward more understanding, not merely knowledge, of what is happening within the organization and its environment ...
> 6. Toward more rapid and effective individual and organizational learning and adaption ...
> 7. Toward development rather than growth ...
> 8. Toward more creativity in management ..." (Ibid.).

Eventually the concept of "user" was replaced by the concept of "stakeholder", and the emphasis came to be on shared values and hence, on consensus, not least due to the shift in strategic goals from intra-organizational relations towards the relation between firm and environment. The basic idea, however, is still the same: the firm must be extremely sensitive to everybody involved with it.

---

26. The stakeholder-model was presented by Russell L. Ackoff in the article "Where do you intend to go now? (Ackoff: 1986) p.11-12. It was also presented by R.E. Freeman in the 1991 book "Business Ethics – the State of the Art" from 1991 (Freeman: 1991).

Therefore the concept of "stakeholder" must articulate the range and the content of all the personal and institutional relations in which the firm is involved in order to master them.

Following its logic of extension, the concept of "stakeholder" denotes in the first place the management and employees of the firm; in the second place it denotes those from whom it buys its services and goods;[27] in the third place it denotes its owners, the shareholders; in the fourth place it denotes the unions; in the fifth place it denotes the lawmaking institutions and those that regulate it in the service of the public. Finally it also denotes nature, the voiceless mammals, the whole organic and inorganic world of used and still unused resources, to which a voice must be ascribed. Finally it denotes the future.

Following its logic of intension, the concept refers to criteria and values, to attitudes and norms, governing the afore mentioned relations of the firm to its stakeholders. But, alas, it does not often point to relations of power and domination. Therefore the stakeholder-model ought to be analyzed as a species of the genus of "subcontracting", and hence, also through the concept of "network", because of its status as a species of the genus of "subcontract".

Whereas the concept of "subcontracting" primarily emphasizes the reciprocal flow of goods and money in a legally formalized setting while making relations of power explicit, the concept of "network-ing"[28] would stress the flow of information, and often in a legally informal way. This emphasis on social relations and, hence, social responsibilities and virtues proper to the concept of "stakeholder", can be caught by the concept of "network-ing", so long as it is not interpreted with too much reverence for functionalism. The dynamical aspect of the term stresses the mutual responsibility, but also the necessity to elaborate permanently on the relation: management is obliged to develop its understanding of the grass-roots groups in the neighborhood of the new plant; it is obliged to comply with the concerns of the public relating to undiscovered effects of pollution from this plant, not just to stand on narrow legal directions of minimal precautions.

The stakeholder-model is virtually global: the ripples of network-ing spread infinitely across the world, not least by way of the internet. But, being species of the concept of "subcontracting", both the concept of "stakeholder" and the concept of "network-ing", can be made the subjects of an analysis stressing both overt and hidden relations of powers and different values.

---

27. The success of Japanese management in relation to the subcontractors of the firm, by tying them to the firm in a long-term perspective rather than playing one off against another through short-term contracts, must have been of importance to the development of this side of the stakeholder-model.

28. The idea to use the term "network-ing" to replace "network" was developed by the Danish scientist of business organization and a philosopher as well, Martin Fuglsang, in his already influential doctoral thesis (Fuglsang: 1998).

Hence, the stakeholder-model, through its meta-concept of "subcontracting" and its emphasis on virtually shared values, can be seen as far more differentiated than the related "Transaction-Cost-Model" suggested by Williamson. It must not be forgotten that the concept of "subcontract", from its Marxian roots, has a pronounced critical dimension, leaving very little room for the idyllic ideology of Williamson (Williamson: 1975). (See below, Chapter 6).

The stakeholder-model probably still favours national and hence, local perspectives, even if multinational structures more and more come to stress international considerations of corporate management. But it is primarily the environment of the market and public relations, rather than the secondary work environment of the employees that has been the most important in marking its fulcrum up till now. Expanding the concept of "stakeholder" to the environment of workers producing raw material to the firm in a country far away seems to have come into focus only recently; it must also be admitted that those environments are still very hard to control, especially when they are integrated in extremely hierarchical social structures. As an exception the coffee brand "Haavelar" sold by the Danish co-op, "Brugsen" could be mentioned. According to the program only beans from autonomous cooperatives are accepted as the raw material for coffee, this being a means to support a democratic development.

But the trend definitely favours the globalization of the concept of "stake-holder". The recent affair with the export of pesticides to Central America by the Danish firm, Cheminova, indicates this. Here it turned out that the workers did not use the pesticides safely, neglecting the precautions prescribed by the Danish authorities. Even if this carelessness might be initiated by the workers themselves in order to keep their jobs, it actually did offend the Danish public – and to a certain degree international circles too – and thereby harmed perhaps the most delicate parameter of the firm today, its public image. As already mentioned, the field of economy can be conceived of as a field constituted by communication through commodities. Transaction-cost analysis interprets communication as a relation by way of measurable commodities, material or mental, and then claims an inherent symmetry in relation to gains. Perhaps this perspective presents a too obvious, or even naive, defence of the capitalist system. However, it might be important to analyze which concept of communication, and hence, of social relations, lies behind the peculiar human relations answering the call of the commodity, and thus the comprehensive movement of information-capitalism to turn absolutely everything into a commodity. This might make our eye keen to simmering reactions against this state of affairs, even inside management. We might suspect that inside this reified communication another type of communication might hide itself.

So let us examine the phenomenology of the commodity a bit closer.

As a phenomenon, the commodity is the bearer of two semantic relations: the denotation of its use-value and its price.

The use-value exhibits a very complex picture, if we choose to examine it through the spectacles of semiotics. "Semiotics" is the designation of the theory of linguistic signs put forward by the American philosopher, Charles Sanders Peirce. Following Peirce it is possible to distinguish between three dimensions of signs as well as between three types of signs:

The three dimensions are, according to Peirce (Peirce: 1955):

"A *Sign*, or *Representamen*, is a First which stands in such a genuine triadic relation to a Second, called its *Object*, as to be capable of determining a Third, called its *Interpretant*, to assume the same triadic relation to its Object in which it stands itself to the same object." (p.99-100)

The important concept here, to characterize the "sign" as a phenomenon, is the "interpretant". Peirce says:

"A *Sign* is a Representamen with a mental Interpretant. Possibly there may be Representamens that are not Signs. Thus, if a sunflower, in turning toward the sun, becomes by that very act fully capable of, without further condition, of reproducing a sunflower which turns in precisely corresponding ways toward the sun, and of doing so with the same reproductive power, the sunflower would become a Representamen of the sun. But *thought* is the chief, if not the only, mode of representation." (ibid)

Thus, Peirce emphasizes the Aristotelian notion that language is a human phenomenon, and a social phenomenon per se: a sign presupposes the ability of thinking and hence a community with the same conceptual framework – that Peirce at the same time has got quite unique ideas about mind and nature shall not be touched on in this connection.

The ideas of Peirce in relation to semantics can be interpreted in such a way that meaning can be conceived of as a relation between three components. A **sign**, "lion" for example, refers to the **object**, the animal, the type of person, the zodiac sign, by way of the **interpretant** only. This interpretant is a sort of filter that ambiguity makes necessary. The interpretant expresses the contextual dependency of signs, and hence, the unity of the semantic, syntactic, and pragmatic aspects of language.

The three types of signs are: the **icon** which denotes via its similarity to the object. An onomatopoeia like "meow", or a portrait, is an icon. Also an individual is an icon of himself, and law is the icon of The Law. If pictures and sculptures are icons, it is easy to see the enormous range and significance of the interpretant. Signs that denote via a conventional interpretant are called **symbols**. For example "Stars and Stripes" or the concept of "mass". Finally, signs that denote via a kind of physical causation by that object are called **indexes**. A smile for example, is an index of a mood, and a "mood" is a condition involving both psyche and soma (Op.cit p.102). I shall not elaborate further on Peirce's semiotics, but just emphasize that his triadic theory of signs, especially his sign-types, creates many problems, because a certain sign often can be attributed to more types, and because **indexes** might be conventional signs too (Morris: 1964; Goodman: 1976)

Well, let us return to the use-value.

The way in which the commodity as a use-value refers to its object is many-sided. Often the peculiar brand is able to collect all those sides of meaning, as when a man's shoe with the name "Lloyd" already anticipates the other possible meanings connected to quality in this special field, such as the material, the durability due to the manufacture, the elegance of design, etc. Employing Peirce's concepts we are able to state that this brand denotes like a symbol; that quality, durability, etc. denote like an icon, through referring to a typical conception about the ideal shoe. For example we are able to examine whether the shoe is welted, and we can touch the leather. In addition, this feeling of the leather's firmness might be an index of its solidity.

The semiotic complex which makes up the price interacts with use-value in a far from simple way. The price symbolically refers through its size to the quality of this commodity, but it probably denotes its actual costs of production through the iconic form. The price-label can also be said to refer, as an index, to the shoe as a unit.

The firm's communication with that part of its stakeholders which are its customers takes place primarily through the balance between these two semantic dimensions – the "use-value" and the "exchange-value" (the price) that Marx named and opposed to each other in "Das Kapital". The brand functions here as a "proto-sign" that unites the many different dimensions of reference. But here we already proceed into a field where forms of non-economical communication dominate. The commodity, recall, is characterized by bearing a name. The brand lies somewhere between the designation of a specific character and a proper name. The proper name denotes persons, places, or events that are all unique. They cannot be reproduced without being summoned in all their, almost infinite, complexity. But this attempt is absurd insofar as we lack criteria of this very complexity. Every time we repeat the names of the city of "Oslo", or of the painter "Edward Munch", or of the "Battle of Waterloo", we change their unique existence. Every individual that uses these words shall add his own world of experience to their possible meaning, tying them to the inaccessible depths of memories. The generality of the word then, our possibility to use it arbitrarily, transforms it into a unique being the infinite sense-dimensions of which we are not allowed to recognize. Seen from this perspective, the word is a grave on which we are standing without knowing it. As soon as we repeat them, we are forced to transform them into symbols, into designations of a specific character defined by the situation in which we speak now, and at least into nouns. They are no longer icons. Modern linguistic philosophy, inspired by Leibniz, might try to escape this epistemological bind by constructing a finite set of possible worlds, each one a correlate to any person's experience of them at any time, but this does not catch the crux of the problem. We still must recognize that the essential aspects of experience are not cognitive, but emotional and conative. It is not possible to construct a "possible world" by way of a knowledge that is inaccessible to formalization.

But the name of the commodity, be it a designation through its specific character, or a brand ("a man's shoe" or "a Lloyd"), differs fundamentally from the name of the person, the place, or the event. Whereas the person is still able to be the same, because he is the same (this must be a truism), the identity of the brand can only be the effect of an assertion. Sincerity, if there is any, becomes instrumental, because there are quite unambiguous, but technical, criteria to verify it: that the shoe is robust, that it is elegant, and that it is a "Lloyd".

To this must be added that a brand can be faked, but it is rather difficult to fake a person.

In principle one could not find such a big difference in relation to other types of consumer goods. Even indicators of quality like the guarantee label of ecological production warranted by the state – in which the Danes at the moment do not appear to share much trust – reveal the same game about sincerity, deception and brand. And it is a game that shall be won by the one who most convincingly can attest to the presence of the beneficial, not just to the absence of the injurious.

If we leave the world of consumption goods, bearing consolidated labels, of consumption goods with explicit demands of quality with legally formalized demands, then the matter looks a bit different because the name of the firm alone must carry the guarantee of an often very complex product or service. "Trust" is a very important concept here, when we are speaking of products that are very hard to return, and where faults emerge late in the process of "productive consumption". For example with products such as extensive construction works like bridges, services like the re-privatizing of hospitals, installing of information systems, the firm must be the icon of its own product. Where information of the product can never be sufficient, because it involves processes in the future, communicative virtues like sincerity, reliability, and trustworthiness must be the symbols of a use-value yet to be realized. The concept of "stakeholder" gains its full significance here.

The rise of "Total Quality Management (TQM)" in the eighties might to a certain degree have been caused by the notorious cases of manufacturing defect in American cars – compared to German and Japanese – during the seventies and eighties. But it was probably the delicate relations between firm and market by the production and sale of the complex capital goods and services demanding a long time to establish, consume and hence, to evaluate, that had the greatest influence on this conception. This new trend in management and organizational settings claimed to prefer quality over an "Economy of Scales". But it simultaneously stressed "Operations Research" and hence, the strategies of Management instead of Leadership.

The apparently greater emphasis on the faculties, the competencies, and the sense of responsibility of the individual employee in relation to TQM-related strategies, and its organizational measures, turned – not unexpected – to be all too strategic and tactic. It was not able to be a genuine means to meet the enormous turnover on the shop-floor, wildcat strikes, slow-downs, and the rather widespread "industrial sabotage" often connected to problems of generational changes, and of integrating different ethnic groups and races. The emerging of the new discipline in the field of the theory of organizations, "Human Resource Management

(HRM)", during the nineties, running parallel to the rise and fall of TQM-strategies, might be seen as a way, if not to heal, then at least to cushion, the effects of the injuries inflicted on the relation between management and employees by the TQM-strategies.

The canonical distinction within classical, political economy (the tradition from Smith, via Ricardo, to Marx) between distribution, production, circulation and consumption of the product, appears to be germane to an analysis of the problems touched upon here in particulary with regard to the phenomenology of the commodity. The distinction between productive consumption and consumptive production proves especially relevant. The decisive point is that the firm must commit itself at all the four levels of the cycle of the product. This means that we must reflect on the communication related to distribution, production, circulation and consumption.[29]

The concept of "distribution" relates to the historical structures of ownership in the society. Ever since the Middle Ages private ownership was the principal axis of the capitalist economy. Today it seems eventually to be under threat with in the democratic societies of the West. The very concept of "stakeholder" might slowly undermine the almost sacred concept of "shareholder", removing the crux of distribution from private ownership of the firm in order to serve it in the best way. Participation comes to be a way to reintroduce earlier, though castigated, forms of cooperation, and communitarianism, within the firm, rehearsed historically under names like "syndicalism". The criteria of distribution, then, is going to change from passive capital-providing to intellectual and social performances to the advantage of the firm. This development is obviously enforced by the enormous importance of radical new technologies and market conditions, setting the focus on human resources, and hence, on inventive cooperativeness on the part of the employees. Modern information technology, and the programmes of knowledge management, cannot be implemented without the commitment of highly skilled employees. Private ownership appears to be almost irrational in that context.

To this development must be added the corporative trends in modern economies, dominating in spite of "backlashes" through the recent political programmes of re-privatization.

A firm, and hence top management, must be able to relate in principle to this development, considering its importance to public relations. The notion of "stakeholder" has an important symbolic value here, however blurred this concept might be.

But today a firm must, so it appears, first and foremost be able to communicate in relation to consumptive production. It must handle environmental problems related to the functioning of the production process: to convince the general pub-

---

29. In his famous Methodological Introduction to the Critique of Political Economy (called "Grundrisse"), Marx unites these three concepts of consumption, production, circulation, and distribution in an impressive vortex of dialectical logic (Marx: 1857/58).

lic and the specific stakeholders about its seriousness in relation to spills, escapes of radioactive material, gasses, dangerous chemicals; but also it must behave responsibly towards scarce natural resources, and threatened species. A firm is today actually obliged to prove its active attitudes on these fields by engaging in problems peculiar to the third world. It thereby convinces the public of its seriousness, even if it does no business in these regions at all.

In the environmental field a comprehensive legislation is emerging, at least in the Western world. But the firm has to prove that it takes its precautions voluntarily. It has to be even more law-abiding than the law prescribes. The story of "Shell" must be presented foremost as the story of the return of the lost son.

But productive consumption which relates to the directly wanted and unwanted effects of the use of the product or the service must also be a subject which the firm is able to justify to the public and to the stakeholders. More and more firms try to argue for the social relevance of their products and services. Or alternatively, they go to the opposite extreme and exhibit the aesthetics of their commodity for the sake of aesthetics, balancing on the edge of a not always suitable irony.

But seriousness, social responsibility, and commodities, seem not that easy to reconcile with one another. The problem is that only custom, long-time relations, hard-earned experience, expensive research, or well-founded trust, can make guarantees as to the real identity of the product or the service and to its quality. The brand generally needs advertising, and even a Rolls Royce needs a salesman – and perhaps a little bit more these days.

The commodity is not able, on its own, to communicate its outstanding qualities. It needs a helping hand. It needs consultancy. The former well-functioning play between the semantic dimensions of use-value and price seems to have reached a deadlock. This predicament hardens when we speak about durable consumer goods where so many brands are so much alike. Here, if we speak about average-price cars, communication about the commodity probably confuses more than it clarifies. It is no accident that the case treated by almost all so-called "Decision Support System Theory", in the youth of this field, was the one of choosing the right car. Not only are there many different criteria here, and hence many problems of weights, but information seems overwhelming, and available data not too certain.

In this general situation the roles of the salesman and the consultant melt together. Many products and services are extremely complicated. One cannot evaluate their potentials, not to mention their built-in faults, without assistance. But the one who answers your anxious questions may be a hired gun. The product and the service are wrapped into a handsome layer of talk.

In the vocabulary of classical political economy the "circulation" of products and services will not be communication just metaphorically, but also in actuality. Everything sold seems to need a justification by way of its technological potentialities and its framework of knowledge. This is not only due to the whole, elaborate system of commodity-specifications demanded by the state, but it is due to the fact that commodities are presented as pieces in the jigsaw puzzle of life. And to this permanent, intimidating allusion to life-style is added the pretentious claim to the appropriation of knowledge. Not only the reading of the right paper, or buying a commodity sponsoring children in Ethiopia, but even using a brand deodorant or buying a lamp simulating the interiors of the sixties, seem to be actions in the world of "epistēmē", in the realm of essential knowledge.

While management might yield to these trends, the leader is obliged to jump off the wagon.

From this perspective it is far more difficult to identify leadership through the customary "proto-psychological" concepts like "empathy, social insight, charm, tact and diplomacy, persuavesiveness, and oral communication ability ..." (Yukl: 1994, p.273).

No doubt it is the task of the leader to structure, trigger and follow this communication, this image-creating demonstration of attitudes. But the crux of this communication is a normativity that only convinces, if it is devoid of the usual strategic and tactic undertones.

In spite of management theory's often elaborate distinctions between skills of a "technical, conceptual and interpersonal character", it is not able to approach the core of leadership.

Gary Yukl (Yukl: 1994) is so cautious that he even refuses to distill an unambiguous set of traits characteristic to the good leader, but he grants the possibility of focusing on some traits of personality indispensable to effective management.

These are, like the skills mentioned above, certainly qualities that are more important to the firm's communication with its surroundings, with the public, the stakeholders and the consumers, than to its relation with its employees.

The leader must step forward before the product or service of the firm. He must stand out. He is responsible to all: to the employees, to the stakeholders, to the suppliers, to the owners; to the public, to the grass-roots groups, to the consumers. But most important, he is the one who is responsible to the future.

Even if his nature is reserved, or reserved on behalf of the firm, the leader has to relate in public to the social character of the commodity, and hence, to problems of distribution.

He has to argue why his firm will not sell vital medicine at a smaller profit; why it will not stop the production of arms, even to countries where the excuse for buying them is "self-defence"; and why he still produces flagrantly superfluous luxury products. He has to get to terms with the increasing moral demands upon products in addition to those meant for war only, such as the recent prohibition in Sweden against films containing scenes of violence; perhaps he even ought to assault on behalf of morals, as the Church of England did when it went into the brewery business in order to vote down the production of alcoholic beverages especially meant for teenagers.

This last kind of responsibility is characterized by the fact that the one who shows it does far more than he is obliged to do. Instead of being content with the cushioning of the adverse health effect of processes of production, he commits himself to anticipate any harm done by production before it is established at all. In this way he transgresses not only the usual common values, but also the customary way to relate to those values.

He undertakes the absolute. Hence, he is able to demonstrate that the leader first and foremost is a human being, and that this is his primary quality before any assignments relating to the firm.

This attitude of the leader is difficult to describe by referring to sets of definite norms or values. We are dealing with an attitude that in its essence transgresses most norms and values, in realizing an unconditioned **Radicality**.

Better examples of this **Radical Normativity**, the prime subject of this book, might be the situation where a human being, or a leader, recognized for his uncompromising fidelity to canonical norms (suddenly) changes his subject of solidarity.

The German generals Rommel and Munch during the Nazi-regime might be examples of military leaders who changed their solidarity and lost their lives. More proper examples might even be those of Martin Luther and Thomas More, both faithful to a God beyond the picture of the ruling institutions of church and state. Or the beautifully designed character of the English archbishop Becket in the play, "Becket ou l'honneur de Dieu" by Jean Anouilh. Here Beckett prefers God to friendship and secular loyalty (to the king), placing one solidarity against another.

It is probably easiest to illustrate the concept of **Radical Normativity**, and hence the so-called **Fourth**, by referring to God, because he is the most obvious image of transcendence. But I do not think that one ought to mix leadership and religion, and I do think that a "profane transcendence" constitutes an opportunity to the leader.

What here is called "the Third" stands for accepted norms and values: fidelity to a nation, love of one's neighbour, love of one's family, respect of every living organism, faithfulness to one's firm or the army; honesty, paying borrowed money back, and even commitment without compromise and the will to self-sacrifice.

In the world of business a genuine expression of the Third could be the new phenomenon of so-called "social entrepreneurship" practised in Seattle, the innovation capital of Northwest America. The "social enterprise" employs junkies and destitutes in order to transform them into former junkies and destitutes. But the point is that this private initiative of charity is done in the context of a very well-functioning, capitalist firm. According to the German newspaper "Die Zeit" (No.15, 8. April 1999), a firm recently established by a former drug-practitioner, David Guth, has a yearly turnover of 55 million dollars, and an income of 2 million dollars in 1998. In this firm 5000 junkies, destitutes, and previous convicts work for an average of two months, but more than a few stay with the firm as permanent employees.

The interesting point is of course that this firm combines capitalism and altruism, just as the "Die Zeit" headline proclaimed. It sells airplane components to Boeing, produces packings, and services within the fields of stocks and even logistics. But according to David Guth, the firm also creates a "social value". This model of combining what seemingly cannot be combined, ethics and profits, is also known to the Scandinavian countries, though on a minor scale. But in the USA the initiative is private. Another example from the article, the firm "Northwest Centre", employing mentally handicapped as house workers, kitchen workers, metal-workers and packing workers, has been part of an initiative sponsored by the public in Denmark under the rubric of "protected workshops". Such "Pioneer human services" "combine the passion of a social aim with the discipline, pleasure of innovation, and power of will, peculiar to the young firms in Silicon Valley", to quote J. Gregory Dees the chief of the Merchant Center of Entrepreneurial Management in Kansas City.

It is important that these pioneer firms have a competitive advantage, because huge enterprises like Boeing want the fact to be part of their public image that they do business with these "Social Enterprises". But what might here be obvious strategic thinking seems to be subject to the "cunning of virtue" – to paraphrase Hegel who spoke of "the cunning of History".

In any event, it seems possible to combine private enterprise with perhaps the most important maxim of Christian Culture: love your neighbour. It thus falls into line with the religious, but also social, virtues of altruism, charity, and humanity. These virtues, and the moral maxims that they reflect, constitute the core of the Third, even if they might be challenged by far more secular norms like frugality and prosperity. Here these opposites seem to be elementary within a happy marriage, and the most common manifestation of the Third, human consciousness, seems to be at peace with itself.

Western culture is characterized by the crucial concept of "conscience". The conscience exists as the cognitive and emotional fact of an inner instance which constantly strives to observe and ensure the association between certain acts and certain values. Conscience can never guarantee that this association becomes a relation, and hence, results in a conception of the good act, because consciousness seems most of the time to be bad.

The fact of consciousness is identical to individuals relating to "something or someone else" appearing within their inner monologue. In actuality this constitutes the core of religion. The unspoken condition of this inner dialogue is the very essence of this "third" in the mind of each of the individuals when they are talkning to each other. This Third could, as an "inner voice", but a voice rather similar in each individual, be the authoritative expression of moral or ethical values – "the generalized Second" which George Herbert Mead christened.[30]

However, the present confrontation in our world of many different cultures, forms of life and points of view, constitutes a rather difficult foundation for the creation of an identical Third between any two persons talking together. Even universal values have to be interpreted by a particular person. This difficulty is rein-

---

30. I am following the rather conventional vocabulary in referring to "ethics" as a more universal set of values in relation to "moral standards", the last ones being tied to limited cultural, social, and historically transient, norms – a way of thinking articulated during the Enlightenment.

forced by the fact that the circumstances under which such values are implemented have become so complex and so surprisingly new that an unambiguous set of rules for this implementation cannot be assumed to exist. The principle of consensus attests to this predicament: one has to agree as to what the value should mean, not just choose the value itself.

But nonetheless, there are countless examples of the mental presence of the Third. The soldiers feeling the glance of the absent general fixed upon them; the group members talking to each other as if the leader were present; the power seeker invoking a hidden legitimacy – most often totally identical to the lack of it, as with in Hitler; or the idealist referring to unconventional norms balancing between subtlety and affectation. The important point from an epistemological or cognitive perspective is that the Third is absent through its very presence: every time we fix it, be it to a value, a maxim, to a mental function, or even personify it, give it a face, it shall be devaluated. This means that the Third cannot alone create the basis of its own legitimacy. We have to be ready for it, to accept to play the game – which means the attempt to make it visible or able to hear. As Kant already knew, the field of morals demands the acceptance of unconditional values. It demands "moral postulates", the readiness to accept the tacit force of acceptance.

But this might not necessarily always be the case.

A normativity could exist that sets one free from canonical norms and values. But this, of course, does not imply the absolute freedom of the individual and hence, the "nihilism" of the absolute right of the will to power.

On the contrary, when the concept of the Third is submitted to a demand of being overt, the concept of the Fourth could then imply a hidden, and hence, far more **Radical Normativity**.

The Fourth is calling. But not in a summoning way. This calling is soft, silent, even gentle. It listens to you even more than it addresses you. It will not deal with power. It shows its force by waiting. It is invisible; it cannot be caught by any image, concept, or name.

Where the Third might be imagined to be omnipresent all the time, even if its/his complexion varies as to context and circumstances, then the Fourth is invisible, listening at most to the pauses in our speech – but being lesser interested in our gestures, I presume. Probably the Fourth will appear as something very personal as he first approaches us, even though he does not deal with the personal. He destroys it little by little. He could never choose sides, nor make any case his own.

He belongs to anybody, always.

The Third is tied to language, to validity, to objectivity. Hence, he is entangled in the same web in which the interlocutors, the "speech-actors", are caught. When validity and objectivity break down, the Third will break down too. He falls with the fall of concepts and names, with norms and values. He falls with the fall of historical realities. But the Fourth does not fall, because he is not standing, but just drifting.

The Third must, in the last instance, be tied to the words of the Prophet, or the Great Teacher, or to The Book, and hence, to authority. The Fourth neither speaks nor writes. Perhaps he is humming? But his medium is silence.

The picture symbolically depicting the place of the Fourth must be a non-place in time and space, a Utopia, or at the utmost the holy place where God denied to be seen by man. One could imagine an elliptical figure surrounding the two prototypical persons involved in dialogue and the Third dwelling inside their minds and hence, as a universal judge, over and above them. So, he is caught together with them within an elliptical figure too. The Third enforces and tries to guarantee validity of thoughts, actions and consensus. He is caught in his own mirror, the mirror in which he catches the two persons speaking, and in which they see each other.

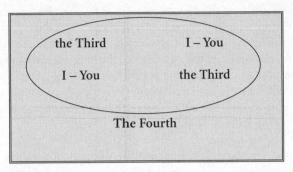

Figure 2

This figure ought to reveal that the symbiosis of the two interlocutors and the Third is destroyed by that very phenomenon of temporality which they try to invoke in the image of eternity.

Nothing can be fixed, so why not fix nothing? The metaphor of "nothing" refers to the existence of something outside this more or less voluntary symbiosis. This alone can constitute the sense of Radical Normativity, as Martin Heidegger pointed out many years ago. But that which dwells outside must always be displaced, forwarded, and left alone at the same time. It is **the other**, the **radical other**. The "Being/Not-Being", which Plato in his dialogue "Parmenides" articulates through such an expressive logic. It is "heteros" in Greek, the opposite of the self-identical, of the self, of "selfhood", of identity, of sameness. Everything that evades thinking and conceptualizing escapes the essence ("eidos auto kath'auto"), and frees itself of identity ("heautō tauton"). It is that which will not be similar to, will not liken anything, the obstinate, the anti-self. It is that which even escapes the trap of opposition, of defining itself through that which it negates, the self. **The other** is itself too.[31]

---

31. Plato,(1926/1996): Parmenides. Loeb-udgaven. Transl. by H.N. Fowler. Cambridge Mass/London. See: 130 B, 139 E. Martin Heidegger names this "other" "Das Sein", "Being"; Emmanuel Lévinas explicitly uses the Platonic expression "The Other" (Lévinas: 1961).

A philosopher of the Middle Ages, Nicolas of Cusa, who lived from 1401 to 1464, phrased this in such a beautiful way: "non aliud non aliud est quam non aliud" ("the not-other is nothing else but the not-other").

The power of the concept is broken by this absolute border. It only appears to us as a trace of an unknown originator. This is the formula of "transcendental immanence", of presence in the capacity of absence.

In other words, sincerity, validity, commitment to the norm, and consensus about the value, can only do nothing about **becoming**. The fact of temporality erodes the firm ground of conceptualization, destroying the foundation of any kind of certainty: each and every time a value is fixed through interpretation and consensus, it will end up as one of the masks which the Third wears.

Only a delicate hint, a gesture of gentleness, a moon-shadow, opening itself to imagination as a clandestine draft of a future, the long-forgotten key to the past, a tender **anticipation**, an undemanding commitment to the almost possible, might help here. This sensitivity to anticipation contains the genuine sense of the possible, a "possibility-sense". This "fifth sense" is able to hear the Fourth calling, and hence, it is the only existing sense of reality.

The Fourth, being outside the ellipse of dialogues, of norms and values, of knowledge, power and desire, even outside the sincerity of consent, and even outside certainty, and hence, even outside reflection, cannot guarantee anything. To relate to the Fourth is to meet contingency with the attitude of contingency. To relate to him is to unleash yourself to freedom. It is to lose yourself. It is to leave what you know, what you want, and as a last effortless effort, to leave who you are. To relate to the Fourth is to yield to the passion of that which cannot be fulfilled.

This frame of reference might transgress what seems appropriate to the curriculum of any business school, but not what is of utmost importance in life.

A leader, being first and foremost a person, a human being, must transgress functionalism, transgress the allurement of victorious ideologies, even the promises of ethics, and set his path for a genuine honesty. He must be able to gamble, not on the shareholders' money, or the security of the employees, but on his own existence.

CHAPTER 5

Of the Concept of Leading

Leading: to lead somebody or something; to be led by somebody; to be led by the hope of something. Or is it to search for? To wit, if you are led by a promise, the one who made the promise must be the real leader. Are you able to be led by that which you are leading? It appears to be contrary to intuition. The one who leads somebody might guide him, and hence, decide his destiny. The one who leads something, must first and foremost know what it is. But that which leads you, might not be in your position, not yet, nor ever, for it might be something lost or something impossible to find.

If the two senses of the concept "to lead", the passive and the active side, were united, then it would match the significance of the old Norse words "leitha", which means "to be at the head of", and "leita", which means "to search for". This signification could be paraphrased as "to try to take possession of something which one does not realize that one already has". This apparent paradox might very well be the secret behind the word "to lead". Then the final aim of leadership would not be directed outward, towards the "objects", but inward, towards the leader's own person. "Leadership" would denote the quintessence of any process of learning: to come to know yourself.

Then leadership would imply steering towards a still unnamed goal. The crux of the matter is to be able to feel summoned. "Summoning" can mean both to challenge the movement, and to ask it for help. But in both cases **movement** is the central issue.

Let us look further into the possible meaning of the word, "to lead":

If leadership is about the faculty of moving others, what then, we might ask, moves a person?

We know that man has got a body, and that the body is able to be moved through contact with other bodies. It is perhaps pushed, and it might be overturned. The collision might be gentle or fatal. But experience shows that the body can be enforced by something outside it, or it can be let totally free to move wherever it wants.

We know that consciousness might be moved by the expectation of reward or punishment. But consciousness is able to move its ends too, thereby changing the meaning of "reward" and "punishment". We imagine that it is possible to enforce such ends upon consciousness, or that it is able itself to choose them from its own free will. Often we make spontaneous use of concepts like "instinct", "need", "interest", "motive", or "desire", as ways in which we attempt to explain actions in ourselves or in others. By this we refer to the expediency of the act. We seek for causes, for effects, for means and ends, we seek the **dynamics** of the act, the significance of movement.

In Greek philosophy, movement is named in two ways, as **kinēsis**, meaning the causality of movement. This concept has been the basis of both mechanics, and of the psychology and sociology inspired by natural science. And movement is also known as **dynamis**, which relates to the "telos", to the final cause of movement, to the possibilities inherent in it. When speaking about "movement" here, we cannot help to combine both meanings.

But there is often an unspoken assumption, when we are speaking about "movement" – an assumption often forgotten by both everyday consciousness and science, namely, that we are referring to a movement primarily caused by two relations:

a. it has the form of the object, or the force.
b. we have not initiated this process alone. Rather it is initiated by instincts and motives as well, insofar as they refer to something not solely created by us, but which has happened to us, or befallen us, or perhaps even taken us into possession; perhaps because we, as children, were easy victims, or during our growth neglected the weakness of our own nature.

Even these mental processes that we usually call "values" and "norms", as if we believed that they were almost static, tangible things, that man himself is able to choose as the possible content of his mind, are movements. Causes and effects ("kinēsis") are transformed into forces that are nothing but gestures of the greatest of all secrets: The secret which we are to ourselves.

But norms and values, through the way in which we conceive of them as such tangible objects, often refer by their conventional logic of intension and of extension to our actions, through the figure constituted by "kinēsis". It is as if they were able to create actions through physical processes of touch, through symbolic pushing. Prototypical series of causes and effects constitute frames in which our blurred everyday actions can be put and from which they can acquire a provisional distinctness. However, even when we sanction the norms and values, appearing as an explanatory setting of our actions, and accept the ascription of the usual, average social intentions, we do not seem to dwell in them. One can only get into a few material things. Or perhaps stated more precisely: They do not fit into our mental space. They do not pervade, invade, or unite.

They are just and simply arranged, if not stacked, and should they disintegrate or even be decomposed because their long residence in our mind's I/eye, then they will mix with the streams of mind, making it lumpy.

When asked, we might produce one of them from the basement or attic of our cognitive system, but we know for sure that even if we do not lie, we will not speak the truth. They just simply function too well in our equilibristic circus of post-rationalization.

But we could think of another kind of movement – an alternative movement through which man certainly is moved, but is able to retain himself as the cause of movement. In this case we already have a hint of this interpretation because of the ambiguousness of the concept of "movement". That is to say that the fact of being "moved" also means to be in a certain mood, to be filled by certain emotions. The one who is moved, is taken possession of, or even seized.

The actions of another person, a story, a film, a talk, a painting, a scenery, or words might incite movement, but the fact of being moved always takes place in one and the same medium: in an event.

That event where man is moved, but still remains his own mover at one and the same time, is what matters here. If such an event were only defined or created by other people, then the individual would not be able to be the one who moves. Such an event cannot be a pre-coded answer, nor can it be an available label which we give to the event, because in that case we would not ourselves be the masters of our emotions.

Such an event must be anticipated by something else that emanates neither from the outside (from other people), nor from the inside (from instincts, needs, or interests not chosen by ourselves). It must emerge simultaneously from something which we are not, and from the quintessence of our being. In other words, it must emerge from something which lies between us and the world. And that which lies between us and the world, binding us, but leaving us on our own, is **mood**.

What is able to move man without making him powerless, is a mood. The word in Greek philosophy answering to "mood", is **pathos**.

Basic to all rhetoric since Aristotle is his definitions, in his "Art of Rhetoric", of the concept of **pathos**. **Pathos** means the "condition of the hearer", and it belongs to the three means of convincing ("pistis"), which are the instruments at the disposal of the speaker, proper to this art. Besides **pathos**, there is the **ēthos** of the speaker, his character, and the matters of fact to which he can refer, the **pragmata** (Aristotle: 1994a, 1356a ff).

"But the emotions ("pathē") are all those affections which cause men to change their opinions in regard to their judgements, and are accompanied by pleasure and pain." (Aristotle: 1994a, 1378a,8)

The instruments of speech are all aimed at changing the mood.

And Cicero speaks of the **pathos** as the "vehementes motus", the violent movement.

The mood, the intersection of the situated emotions, unites the body with consciousness, because the mood exists in both places/spaces. In modern philosophical vocabulary one often speaks of a "decentred intentionality" that neither establishes a compulsion from without, nor an inner world of coercive objects (instincts, needs, desires). It does not get its content from values.

The mood has the three following qualities:

a. it forms the reality which we perceive by being of the same stuff as the blood of the event, "the blood of the world", to borrow an expression from Hegel's "Phenomenology of Spirit".
b. hence, it is able to change this reality.
c. it cannot have the status of the subject of experience, nor of an object, because it "anticipates itself". It is memory as living experience, and living experience as memory.

If we combine the concepts of the event and the mood, we are able to see how well they match. Because the event is taken into the mood, it assumes its colour, its taste, its movement, its tune, and at the same time the event widens the mood. They inspire each other. They are the mutual co-creators of their collective movement.

First Thesis

Leadership is the name of the movement whose fixed point is the right moment and the right mood.

The analysis of the right moment, and of the right mood, must concentrate on the range of meaning of these concepts (in Part IV we shall analyze the relation between the right "moment", and the right "event", here we only touch on the distinction).

From the point of view of any individual the right moment/event, be it as the space of starting, continuing, or ending, and the right mood, take off from the world of this individual.

But no individual lives in isolation. The event expresses, as a phenomenon, the place where your and my world meet. As far as they meet **in** time, and because time must be anticipated, and itself anticipate the right mood, then their space in common is the **moment**. The moment contains the event. Hence, the moment itself cannot have any definite sense – or else the event would not be able to. The event is like the action on the stage, the moment is like the spotlight.

The main problem of the right mood, and the right event, is how we are able to judge the right moment without just simply projecting it through the mood? How does the mood of the right moment feel?

The leader has to know that he shall be in charge of the right movement towards the right moment. He has to know the mood – that belonging to anybody, as well as his own. Because, after all, there is no other way to know when the right moment has come.

Second Thesis

Leadership must, as the subject of a frame of analysis, first and foremost be KAIROLOGIC, the study of the right moment, of timing.

If **kairology** should be able to assume a theoretical and empirical position as a research field, it must found the basis of examining the possibilities that we possess to analyze the relation between event and mood. Here one shall find many metaphors to describe all the possibilities, but the best one is that of the theatre, because it is most close to the event and its content as a communicative occurrence; it also, in one and the same movement, confirms reality and transgresses reality by repeating it through **mimēsis**.

Third Thesis

The right event, as well as the right mood, must have a beginning, but any genuine beginning is an origin that must find its justification within itself, because only through its conclusion it can be corroborated.

The leader who is able to initiate the spontaneous beginning that needs no justification, I shall call the **hodegēt**, the word originating in the Greek words "hodos", "road", and "geisthein", meaning "to guide, to lead".[32] He dares to launch something. He dares to walk a way that might not be new, but which has been hidden in the grass. As a sensitive wanderer in the woods, on invisible forest roads, he might even walk out of the picture of Heidegger's honest Schwarzwald-farmer with his staff, the pilgrim seeking his religion, and into the picture of Gilles Deleuze, into the shape of the inspired nomad, moving from circle to circle, through ever-new circumferences, as if he were jumping from floe to floe, preferring the fields to the forests, the ocean to the fields, yet never falling victim to the illusion of concentricity (Heidegger: 1950; Deleuze, Guattari: 1994).

In contrast to this figure we find the leader that only accomplishes processes

---

32. Aristotle defines a beginning in the following way in his Poetics: "A beginning is that which does not itself follow necessarily from something else, but after which a further event or process naturally occurs." (Aristotle: 1995a, 1450b, VII, 25)

already begun, however meticulously. To him I shall give the name of **kategēt**. He is the one who writes the catechisms, he loves to guide, to teach, to evaluate.

The fundamental difference between the **hodegēt** and the **kategēt** is that the **kategēt** always shall refer to accepted sets of values, the content of which is functional, however lofty, and whose communicative potency remains at the strategic level. The **kategēt** shall always legitimize his behaviour through a rationality that never transgresses the clean economical and technical horizon. His aims must always be, however great, the canonical ones. He is an equilibrist when it comes to reading through the spectacles of the establishment, but no matter how law-abiding and pious, no matter how dedicated to consent, his final criteria shall always be success.

At the bottom he might even show an almost perverse obsession with transforming values into tangible objects, available to measurement and evaluation. He uses a nano-scale, and he uses it strictly. But the last thing he would do, would be to admit to the smallest trace of cynicism. Yet when he chooses to enhance the autonomy of the employees, via the establishment of self-organizing groups, gives rights to further education, or expands the area of employee responsibility, he only returns this "original form of cooperation" to his employees, because he has been estimating, with the utmost calculation, how much this granting will augment the efficiency of production and the quality of the product.

Even if he explicitly refers to humanism as his motivational horizon, he shall always opt out of the human considerations, however discreetly, if they should contradict the fundamental control of the production processes and the refining of discipline as universal means to progress. He cannot be reached by outside influence; he remains a conservative who would always be inclined to place the consideration for society over that of the firm, and the consideration of the firm over that of the individual. He is a master of the legitimization of layoffs. He is not an emperor, he is an archbishop. The **kategēt** is a devoted follower of the Third. His religion is progress, and in that his conservatism triumphs: the rise of Western Civilization in the fields of science, technology and evoking an ideal of enlightenment guided by a "ratio" that pays due respect to a moderate humanism. Therefore it is no paradox that his creed is "innovation". But exactly in this particular game, there may be no chance of confession, no restoring to favour, once the sins have been committed.

The **hodegēt**, on the other hand, being a nomad, and very far from the shape of the pilgrim, looking for no established or even secret authority, does not take seriousness seriously. In the circus of life he would always prefer the fat, little clown with the all-too-small jacket, and the by far too long shoes, to the pompous, white clown with the caricatured, majestic manners of the **kategēt**. But normally the **hodegēt** tries to avoid the show. He is content with being an **example**.

Really to be an example means that through one's behaviour one refers to qualities, and thereby transgresses this very behaviour itself. To be an example, is to be, at the same time, a gentle admonition, and an enigma. The **hodegēt** relates to the Fourth.

He shall always be a human being prior to being the man of society, the nation, the institution, or the firm. His favorite tale is of the king who walks among his subjects dressed in a beggar's clothes.

The qualities of the **hodegēt** testify to genuine human capacities, but we are here referring to capacities that can never be studied as objective qualities through any science. His conception of man comes close to seeing him as a harlequin that through his costume's colour-play reflects the ever-changing contexts of the traveller, and certainly not the tactics of the chameleon. He sees man as the master of mimicry, yet he sees him as the one who is on the point of showing his face. But he is not at all supported in this process by any science of any kind, nor by any communicative techniques, nor by any collective therapeutic devices.

The actions of the **hodegēt**, his way of speaking, should then show a gentle obligation, a sort of kindness not so much proper of the exiled, as of the person who knows that it is very hard to acquire any true knowledge. But this is not identical to relativism. On the contrary, it is the utmost respect of knowledge.

This respect of knowledge that contains the shyness towards the other person too, must then imply the respect of this otherness too. Being a nomad, the **hodegēt** does not want followers, but he shall be followed indeed.

This Socratic attitude, this qualifying suspicion of qualities, is the quintessence of that which we, ever since Greek Philosophy, have called **virtues**.

But the virtues of the **hodegēt** are not demonstratively stated through his way of being, they are just indicated. He is not playing with charisma, exhibiting no shrewd strategic game of authority. He works on behalf of otherness. He is walking hand in hand with nothing. He refers to something greater than himself, but impossible to invoke.

Let me give some examples of the **hodegēt** as a closing of this chapter, examples fetched in a more prosaic zone, and still at the edge of the possible:

---

a. As a top manager he shall never be satisfied, even if the products sold by his firm do match the restrictive demands of the state. He shall establish his own standards of quality, demands that far surpass the demarcation lines of possible health or environmental damages pointed to by institutional research. He shall here listen even more to grass-root researchers in trying to prevent problems. Any well-founded doubt is enough to him. He shall not try to hide behind any kind of so-called "objectivity". He shall withdraw the product. He is ready to lose money, and his face.

b. As a chief of production he shall not conceive of the individual employee as an instance of a production function, but as a fellow human being. In his world there do not exist any anonymous job-functions, but only living persons, the working time of which is the largest and most important part of their lifetime. To him the changing in techniques is first and foremost a restriction of, or an increasing in, competencies, skills, knowledge and qualifications of his employees, and as changes in

---

their time of life. He shall not count units of time, but relate to moments of life. He shall see technology not only as the other side of education, but as the formation of personalities too. When it is able to benefit the workers, he shall choose the more expensive and more uncertain solutions too.

c. As the chief responsible of organizational structure, he primarily perceives the organization as a communicative reality that must be shaped in the picture of pre-existing, informally created, cooperative competencies. Organization must strengthen this autonomous cooperation. It shall not be subjected to strategic goals.

d. To him nature and environment are not mere resources, and cannot be seen as parts of the firm's basis of production. On the contrary, they are a living "otherness", and they cannot, and they shall not, be conceived of as objects. Their otherness shall be met as a real otherness. They shall be met with as others who themselves must be able to choose whether to grant him the rights, he is forced to usurp from them. To him, "sustainability" is an opportunity to analyze contexts and circumstances, not a legal safety net of minimizing costs.

e. As a top manager he shall conceive of his firm as responsible to the normative construction of the relation between all the four links of the production cycle: production, circulation, consumption, and not least, distribution. To him the firm must be socially just – and concerned with the justice of other firms and institutions too. He sees a firm as an instrument for implementing a fair distribution of the social surplus. He sees the corporation as co-creator of social reality. Thus the leader is obliged to reflect on the social necessity of the commodities his firm circulates. And this does not solely relate to the collective resources saved by the methods of production or to the increase in quality of products. He has to ask himself whether this type of commodity has any use at all. He must ask about the consequences of it, as well as about the preconditions for it, in relation to the stakeholders, and especially the subcontractors. He must be able to "think in social networks". He must ask how it will influence both the consumer's mind and the future. He must, in other words, give up any idea of the market's ability to solve normative questions on its own. Hence, he must be a politician in the broader sense of the word: he must take on a responsibility to the democracy of his own society and of others as well.

f. As a CEO he shall choose the responsibility to those parts of the stakeholders directly involved in production and consumption, before he will be answerable to the shareholders.

Put simply, he must at any time be ready to risk his own position.

CHAPTER 6

Management, Innovation and Cooperation

6.1. The Origin of the Capitalist Production Process

If there is any important lesson to learn from studying the management of today's high-technology firm, it is **the dependence of innovation on cooperation**.

To acknowledge this as more than a trend-based relation demands the ability to relate topical phenomena of production to their historical roots.

Primarily a willingness to look through the glasses of history is able to make us realize that modern industrial society, due to its basic structure, is – expressed in a rather solemn way – to blame. It is guilty of the destruction of the phenomenon of **cooperation**. Now it is time to mend the crime, and bring it back again. Not because this industrial society feels a deep repentance, but because cooperation is the only thing it really needs. Cooperation is the only answer to the problems created by technology and education.

From the perspective of the townsman this "guilt" was the price of freedom. It was the townsman, in German "Bürger", in Danish "borger", in French "burgess", later the "bourgeois", which Rousseau transformed to mean the individual, with his egoistic interests, who was the contrary of the "citizen" (the citoyen). He alone was capable of relating to the community and to the state. This distinction was later overtaken by the socialists and communists who used "bourgeois" as an invective. The "bourgeois" settled in the town he built outside the walls of the "burg" ("castle"), by the mouth of a river, already during the eleventh century.[33] His motto was "Handel macht frei!" (trade makes one free), and the town did indeed secure him against serfdom, but his individual freedom was directly proportional to the quantity of those insignia that symbolized it: money and capital (Simmel: 1930).

Through this perspective the creation of industrial society, ever since its first appearance in the fourteenth century has always been identical to usurpation of the traditional trades of production. These trades were organized through a natural

---

33. See Pirenne, H. (1965): Economic and Social History of Medieval Europe. Routledge & Kegan Paul, London. Chap. II. The Towns. Pirenne refers to a "first industrial revolution" here: "If the first beginnings of commercial capitalism partly evade our notice, it is much easier to follow its evolution during the course of the 12th century. In the vigour and relative rapidity of its developement it may, without exaggeration, be compared with the industrial revolution of the nineteenth century." p.49

cooperation, with the aim to structure and systematize the production of commodities with an existing market.

Karl Marx defines the concept of **cooperation** in the following way:

"The form of labour of many persons, methodically working together and alongside one another in the same production process or in related production processes, is called co-operation."[34]

Natural cooperation, being the original form of production in these trades, became the target of merchant capital. Management quickly grew into the practice of submitting existing forms of organization, including crafts and guilds, as well as production techniques, knowledge, skills and qualifications, to an alien rationality. It was alien in relation to their natural, organic physiognomy in local communities based on principles of collectivism. However, as far as these production processes were based on handicraft, the first period of capitalism, the period of **subcontracting**, did not change these processes, but only the relations of ownership and income. A merchant with some capital would usually take a master, or a farmer with his family, into his service. He would deliver the raw material, but not always the instruments of work, and he would either buy the finished products with a reduction for material, rent of instruments, etc., or pay some kind of wage. He did not need to provide buildings, or even always to buy instruments (e.g., a loom). The subcontractor was still a free man, able to manage his own labour process, but he was usually kept poor. Management then, did not mingle with the production process itself until the system of **manufacture**, where re-structuring of the labour process through the division of labour placed management in a far more important position.

At this stage management began removing craftsmanship from the workers, and to implement the skills into frameworks of organization and into machinery.

The main part of all production far into the 19th century, when scientifically invented processes of innovation began to create new trades (chemicals, and especially petro-chemicals), took off from this handicraft-based production. Manufactures and mines, and even the first factories, did not actually create new processes, even if they did create new products, like steam engines, locomotives, machine-guns and telegraphs. They just put existing handicraft techniques into new settings through the principles of the division of labour, and eventually the power of steam. Adam Smith makes the former the **sine qua non** of any wealthy society, and Karl Marx makes the latter the prerequisite of industrialism. However, the chain of causality is limited by the fact that "The revolution of the working machine, on the contrary,

---

34. Marx is here quoted in the English from Engels, F. (1972): Engels on Marx' Capital. Moscow, Progress Publishers. p. 80. (Engels quotes from p. 306, of the First Edtion of "Das Kapital").

first made the perfecting of the steam-engine a necessity, and then also carried it out."[35]

This stands as yet another example of the fact that organizational changes cause technical ones, and not the other way around.

Manufacture and factory, the development of division of labour, of work-machines, and of power-machines, and hence, "large scale production", became the capitalist societies' contribution to history. But management was for a very long time nothing but a necessary evil.

Management was alien to the production process because the workers themselves and machines appeared to be enough to regulate production. It was strange, too, because management had the will and the ability to create its own necessity. In any events the capitalist and the manager were almost always one and the same person. Hence, management appeared as sheer necessity. It was not necessarily for technical reasons, but more because of the unlimited possibilities of valuation of capital, of profits, and the demand not to waste capital. This general feeling of the preciousness of capital does not come from the fact that it is a way in which the labour of the community exists. Rather it arises from the individual's worries about his property. Hence, it appears as the necessity of the valuation of capital, and thus of a management that does not waste the good money used on wages and machines, on buildings and raw-materials, on storing and on transporting. This condition of capitalist production is important to grasp prior to deducing management from the problems peculiar to a species of society called "industrial".

In the past, management could be understood as one means to satisfy the needs of a growing population and an increasing market; it could be understood as necessitated by the demand to combine man and machine; it could even be understood as an untouchable, sacrosanct pillar in the temple of Western Civilization, as a spiral-shaped and successful Tower of Babel. Even if this new metaphor of spiral-shaped growth overtook the spiral of money and capital, of assets and profits, more profits and more assets, only a few dared to question its value.

Management appears heroic: the will of the strong individual uniting with public benefit. Profit is the reward of the industrial general who has already merited rewarding through the effort of thrift that first brought him into business.

It is crucial that we are able to find a management not necessitated by mere technical demands of production. On the contrary, a peculiar type of **organizational intent** is presupposed.

This lack of technical necessity can be unveiled through an optics that on the one hand places existing, "organically" grown forms of production as pictures of contrast (without, I hope, making them too idyllic), and on the other hand constructs an alternative, even utopian, organization of production. This picture of contrast is able to cast light on the development of capitalist production so that it is not automatically legitimized by its enormous advances in productivity.

---

35. Engels, op.cit. p.87. (Das Kapital, 359-60, and 361-62)

The primary insight, then, will be that the production process making manage-ment into a technical necessity is itself the result of a certain principle of organiza-tion: the division of labour and the destruction of "natural", or "organic", cooper-ation. Organizational procedures precede technical innovations because capital precedes the production process: power and private property set the conditions of an apparent technological neutrality on behalf of Civilization.

Engels paraphrases Marx in the following way:

"Now, wage-labourers cannot co-operate unless **the same capitalist** employs them simultaneously, pays them and provides them with instruments of labour. Hence the scale of co-operation depends upon **how much capital a capitalist has.** The requirement that a certain amount of capital be present to make its owner a capitalist now becomes the **material** condition for the conversion of the numerous dispersed and independent labour processes into one combined so-cial labour process.

In a like manner, capital's **command** over labour was up to now only the for-mal result of the relation between capitalist and labourer; now it is the **necessary prerequisite** for the labour process itself; the capitalist represents combination in the labour process. In co-operation, **control** of the labour process becomes the **function of capital**, and as such it requires specific characteristics." (Op.cit. p.81. Das Kapital, Volume I, p.312)

The concept of **control** is the analytical media through which the logic of deducing technical advances from organizational goals is able to be understood. But like "power", "control" is an ambiguous concept, referring at one and the same time to man's need to dominate nature as well as his wish to dominate his fellow man. It is a concept split by normativity, pervaded by antagonistic rationalities, and constant-ly re-interpreted. Philosophers from Schopenhauer to Foucault have looked at its negative aspects, while its promises of the pleasures of free time have been empha-sized through its positive interpretations from Comte to Artificial Intelligence. Par-enthetically, for reasons always opaque to me, Marx seemed to perceive "control" primarily in its technical aspect, as a species of the so-called "forces of production". For him the historical task of the phenomenon of control was to liberate man from the yoke of labour and of domination. This aporia is the fatal mistake of Marxist thinking, through which the doors to totalitarianism were opened wide.

However, let us return to the problems of the historical destruction of natural cooperation that was to establish the control of cooperation, and of the skills and qualities of handicraft labour – the core of Josiah Wedgewood's programme, as a pioneer of the modern factory system was explicitly that. Wedgewood did devel-op the principle of a total re-structuring of the production process of potters, but without the aid of machines. Hence he demonstrates how organizational struc-turing anticipates the spectacular technical ones. His means were the creation of discipline through specialization on the basis of early training, meticulous defini-tion of every function of labour down to the finest detail, the construction of a production-flow through systems of rewarding and fining, and by way of a corps of loyal foremen. The aim was, "to make such machines of the Men as cannot err."[36] Here, the work of the French philosopher La Mettrie comes to mind, who in his famous book from 1748, "L'homme machine", anticipates the conception of man as the living machine that soon became the programme of the factory system.

It is important to realize, in order to understand the rise of industrialism, that the machine which is normally identified with "the technical" **per se** presupposes a specific organization of work: division of labour on the shopfloor and between trades, detailed description of tasks, and the concept of a combination of divided time and space, the "flow". The development of organizatorically rather advanced divisions of labour is historically well-known. From the early types of societies we know the coordination of very different kinds of labour by huge tasks of production with great demands to space and time, like drainage, roadbuilding, dam construction, etc., tasks that from technical reasons are only possible through large scale cooperation (Engels, op.cit. p.81. Das Kapital, Band I, p.310)). To these examples must be added the building of temples and cathedrals, first and foremost, however, the tasks necessary to the creation of the first feudal societies must also be noted: making an army function, making a town into an organic unit through cooperative tasks laid down by administration, and primarily perhaps the church. These organizational forms attest to a technical necessity, without them the tasks could not have been accomplished at all. This technical necessity is more difficult to stipulate as a universal principle in relation to the capitalist divison of labour.

Modern industrial society originates in the individual expropriation of cooperative productions, in local communities with complicated organic, social ties, and "cultures" of their own. Most often individual, capitalist enterprises have usurped handicraft-based production processes with their highly developed traditions of craftsmanship. In the first place, this is only possible through the liberating of traditional ties, and hence, re-institutionalization of private property, taking place during the Late Middle Ages by way of a legislation making the sale of land and hence, expropriation possible[37] – an expropriation that gave birth to the early labour force through legal rights to usurp the farmers' common land.

In the second place, it is only possible by securing the serf against the landlord as a free member of the town's community. This process creates the foundation for the transference of rights of private ownership of lands, buildings, machines, and raw materials, into the rights to the products of the production process. And it

---

36. See: (Mckendrick: 1971, p.67). The fact that Wedgewood was well-known both as a protagonist of democracy, and and as an opponent to slavery, just reinforces the picture of the firm as a new kind of no-man's land outside the norms and values of the surrounding society. See also: (Mantoux: 1973, p.399-406).

37. A property is "private" because it is no longer tied to the phenomenon of "fief", i.e., to mutual obligations and rights, to complicated claims of many family members, and to the "mores". See: (Bloc: 1962).

creates the "free" labourer, "free" in a double sense: free to perish and free to sell his labour power – the bitter observation by Karl Marx.

In the third place, the creation of relatively free markets based on the economy of money is indispensable to the rise of industrialism.

In the fourth place, this type of society is dependent upon the creation of the phenomenon of "capital good". This opens the possibility for the material elements of the production process to take the shape of assets, of "things", whose magnitude is measurable through money.

In the fifth place, modern industrial society arises from the creation, legitimization and consolidation of merchant and money capital. Hence, of the phenomenon of "rent" emerges banks which causes the development of stock exchanges, companies, corporations, paper money, and gigantic national debts.[38]

Industrial history demonstrates that most of the pattern-forming enterprises during the "Gründer-period" of the 18th century rested on pre-existing productions of a cooperative nature. The enterprises were textile production; and mining; potteries; shoes; glass; porcelain; hardware; clothes; and building materials (Pollard: 1965).

But the fact that cooperation is changed, and even destroyed in every detail of its original form, does not mean that cooperation itself as a phenomenon is abolished. Karl Marx emphasizes that:

"Co-operation ... in its **elementary** form, coincides with production on a larger scale, but it does not constitute a fixed form characteristic of a particular epoch, or of capitalist production, and it still exists today, when capital operates on a large scale without division of labour or machinery playing an important role" (One wishes to go on: "as in high-technological and consultancy firms, and in information technology-based firm-sections in the last decade of the 20th century. OFK") "Thus, although co-operation is the basic form of the whole capitalist production, its **elementary** form appears as a particular form alongside its more developed forms." (Engels, op.cit. p.83. Das Kapital, Vol I, 318)

Cooperation is necessarily built into the machines, even at the power station with its ten highly educated white-collar workers.[39] Cooperation is not a relation that can be eliminated entirely through any kind of task or time studies, not even through Taylorism.

---

38. C.B. MacPherson develops an ideal type model of this kind of a society on the move from feudalism to capitalism. This type of society can be empirically identified with the English society in the 18th century. The most decisive and distinctive traits in relation to fully developed capitalism is a rather limited labour market, and the feebly developed factory system. See: (MacPherson: 1970).

39. "the co-operative character of the labour process is now a **technical necessity**." (Engels, op.cit. p.88. Das Kapital, Volume I, p.372).

The atomization of every slight movement by every soldier in Frederick the Great's Prussian army into fractions of seconds does not help a bit when the truly important factor is how they are able to combine these fractions and cooperate with other soldiers in a time of emergency (Foucault: 1975). The secret of Napoleon was his ability to create "self-organizing groups", capable of functioning spontaneously in accordance with the original plan.

This does not furnish us with reasons to deny that manufactural production with its cunning division of labour and transformation of the formal systems of cooperation, plus the emerging mechanization of production, did create gigantic potentials for increasing the productivity of labour. Or that we would be correct in denying the great reduction in the waste of time and raw materials achieved by manufacture in relation to the former systems of subcontract. Or that we should disregard the amelioration of products and the emerging of many important new products. However, products by which the demands to quality were extraordinarily severe, as in the parts of iron industry producing machines, and, most important, machines meant to produce other machines, were still, during most of the 19th century, totally dependent on very skilled handicraft workers, and hence, on their will and ability to organize on an autonomous basis. The wages of instrument workers and metalworkers attest to this. It is said that the entrepreneurs were lying in wait outside the gates of Boulton and Watts to buy up craftsmen with offers of far higher wages (Pollard: 1965).

It would be impossible to deny that especially durable consumer goods and means of transport were created, exhibiting a mixture of fantasy, skill and exuberance, that no renaissance prince, nor inventor, such as Leonardo da Vinci, could have imagined in their dreams.[40] Nor would it be fair to deny that new trades and new occupations, new functions and new knowledge, were created, and hence new types of work and related qualifications.

However, as the programme of industrial society, capitalism has too often undermined its true basis, cooperation, no matter how far it developed the powers of social labour. Even totally automated production presupposes it, because cooperation between trades, and complicated systems of subcontracting and "networking", are built into this very human-free systems of machines. Cooperation becomes indirect. The development of the iron and metal industries during the 19th century demonstrates the dependency of this trade, in which the means of mechanization and automation of work processes must be created, on the very labour that it aims to make superfluous (Dobb: 1963).

---

40. If we were to be buried in the same ways as important people in the Bronze Age, we males would probably get an electric shaver, an electric tooth-brush, a glass of vitamin pills, a pocket-computer, a cellular telephone, a football, a bottle of aspirin, a bottle of brandy, a radio, a ... What could the criterion be to make us stop somewhere? Or must the burial place be a hangar?

As soon as capitalism has given industrial production the shape of both producing commodities for markets with intense competition, and being forced to fight hard for the resources essential to this production, then the innovation of the production process, as well as of the product, becomes the decisive factor: who can make the most precise turning lathe? Who can fabricate the best soluble oil? The fastest steamer? The heaviest guns? The lightest and most resistant armour? Who is able to fabricate the fastest and most efficient printing press? The most durable camshafts? Who can create products that make cleaning more easy and more safe? Who can produce nutritious foods that are not fattening?

But markets are beginning to be saturated during the last two decades of the 19th century, because the huge waves of production for infrastructures have run out. In the overseas areas these infrastructure-projects, railways, harbors, were often financed by the producers in the centres of Europe through investment and loans. In this manner imperialism came into being. Then, at the turn of the century new demands were made to the organization of production. The influence of Scientific Management, or "Taylorism", as it was called after its creator, Taylor, arriving on the scene and demonstrating, the victory of a universal strategy of management, conquered the production of large series of identical products.[41] However, it must be recalled that hardly any of the big companies really introduced Scientific Management on a large scale. They did not want to further increase the tension between workers and management, given the background of the necessity of a safe depreciation of huge investments of fixed capital. In any event, the gigantic profits that the First World War ushered in for American industry, and the possibility to use almost martial law against striking or recalcitrant workers, did not make Taylorism that necessary.

The fact that Lenin took over Scientific Management at a very early time testifies both to the limits of his visionary power and to the fact that the former USSR never actually belonged to the workers. Perhaps this contempt for the workers, often even excluding the right to a shop steward, might be one central reason for the fall of Russian despotism?

Well, the shadow of Taylorism accentuates the guilt of capitalist society, for it has failed to realize that cooperation, development, and implementation, of technology belong together. The one who destroys cooperation in the name of private interest, or through the pretension of the interests of a "collective" state, destroys the most important trait of production: the power of innovation.

---

41. A classic introduction, and severe critique of the three chief works of Taylor, (collected in the one volume "Scientific Management") is to be found in Bravermann: 1974.

6.2. Cooperation and Innovation

In the previous section we pinned down the concept of "cooperation" in a historical context. Let us now look more systematically at it, and at the concept of "innovation" that is dependent upon it.

"Cooperation" can be defined in the following way:

Cooperation is the will and the ability by the workers who are working directly together, to maintain, or to maximize, the human and technical sides of this production in relation to a stable or increased production at the same, or at a higher level of quality, without any augmentation of the existing relations of domination. It is presupposed that they must work in the same space and time, on the production of a product/service, or on the development, innovation or implementation of a new one, on their own initiative, or spontaneously.[42]

This is meant to be a "regulative" or normative definition.

I have chosen not to follow the meaning of the concept "of domination" in any depth here. But if the Jewish philosopher, Avishai Margalit, is right in defining a "person" as somebody who can be humiliated, then "domination" could be seen as a relation that legitimizes humiliation (Margalit: 1997). It is important that humiliation must take place at all levels of our mental capacities, the conative, emotive and cognitive levels.[43]

By this definition it must be the case that the person kept out of information, or who is not allowed to develop his abilities or his inclinations, is said to be humiliated. Hence, the history of working life is the history of humiliations.

It is important that this criterion of domination presupposes that the **possibility** of experiencing and recognizing this humiliation is present. Here a society would only be able to secure these possibilities under some circumstances related

---

42. Karl Marx defines the concept of "cooperation" in the following way: "The shape that labour takes on, when many people work methodically together, side by side or with each other, within the same production process or in different, but coherent product processes, is called cooperation." (Marx: 1969, p.344) It is obvious that this definition is shortened a bit by Engels (see the previous chapter). Engels misses the point that Marx, by talking about "different, but coherent production processes" opens up the concept of "indirect cooperation" that extends the concept of cooperation to mean other types of relations than directly, physical contact, or being tied to the same shop floor. Connections of work tasks across trades and sectors can be cooperation too, through direct interactions, or mediated through products. Hence, subcontracting is a species of cooperation.

43. Hence, a creature without a will, or without emotions, or without any kind of knowledge, cannot be humiliated, and therefore not dominated either. Thus, it is probably not apt to speak about the domination of animals, unless one shall insist on their cognitive capacities, even if they have both emotions and a kind of will. They cannot be humiliated or offended, but of course they can be hurt, and they can suffer, and they can be victims too.

to the cognitive aspects, probably, neither those related to the conative nor to the emotional, because childhood cannot be programmed, however good the intentions might be.

If **cooperation** is seen as primarily informal, i.e,. not rule-governed, then it is characterized by the fact that its pattern of interaction, in all possible constellations between individuals and groups, does not allow for humiliation.

The definition of cooperation presented here does not in any degree refuse to take into account **indirect** cooperation, i.e., cooperation between firms, trades and sectors, cooperation in networks, or with subcontractors. But it focuses on the direct "physical" contact, meaning mutual settings for speaking and acting, and, most important, the experiences of sharing the **same** space and the **same** time – which most often will mean "the same corporate space," i.e., the same firm. Trade unions will be of little importance to these kinds of experiences today. However, networks and relations to subcontractors will certainly gain increasing weight, thereby changing the range of the meaning of "same" in relation to ascribed membership of the "same cooperative unit".

The above definition emphasizes the natural urge within cooperation towards innovation (the distinction between innovation and invention is not important here). It also underlines that the aim of cooperation does not need to be a product in a narrow, functionalistic sense, but relates to the product as a concept, as an idea. This means neither that the cooperative unit always must identify with the managerial "mission" and "visions" of the firm, nor that a directing of cooperation to very fixed goals would further innovation. The distinction between **formal** and **informal** cooperation might cast light on these problems.

If "formal cooperation" is defined very narrowly as a rule-based specification of individual tasks and their combination, then the so-called "symbolic paradigm" of management theory and organizational theory would seem to suggest a very loose structuring of the production proces. This would, in turn give a wide space to "informal cooperation" in which it could spontaneously grow procedures and interactions during work. The direction of the production process must, according to Edgar Schein, be made (indirectly) by the "culture" of the firm, by artifacts, values and basic assumptions (Schein: 1985). But in Schein's universe, managers seem to be the priests of this culture. They are the ones who have the right to interpret this culture, and hence to construct the language in which these intangible entities are brought up to the surface. But the hard lesson learnt might be that, like love, culture cannot be invoked by the will, and that the important phenomenon of solidarity, in all directions, might be something other than a species of the genus "corporate culture".

From this perspective, **informal** cooperation must mean something quite different from "organizational culture". The core of informal cooperation is not the firm, but the **anti-authoritative** group, or team, as a resource of the task force.[44]

---

44. It is of utmost importance to emphasize that the group might establish organizational

Hence, it is a combination of personal relations, technological knowledge, and technical skills. Whereas formal cooperation, and its precious relations to innovation and implementation, are the explicit goals of management (whether through organizing of autonomous groups, by way of bonus systems, or by way of "culture"), informal cooperation in its essence always escapes managerial strategies.

One might say, on the one hand, that there exists an informal cooperation fruitful to innovation and implementation, and then management must be happy and try not to disturb it – and why should they disturb it, after all? The employees often know very well what the overall aim of the firm is, unless it is changed drastically by inner or outer factors. This knowledge is part of the socialization on the level of informal cooperation. Informal cooperation consists in a combination of devotion to technical problems, and a "crude language of the heart", having its origin in groups whose members are bound together by a mixture of this technical devotion. But it also originates from the common experience of being only, after all, employees. They thus often share a common social and educational background, as well as general "interests", conditions, and prospects of life.

On the other hand, if informal cooperation does not rise to a certain level, because group-members are too heterogeneous, or technical problems not challenging enough, or managerial traditions in the firm all too scrutinizing and interfering, then there is very little management can do without virtually reorganizing the firm.[45] One must not forget that under the pressures of innovation and implementation of knowledge technology, personal politics has become a very delicate affair. However, management is able to anticipate the dead-locks of informal cooperation by granting comprehensive "social" rights on the shop-floor.

The question is whether management had to interfere directly at the level of informal cooperation, even if it could?

Perhaps it is worth remembering what Marx pointed out: that cooperation is the product of, and itself reproduces, "the inevitable antagonism between the exploiter and the raw material of his exploitation (i.e., the worker. OFK)." (Marx: 1969).

This is the antagonism between a technical and a social necessity of directing the production process, and hence between a neutral, universal level, and a historical, if not contingent, level of work organization influenced by power.

But even if the "technical" level cannot be abstracted from historical forces, these forces inhibit not just every innovation, but probably every invention, too. There

---

traits on its own that come close to the negative sides of formal cooperation. Groups and teams might often show authoritative structures with the result that individuals are dominated accordingly. Hence, informal cooperation can only be identified with some types of groups and teams, namely those that exhibit distinct anti-authoritative characteristics. See: (Janis: 1972).

45. Pascale Gagliardi, director of ISTUD in Stresa, Italy, has been working with the problems of corporate culture in theory and practice, especially in relation to changing this culture. See: (Gagliardi: 1986).

seems to be a hidden inertia in technology that could be able to combine with the maximum of autonomy on the sides of the workers – be they white-collar or blue-collar, business economists, engineers, or from the humanities.

The crux of the matter here is that informal cooperation today, in its close relation to innovation and implementation of technologies, has two demands in order to lead to innovative processes: a free space and a free time. This freedom primarily means that autonomy on the shop-floor is substantial enough to give even comprehensive activities of innovation and implementation a chance to develop, and to be realized – and this goes for research activities too.

Thus, the amount of uncertainty, based on a great difference between the levels of formal and informal cooperation which often scares management, might be the very basis of innovation.[46]

The central point is that the technical aspect of the informal cooperation on its own can never support innovation. What top-management can do is to secure the following rights and duties on the shop-floor, which stands as the quintessence of free time and free space.

The German philosopher Immanuel Kant emphasizes three "maxims of the human mind" in his Aesthetics ("Kritik der Urteilskraft") Paragraph 40:

a. Autonomous thinking.
b. Empathy: to be able to think, as if you were any other person.
c. At any time to be able to think in harmony with yourself: self-management on the basis of self-insight.

The last maxim is placed as the most important by Kant, being the precondition of the two first ones. (We shall return to these problems of philosophy in the next Parts of this book).

The following social aspects of organization are also emphasized by Kanter as indispensable to innovation: relations such as support, acknowledgement, backing, appropriation, and trust between management and the shopfloor. The important factors of will and ability need not be technical entities, but may originate in patterns of social interaction, constituting the core of "collectivism".

Perhaps, one should add the following here: much research has been done during the Sixties, Seventies, and Eigthties in informal cooperation and in worker collectvism on the shop floor. Often this research was politically biased, being done by left-wing researchers, or initiated by the unions, so long as these two groups did not conflict, as was frequently the case. Katherine Stone's influential article: "The Origin of Job-Structures in the Steel Industry", or Stephen Marglin's "What do bosses do?", both published in the rabid left-wing journal, "Review of Radical Political

---

46. R.M. Kanter emphasizes that the innovative firm does not try to repress and master uncertainties and conflicts, it knows how to use them to enhance overall responsibility and to stimulate informal cooperation (Kanter: 1983).

Economics", tried to challenge both the rationality of management, and the legitimacy of trade unions in relations to "genuine" worker interests. However, some of their insights might be equivalent to the ideas of the upcoming schools of "soft" management within organization theory, (the legacy of the "Chicago School" which had "job-enrichment" and "humanization of work" on their agenda). German industrial sociology developed in this wake with the works of Kern and Schuman, analyzing the physical and psychical consequences of overspecialized and repeated work-operations on the shop floor, through mechanization; the meta-sociological studies of the concepts of "work", "knowledge" and "learning" in capitalism by Negt and Kluge from Hannover stand as another example. In Denmark it caused a series of historical studies in the labour process to arise, the intentions of which were to testify to the important influence of workers on the development of the technical sides of the production process ("The Society of Workers History").

However, today management theory realizes that the antagonism between management and employees might be fruitful, in its appearance as the difference between formal and informal levels of cooperation – the attempts at abolishing these antagonisms through legislation and symbolic gestures, in the so-called "socialistic" regimes, seemed a disaster to innovation and implementation on the shop floor.

This antagonism implies that cooperation in its totality is always more than a formally constructed and hence, analytically available force. The informal cooperation is the level of "one's own initiative" and of spontaneity, levels often dependent on "embedded" knowledge, a knowledge that is specific in relation to production processes, or even to the situation of production, but that certainly must be recognized as a "specific application" of general knowledge too. This kind of knowledge might be called "tacit knowledge", in the terminology of Polanyi, and it is connected to mental patterns of spontaneous cooperation, and to non-codified competencies, or even to competencies that cannot be codified at all.

In other words, cooperation has the potential to build technical competencies into social settings.[47]

This means, as already stated, that the phenomenon of cooperation must include not just motivation, and practices of informal problem-solving, but also mutual respect, the care of mutual worthiness, collective commitment, trust, and even

---

47. The managerial movement of TQM (Total Quality Management) was, and still is, carried by this knowledge. The left wing academics writing about industrial work during the end of the Seventies and the beginning of the Eighties, were very well capable of phrasing the programme of TQM prior to its actual breakthrough. For example in Cressey, Macinnes: 1980: "To develop the forces of production capital must seek to develop labour as a subjective force to unleash labour's powers. Thus in the use value aspect of its relation with labour capital will seek a purely cooperative relationship in order to abolish the antagonism between the worker and the means of production that its capitalist form throws up" p.15.

passion. This cannot be brought into life through a liberality in relation to the flows of information and resources on the side of management only, it demands a "tacit culture" – a culture that is able to reconcile individual ambition with social virtues.

This tacit culture cannot, and ought not to, be the subject of managerial strategies. Hence, it is relevant to distinguish between "real" and "unreal" autonomy of work within the processes of invention, innovation, and implementation. The recent program of "Empowerment" seems to aim at this, recognizing the importance of genuine responsibility of the design, and realization of processes and products, on the side of the employees. It might also establish a proof of the great importance of organizational structures and managerial practices to the content of "the technical" per se. However, this should not be interpreted in a way that propagates the total lack of significance of formal cooperation to the development of innovation-structures: the last thirty years of trying on different levels and in different ways to establish the setting for self-organizing groups attest to that. The power of analytical prognostication seems rather weak here, and rule-governing must yield to governing through the creation of settings, or even "circumstances", and to a focus on the process, and not that much on the goal. However, where goals are rather loosely defined, processes might run astray. A way to stimulate innovation through a mild form of structured cooperation, on the side of management, could be the introducing of "dialogue-directed" groups. It was pointed out that dialogue could function as a filter to "clean" the group of undisciplined members.[48] However, the problems of whether such a procedure breaks with the democratic ideals of cooperation are complicated.

Formal cooperation expresses an opposition between the technical and the social aspects of management that cannot find any reconciliation. So the clever manager will try to make formal cooperation invisible, or, as an emergency solution, so rough that it will be easy for informal cooperation to grow and emerge inside of it.

However, the possibilities of action vary in relation to the dominance of mechanized and automated processes within the firm: in trades where machine-systems are the rule, formal cooperation will leave few opportunities for informal cooperation, whereas trades with much "knowledge capital" directly force the manager to stimulate informal cooperation. In this case a high degree of self-organizing is a necessity.

The good leader has to accomplish a balance here between the built-in antagonism of capitalist production of which Marx spoke: its technical and social dimension. This distinction manifests itself on the level of formal and informal cooperation, as the distinction between autonomy and heteronomy. The excellent leader

---

48. Professor Henrik Herlau from Institute of Management, Politics and Philosophy at the Copenhagen Business School has emphasized this through his socalled KUBUS-model. He has practiced this model through a simulation of inventive cooperation in groups of workers at many levels.

is capable of making the cooperative units work for the firm, as if they only worked for themselves, and yet still not be liable of any accusation of manipulation, i.e., he has to cancel and maintain the antagonism at one and the same time.

This balance invokes the concept of the invisible leader and hence the question of the need for any management at all. But at the same time it seems to call for the most visible leader to incorporate the crux of this balance and hence the crux of modern leadership and management.

That it can only be solved through the concept of **managerial virtues,** is the principal thesis of the present book.

6.3. Innovation: The Dilemma of Management

The manager of the 21st century must face the fact that cooperation always was, and still will be, something unique. Neither the right of private ownership to direct and distribute work, nor the attempts initiated by the unions and the state to represent cooperation from a perspective of the employee are satisfactory. His transformation from a manager to a real leader can only take place through the serious growth of a moral character on his behalf, from which the peculiar combination of genuine human virtues and dedicated leader-virtues can arise.

The potentials of human labour lies in its ability, through an optimum of freedom in cooperation, to create, conceive and produce more than each individual could ever do, no matter how furnished with technical devices or organizational experts. But "more" must here be understood on the basis of qualitative, not quantitative, criteria of production. Informal cooperation is the vital principle of the innovation of products and processes of production.

These considerations must be seen in the light of the concept of "innovation". Too often innovation is conceived of by way of conservative schedules, constructed through the ideal of scientists, researchers and entrepreneurs. The social factor is easily forgotten – a fact Peter Drucker already pointed to in his famous "The Concept of the Corporation" from 1946, and elaborated further in "Innovation and Entrepreneurship" from 1985 (Drucker: 1985). Schumpeter's apotheosis of the entrepreneur only reflects banal, but apparently viable fantasies, where people, like Edison, are always pulled out of a hat. The fact that he would be almost nothing without the fabrication of usable glass, usable filaments, usable sockets, usable flexes, usable switches, usable power plants, and behind it all a usable national state is forgotten. Chandler's perspective on industrial growth emphasizes that (Chandler: 1990). He would be nothing without the vital, but often hardly visible, networks of intentions, promises, aspirations, demands and visions, surrounding him in a certain shape: the light bulb was on the point of happening almost everywhere.

Of course, it could be argued that it is the very invention and innovation of Edison that creates the innovatory horizon of all the other products and processes.

And that he, all by himself, was able to pose a general problem so concretely that it forced through the solution. But this is not the only aspect of the matter. It is more likely that existing, but latent, "know-how" is delivered as the concept of a definite product. Innovation makes unused knowledge topical. Because we cannot demand that inventions, and hence innovation, should contain the idea of something never seen before by any person – that they somehow have been visualized in the mind of somebody is inevitable, of course. The story of the steam engine demonstrates this. To this must be added the fact that it is the amount of capital, and hence the scale of production, through which innovation often has been actualized, i.e., a corporate success.[49]

From a philosophical perspective the problems of defining innovation might be similar to the classical epistemological problems already haunting Plato of defining "new knowledge".

The predicament here is that insofar as the knowledge is really new, we should not be able to perceive it – the solution of Plato was consequent to his ascribing this genuine kind of knowledge to a knowledge "remembered" from an earlier life.

In a more concrete, empirical context, this discussion must focus upon the level at which innovations are recorded: firms, trades, sectors ... and finally on code numbers and Patents Acts; but also on the relations between innovations on the one hand, and research and implementation through processes of production on the other.

Decisive beyond all these considerations of levels of economical operations is the fact that an innovation is a symbol. It is about continuity and about breaking it, because it is about the actualization of a carefully prepared fantasy.

Then innovation is about something coming in the right moment, **kairos**, and creating itself and this timing at one and the same time. Innovation is the first spectacular condensation of the time and space of corporate reality, of the fusion of processes of informal and of formal cooperation.

When it is hard to repress our knowledge of the dependency of apparent coincidences which so many of the new products and "great inventions" result from, how on earth should a leader then, trying so hard to keep everything under control, be able to contribute deliberately to these innovations? But the ability to keep all reins in one hand presupposes, after all, only a few horses. The simplification, standardization, clarity, and manageability that are so important to the exercise of power hinder the utilization of the most important factor to innovation of all: It is chance that creates; a successful leader must exploit the force beneath apparently indifferent coincidences. Innovation then, can be seen as the moment when the

---

49. This should not be possible to extrapolate from conditions dominating innovative markets of today to a general theory of economically driving forces: "It was investment, not innovation, that determined entrepreneurial success or failure in the new industries of the Second Industrial Revolution". Chandler, op.cit. p.63.

intangible competencies, prepared during cooperation, find their real shape through the combination of chance, cleverness and skills.

This spontaneity has been built into cooperation, a spontaneity that alone the experiential attitude makes possible. Definition of tasks, time-studies, hierarchial organizing, lay offs, orders, regulations, nervous rehearsals, visions repeated without fantasy all destroy the experiential attitude.

From this perspective the worst enemy of the manager, in relation to his becoming a leader, seems to be himself. Here he is somehow forced to direct and distribute work in a way that transforms "labour" into its original meaning in Middle Age language: "arebeit", "suffering", "pain". The easiest thing in the world of business seems to be to separate the identity of a person from the processes of work. He is told exactly what to do. And the more precisely this is done, the more he will be like a zombie, and at the end of a process like a machine.[50] Through this process the horizon of the possible, the utopian urge, is destroyed. This means the the most important questions cannot be posed due to torpor, or due to the total absorbtion of the attention trough systems of piecework contracts and bonuses: the question of another reality of products and production?

But this does not mean that everything points to the invisible leader as a universal solution. Management does not, of course, operate in a historical or cultural void, it entangles itself in pre-existing relations between bosses and labour. The manager who as a real leader wants to set cooperation free, must make himself very visible as the guarantor of this freedom.

This is only possible through his personally embodying, as the example on all levels, the genuine virtues of the leader. No compromises are possible here.

Capitalist society and hence, the firm, still has a kind of organization that the freedom granted to informal cooperation must be given from the top. The employees should never be allowed to take it by themselves.[51]

A manager that chooses to guarantee this freedom, must himself be able to legitimize it to the stakeholders – and, alas, to the stockholders and to the shareholders. If he chooses to grant such a degree of freedom, ignoring capitalist rationality, then he will not even be a missionary, but rather a "kamikaze-pilot", a suicidal member of the community of the mad. However, he might also be a saint. And to my knowledge nobody ever proved that the position of the saint was not the role that he was destined to play, if he were to follow the calling.

---

50. "Indeed, the more jobs are "formalized", with duties finely specified and "codified", the less innovation is produced in the organization." (Kanter: 1996, p. 102). See also: (Borum: 1990).

51. This statement is not an **a priori** argument, but an **a posteriori** one. It relies on historical experiences with demands to autonomy reflecting the fact that rights fought from the bottom, i.e. self-organizing, very rarely can be kept. Perhaps due to the shape of this fighting: It challenges power too boldly by questioning its silent reference to its own rationality.

6.4. Some Aspects of an Idea of Ideal Cooperation

The problem of the connection between management, cooperation and innovation can be sharpened through the following question:

Does there exist a kind of cooperation that is also optimum for innovation, and makes the hitherto known organization of work superfluous, and hence, the capitalist concept of management?

When one enters this field of problems, two issues are of importance: on the one hand, whether one conceives of the production processes, and of the spectre of products proper to the ultra-modern industrial society, as the articulation of social relations in absolute contrast to a fundamental notion of civilization. On the other hand, whether one conceives of the overriding organization of the social processes of work and distribution, realized through the market and the formation of capital as functionally inappropriate and/or morally objectionable.

The first perspective contains the vision of the great return to pre-industrial production processes. It is primarily seen in ultra radical ecological movements, and in the idea of establishing small, collectively organized, local communities based on handicraft (sometimes even with the "computer-craftsman" secure from management behind his own walls).

The problem with this alternative is, that at the one side, it is hard to take seriously as a proposal for a national or even global solution to modern economical problems. On the other side, it has often reintroduced – as far as it is based on ideology, and collective units seem to need that – hierarchical forms of management, formal or informal. Its innovative potentials do not seem convincing either. Its conservatism, or even its "restoratory" urge, are too great.

The other alternative seems more serious. First and foremost this is due to the fact that the questions about possible connections between cooperation, innovation and management here can be posed on the basis of the status quo of production.

We are able to ask here about the existence of an alternative, but altogether tangible, rationality to capitalist principles. It would be a rationality changing the view of how one applies science and technology, knowledge and qualifications, skills and social competencies, collaboration and coordination.

This alternative rationality will emerge through a different shape and hence, a different development of firms, trades, sectors and their interrelations.

Neither "socialist economies", nor socialist movements in Western Europe, have demonstrated any convincing model of this alternative rationality. Especially socialist movements inspired by Karl Marx were subject to capitalist rationality, because of their trust in the liberating power of "the productive forces", i.e., science, technology, and knowledge. The protagonists of an alternative rationality would more often be found among syndicalist movements, and in alliances between the Social Democrats, communitarianists and syndicalists, as in England during the first third of the 20th century.

Syndicalist movements were always keen on demonstrating the gains in relation to productivity and quality of products within the capitalist framework of production that resulted from self-organizing cooperatives. They would usually argue that many of the barriers to effective production, due to the antagonism between workers and management, would be removed through self-organizing. Any managerial technique would prove itself inferior here. To this was added the reminder of the gigantic gains to society from expropriated profits and abolished burdens of interests. One even imagined a reduction in the level of crisis of modern economy, and a reinforcement of social justice.

From this point of view, management as a phenomenon could be blamed for everything and hence, rejected as a relic of the injustices of capitalist production. Civilization could do without capitalism.

From workers' collectives in Katalonia, via the red areas of Northern Italy, dominated by communist unions, to the Yugoslav cooperatives of Tito, and to the English protagonist groups of "Workers Control" during the Seventies, did sound the arguments for better utilization of production machinery and production techniques, and of faculties, skills, qualifications and motivation. When management was chosen by the workers themselves, and not by shareholders, it was objected, the workers must be able to deliver ten times the amount of what was produced during the reign of capitalist management.

However, this did not seem to be the case. They did not create an alternative to management, not even an alternative management. Perhaps they still suffered from the belief in omnipotent management, or just from the prosaic fact that they could not raise any capital or get any costumers.

But concepts rather close to today's programme of Empowerment arose in these settings, and conceptions quite close to many important and alternative initiatives of today: the idea of "socially useful products", or the idea of "sustainability". For example, "Workers Control" in Nottingham launched the idea of a reorganization of the huge "Lucas Aerospace Factories" where English war planes were produced, into a production of amphibious vehicles, invalid chairs, and pace-makers.[52]

However, in the light of the rationality proper to capitalist production, a concept of change in production through innovations of products was developed here, a concept that is on the agenda now, in the late Nineties. But it would be wrong to believe that these historical experiences were of great importance to the new conception of cooperation within management theory. The great inspiration and hence, influence came from Japan: here a combination of respect for worker-initiated cooperation, comprehensive systems of subcontracting, quite new con-

---

52. The "Institue of Workers' Control" in Nottingham was an organization that started on the initiative of the English trade unions, shop-steward commitees and the left wing of Labour. Its roots were syndicalistic, probably mingled with the legacy of the Fabian Society, and financed through the Russell Foundation. Its research was directed by its aim: to support workers' self-organizing activities, the establishment of cooperatives, and the conception of "social products."

cepts of the management of time and space of the corporate firm, complicated cultures with communitarian traits, an extremely able use of innovations in an economy of scale, mass-production, and product-quality, and quite unknown systems of responsibility towards the workers on the side of the firm ... all caused the managers of the Western world to gape during the Seventies.

Left-wing self-organizing cooperatives were drowned in problems of management, of administration, in the lack of highly educated employees, lack of marketing-expertise, but most of all lack of capital – the last item rather undeserved, I presume. The Japanese, on the contrary, succeeded at all levels.

It is important to notice that one factor of the last quarter of the 20th century pressed management into serious considerations about the blessings of self-organizing cooperation: the computer. The full utilization of the potentials of this machine seems to demand a rather wide granting of autonomy. Computer-work is hard to standardize without loosing innovative potentials. And it needs highly educated, and rather self-assured labour power, and a flexible, and definitely non-hierarchical distribution of tasks, functions and privileges. Customs and rule-governing, as a means of protection against sudden pressures in production, had to yield to the need of this new "open sesame" called "flexibility". The perhaps greatest problem to the leader today might be his lack of knowledge in relation to the technical sides of production: he does not always know the code of techniques and skills that is able to transform his intentions and directives into new initiatives and hence, into customs rather than mere routines This places him within the dilemma between aggressive impotence, and the "generous" granting of autonomy.

Here the picture of cooperation through the twentieth century is thrown into relief, because cooperation has been conceived of as both concretely and symbolically represented by one person, the mid-level manager. Like the sergeant in the army, he is the one responsible for implementation at all levels of direct action. The level delimiting cooperative units in relation to organization and techniques is exactly that of the mid-level manager. But the focus is increasingly on re-structuring production, and hence, on task-forces and ad hoc teams, instead of on rather stable groups. There is a quest for qualities and faculties of flexibility, instead of those of rigid professionalism in relation to implementation of rules and customs. An imaginative interpretation of directions and circumstances, not conservative loyalty and the guarantee of continuity, is the subject of demand. This development is beginning to make the mid-level manager superfluous, or even a hindrance. The mid-level manager, standing at the point of intersection of formal and informal cooperation, securing group-borders from without, now seems to be an impediment to progress in self-organization from within.

During the movement of the TQM, the mid-level manager was still able to hold his position as the one who passed on knowledge about technical and social limits to projects higher up in the corporate system. He was able to guarantee that self-organization and hence, autonomy, was kept inside the boxes of firm-visions. However, the mid-level manager now had to be managed himself in quite a new way: directed, motivated, taught to sense new signals, taught to interpret signs from above and from below, or be laid off. The mid-level manager had to acquire new kinds of social skills closely related to the new kind of labour in his care. He had to be the catalyst of innovatory potentials, not the factor of their dissolving.

In the USA management decided to get rid of the mid-level manager during the last years of the Eighties. The final influence came from the so-called "Re-engineering movement", the management-theory wave succeeding the TQM. TQM was defined as a management program based on the continuous improvement and development of processes, as well as on the focus on customers and involvement of employees. This refined new type of "Scientific Management", "re-engineering", had been developed at the Sloan School of Management, at the Massachusetts Institute of Technology.[53] The promises inherent in computer-systems, as the material core of the information-flow inside the firm, were a means to this programme, i.e., direct contact between management and every individual employee across groups and formal hierarchies and team-work on the basis of projects (task-forces), rather than a distribution of work in divisions and without what Mintzberg called, "the middle line". But this aggressive strategy towards forcing the "Adhocracy" into existence had its costs (Mintzberg: 1979).

The attempt at constructing the patterns of an informal cooperation, transgressing organizational structures of dividing and combining work, proved to be a hazardous project. In theory it seemed to yield a wide scope to the initiative of the individual, integrating him at the very same time into what at the surface might appear as an almost "communitarian" community of communication in the firm. Re-engineering showed how important the mid-level manager was to these processes. The notion seemed fatal that without him and, hence, with a fewer steps between top and bottom, management could be more direct, more intense, and more tight, and shopfloor resources more easily get at in order to release innovative creativity. The tremendous gestures of symbolism and the talk about "missions" and "visions" (old Jesuit language) of the firm could not solve problems composed of intricate mixtures of the technical and the social.[54] From the level of a "language of symbols", speaking in terms of missions and visions, of corporate values and of personal attitudes, there is a long way to the language of innovations. The whole promising project of "Corporate Symbolism", both in the universities and in the firms was to meet its Waterloo in the Re-engineering movement. The weaknesses of "Corporate Symbolism", in underestimating the role of language (discourse) and the role of

---

53. The movement of "re-engineering" was suggested through the best-seller "Re-engineering the Corporation" written by M. Hammer and J. Champy in 1993.

54. The concept of "vision" seems to create problems to management, insofar as it has to articulate a rather delicate balance between two opposing conceptions: the first one being "pre-discursive", almost "innocent", images of the aims and identity of an organization (often named "values"). The second one being rather elaborated strategic scenarios, depicting the future as distinct states of successful accomplishment (Thyssen: 1994; Nymark: 1999).

hidden power as an enormously destabilizing factor, were to create marked changes in management theory. These changes took two directions: the one led towards business ethics as value-orientation and consent; the other interpreted postmodernism rigourously, and faced the realities of power and the shallowness of managerial languages (we shall return to this in the next chapter).

Another lesson that was hard to learn was the fact that information technologies did not keep their promises at all. They often created more problems through the processes of implementation than they did solve. Computers cannot transfer commitment across the organization. The mid-level manager is extremely important as the one who communicates commitment, if not "euphoria", in a strange combination with technical soberness. So, instead of laying the mid-level manager off, top-management had to grant him structures of support. An example here could be what Davis and Lawrence already in 1977 called "matrix organisation structures" (Davis, Lawrence: 1977). The mid-level manager must here refer to the identity of both a project- and a function-manager (Kanter: 1996, p.100). Besides, the mid-level manager motivates at a symbolic level by being an object of identification for the workers, and by being "the one" whose place an ambitious worker might eventually assume. The mid-level manager is a living paradox in embodying simultaneously a whip and a carrot, a means and an end. The managerial virtues shall certainly be important as attitudes for him to incorporate.

It is the task of the manager to preserve and strengthen cooperation as the basis of innovation. But it is the task of the leader also to protect cooperation for the sake of the employees. What can be done?

Literature about innovation, and about the rather new field, "management of knowledge", as well the concepts of "intellectual capital", "ethical and "green" accounting", the increasing analysis of "organizational learning",[55] of "tacit knowledge", and networking, have cast new and different lights on the processes of innovation. The authors try to direct innovation towards much more collective goals, and to reinforce the responsibility in relation to man and nature, to the future, in management, scientists, researchers, planners, workers and in the consumers.

One of the first to emphasize the crucial role of autonomy to innovation was Elisabeth Moss Kanter in her book "The Change Masters" from 1983, where over a period of five years she analysed about 100 companies (selecting six to examine more thoroughly).

Her aim was to diagnose "the innovative firm". She concluded that firms ought to try to create units functioning on the basis of informal cooperation.[56] This can

---

55. On the concept of "organizational learning", see: Argyris, Schön: 1996. And Nonoka: 1995.

56. (Kanter: 1983). When the creation of informal cooperation is the strategic goal of management, it often speaks about "team-work". And Wilson: 1996, Chap.7: Team knowledge as a business resource.

be seen as a radical rebellion against the idea of a technically and socially omniscient management, which organizes the firm through a functional outlook. Kanter stressed the following parameters:

a. "Kaleidoscopic thinking": the metaphor evokes the fact that an organization can be changed by being shaken. Through this effort the same elements are re-arranged: "Often, creativity consists of rearranging already existing pieces to create a new possibility" (Kanter: 1996, p.99). Kaleidoscopic thinking is charac-terized by a stimulation of ideas beyond the borders of the firm. Thus innova-tive units in the firm are characterized by a larger surface of contact and a more intensive practice of contact with the world (ibid. p.98). They are characterized by more open communication, and can be given more liberty of action and more freedom. An example from Peters & Waterman (Peters, Waterman: 1982, p.232) might illustrate this liberty. The firm 3M does very little to control the intiating phases of innovation: "An NBVD product is never justified on the ana-lytic case; it must be based on belief," says the manager of SM's New Business Ventures Divison".

b. The creation of smaller, cooperative units that work together across sections of the organization. This opens up the possibility of interdisciplinary teams, and through this more perspectives on the topic are activated. It is important that the informal unities activated here actually are of an informal character – that they are "based on a common end use goal but not around function or specialty" (Kanter: 1996, p.101). Hewlett-Packard, for example, has followed this strategy for some time.

c. With a wide area of functions. This refers to expanding the field of functioning, and the content of qualifications and skills.

   "This, in turn, gives people the mandate to solve problems, to respond cre-atively to new conditions, to note changed requirements around them, or to im-prove practices, rather than mindlessly following procedures derived from the past" (ibid).

   Such broad definitions of jobs imply that tasks overlap. Through this people will be integrated at an interdisciplinary level, giving each employee the respon-sibility of the whole product – a factor that will stimulate innovation too.

d. A general atmosphere of innovatory expectancy within the organization.

The attitudes of the organization towards innovations are decisive factors of innovatory practice. This might be the existence of "innovation-funds" that can be employed when potential innovations are discovered, or the possibility of getting enough free time to follow an idea. In addition, mid-level managers must be granted a certain autonomy in letting people on the shopfloor go their own way.

The values of management and the customs or "culture" of the firm are important here. The empirical fact that new firms have higher rates of innovation than old ones full of traditions attests to this. However, this might be due to the kind of products sold by new firms, e.g., software and consultancy. But firms that grant more liberty of action to their employees, and with a lesser threat of dismissals, also have a higher rate of innovation. "Downsizing" – as it euphemistically is called in the American business slang – is fatal to cooperation and innovation if it affects groups other than obviously superfluous or administrative personal:

> "Thus, organizations with 'cultures of pride' in the company's achievements and in the achievements and abilities of individuals will find themselves more innovative ... It is a self-reinforcing upward cycle – **performance stimulating pride stimulating performance** – and is especially important for innovation. Change requires a leap of faith, and faith is so much more plausible on a foundation of successful prior experience." (Kanter: 1996, p.105)

Following Kanter, the factors stimulating innovation do not focus on any special technology. However, the full utilization of the potentials of the computer still haunts this ideal model, and in two dimensions: in the first place the ideas of Kanter seem primarily realistic when we speak of employees working with computers in a potentially innovative way. Liberty of action is an evident organizational strategy. In the second place however, cooperation might be rather difficult when people are working with computers. The discipline of CSCW (Computer Supported Cooperative Work) testifies to this, because it examines the changing conditions of the "bodily" foundation of "the cooperative experience" resulting from hyper-intellectual computer-tasks.[57]

The famous research-project "Artificial Intelligence", with all its connotations of science-fiction, supported by its meta-discipline, "Cognitive Science", can very well be seen as an attempt to automate the innovative processes through the simulation of individual, cognitive processes of innovative behaviour, i.e., inference by analogy, tacit knowledge, conclusions from too few premisses, intuition, etc.. The computer seems to fit managerial strategies almost all too well.

Kanter shows us further that the manager has quite new roles characterized by the following items:

The ability to strengthen the positive relations and competencies that mark gen-

---

57. See for example: "Proceedings of the Conference on Computer-Supported Cooperative Work". Oct 7-10, 1990, Los Angeles. The Danish researcher, Kurt Keller, has contributed to this field by using the phenomenology of the French philosopher Maurice Merleau-Ponty, to examine the bodily experience of cooperative work and its modulation through the computer as the axis of work. Merleau-Ponty centres his phenomenological philosophy in the examination of the body.

eral communication and social intercourse – after all they are the core of cooperation, not the technical aspects.

This primarily means the ability to incorporate **values**, to guarantee **validity** of the firm's intra- and inter-communicative settings: the will to adhere to truth, i.e., to give available information to the public, and to accept the judgments of impartial, or even antagonistic, expertise. And finally the manager needs the will to direct the process wherein norms and values are interpreted, under absolute guidance of these norms and values, in spite of firm-interest.

This refers to the ability of the leader to **be an example** of a special kind of goal-directed behaviour where, what is meant by "goals", can never be narrow business interests, but always must integrate public concerns within them. Technical and economic considerations can never be excuses in this context.

When approaching managerial functions so close to general social competencies another picture of the successful manager, or better, of the good leader, appears. The qualities of the "leader" presented in "Stogdill's Handbook of Leadership": "Autocrat, Missionary, Compromiser, Bureaucrat, Benevolent Autocrat, Developer, Executive", no longer seem sufficient (Bass(Ed.): 1981, p.23). The recently emphasized qualities of "coach" or even "mentor" do not work either – as we shall see in section 6.6.

These general social competencies are directed towards the organization itself, towards the employees. They consist of the abilities to stimulate, even to urge, to catalyze commitment, solidarity, fantasy, and to create enthusiasm and even "euphoria".

Such qualities of the leader are definitely **managerial virtues**, however general they might seem.

These competencies relate to the customers too. The manager must be able to act as an interpreter. He must translate between the languages of the firm and of the consumers, between technical and economic "realities", and the differentiated worlds of infinite, and sometimes even, sophisticated needs. These needs, after all, do not so much answer to questions posed my human nature, as to questions posed by "needs" already the result of technical interpretations of human possibilities. He must be able to stand the speed in the astronaut-centrifuge where the infinite transformations of no longer identifiable needs into demands are staged. He must first and foremost never seem a pretender. He must never appear as a rhetor, or even worse, as an actor. He must seriously and honestly try to think of the 20th simulacrum of simulacras, the product that is going to revolutionize markets, without being allowed to develop schizophrenic, nor schizoid traits. He must be relaxed, but never apathic; keen, but never obsessed. He requires the gentle mania of convincing.

The social qualities of the manager are directed towards the rest of the network of stakeholders too: suppliers, consultants, trade unions, stockholders, shareholders, public servants, newspapers, trade associations, the lawyers of the other firm's consumers, minority groups, grass roots groups, town planners, patent agencies, advertising agencies, bankers, the ministry for taxation, customs authorities, the Factories Inspectorate, a local politician, as well as the participants of a strike among transport workers in Bombay. He has to be lithe, but at the same time hard. He must be a diplomat, trustworthy, patient and yet resolute.

To develop a "meta-quality" here seems to be rather urgent.

A quality through which this insisting world can be kept at arm's length and yet, as the world of one's fellow man can be committed to without the posture of the affable or blasé. An honest bird's eye view. This mental quality is often called **euboulia** by the classical Greek philosophers. It means a devoted, but cool overview, taking into considerations the interests of individuals, the public, the future and the past.

Demands to management, subject to such complex conditions, might seem to transgress the horizon of discursive logic and to challenge reason. The manager must have a sensitivity to spaces, to moments. He must have a sense of arranging and of timing, of timing arrangement, and of arranging timings. In a way, the good leader must be allied with the future. It is as if a concealed force presses us to admit that he must be a follower of the magician's art. **Invocation** suggests itself, because the leader must create results in a world invested with technical realities that he cannot understand completely. It is a world characterized by mental forces, to which he has to relate both deliberately and spontaneously, but without the ability of an analytical preview. Even if he tries to create the settings of informal cooperation, he seems forced to invoke reactions, even to summon happenings and hence, results. He has to "create" the things that cannot be created, or be extremely resistant to the temptation of trying to construct deliberately, passions, culture, and the **kairos**, i.e., "the right moment". He has to discover them, but by means that often seem to be beyond reason. So perhaps **invocation** might be a managerial virtue after all?

It is the burden of the leader to be split between the considerations of human rationality and capitalist rationality; to be split between the considerations of stakeholder rationality, and the considerations of the needs of the individual and of the public, between the realms of God and the emperor.

In 1994, the great year of re-engineering, the profit of American firms rose by 11%, while 516,069 workplaces were closed down. The manager obliged to close down workplaces during times of prosperity, if not even booms, is not someone to envy. When Danish banks mounted the wave of re-engineering in the mid-Nineties, many a middle-aged employee was dismissed without the possibility of retirement. This cut in salary spending seemed suspect, because it coincided with great losses of money due to faulty and hazardous investments: management demonstrated a lack of responsibility both towards individuals and society.

However, the important new fact of managerial behaviour today is the ability of this very management to be conscious of this dilemma. If the metaphor of the story of the firm as a drama is relevant, then it would be unrealistic, if not childish, to ignore the insight that many a drama has already been staged as a tragedy, and probably shall stay that way for yet awhile.

Let me finish this section by quoting G. Burrell. In his recent book, "Pandemonium – Towards a Retro-Organization Theory" he plays with this thought of the corporate room as the stage of the human comedy and tragedy:

"the lived-in world of past, present and future organizations is indeed full of lust, despair, death and mayhem. Yet we continue to deny this. In much of management theory and the analysis of organizations there is a turning away from dealing with such issues. The managerial props which are often used in conventional denials of this de Sadean picture are very "handy", but they sacrifice any understanding of what lies and lives beneath the rim. As Kundera has argued, there is an aesthetic ideal which is well established in the Western world where shit is denied and everyone acts as though it did not exist. This aesthetic ideal is called kitsch ... kitsch excludes everything from its purview which is unacceptable in human existence. In this sense at least then, organizations studies tends to be kitsch because it ignores or, worse still, consciously hides that which is thought to be unacceptable in polite company. There is little mention of sex, yet organizations are redolent with it; little mention of violence, yet organizations are stinking with it; little mention of pain, yet organizations rely upon it; little mention of will to power, yet organizations would not exist without it." (Burrell: 1997, p.51-53)

6.5. "Technology of Knowledge": Knowledge from the Point of View of Management Philosophy

A short and provocative chapter on this topic is relevant as a demonstration of how Management Philosophy could proceed.

Let me begin the examination of this issue with a claim: there only exists a very problematic concept of a so-called "technology of knowledge" that is acceptable in any serious sense to Management Philosophy.

Such a claim seems rather strong, considering the flourishing fields of science recently used to qualify business economics: sociology of technology, cognitive science, and the theory of science. They can all be seen as modulations on the theme of "the technology of knowledge".

The Greeks, of course, could teach us that the two concepts, "technology" and "knowledge", are opposites. They are not mutually exclusive in relation to each other, but technology, the **logos** of **techné**, cannot in any way comprise "knowledge", i.e., **epistémé**. **Techné** might be a step towards **epistémé**, but only as an aspect of **hexis** ("habitus", "moral character") of the climbing towards virtue, because they both belong to the so-called "dianoetical virtues".[58] But **techné** belongs at the lower level. It could never form a genetive relation with so noble a subject as **epistémé**. Hence, there could be a knowledge of technology, but never a technology of knowledge. Knowledge does not in its centre of significance share any meaning with the **logos** of **techné**.

Aristotle's argument would perhaps run like this: **techné** has another **logos** than **epistémé**. **Epistémé** is in its very essence **normative**, because it is a kind of knowledge that springs from the right **hexis**. You must have developed into a certain kind of person in order to expose it.

Techné refers at its utmost to the ability to practice something that presents one with a limit, because in the most elegant time- and energy-saving machines, or in the most beautiful works of art, it invites us to join the experience of the world's "inside" nature or to enjoy the harmony of form. Hence it demonstrates the immanence of transcendence, but it does not force us to confront this immanence, because it compels us to question neither the logic of functioning nor of form.

Epistémé, on the other hand, demands that we pose this question. We must ask for the "function of function", as well as for the forms of forms, and we must be able to face the fact that there may be no answer at the level of verbalized thought.[59]

But we are, of course, obliged to give arguments here that are different from

---

58. The **dianoetical** virtues that Aristotle mentions in the Nicomachean Ethics are: **techné**, **epistémé**, **phronésis** (practical wisdom), **nous** (spirituality) and **sophia** (ultimate wisdom). See Part III of this book.

59. In Plato and Aristotle the word "dianoetical" always means that the epistemological and ontological content of a thought must have a normative implication too: only the ethically developed person is able think it for real.

those that rest upon the authority of Greek Philosophy. Let us then try to pursue another claim:

Knowledge can, due to its essence, never be a commodity. Hence, it can never be integrated in a relation between people built on exchange.[60]

The consequences of this could be far-reaching, because it could mean that a field like "knowledge management" might change its face completely. If it is wrong to speak about "technology of knowledge", then it also might be wrong to speak about "knowledge management". Perhaps this discipline is a phantom, because knowledge is of a character that cannot be managed at all; any manageable knowledge is a secondary knowledge. Knowledge invested in machines is only to a certain degree a knowledge that belongs to us.[61]

Or let us look at it from the opposite perspective. If knowledge management should be a genuine field of its own, then knowledge should be accessible to the canonical, **direct** strategies of management, which presuppose:

A. the generally discursive character of knowledge.
B. the possibility of eliminating knowledge as a tacit phenomenon by expropriating it through procedures, rules and manuals.

The full consequences of the two first issues are

a. that knowledge, in its intensional and extensional totality, is transferable to a computer-system (Turing's Principle of the universal machine).
b. that knowledge is not situated, and not incorporated, i.e., not tied to persons, experiences, norms or values. This means that knowledge should be able to be separated from its historical, social and cultural context. And it means that knowledge can be conceived of as an anonymous technique, and the conditional framework of its application can be seen as technical in itself. Hence, knowledge is not conceived of as bound to a person who knows.

C. that knowledge exists outside the settings of communication between human beings.
D. the "naturalness" of treating knowledge as a commodity.

The modern theory of leadership, and even of management, and certainly recent organizations theory, shall only partly subscribe to this picture. They shall focus on tacit knowledge, on technology as a function of organizational structures, i.e., espe-

---

60. Williamson articulates already in 1979 the opposite view: knowledge can be thought of as a commodity by distinguishing between investment specific to equipment and to knowledge. See: (Williamson: 1979, p. 233-61).
61. The field of "knowledge management" is examined in (Wilson: 1996; Grant: 1996), and in the contributions in (Alverez: 1997).

cially of situated learning, on development of human resources, and on the crucial factor which the individual and her inventive/creative cooperation constitutes. Postmodernism invades business economics (Cooper, Burrell: 1988; Burrell: 1997; Berg: 1989; March: 1988; Morgan: 1988).

This insight is underlined by the intrinsic and complex relation between technology as a **process**, and information technology. The computer makes it impossible to look at technology as "know-how". Instead technology must be seen as a hitherto rather unknown field of "knowing-how", rather than as a receipt, as a "knowing-that" – to recall of the old Wittgensteinian distinction between forms of knowledge in the phrasing of Gilbert Ryle.

Hence, business economics that has a sense of normativity is to a rising degree aware of five aspects of the phenomenon of knowledge and its functioning inside the firm today:

a. it is a process.
b. it is tacit.
c. it is bound to a "possum", an "I can", to Somebody's "knowing-how".
d. it is contextually delimited and hence also constituted and nurtured contextually.
e. it is closely related to the right utilizing of information technlogy, ie., using the computer to support human invention and innovation, not to replace it.

Such considerations are of course able to concentrate attention on the development of the most fertile and fruitful managerial and organizational strategies, under the auspices of which technology as a potential and hence as an intrinsic energy of the firm can be furthered and realized. The crux of the matter is the strategies through which to manage knowledge workers – "strategies" that should come close to abolishing the very concept of strategy itself.[62] Perhaps the right motivation could be

---

62. Mahen Tampoe mentions four factors of motivation best fit for knowledge workers, (Tampoe: 1996, p.184):
   "1. **Personal growth** – the opportunity for individuals to realize their potential, supporting the hypothesis that knowledge workers were seeking intellectual, personal and career growth.
   2. **Operational autonomy** – a work environment in which knowledge workers can achieve the tasks assigned to them within the constraints of strategic direction and self-measurement indices.
   3. **Task achievement** – the achievement of producing work to a standard and quality of which the individual can be proud. There is a need for the task undertaken to be relevant to the organization.
   4. **Money** – earning an income which is a just reward for the contribution made and which enables employees to share in the wealth created by them, through incentive schemes geared to their company's success but related to their personal performance."

best achieved through the construction of "Socratic dialogues" (See Part II). Through these differences of values, interests, and intentions, could be made explicit, condensing the group, concentrating on definite operational tasks, but without the regulating goal of final consent. Hence, the forces of conflict could still be utilized.

These strategies could be the creation of multi-disciplinary, autonomous groups, or ad hoc groups on factory level. They could be the complicated strategies for supporting the originating of problem-dedicated networks between equal firms, or between subcontractors and entrepreneurs. They could be about the integration of public research and private enterprise, or about the optimum utilization of the firm's research units, and its overall policy on consumer and financial markets. However, it all comes to one thing: to be able to create the problem to the solution of which the human resources of the firm could concentrate. The inherent views of business might be transgressed, and diagnoses made, which perhaps are hardly possible to accomplish analytically at all. The challenge is to make a question that changes existing answers.

But what often does not seem to be considered too well is the repressed fact that the most important factor in developing knowledge is the **normative** one.

The scientific culture, and much of the philosophy following in its wake (yielding to its claim to know reality) generally define knowledge as something that is founded by an "is", and never by an "**ought to**".

This culture has created an imperative that tells us that knowledge consists of techniques to describe and prognosticate an already existing reality. But the core of knowledge consists in "co-creating" reality, i.e., making possible worlds real.

It would be untrue to claim that management theory and organizational theory have not been aware of this fact. The metaphor of the theatre recognizes the importance of the "unreal", of vision, in relation to the form.

The Jesuits already knew and utilized the knowledge of the relation between vision and mission. They used a component of actor-education with their would-be missionaires.

What combines vision and mission, i.e., what makes them into a mutual devotion, is fantasy. And fantasy is always normative.

"Normativity" here means that any new technological solution presupposes a problem posed in such a way as to be able to be directly related to a concept of humanity that is determined by the Stoic concept of "the great logos": that only the uncompromising love to our fellow men (the dead, the living and the ones to come) is able to realize our nature.

This, of course, would exclude war technologies, technologies that continue pollution, that expropriate common resources, etc. Hence, it points to the fact that "normativity" demands interpretation, because the concept of "the great logos" demands it. An interpretation even more radical than is implied in the concept of "sustainability".

It is the task of Management Philosophy to anticipate the negative forces and consequences of knowledge, and hence of technology. To decipher the dark side of knowledge that is the negation of normativity as a whole, or even an aspect of it.

So it is the task of Management Philosophy to inspire the creation of an organizational setting where normativity in all its aspects, the dark values and the negligences are forced to the surface.

Here we really find the raison d'être of the talk about managerial virtues that are more than mere social or communicative skills.

From this point of view we are able to state that real knowledge is always personal knowledge, because it is normative knowledge.

This means that the task of the manager is to re-unite and re-integrate the "managed person" with the wanted knowledge. The manager must in a way "reconcile" the employee with knowledge. And this means creating a scope of critical possibilities for the employees; but a critical scope, a space, the horizon of which is normative, rather than tactical or strategic.

To reconcile, to make re-appropriation and re-enchanting of knowledge possible, with the aim of overcoming the barriers of using technology in another way – barriers of a organizational and managerial kind – would fit the managerial virtue of **maieutics**.

"Maieutics" means the art of the midwife. It is the famous way in which Socrates named his own communicative project. A project with the core idea that everybody has the right knowledge, if he has the possibilities to find it in himself.

But this kind of knowledge can neither be technical nor scientific knowledge, nor a kind of specialized skill, of course, even not a generalist one. It has to be another kind of knowledge, or perhaps a more fundamental knowledge, deeper, but also more comprehensive than technological and scientific knowledge. It cannot be mere common sense, either; and it cannot be simple social skills. It has to be something else.

It is **epistēmē**, as Aristotle spoke about in his Nicomachean Ethics. And what else can that be, but the ability always to have knowledge about knowledge. Knowledge about knowledge can only, as far as it should not rest on expertise, be **normative**.

So here we have another managerial virtue, **maieutics**:

The ability to create a context in which people relate critically to knowledge.

It is the knowledge that is fundamentally impossible to address as "knowledge technology" and "knowledge management", or even as "intellectual capital". There are only people **with** knowledge, and with a living mind, a mind and a knowledge that can be set free. This, of course, is also an eminent "social" quality in the manager.

6.6. To Re-create Cooperation: Subcontracting as a Necessity

Subcontracting and networking are able to enrich the concept of cooperation today, but its dynamics consists of economies of scales. If a firm's quote of investment is high, it is interested in tying the consumers. When they are firms themselves, or part of the state, this aim is realized most effectively through contractual relations, so as to keep marginal costs low. A network might be the solution here.[63]

The concept was, among others, introduced to modern management theory by J.P. Kotter in 1982 in the book "The General Managers" (Kotter: 1982). A "network" is a structure between the firm and its stakeholders, formalized by contract to a more or less degree. The relation can be horizontal or vertical. Its aim is to reduce uncertainty created by dynamical surroundings, contingency, and increased complexity. Controlling subsuppliers is an important subject here. Japanese management inspired it through the principles of "just-in-time", but it served the purpose of reducing the inner pressures of the firm. It also aimed to allocate them outwards by buying products instead of producing them. Postmodern writers on business economics, like the Danish scientist Martin Fuglsang, moves the centre of gravity in the analyses of networks away from the concept of deliberate planning into the area of the narrative, the fable and the myth: networks are not constructed, they arise through processes that never end as result of "network-ing" (Fuglsang: 1998). Micklethwait and Wooldridge quote that more than 20.000 new alliances were entered into during 1987 and 1992 in the USA. These alliances comprise research communities, giving firms possibilities to relate to competencies, based on research which they would never be able to create themselves. And they contain at a global level cooperation between firms[64] that were traditionally competitors about the improving of the product, subject to their competition. For example, the cooperation in the car industry between Mazda and Ford, Daimler-Benz and Chrysler, as well as the "pill-pact" between Rhône and Hoechst. Today such collaboration might often be formalized through mergers or the like.

Such complicated trends in subcontracting will perhaps still be called "networking" even if they play with the breaking of anti-trust laws. Information technology, no doubt, makes these close alliances possible, by letting the merging of two different organizations be easier. Yet, this does not mean that unification of computer-based knowledge does not create problems of its own.

Subcontracting is a very old phenomenon of capitalism; we have already treated this issue. Generally it has been used as an instrument of production to introduce new products onto not-yet-established or very small markets.

To claim that the essence of subcontract is understood by transforming it into a

---

63. The concept of "network", in relation to processes of self-organizing through networks, is defined in (Nohria, Eccles: 1992).
64. "The first distinguishing trait of knowledge links is that learning and creating knowledge is a central objective of the alliance. Knowledge links can help one company learn specialized capabilities from another, they can help a company combine its special capabilities with those of another organization to create new embedded knowledge; and they can enable one company to help another organization build up its skills and capabilities in ways that will benefit both companies later on." (Badaracco: 1996, p.134).

general principle of "transaction", and deducing it from there, is not an acceptable procedure. Subcontract is a metaphor of a wide concept of cooperation. As a concept it is a way to introduce the importance of social interrelations, through techniques and technology, into the world of business economics. Williamson's perspective is wrong. Subcontracting cannot be viewed as a species of the genus "transaction", and, hence, a theory of the relation between capital and labour and capital and capital as one of "exchange". Rather, subconstracting is a function of managerial problems. On the one hand, it is a function of the problem of creating control and discipline. On the other hand, it is a function of meeting opportunities and demands on very uncertain, fluctuating and chaotic markets.

The first item has to do with the organizational problems posed by knowledge and technology, and hence, with situated and incorporated knowledge, levels of qualifications and skills, in relation to techniques, not mastered by the entrepreneur, and perhaps even just new and untried. The other problem has to do with buffer mechanisms that are able to mitigate the beats of unruly markets.

Re-creating the workteam as a fundamental unit of management and organization has to do with the need to develop a competence characterized by the disturbing fact that it is purely and simply not mastered by the firm. The case of interest here appears when the competence is not mastered by any firm yet.

Here of course you have to ask: how does management come to know about such a competence? The answers differ by contexts:

a. if it is a technical one, it might be deduced from some sort of intrinsic, technical "logic". E.g., we have a "sense of" the arrival of a computer interface based on the spoken word, not on text. Or it might have been developed through rather severely organized search-processes using probabilistics which simulates the contextual frameworks of earlier, significant inventions, and so on. Thus, we might have more than just a hunch about the nearfuture arrival of bio-chips.

   Such "purely technical" competencies, however, are always nurtured by some typical social setting, and most often with a distinct organizational profile: The research union of a larger firm is a rather uncomplicated example of subcontracting within the same corporate space with the explicit aim at creating new technical competence. The cooperation between, e.g., medical research at University Hospitals and firms within the electrophysical industriy might be a case of subcontracting too, however far more complicated in relation to the forms of control, not to speak of the legal setting.

   However, subcontracting is the perfect solution to the development of competencies that are more than suspected examples of what I choose to call "**imminent competences**". The imminence comes from the fact that the firm which succeeds in getting to them first, may have enormous competive advantages.

   The development of these kinds of competencies has to be balanced against the risk of over-invention and even "hyper-innovation". This phenomenon is creating vast overcapacities in many industries with a high level of competition on the open market, for example in the car-industries.[65] Perhaps the recent fusion of Daimler-Benz and Chrysler might find one aspect of its explanation in the attempt to alleviate this predicament?

b. if it is a communicative one, the competence might be the vague conceptual answer to a demand, be it from low sales or from the feeling of lost opportunities. But it may also reflect – and this is by far the most prototypical situation – the general demands born by the complex, and reciprocal, relation between production technology and consumer demands. Culture is also an important parameter in shaping these demands. "Culture" here means education, i.e., the general level of consciousness in relation to the both social and subjective conditions and consequences of the satisfaction of needs which might involve a general suspicion towards the ontology of needs: is the commodity x really necessary? Would it not be better to abolish product y and hence to evade consequence z involved in its production? ... One communicates about products because one must.

This is not just a demand from the state, requesting information about brands and often a certain level of information in relation to the ingredients of a product. It is also due to a peculiar fact which I shall try to diagnose.

To understand it, we might at first touch upon the distinction between the prototype and the unique.

At the first level this distinction is almost too evident:

Every car, with one exception unimportant to our perspective (Rolls-Royce) is a prototype. One vintage model of a certain brand has to be exactly like the other. It has to be unique in relation to almost exactly the same type, model and vintage of another brand.

Within the same brand a product manifests the prototypical. Every exemplar must look and be exactly like some single exemplar made as the prototype, the "arch-model". But probably this prototype does not exist as such. Here it shall just be the very first produced exemplar, or the last test-exemplar in a line. As a unique phenomenon, it only exists on the desk of the designers, or as a collector's item.

Between brands every exemplar should refer to a uniqueness; not a uniqueness inherent in it as an exemplar, but only attributable to it as a copy of the original model.

What we at first could concentrate on here is the fact that when a product is very expensive and looks rather close to its range of substitutible products, it becomes clear that its uniqeness has to be constructed through speech. Watching, listening, touching, or even smelling, are not enough here.

---

65. Volkswagen's attempts at reducing pressures from overcapacities by selling cheap models on extremely competive markets and buying the traditional élitist productions, Rolls-Royce, Bentley, Bugatti, and Lamborghini as buffers, might prove to be a bad strategy too.

Speech has to warrant that the copy not just "is" what it looks like, but looks what it is like.

Speech has to refer the copy to the "arch-model".

Even though this is most evident in expensive consumer products, it also holds true for bikes or even biodynamical bread.

Subcontract is an obvious managerial and organizational tool here, to develop the competencies related to that kind of information which has to be far more than information. It is the constructing of the uniqueness of the product, which means the "finding" of the criteria needed to establish this uniqueness, where it might seem less obvious.

This is due to additional reasons:

1. One person is unable to anticipate all the necessary arguments to meet the objections, because objections are tied to social levels, social groups, social and individual histories.
2. It is possible perhaps, but inexpedient, to present one or two persons with a task that cannot be sufficiently described from the beginning.

Advertising companies often fulfill the task of communicating that a given prototype is better than another, but they seldom argue how and why this is so.

The problem might be that the consumer at the beginning will join the game of the significance of small differences, but at the end demand that outside looks be transferred to inside quality. Of course, a car company has to rely on salesmen and mechanics here, but there seems to be an aura around every brand that is far more than could ever be established through the typing of presentations, instructions and even manuals.

The problem that we are facing is the predicament of the new consumer: that she expects products to convey some meaning.

This does not imply the trivial observation that consumer goods, primarily the lasting ones, might substitute for or even "solve" existential problems. I think this point is too superficial. But it means that a product is "read" in a way as to solve some problem. So, to experience the product is to search for the problem.

But the problem might more than often be interpreted outside of a frame of simple "use" or "function;" it might be interpreted as bearing upon a form of life. But this implies more than the trivial concept of "life style", or even "segments". It leads towards the border of the "lifestyle".

Psychology, anthropology, and ethnology are able to tell us a lot of the significance of products in relation to forms of life. The symbolic value of products has been utterly exploited by business. But here I am thinking of something else. Because every product cannot help but pose the question: **what is a thing?**

A thing is everything and nothing. So closely related to the senses of sight and touch, it covers almost any phenomenon not confined to the mind. A diskette, a lighter, the distance between the kitchen and the living room, an advertising spot on TV, an evening sky, my hand, the glance and the eye, summer and winter, a hammer and a nail, the minutes she was late, and the travel to Venice last summer. A thing? Might it be something that protects us against nothing? The world with no things in it is terrifying. The world in which every thing is close at hand is boring. Might the domain of things be the space between boredom and terror?

What is the middle between boredom and terror, if they could be conceived of as points demarcating a line? Could it be passion?

Then a thing is that which in this moment is standing in the spotlight of passion.

But what, then, is passion?

Could it be the intentionality of desire?

The thing which we see, touch, hear, smell, taste, because we want it?

Then products are unimportant; what matters is the attitude.

But we cannot be satisfied with that. We have to mingle with attitudes and perceive them as parts of a game: the pride of destructing and constructing attitudes and hence, things. Business science knows this all too well. To influence, to shape, to create, to construct attitudes, ways of life, lifestyles, to imitate the creator, is it not too smart? It has aleady for some time been a game to believe in this game – the ironical meta-level of advertising, testifies to that. But a serious alternative is far from easy.

We have to search for the thing, in earnest, because we cannot exist without it.

Attitudes must be destroyed, intentional fixations dissolved, spotlights broken, optics split, clear-sightedness blurred.

We must be responsible to a "transcendental realism" that summons the thing. This stands as the contrary to invocation, because the thing itself is the author of the magic.

But then "subcontracting" seems to alter its meaning. It breaks through the world of business economics into the original environment of any "technical" activity: the lived-in-world (das Lebenswelt). Then subcontracting comes to conjure up the primary band between human beings, and between us and the whole creation (blurring any rigid distinction between the organic and inorganic dimension) constituting the basis of reality, the "concordia", the mutual devotion to something that could never be worshipped through any other name but "The Real".

c. if the competence consists in a combination of technological and communicative skills (and I guess this is the only way to describe much consultanty services) then subcontract is also evident as a managerial and organizational solution. We should actually conceive of the more and more influential phenomenon of networking as a special way to organize subcontracts, where this combination of technological and communicative skills are involved. But consultancy is difficult to grasp as a by-product. If the product, e.g., a new computer system, actually is faulty, how far should the consultant go in solidarity to his firm?

This depends, of course, on the level of malfunction.

But the consultant is always tempted to ally himself with the customer, in his own interest, or in the name of justice.

We have a complicated relation here, on which to test the concept of leadership the consultant as a leader of himself and of the customer, and the manager of the consultant as a leader of him and of his relation to the customer.

We here touch on the delicate problems of the leadership virtues of the co-directed – one of the most important problems of Management-Philosphy. But answers might not be that difficult, because while managerial functions are not easily inherited downwards through the organization, it must definitely be possible to delegate managerial virtues all the way down to the shopfloor, and hence, to let leadership constitute the potential "lifestyle" of any employee.

As was already touched upon, leadership is an attitude, a mental state, far more than a formal position – but of course we are treating it in the context of this book as a formal position.

The consultant creates himself as a leader in the minute when he chooses to take on the customer's interests, and not that of his firm – as far as the product has a rather serious fault. This opposition presupposes that the manager of the consultant does not act as a leader. Hoever, it is important that the reactions of the consultant cannot be interpreted as a betrayal of expected solidarity towards the firm.[66] But we are balancing on a knife's edge here.

After all, the removing of the centre of cooperation towards the customer shall have its price. A company such as IBM, whose slogan is "the customer is always right," or "there exists no unreasonable customers," cannot sue too many of their own consultants. So, to a certain degree functionalism supports self-leadership. But it too has its limits. And here, on the border, the managed shall teach the manager the virtues of leadership. By this all the virtues of management and hence, of leadership, are not implied, but only the fundamental trait of the will to radical normativity. The important difference here would be that the employee, placed at a position low in the hierarchy, would justify his action through the gesture of his duty as a human being, while the manager more probably would refer to his position as a manager, or to his loyalty towards the firm – and that might more than often prevent him from approaching the threshold of leadership.

Which virtue should fit the manager's ability to be able to create and withhold subcontracting under these three different conditions? And here I am speaking of a form of subcontracting where the changes in knowledge, technology, interrelations,

---

66. People who choose to benefit the public with knowledge of the firm's production process, following their consciousness, have in the time after the last war often been accused, and convicted, of "industrial espionage". The sentences have at times been utterly severe: ten or more years in prison.

communication, and marketing, demand an extremely high degree of autonomy. Is this virtue, or are those virtues mere social skills, general virtues responding to democratic ideals? Or are they something else?

If we look at the managerial roles which business science has focused on recently, it would be the "coach" or the "mentor".

The concept of "coach" is still working in the world of sport, amateur as well as professional. In it is implicated the conceptual framework of "game", of "teamwork," of "extreme competition" and of "winning". The connotations are to the one who can convey the feeling of "team spirit", of "mutual responsibility", of "the will to self-sacrifice", of "almost limitless generosity". Those are social virtues of high distinction. But the goal, or better, the ontology of losing and winning, is never questioned.

A coach is nearly always a person who has practised the game which he is now managing at a level of excellence. Most often he would belong to another generation than the people whom he manages. But in this, one might find both an advantage and a hindrance, in relation to his way of functioning. The advantage is pure and simple experience. The hindrance lies in the fast changing of games, in the mixing of games, and in the extinguishing of games – the latter relates to games which you still think exist, but that do not. Perhaps the coach is a little bit short-minded, or even obdurate? But one thing is almost certain: if the coach is wise, then he is only wise to a certain degree. Or if we must call him "wise", it is only in relation to **technē**, not in relation to **epistēmē**. Even if he might choose to nurse you, he is "wise" inside a very restricted domain.

In the metaphor of the coach lives a mixture of the senior sergeant and the school master. He thinks it proper to interfere (he would never question his own right here) and he is watching and permanently evaluating. It is important that the coach is forced to evaluate, and that he himself, as an evaluator, is constantly evaluated.

The evaluated evaluator is an image that describes everybody in business, from the CEO to the hourly paid employee. But its genuine field of application would probably be the range from "assistant manager", "mid-level manager", "group manager" and downwards to the "supervisor" of the factory floor.

But I think that the picture of the manager which we need here has this one distinctive feature: as a leader, the manager is **not** an evaluated evaluator.

The manager must not only relate to The Third, to the overt criteria of culture, to the hidden criteria of complex games, to the unscrutinizable goals and values of communication – in short to money, power and passion. The manager must relate to The Fourth, i.e. he must be a leader.

This means that he must be able to question any standard of evaluation, including that of money, of profit, of strong positions, of strong business connections, even of excellence, the power in the name, the beauty in buildings, in the plant and in the artifacts. But he must be able to question this very questioning too, being aware of its puritanical snares.

So this type of manager must possess some special fan of virtues.

And we could certainly call him **wise**. We have already been introduced to the elaborate analysis of the concept of **phronēsis** in the Nicomachean Ethics by Aristotle. We shall return to that in Part III.

Another metaphor for the manager that has been launched recently is the "mentor".

"Mentor" was the name of the teacher of Telemacheus, the son of Odysseus. In this concept we find the tenor of age, of wisdom, we find the advisor and the teacher. But there is an air of distance to the goals and passions of life in this word. "I Tiresias, old man with wrinkled dugs Perceived the scene and foretold the rest –" as T.S. Eliot sings in "The Waste Land". But the manager is tied to the burning life. He must be involved, not retired. He must be engaged, and to such a degree that he is still able to get hurt.

But which fan of virtues and which core-virtue can satisfy these three fields of functioning which the manager must relate to as the subject of subcontract: technology, communication, and consultancy?

In the language of Greek philosophy the game between voices trying to climb to the truth of some matter, **logos didonai**, the different hands in the game of truth (and **eristikon**, competition among arguments) would correspond to communication. The concept of **euboulia** would respond to a broad concept of "consultancy", approaching the concepts of "therapy" and "moral guidance". What matters are moral and political questions, not those proper to technology.

The Greeks did not conceal the fact that communication was competition. In Plato and Aristotle one often finds the concept of "discussion" related to the word "eris", "fight", "competition". Honour is at stake. This is of course important to the understanding of the dialogue. And it sets the other metaphor of discussion into contrast, that of the game.

I think that by the first virtue, the one related to **technē**, the essence must be found outside the context of this very **technē**, in the world of fantasy. This virtue was called **prolēpsis** by Epicurus, and is still familiar today, in its Latin translation

---

67. The fan is a special kind of metaphor. Inside the fans of the Baroque and the Rococco ages pictures were painted or texts written that emerged in different but wonderful ways when the fan was opened in front of the face. This is a metaphor of reflectivity. Also, the outside of the fan differed from the inside – like the structure of human experience. But at the same time the fan is a prolongation of the arm, it is an instrument of gestures, of the possible grace in hiding and uncovering, of more than a functional tool for cooling the passions that emerge on the outside of the face, on the skin. So in a way, a fan is an interchangeable tattooing, substituting the skin and usually being just as transparent and light in its bottom colour as this arch-human clothing. But most of all, perhaps, is it a projectable eyelid and hence a widening of sight?

to "anticipatio". It is the ability to visualize future scenarios, without being able to explain exactly how.

The second virtue would be the ability to communicate critically, **logos didonai**, because here the manager is searching for something pushed away by his very taking hold of it. This is a genuine cooperative quality. To hunt alone is to hunt in vain. This is actually a theatre, but no play exists. Instead everybody improvises. Voices mingle, and the performers hand something to each other, and as they are singing, they follow the thing. Perhaps this object was all the singing was meant to be about, or it might only have been a prop, the role of which somebody (a non-existent author?) must have known after all. But this thing could of course be a football that just happened to look like an atom bomb, or an atom bomb that looked like a football, and hence, rather dangerous to desire – to remind of John Delilo. So the appropriate virtue here ought to be patience. But not just any kind of patience. A firm and resolute patience is demanded here. In the Greek this is called **hypomonē**.

The third virtue would be that of **euboulia**, the ability to give and receive advice. And, most importantly, the faculty to follow the obligations of duty towards society, whatever the costs. There is not a grain of opportunism, not even of pragmatism, in the virtue of **euboulia**. The genuine case of this virtue would be the bold leader leading his consultant to betray him (the leader) and the firm out of duty to "the great logos". In the alternative case, where the consultant is isolated unjustly as the traitor to the firm, the guts demanded on the leader's behalf would answer to the virtue of **maieutics**: the voice from the other person that challenges you to be the one who you "are", assisting with the birth of your "real you". Now the voice has to be one's own, the "inner voice", but still it is **maieutics**, even if the midwife has got no face.

However, it is important that the co-directed is able to be the example through which his manager can learn what it means to be a leader.

We shall return more systematically to these virtues in Part III.

Part II

Dialogue or Metalogue

CHAPTER 7

The Machine of Dialogue versus the Organic, Inner Monologue

Let me begin this investigation of the phenomenon of the dialogue with two items:

The first one is to recall what is going on in the earlier Yugoslavia now, while I am writing these words (April to June 1999): NATO has finally succeeded in forcing the Serbs into dialogue. We were doing almost everything possible in order to weaken the Serbs, to a degree that leaves no other alternative than to find a solution through speech. Hence, it seems as if only power, the play between omnipotence and impotence, is able to make dialogue possible. Dialogue is the child of power; the offspring of force.

The other one consists in two quotations from the work of the German philosopher, Arthur Schopenhauer, from "Parerga und Paralipomena" (Supplements and Writings left behind), Chapter I. "Über Philosophie und ihre Methode" (Of Philosophy and its Method).[1] The first quotation is from the Paragraph 6, which deals with the phenomenon of dialogue, where Schopenhauer confronts the "machine of dialogue" with the "living organism of inner monologue or contemplation". The next Paragraph deals with the relation of thinking through personal inner monologue versus thinking through dialogue as a means to insight into life.

Paragraph 6

"The **dialogue** with another person about our own serious meditation and inner perception of things, relates to the latter (meditation and perception. OFK) like a machine to a living organism. Because it is only in the latter that, everything emerges as one single piece, or as if played in the same tune; this is why it is able to achieve total clarity, conciseness, and a true coherence, yes, even unity. The machine, on the other hand, results from the combination of heterogeneous pieces of very different origin, and the enforcement of a certain unity of movement which often might get unexpectedly stuck. After all, you are only able to understand yourself completely. Other people can only be half grasped: you are

---

1. I translate from the Edition of "Arthur Schopenhauer's sämtliche Werke" (The Collected Works of Arthur Schopenhauer) by Paul Deussen, from 1913, R. Piper & Co., Verlag, München. Vol. II. P.11-12.

at most able to establish a common conceptual framework, never a recognition of the intuitive perception, that serves as the foundations of these concepts. Hence, profound philosophical truth is hardly ever conveyed through common thinking, through dialogue. But this phenomenon could be of great use as an exercise, as a tracking down of problems, as a ventilation of problems, and afterwards as a means to control and critique of the established solution ..."

To Schopenhauer the first problem of dialogue is the fact that the linguistic media refers to different experiences (different bodies, different events), even if the very same word is agreed upon. There is no overt criterion of the fact that we ultimately are speaking about the same thing. In other words, strong consent and agreement might cover a tremendous, communicative or hermeneutic, illusion. Dialogue, hence, can only be a means to sense and pose problems, never to solve them.

Paragraph 7

"Neither our knowledge, nor our insights, shall ever be much increased by comparing and discussing what others have said:
    Because this is always just as if water was poured from one cask into another. Only through our very own contemplation of the things in themselves is it possible to enrich insight and knowledge: because this alone is the permanently ready and always present and living spring ..."

To Schopenhauer the other problem of dialogue consists in the fact that knowledge springs from personal experience, from the hard work of contemplation, not from the "idle game" of talk. And dialogue is to him a game, because the use of language is a game, and from a game no real insight can originate. Dialogue might be a serious game, but it is nothing but a game after all, and this counts even for the "written dialogue" of Plato too: his legacy is the skepticism of the "Second and Third Academy"; even poetic dialogue is still a game, however great, with truth.

Let us examine these items and these claims in the following chapters:

"The pill-pact between Rhône-Chef Fourtou and Hoechst-Topmanager Dormann might break." This is a headline in the German Newspaper, "Die Zeit", from February 1999.
    To make a pact, a treaty, is the work of dialogue.
    The long talks behind closed doors between Daimler-Benz and Chrysler, the prolonged talks between Rhône and Hoechst, attest to this. Many more of these kinds of negotiations will emerge, because the big companies know that they shall not gain anything from waging war against each other. They have common en-

emies, the consumers and the state, and they only try to win the favour of one stakeholder: the future.

This says, among other things, something about the quintessence of dialogue.

The dialogue belongs to the initiated ones. This might be its very first trait. The dialogues of Plato attest to that. Here the philosophers, the wealthy, handsome, and perhaps even well educated young men, and some carefully selected Sophist, are enacting. It is a closed circle. People talk to each other, people sharing the same status, the same privileges, the same language, the same frame of reference, and the same sanctuaries. Hands on the table, palms open, put into the middle, not behind the backs – most of the time.

The facts that opened these closed circles of the initiated were mostly violent transformations of social structures, involuntary delegation of power, and much later, the projects of general education, democratic rights, and the press. Benevolence in itself never opened it, but social pressure; **ananke**, alas, almost never **erōs**.

"Unions in dialogue with big business." "USA in dialogue with Saddam Hussein." "Small entrepreneurs are now in dialogue with Silicon Valley." "Hospitals in dialogues with patients."

The opening of the dialogical circle did not liberate the dialogue as a phenomenon. The so-called "open dialogue" was always kept close to the body of power, and as time went on it became the best instrument power ever had of maintaining itself.

No doubt, dialogues might set free, and they might domesticate. Dialogues might reconcile with the human condition, and they might reinforce ressentiment and even anger. Dialogues might confirm your impotence, and reassure you of your omnipotence. Dialogues might teach you so much, but also make you more stupid. Dialogues might get you closer to action, and remove you from it. Dialogues might enhance your level of reflectivity, support and rise the "meta-". Dialogues might enlighten, and through this effect place the unbearable within the circle of acceptance, and dialogues might unite a small community of people around the collective feeling of a destination beyond all means. Dialogues might compensate for pathos, or dry life up. Dialogues might involve the body, through gestures, or yield a refuge to it, as the yet unopened gift, or the still unrealized violence, and dialogues might almost abolish its existence. Dialogues might be extremely boring, and be the thing you look forward to all week. Dialogues might be hard, straining every nerve, totally exhausting, and they might be amusing and relaxed. Dialogues might be without sound, inside a mind, but roaring like ocean breakers or airplanes diving in this secret room where the soul is divided against itself.

Perhaps there are so many ways to talk together, so many communities or groups, so many circumstances and contextual settings, so many frames of references, so many horizons, and so many places, so many lines through time, that one cannot speak about **the** dialogue?

There is the priest talking to the dying. The mother scolding her child. The potential lover trying to convince the shy beauty. The salesman at the door praising his bad encyclopedia. The judge seeking the accused person's eyes. The dentist with the hearing-aid, and the offender evading his victim's eyes. There are the three teachers talking low-voiced about your child. There is this carefully prepared letter that you never opened. There is the gossip about you, but meant for you to hear. There is the ignored kindness of an unexpected voice. There are the resounding commands. There are the whisper, the decisions, the most important ones, that you cannot hear. There is the long time no seen. There is the beloved book in which you hear your own voice. There are the last and the superficial good-by. There is the silence of the telephone. There is the e-mail fired at all too many. There are the sacraments, the reception of the last rites. Words and gestures combine, bodies and voices co-merge, light mixes with darkness, artifacts mix with flesh, loudness with silence, life with death.

I have to ask: Is the talk about dialogues a dialogue? I doubt it! It is a monologue about dialogue. It is a one-man-talk about the very best of managerial tricks, a tactic that excludes loosing. On the surface it looks like the very serenity and seriousness of the big blue, but it is mask, a gimmick.

Is it a first breathing of a new morning? We have to leave Plato and Greek thinking here – for the most parts, at least – in order to take a stance against the old air of dialogue.

Everybody seems to want to consent, to be one mind, to agree entirely about that which suggests itself as the evident. Disagreement, struggle, dissent, only mean something on the background of consensus. We are almost all "cupboard-communitarianists". But let us go straight to the point: what is a dialogue?

From Plato to Lipps, Wittgenstein, Austin, Searle, Strawson, Apel, Habermas (no one deserves the comparison on his own, and of course I missed several important contributors) there has been this focus on doing something **with** words. Speaking and acting melt together, matching the Greek word "pragma", in order to conquer posterity – which, alas, does not seem identical to re-expropriating a knowledge that already belongs to you.

It would be rather easy to focus on quasi-axiomatic conditions of speaking here, because it has been done by so many, and by so brilliant philosophers: on intentionality, on purpose, on the ability of expression, on reciprocity, on interaction, on cooperation, on coordination, on all the levels of mutual understanding, on strategy, on tacit knowledge, on common values, on implied intentions, on transferred emotion, on hidden discourses, on secret desires, on forces, and on structures and on spirits ... All these are modern and highly elaborated, theories within the domain of rhetoric – even if they claim to be philosophical after all (and that means to be un-rhetoric during Modernism).

And they certainly have their questions, from Austin to Grice, from Apel to Sacks, and I am sure, that they are all relevant. But I only want to ask one question:

"What is the criterion of the fact, that you know, what you yourself are saying?"

If this question is answered negatively, there shall exist no dialogue, but only "blather" among carnal machines.

But the fact is that there is no such criterion. Thus a dialogue is only "blather" among machines, or – conceived of most benevolently – the victory of the talk as a machine, as machine-talking. Hence, a manager, who wants to manage through dialogue, has to accept an identity as either a very bad magician, or a communicative engineer, or just to stop such futile strategies.

I shall show in the following that there is no such criterion to secure that a person knows what he is saying. But I have to calm you: it does not abolish the phenomenon of dialogue in any way, it just removes it, indeed, to its proper place.

Let me begin with this simple, but too often forgotten fact, that dialogues only consist of voices, because voices come from bodies. In this truism so much is said that it is hard to grasp.

7.1. Of Bodies and of Voices

It is often both stated and theoretically claimed that speech is "symptomatical", that gestures can be conceived of as linguistic expressions that refer to the existence of a language of all those phenomena, that is not dependent upon voice; i.e., that the body could be conceived of as an autonomous area of articulation separated from the voice. Now, talking about "body language" has been more and more usual during the last decades, and hence less and less binding from a theoretical point of view. Especially American management and organizational "theory" has indulged in this phenomenon.

But it is often forgotten that so-called "body language" has been the object of a thorough investigation for 2500 years of philosophical thought. In the Greek, Roman and Renaissance discipline of rhetoric, and in the theory of the theatre generating with the famous Poetics of Aristotle, the body has been analyzed as a vehicle of regulating expression and articulation. Even the Jesuits were obliged to act on the stage in their famous schools during the time of the Counter-Reformation, in order to acquire the ability to master their emotional expressions and bodily gestures.

So, replacing the body from the scene of spontaneous expression to the scene of deliberate articulation was the aim of those schools. The core concept here is the Greek word **pathos**. In the rhetorical tradition it meant the emotional condition stamped into the listener's mind by the words and manners of expression through the speaker. But it was only from the Hellenistic period and onward that it came to mean something connected to a conception of morally bad strategies. In the area of classical Greek philosophy it did not refer to a phenomenon opposed to ēthos. Today **pathos,** through Stoicism and its translation into the Roman world, as well as by its rejection and acquisition through the scholastic Christian tradition, has come to mean the process of suffering, the condition of being an object to something that overwhelms, in coming from the outside or inside world. Hence, the concept of "patience": to master "pathos". The one who did not manage, was a sinner against both sacred and profane rationality – or later, in Nietzsche's new quasi-religion, a sinner towards the innocence of force, a bitter bearer of "ressentiment", because he even tried to manage it.

But between the body conceived of as the media of mastering conversation, interrogation, as a strategic instrument, and as a media of aesthetic articulation on the stage, **and** the body as the domain of symptoms, there is an important gap: that of consciousness, of self-reflection.

I think, to state this most precisely, the concept of the dialogue as a mutual, re-ciprocal, highly enlightened place of consensus through discourse, presupposes that speaking can evade being **symptomatic.**

So the first way to destroy the whole framework of the dialogue would be to demonstrate that speaking is symptomatic.

But first a very important point about my particular approach should be men-tioned:

If speaking is symptomatic, it does not have to be symptomatic of anything else, but of **nothing.**

This ought to place my monologue about the character of the dialogue outside psychoanalysis, outside functionalism (including Niklas Luhmann and the hyper-cleverness of systems science), and outside discourse-analysis and post-structuralism, (perhaps with the exception of J. Derrida, and some works of M. Foucault and G. Deleuze).

To a strategic theory of the dialogue from the perspective of Management The-ory, this is devastating: all those clever strategies, all those money paid to the gurus? All those serious purposes? All these appeals to values? All that carefully con-structed responsibility? All those devices to mirror the hands of the actual and potential consenters, the so-called "stakeholders"! All those serious talks on all levels of the organization, and between these levels, and between the functionally defined sections in the enterprise, and even between divisions. And the attendants, and cheer-leaders, and stern servants of a hidden, or perhaps buried, canon of truth within those talks, those conversations at the abyss. Money lost? No, because first and foremost there is the acceptance of the victims of bad management who agree to be fired. The serious, but short speeches spoken from one person who owns twenty million dollars to lay off 10.000 people. At that price dialogical rationality can always be produced provided that a "dialogue" could last half an hour where the victims are allowed to raise their fingers to the executioner and get a formal description of the gallows, but – like in the universe of Kafka – never of their crime.

The phenomenon of the symptom creates very peculiar epistemological problems, because it nearly always seem to presuppose an ontology: it is claimed that a thought or an action can only be caused, and hence explained, by a particular force or instinct regardless of the way it is experienced by the one who is thinking or acting. For a century this "program" has been advocated by psychoanalysis, but the symptom certainly belongs to philosophy, and hence to the manager as a philosopher, not as a follower of psychoanalysis, or as a client of some course on "psychodynamics".[2] The only two subjects of management courses that cannot be expropriated are "to think" and to "learn virtue". So, why should anybody actually take courses in management?

But let us turn to our question, and proceed into the conditions of how you should be able to know what you yourself are saying.

Let me begin with an assertion: we do not **have** a mind, nor do we **have** a body. Rather we **are** minds, and we **are** bodies.

Instead one ought to say that we are **in** a mind and **in** a body, and at the very same time. In the classical Greek tradition there is a very special conception of what it means, after all, to be **in** a mind. Aristotle phrased this condition in the famous and ambiguous concept of **noēsis noēseōs**: the **mind's mind**, the **thinking of thinking**, from "De anima" – his contribution to a field that comes close to today's "psychology".

The existence of the mind, Aristotle says, is bound to the actual process of thinking. The mind knows itself through its thinking of its thinking. But to think, is to think of something, hence, the content of thinking must be of such a kind that the mind is able to recognize itself in the **forms** of this content. The content must present itself in a way inherent in the concept of thinking itself, it must be of the same form as the thought (**nous**) which thinks it. Hence, it seems terribly important what exactly you are thinking of![3]

In the works of Aristotle one can distinguish three ways of conceiving **noēsis noēseōs**[4] (a remark: if you find this exposition too concerned with Greek philosophical terminology then please proceed to the next section!):

---

2. I shall neither relate to the thinking of J. Lacan, when using the concept of "symptomatical reading", nor to L. Althusser, nor to the legacy of structuralism. My frame of reference in this book is strictly phenomenological, and it does neither fetch any important ideas from psychoanalysis, nor from structuralism.
3. The relation of **nous** to **logos**, and the translation of **logos**, **nous** and **eidos** to the Latin concept of **ratio**, through the Roman and Christian philosophers, and hence the origin of "reason", shall not be addressed here. I translate **nous** to **mind**, or to **the process of thinking**, but not – as is most usual in Latin philosophy (Cicero and his legacy) – to "intellectus", due to the fact that after Modernity the connotations of this word are very strong, and mostly misleading.
4. Aristotle (1936/1995): De anima. The Loeb Edition. Transl. by W.S. Hett. Harvard University Press, London. 407a og 429 b. And Aristotle (1936/1996): The Metaphysics. The Loeb Edition. Transl. by H. Tredennick. Harvard University Press, London. XII, viii, 18-ix, 1074b.

a. **nous kat' energeian, nous entelecheia**, in the Scholastic tradition translated to **intellectus agens**. This means thinking as the practising of thought, mind as the **activity** of thinking of something.
b. **nous dynamei, nous pathētikos**, in Latin **intellectus possibilis**, the possibility of thinking. It is "the sleeping thought", as Aristotle says, the thinking, which **has to** be there as a possibility, if thinking as a practical ability should be possible at all.

The connotation of **activity** in thinking is very strong here. "Thinking is doing." But Aristotle would not subscribe to the continuation of the phrase: "Thinking is doing things with words." He just focused on rhetoric in the very last years of his life. But Plato would subscribe to it, indeed, which the dialogue "Cratylus" demonstrates.

But there is a last configuration of the relation of the mind to itself in the works of Aristotle, this is the **nous**.

c. **aition kai poiētikon**, the **"poietical"** thought, "thinking that thinks" by creating the content of thought out of the material of perception. The metaphors Aristotle uses here are the metaphors of **phaos** and of **phaino**: the ability of the mind to be the source of the light in which it perceives the phenomenon, i.e., **to see the sound** – and reminds us of Goethe.

Then thinking of thinking, the mind's mind, could mean something quite different from formal self-reflection, from the pure process of registering one's own process of "thinking thought". It might also be interpreted as an expression of the fact that the condition of existence is the condition of thinking. Because every act of thinking manifests a being here in this world, a **tode ti**.

What presents itself in the process of thinking is the presence of something other than thought. This otherness is the presence of the body as the "grounding" of thinking in time and place. What present themselves are motivation, intention, strategy, all the beloved words of the theory of speech acts, and of modern pragmatic linguistics. But one thing ought to be noticed here: there is a very tense awareness of the role of – what we today would call – **emotion** in these conceptualizations of the working mind.

Interpreting Aristotle, – and perhaps without the usual reverence to the canon – those concepts of **nous** might say the following about thinking:

a. thinking is deeply involved in action, in everyday life, in the situation and its context.
b. thinking can be in a state of sleeping, and then perhaps dreaming too.
c. thinking makes something that we call "reality" (but this is the only thing that thinking does not know of, so it is a genuinely intuitive statement). It creates phantasms, images, it is pure imagination ("Vorstellungskraft").

If there is anything to which a dialogue adheres, as to the most firm ground, it is to the metaphor of being awake. And being awake, one is able to abolish the opaque sides of the relation between speech and action (understood as the practical relation to life); and one should be able to lay out into the open every supposition, through the presentation of well-formed, unambiguous propositions ("apophansis" in the language of Aristotle). Propositions are in the last instance subject to "Ockham's razor": a proposition is the linguistically most intense, most necessary clothing of a single, clear, unambiguous, and economically sculptured thought.

But the just presented principles of Aristotle destroy these canons.

Thought is busy, daydreaming, and totally imaginative. Then words have to be the same, the use of words and concepts has to be too, and hence, the producing of propositions.

But then, dialogue is either a far more complex phenomenon than we think, and hence, as far as it is practised, a mere strategy. Or it is an old version of the Monty Python's Flying Circus.

This point could be underlined by stating that the mind is never an object to itself, neither as a mind, nor as a body, when it thinks. It is a circle, it is self-contained, it is a snake biting its own tail. Hence the body emerges as **that** which thinks. The body presents itself to the mind as the ability of thinking the process of thinking. The **mind's mind** and the **mind of the body** are one. It is a fact that you are unable to think your own thinking. Likewise you cannot think your own "wording", because you cannot word your own wording – this is what the body does for you.[5]

Or to put it in a more terse manner: the mingling of bodies and voices makes dialogue impossible as a place where thoughts, ideas, values, intentions and interests do compete for the prize of truth. A prize consisting in the unambiguous consent from the losers – who somehow seem to realize that they were the real winners.

So get Thee a radio, Ophelia, or a telephone, or an e-mail, or some even more new device, like the artifacts of video-conferences broadcasted in real time, where there are only voices and no bodies. And hide yourself in Hamlet's old armchair, armed with a packet of books on philosophical pragmatism and some magna opera on didactics, and talk through the endless days. You shall get your agreements after all, and even consensus.

Let us make this horrible conclusion:

There is no genuinely rational, i.e., conscious, way to speak, or to mean. There is no totally deliberate way of speaking. This means that there is no totally deliberate way of understanding. Speech is always symptomatical.

Hence, dialogue could never be transparent, never belong to those who take part of it.

We would always be the victims of our intentions, and when we think that we have caught them, and put them into words, and thrown them into the dialogues' ring, we are still the victims of this last intention that always escapes us: to want to speak.

---

5. My doctoral thesis had the title: Kirkeby, O.F. (1994): Event and Body-Mind. A Phenomenological-hermeneutic Analysis. Modtryk, Aarhus. Here I developed some of the ideas presented now.

But if we cannot rely on dialogue as the means to warrant liberty, equality and fraternity, there has to be something else, has there not? Because there always seems to be "something else". Till now this has been the secret "open sesame!" of our culture, which has stood a last opportunity rather than a benevolent referee?

Let me conclude:

If Aristotle is right, then it would be impossible for any human being to know what he says before he says it.

To speak is to search for meaning, not to have it in the form of a thought before you speak.

Then somebody might say: "All right, I accept that there are no "thoughts" inside your head before you speak because what should they look like? Images, some kind of "semantic tensions" or 'semantic fields'? Or resemble some kind of "emotions"? No, to accept that is impossible to me! But if a thought does not look like all this, it might simply be a proposition "inside your head". Why should you not be able to know it before you speak it out? Look at James Joyce, for example, he just writes his inner monologue down. Does that not prove that you are wrong?"

"No!" I shall answer. Because he writes it down in order to know it. The point is, of course, that there is no witness who can confirm that the words inside his mind are the same as those written down by his hand, or even spoken out into the air to himself. There is normally nobody else inside one's head!

There is no such criterion, and this is what gives dialogue this character of uncertainty. The speakers "sound the depth", so to speak.

This condition of the way in which thinking and speaking relate to each other, I call The **Principle of translocutionarity**. It can be expressed in its most precise formulation in the following way:[6]

"I do not know what I mean until I hear what I myself am saying."

It is obvious, that such a principle evokes the collectivism of meaning-production. Wittgenstein's famous conviction that there is no private language can be reinforced to say: there exists no private meaning – the canonical interpretation since Kripke.

To speak presupposes a kind of **preconception**, or **pre-reflectivity**, or an anonymous "common sense" identical somehow to the total "language game". It anticipates every reflective activity. This anonymous "sensus communis" has a form similar to a semantic lexicon of possible meanings within an area. But these meanings are not at all definite.

So, speaking might certainly look quite like playing some musical instrument:

---

6. The origin of the name of **the Principle of Translocutionarity** is explained in the next section.

you have to play in order to feel the phrase – even if you hear the tones in your inner ear. There never was a piano or a violin of the mind – even to the deaf Beethoven.

By examining The Principle of Translocutionarity somewhat closer, the following sections are of importance to a book on Management Philosophy for three reasons:

In the first place, they draw up a picture of the basic conditions of man as a linguistic being, with decisive bearings on theories of the relation between thinking, planning and acting. Hence, they bear upon the understanding of the phenomena of speech and of communication.

In the second place, the Principle of Translocutionarity establishes the epistemological foundation of the myth and the narrative, phenomena of rising importance to business economics and to the practice of the firm. At the same time, translocutionarity emphasizes the metaphor in opposition to the concept.

In the third place, translocutionarity enables us to make a principled and fundamental critique of discursive ethics, and hence, to lay a distance between Radical Normativity and business ethics, with its main emphasis on rational consensus.

Discursive ethics is the philosophical basis of the scientifically sound conception of an "ethical accounting", and the related concept "value-based management".[7]

This critique of discursive ethics makes it possible to examine the concept of "ethical accounting", and to get to the epistemological bottom of the concept of "value-based management". A more comprehensive critique of existing "ethical accounting" seems to me not to be necessary in the context of this book. The issue here must be the basic foundations and hence, the raison d'être of this program in relation to Radical Normativity.

---

7. The concept of "ethical accounting" is developed by Professor Peter Pruzan at the Institute of Management, Politics and Philosophy ind The Copenhagen Business School. Professor Ole Thyssen, and recently, associate professor Anders Bordum, both from the same institute as Peter Pruzan, have been important contributors to this theory too. In the English language is published: (Evans, Pruzan, Zadek(Eds.): 1997) As has already been mentioned, ethical accounting depends on "discourse ethics" as an epistemological program. Jürgen Habermas was the driving force here, but Professor Thyssen has tried to combine it with Niklas Luhmann's theories – a difficult project when one reflects how different their universes are.

7.2. The Principle of Translocutionarity

If management theory generally seems to be troubled by relating theory to practice, many explanations of this predicament are possible, and some, no doubt, are similar to the explanations of the social sciences. But one important reason could be that the "paradigm" through which the relation between thought and language are treated is misleading. This "wrong" paradigm might imply the conception that it is possible to control language, to master the phenomenon of speech completely, to subordinate words to thoughts as if this were a deliberate process implemented by "somebody/something", hovering beyond these words and those thoughts.

But considering that both management and leadership are essentially communicative processes, giving orders, approaching, committing, listening to the secretary, bargaining, making deals, excusing, advertising, talking in telephone with the Far East, suing somebody, filing tax forms ... it is rather important if it became evident that management theory were based on a concept of communication which is wrong.

Perhaps we all are victims of one great illusion about the cognitive functioning of language? This illusion, which I have already pointed to, consists in the notion that speech generally expresses a meaning somehow existing inside our mind before we choose to speak.

The creators of Western Philosophy, the Greek philosophers, did not care much about the written word. To them speech was the central, communicative function. But speech was always personal, committed, bound to the event, bound to the personality of the speaker, to his voice (phōnē). So far as the person was the servant of something greater than himself, the eternal truth (alētheia), his personality only mirrored this greatness. So he did not speak on behalf of himself, and then the effect on the hearer of his words was legitimized by this truth. The art of convincing, **rhetoric**, began in the art of instruction (paideia), the end of which was to set the listener free. Not until Hellenism and the Roman Empire was rhetoric transformed into an instrument of demagogues and overly erudite philosophers.

Even if the classical Greek philosophers, such as Plato and Aristotle, believed in a thought existing before and outside language, and even if they were extremely conscious of the means of speech and the rhetorical figures, then they did not claim to possess any knowledge themselves as individuals with an ego. They only expressed a knowledge of which they were the media – if they happened to be able to think in the right way.

The Stoic philosophers made a distinction between inner monologue (logos endiathetos), and sounding speech (logos prophoricos), but they did not stipulate a fixed and precise meaning before the choice of words. On the contrary, words had to be the door into the realm where words were superfluous, and Stoicism was obsessed with words and their origin.

This conception, the firm distinction between pre-linguistic meaning and the couching in words, is a product of the Baroque, of the 17th century. Words must be loosened from speech, from the person, from the speech act, and from the event of speech, from what you might call the "holy dimension" of speech. This "holiness" in speech emerges not only when the one speaking expresses a truth greater than himself, but when he, through his words, commits himself to something beyond this world. This is the secret of the "kerygma", of the holy word, and hence, the power of the sermon, and the condition of the prayer, the invocation, the confession, and the blessing. And it would be wrong – however unpleasant – not to acknowledge that the relation between management and employees gradually tends to be identified through concepts of the just mentioned type, which express trust, commitment and confidence, and hence, the demand of sincerity, honesty, willingness, and readiness. Will today's factory, without sweat, oil and noise, and with the rooms of the firm furnished with beautifully designed artifacts, without any trace of functionality, become the church of the next century? Ritual and recently, magic, belong to the vocabulary of organizational and managerial theory.

In the Baroque, speech is separated from this binding to personality and to the possibility of an implied transcendence. Words and concepts become instruments only occupying the place between consciousness and world. These words must be deprived of the inevitable contribution of the speaking person, **pathos**, the emotion, and the mood. And they must be deprived of the peculiar individuality of voice, of the subjective power of expression, of **style**. Through this deprivation it is possible to conceive of words as labels, as instruments to articulate already existing thoughts, independent of time and place, of person and emotion, and even of perspective and attitude.

This conception of words as instruments presupposes at least two things: the development of the art of printing in the beginning of the 15th century, and the transforming of mathematics and logic into the universal ideal of thinking, as "the process of thinking accessible to sight", because those disciplines have to be written and hence read – contrary to thinking through the voice and hence the importance of the ability to hear. Thomas Hobbes identifies thinking and "computation".

Logic and mathematics become tokens of the exact thought, but only as its instrument under certain circumstances: that thought must be functional in relation to the concurring and dominating of the world, of man and of nature.

Seen through the spectacles of this new conception, speech must be evaluated as an imperfect media of communicating the truth. People shall try to approximate speech to the form of logic and of mathematics. Try to determine it analogous to writing and to print, but attribute to it a far lesser importance. In the so-called "vanitas" pictures of the Flemish Baroque the carefully painted skull beside the book, the sheet of music, the glass of wine, the pack of cards and the globe, has very often lost its jaw, or the jaw is juxtaposed, as another object. Man has lost speech to printing.

In this way the illusion about the speech-independent thought is able to arise, through the projection of the relation between thinking and writing onto the relation between thinking and speaking. Because he who writes has an inner monologue running before or while he is writing them, thinking is mistakenly believed to accompany speaking, as well. Even if speech often goes too fast, it seems possible to fit it into this conceptual pattern: that we already, before we speak, have a finished and precise model of it inside our consciousness. Perhaps even the metaphor of "reading one's own mind" might work? The only problem is that this model is wrong.

In modern philosophy it survives within the so-called "formal pragmatics" tied primarily to the name of the German philosophers, Jürgen Habermas (1929-), and to Karl-Otto Apel (1922-). This "formal pragmatics" is the epistemological basis of the important "discursive ethics", which forms the core of any scientifically sound business ethics.

This frame of reference presupposes that it is possible to explain, (sic!) the meaning we are going to articulate and the intentions governing our speech, **before** we begin to speak.

A genuine understanding of the possibilities given to any man, and thus to the manager and the leader, to use speech presupposes a destruction of this illusion. It demands the ability to adhere precisely in theory to what our thinking owes to the words we use, and hence, to the language games. It demands the ability to explain the contextual setting of thinking, its intricate dependence on the situations wherein we speak. Finally it demands the acknowledgement of the role played by the voice, and hence, by the personality in thinking. The word "person", originating from the Latin "persona" meaning "mask", emphasizes the sound: as the mask is anonymous the identity of the person is established "through the sound", "per sona".

Perhaps Habermas' emphasizing of the three, so-called, "formal pragmatic criteria" is well-known. They are claims of validity to the consensus-oriented dialogue, and they all presuppose the intelligibility of the said: objective truth, normative acceptability, and sincerity. The central perspective of Habermas here is that when these three criteria are followed, it will be possible for those communicating to reach consensus. This consensus is based on an actual balance between all three parameters. But the conception of this balance presupposes a matrix that betrays a decisive lack of fulcrum in each criterion (Habermas: 1981).

Following Habermas, there must exist clear, unambiguous criteria of this balance that are possible to make objective. But these criteria cannot be determined by dialogue itself, because this would reduce the criterion of balance to the relation of power within the dialogue itself.

This anti-rhetoric model of the dialogue must then presuppose that something exists outside this linguistic form, outside the speech-acts wherein they are expressed. This "something", then, is able to be balanced by the expression it is given in the particular situation wherein it is communicated.

Habermas develops his idea about a balance between a mental and a linguistic dimension via the linguistic philosophers John L. Austin and John R. Searle. These philosophers develop a conceptual framework to identify so-called "speech-acts" through the distinction between different intentional attitudes in the situation of speech (Austin: 1962; Searle: 1974).

Such intentional attitudes must of course express a distinction between a mental dimension, a dimension of thought, and its linguistic couching. Alternatively, one would not be able to ensure oneself of which intention actually is put into the said. Such "intentions" seem to constitute a "mental language" beyond the grammatical form.

Austin distinguishes between locutionary, illocutionary and perlocutionary speech-acts. A "locutionary" speech-act refers to a proposition stating that something is the case (this category is peculiar to Austin, from whom Searle inherits his conceptual framework). An "illocutionary" speech-act refers to a proposition where the intention of the speaker is the subject of reflection. This intention consists primarily in the aim to make the hearer understand the content of what is said, e.g., a promise, reminder, or threat. Finally, a "perlocutionary" speech-act refers to strategic intentions, where one wants to make the hearer react in a certain way. This is the world of anticipatory, if not manipulatory, rhetoric: certainty and sincerity are often used as means to conceal and legitimize the interests of power; even validity and truth can be thrown into the game.

If this model of speech-acts is criticized in the same way as the mentioned figure of "translation" – because of its distinction between a mental dimension of thought **before** the couching within words – then it is possible to develop yet another mode of speech-acts. This shall prove to be the most decisive one.

We could give it a name that reminds us of the just mentioned modulations of the Latin word of "speech" or "the act of speaking", **locutio**, by Austin and Searle. Let us call it **translocutionarity**.

Trans, "through"; **locutio**, "the way of speaking". This "through" expresses a movement, a break**through**. But, what breaks through the way of speaking is not the pre-linguistic world of the subject. On the contrary, it is a world of meaning given only through the words and their articulation. Meaning originates within the said and the written. The one who speaks, and the one who writes, is in a certain way a stranger to his own product of sound and letters.

There is a "that" and a "there" playing within the said and the written, which contain a "more than" in relation to the cognitive world of the subject. At one and the same time it summons an anonymity in speech and writing, and it introduces a surplus of meaning.

The Principle of Translocutionarity could be phrased through a number of theses, at different levels of abstraction. We present them here, but rather shortly.

Level I:
The Cognitive Picture

a. the linguistic character of experience: perception is propositional.

  This means that it is very complicated, if not impossible, to speak about an "objective world" given by the senses that can be compared to the proposition and the words within it.[8]

b. the relative contingency of the individual amount of experience in relation to "language" as the encoding "of total experience". "Total experience" here means both the historical experience with words, how they have been used, and the possible worlds containing their use. This indicates that one can never know so awfully much about the words to use, simply because I, as an individual, was neither present at their birth nor involved in their upbringing. Hence, the scope of the transfer of experience into meaning available to me is very narrow.

  In "Philosophical Investigations", Ludwig Wittgenstein says that "the word watches us": it is just as alien, strange, full of secrets, like a picture, and to a high degree, not anything that belongs to us."[9]

c. the transcendence of the meaning of the meaning of language games.

  This follows up on 2., but states the fact that you cannot define meaning sufficiently through meaning. Or, you cannot mean meaning. We can perhaps "use" meaning, but we cannot create it from nothing, nor annihilate it. Our language games presuppose the concept of meaning. We are in a way "played" by those games.

  This is beautifully expressed by Martin Heidegger on the last page of his essay "Der Satz vom Grund", when discussing the early Greek philosophical concepts of Heraklit: **logos**, **physis**, **kosmos**, and **aion**:

> "The destiny of Being, it is a child, playing, playing on the draughtboard; the kingdom belongs to the child – ...
>
>   Thus there are also big children. The biggest, a royal child due to the soft-

---

8. This notion is put forward by both Maurice Merleau-Ponty, in his central opus, "Phénomenologie de la perception" from 1945, and by Hans Lipps in "Die Verbindtlichkeit der Sprache" from 1958. Lipps phrases it tersely: "the way in which my conception of things is anticipated through the language I receive." (Lipps: 1958, p.96. translation mine).

9. Wittgenstein, Ludwig(1989): Philosophische Untersuchungen. Teil II. Werkausgabe, Band I. Suhrkamp Verlag, Frankf. a.M. p. 501. The paragraph sounds, in the translation by G.E.M. Anscombe (Wittgenstein: 1974, Part II, vi, p.181): "Though – one would like to say – every word has a different character in different contexts, at the same time there is **one** character it always has: a single physiognomy. It looks at us. – But a face in a **painting** looks at us too."

ness of his playing, is this secret of the game, in which man and his lifetime are placed, where his essence is set at stake.

Why does this big child which Heraklit catches sight of on the aion ('the bow of eternal time', OFK), play the game of the world? It plays because it plays."[10]

d. the dependency of words in relation to context.

Words have to be spoken within a context, to reveal their meaning. And a context is first and foremost a situation, and hence, potentially, an event. In situations, you are seldom alone. Hence, thinking is a collective phenomenon.

e. a word is a kind of "echo sounder". Speaking is involved in the "haptic", "synkinaesthetical" use of words – exemplified through metaphor, where meaning is immanent, but with a tangible dimension.[11] Meaning depends on a competence, on ability, on a **possum**, "I am able to". This is implied in the concept of speech-act, but this ability is transcendent to thinking itself. The words appear through my mouth. The written word emerges from my hand. The Cartesian "cogito", "I think, therefore I am" must be substituted by an "I can, therefore I am".

f. what could be called "the nominalistic character of meaning-production". There exists no a priori criterion of **the same** concerning the relation between a proposition and the thought articulated by it: thoughts are identical to their unique existence within propositions. The concept ("das Begriff") might be more than a word, but it can never appear as anything else. Even its existence as something transcending the word is nothing but a relation within the word itself. Although we can have the inner feeling of meaning the same thing, it can never be finally corroborated.[12]

---

10. Translation mine, from (Heidegger: 1957) The German text goes:
"Seinsgeschick, ein Kind ist es, spielend, spielend das Brettspiel; eines Kindes ist das Königtum – ...
Somit gibt es auch grosse Kinder. Das grösste, durch das Sanfte seines Spiels königliche Kind ist jenes Geheimnis des Spiels, in das der Mensch und seine Lebenszeit gebracht, auf das sein Wesen gesetzt wird.
Warum spielt das vom Heraklit im **aiōn** erblickte grosse Kind des Weltspieles? Er spielet weil er spielet.

11. The concept of "haptic" origins in the Greek word "haptein", which means to be in direct contact with, to seize, to fasten to, to stick to. As an epistemological term I use it to indicate the union of all the senses in the bodily motion towards the world. This meaning is also implied in my neologism "synkinaesthetical", where reference is made to the combination of the senses through movement, and to the ability of the senses to express each other's images of the world (e.g., to smell a colour).

12. This implies that there cannot exist a language of thought, neither in the Fregean, nor in the Husserlian sense, nor a language of mental images; a Chinese box language inside the mind cannot exist either.

Level II:
The Social Framework of Talk

g. through speech, text, gestures, or – more seldom – silence, the other has to ful-
   fil the meaning of our meaning. The social setting of speech, then, the situation,
   and hence, the event, grants an enormous importance to the realization of
   meaning. This is perhaps the most significant lesson taught by The Principle of
   Translocutionarity: that the event is the real author of meaning here. That it, at
   one and the same time, creates, anticipates, and fulfills a meaning that it obviously owes to the individuals involved within it, because they borrow the meaning of meaning from the event.[13]

h. speech is symptomatically related to personal identity. The will, and emotion or
   emotional habitus (mood, "Gestimmtheit"), are the dominating cognitive factors of speaking. Words are always combined with gestures, voice, tone, fulfilling
   the creation of identity in the very act of speaking. I create myself as the one who
   speaks through my words. This "one", who is created through my speaking is
   partly unknown, and not identical to the content of the reflective I, or the intentional consciousness.[14]

   Immanuel Kant supports this view in his "Kritik der Urteilskraft", his "Aesthetics", when he in Paragraph 21 reduces the concept of reality, our common
   sense, to a "Gemeinsinn", a "collective sense" the core of which is emotion. Only
   emotion can guarantee the possibility of communication:

   > "If insights ('Erkenntnisse') should be able to be communicated ('mitteilen
   > lassen'), then it must also be possible to communicate the **mood** ('Gemüts-
   > zustand'), i.e., the emotional motivation ('Stimmung') of the faculties of
   > knowledge towards an insight ('zu einer Erkenntnis') at all, and hence in that
   > proportion needed to such a conception (through which we are able to con-
   > ceptualize an object), in order thereby to create knowledge; because without
   > this [emotional motivation. OFK] as a subjective condition of knowledge, this
   > knowledge would not be able to emerge as an effect."[15]

---

13. This logic, belonging to a peculiar kind of dialectics between the event and "its" individ-
    uals, is far more complex than the famous "Principle of double contingency" presented
    by Talcott Parsons and Niklas Luhmann (Luhmann: 1985). The Principle of Translocu-
    tionarity might be conceived of as a "reinforced communicative double contingency", but
    it is important, and it marks the distance to Systems Science, that the "double contin-
    gency" involved in The Principle of Translocutionarity cannot be controlled through any
    kind of media.

14. See: (Merleau Ponty: 1945, pp.445-446, and p.448). The German philosopher, Hans
    Lipps, spoke about "Sicht" ("sight"), which both refers to optics and to shooting, mean-
    ing the anticipated, intended, content of perception. Perhaps it is relevant to recall the
    fact that Plato, in his dialogue "Cratylus", remarks that the concept of **doxa**, "meaning",
    often "not-demonstrative", "uncertain", knowledge, originates in a metaphor from

Level III:
Consciousness as a Text

On this background it seems possible to conceive of consciousness as a **text**. I find this metaphor apt because of its connotations to the tension between a spontaneous anticipation of meaning through the authoritative sequence of signs, and that which must be interpreted although it "already always" gives sense immediately. But also because of its connotations to this "body of meaning" called "experience" that belongs to us, but whose author we do not know. That self-reflection is a hermeneutical project must be obvious, but also remembering is, after all.[16]

7.3. The Illusion of Representation

The Principle of Translocutionarity was phrased in the following way: "I do not know what I mean, until I hear what I myself am saying."

One of the reasons why this principle seems strange or directly wrong to perhaps most people might be that we have acquired the epistemological habit of identifying mental activity with **representing**. To think, is to handle mental objects and their relations. To feel, is to handle mental complexes. To intend, is to handle mental objects. In making reality a place outside the subject, but guaranteed in its objectivity by this subject, we identify reality with the form of the object. Reality is "constructed" by the subject in this act of representation, but the subject is also "constructed" by its very representation of reality. We also used to put inner and outer reality on the same footing. The principle of representation consists in the concept of a presence possible to handle, "re-present-ation" (Heidegger: 1957; Heidegger: 1963) Here the object, inner or outer, is given its immediate appearance through the senses. When they are functioning at their best, they disappear in front of the appearance. Thus the best sense of all is thought: **cogitatio**. Intuitive introspection, clear and cool. The ideal of Descartes.[17]

---

archery, **toxon**. This is also the case with the concept of "intention", **boulē** from **bolē**, "shooting". Op.cit. 420C. Thus the metaphor of "sight", used to indicate the anticipation of the meaning of experience through intentionality, is already conceptualized by Plato.

15. "Kritik der Urteilskraft", op.cit. p.157-158, translation mine.

16. En passant: The Principle of Translocutionarity is much easier to accept if we relate it to the arts. The French sculptor, Auguste Rodin, spoke about "the liberating" of the figure hidden in the stone. Non-figurative artists seem to calibrate themselves towards a motive which does not exist in advance, as such.

17. The ideal of Descartes contains an aporia. Here naming, the "onomata", the names of things, can only be labels contingently related to the mental objects. They can have no intrinsic relation to the essence of this object, because the essences of objects lie in the external, well-observable qualities which make them obedient to laws, or in the clear, mental images of them, and they are subjective or private, and hence contingent in relation to the word.

Here you shall find mental images referring to one and only one object. From this perspective The Principle of Translocutionarity seems futile, because you are able to visualize, intend, and name an object, before you speak of it.

But if the figure of representation does not work, then The Principle of Translocutionarity seems much more obvious. The word might, through the very pronunciation of it, reveal much more about the object than could ever be conceived of in a single mind.[18] One might sense a concealed, if not sacred, relation between name and thing, as implied in Walter Benjamin's famous criterion of distinction between the language of things and the language of names. The name might contain the secret of the thing, giving an immense importance to the very pronunciation of the words that invoke it.

If the subject reigns over the objective world, its supremacy involves full knowledge of those objects. Their names must thus be totally transparent, and at best trivial. Language has to be a conventional media, and words contingent or chosen labels.

In opposition to this, if wording is a necessary condition of the meaning through which the object appears to the mind, a meaning which the word reveals, not to speak of its being the only condition of it, then representation is abolished in its strict sense. The implication is obvious here that the world is a social phenomenon in which the words are laid like pieces in a mosaic, or constituting an intarsia, producing more dimensions to experience than it consists of itself. There are deeper relations between words and things than we seem to know.

But far from placing language game relativism or constructivism at the heart of epistemology, the passions inherent in the word towards reality testify to the fact that it is more than an image or a phantasm. It might also re-introduce a positive kind of metaphysics beyond postmodernism, a "transcendentally immanent realism", where both the mind, its world, and the media between them (language) are deeper than figured out by the daylight of representation and its transcendental subject.

7.4. Further Epistemological Consequences

When exposing this Principle of Translocutionarity it is important to make the levels clear on which we are speaking, both ontologically and epistemologically, relating to cognition and to method. Let us start by looking at the literal meaning of this first paraphrasing of it, that "I do not understand what I mean, until I hear what I my self am saying."

---

18. Weick's concept of "retrospective sense making" could be thought of as a concept to which "the Principle of Translocutionarity" was an epistemological basis, and a meta-concept at all levels (Weick: 1979).

Crucial here is the redefinition of the notions of understanding and meaning, as well as the present participle form, functioning in the phrase "until I hear what I myself am saying", which denotes the passage of time.

Most people shall probably find it obvious that one first thinks about something, before one puts it into words. It seems perfectly possible to mean something without the words that express it. It also seems evident that one can mean something exactly and in a finished form, before one says it, so that it is rendered unambiguously through the words chosen. It also seems uncomplicated to choose the words: the one who reflects the meaning, and the one who puts it into words, seems to be neutral, most often his own judge. It also seems as if the words chosen are able to translate this pre-verbal meaning uncomplicated into the understanding of it by the other(s). There is a metaphor of "mind-matching" here.

Nevertheless, this presupposes at least two phenomena: that thinking precisely without using words is possible, and that thinking one's thoughts outside or before a situation is possible.

Let us take the almost trivial example of a person reproaching another person by saying: "you do not behave well!"

Besides the wellknown fact that the effects of these words might create a quite new situation, because they passed some kind of threshold between the two persons, then how do you think about it before you say it?

I believe only the following possibilities can be found.

A. As a state of mind.
   This state of mind can be
a. **not** expressible in any kind of words, nor thoughts, but in spite of this, it has a reflective character, i.e., you know that you have it, and you can distinguish it from any other state of mind. Here the criterion of what it means to mean, what is expressed through the selected wording, seems difficult to handle. How can you be sure what your state of mind was, until it has been worded? Not to speak of how you would explain to others what your state of mind actually was?
b. **not** necessarily expressed in any kind of words, nor thoughts, and non-reflective. This would perhaps be the perspective of a super-naturalistic view of the mind, where "brain-states" are thought of as correlatives to thoughts. The relation between those and the actual wording through speech would be a causal one, but the criterion of correlation seems contingent.

   Yet, here your own knowledge of your own mental processes would have no final relation to their truth value. Not even communicative, consensus-related processes would probably be able to create any judgements of the validity, i.e., the sincerity and reliability of statements.
B. As some forms of mental images. Such a kind of pre-conceptualization of any thought, possible to put into words, should have its own image or image-constellation (a moving or floating image, perhaps). This amounts to the mind being an immense catalogue of icons, an "iconery" with a structure exhibiting

traits almost similar to the spoken language, hence similar to a "rebus of rebuses". This Chinese alphabet analogy of the mind seems very clumsy to me, and rather problematic as well, because it presupposes both a universal, transcultural idea of consciousness and very extensive ideas of our ability to produce an inner exemplification of the ability of meaning.

C. As a reflective, discursive notion. This would imply the idea of mind as a linguistic system where mental processes would be proto-linguistic – a position perhaps similar to that of Donald Davidson, or Ernst Tugendhat. Still, you would here confront a problem of translation, where one and only one formulation of a thought exists, and every shade of sense is similar to a derived propositional thought. The process of thinking should probably be strictly rule-governed. Also the genealogy of the thought must be reflective in some way, i.e., the thought put forward in your speech can never be misplaced or wrong in relation to your intention. Which would mean that the idea of intention is superfluous. But speaking would be genuine repetition. You would be your own parrot.

D. As a non-reflective, discursive ability, which only shows itself in your overt speech, but the existence of which can be inferred through deduction from the former. This would probably come closest to a computer metaphor of the mind. Here you must have a whole system of transformation rules. A system unlikely to exist when compared with the flexibility of expressions of – what in communication is experienced as – "the same" thought.

To everyday consciousness, case A.a. is by far the most plausible perspective. We find it widely documented in the phrases of everyday language that meaning exists as a kind of mental state. We assume that we can search for the right word; try to express our feelings; fail to say what we really mean; want to be more clear; wish to be more exact; be able to express what we truly experience and what we truly feel, and so on.

Thus, there may be a small interval of time between a state of mind and its wording. Nevertheless, this does not necessarily imply that we can search for the word without already having the word in mind. On the other hand, it makes little sense to say that we "consciously seek the word", because we are not able to describe such a procedure. This afore-mentioned short interval of time is more likely to imply that the right word needs some time before it is felt right. It is as if we had to exclude possibilities. The final choice is not the choice of the right meaning, but the "meaning's choice of the right word", to phrase it as an aporia. The meaning arises as exactly this meaning, only in and through the word. This is why it can be a right or a wrong word. This is why your own word seldom directly surprises you, even if it confronts you with the fact of your own mental reality. Words make your own states of mind real.

So The Principle of Translocutionarity seems far-reaching.

It transforms the criterion of meaning.
It transforms the picture of dialogue.
It transforms the picture of the working of the mind.
It changes the picture of economic man.

Uwe Jan Heuser illustrates this in his article in "Die Zeit" with the title "Poor Homo Oeconomicus" (No.9, 25 Feb. 1999). Referring to the results of the receiver of the Nobel Price in Economics, Reinhard Selten, from Bonn in Germany, Heuser tells us that we could never understand our own decisions completely, and hence not control them. The "bounded rationality" of Herbert Simon is at work more than ever. Decisions depend on canonical "irrational, cognitive elements" like "emotion", and of the contingent row in which options are presented to you. Decisions depend on the amount of efforts already invested in the solution of it, e.g., why else wage war at a time when everything is lost already, and absolutely nothing can be gained? And Heuser continues:

> "People might even sometimes prefer product A to B, B to C, but again C to A – rationally a monster, but to us quite normal.
> And this behaviour cannot be cancelled or abolished through training, as the psychologist Daniel Kahnemann and his colleagues again and again have been forced to realize. Behind this we can see patterns rehearsed through thousands of years, perhaps even neuronal relations in the brain. We are not able to cope rationally with probabilities. For this reason we are not able to decide sufficiently what would correspond most perfectly to our goals. Often people try to describe their behaviour as rational afterwards, Richard Selten thinks – because of the lack of knowledge of their own motives and inadequacies. But it is important to come to terms with that.
> But this is difficult. Because in order to make the most of the sunny sides of the new economy, we are forced to continuously examine and optimize our own decisions. It would not be especially odd to conclude that other parts of our personality might lose significance – for example the demand of autonomy." (translation mine).

7.5. But What about Dialogue, Then? And Management via It?

Perhaps the most important consequence for the dialogue of The Principle of Translocutionarity is that a "naturally demarcated" dialogue does not exist. On the one hand, every member of a dialogue is contingent in relation to circumstances and these to contexts (they are in a sense contingent too); the one's whole family is invisibly present in the room, the other's whole clan is lurking – as "Romeo and Juliet" makes vivid to us. There is no "pre-communicatory" choice that can make the dialogue a genuine experience of face to face. On the other hand, the members of the dialogue are always chosen through some criterion – power, what seems reasonable at the time, some political process of selection, religions, view of the world, education, experiences, age, gender, prices offered by travel agencies ... Thus any dialogue needs another dialogue to be interpreted. It needs a **metalogue**. There is an infinite regress of hermeneutical procedures involved in mutual understanding, not to speak of consensus, or even a vicious circle.

The space and time of dialogues cannot be properly defined. The sets of possible dialogues encircling any dialogue are almost infinite. The sets of possible **metalogues** cannot be gathered in a final set.

There is a mild version of an aporia at play when we try to submit the dialogue to an evolutionary logic. On the one hand, we believe that dialogues are able to move culture in the right direction – even if the concept of "right" is hard to define. On the other hand, we certainly conceive of dialogue as a phenomenon not obedient to any crude principle of power. If the most fit survive, then it is not because of dialogues. We either conceive of dialogue as subject to reason, in the sense of "the interests of humanity", or as subject to a "reason" only approximately touched upon by our values. Dialogues are the quintessence of democratic principle, protecting minorities, but they also serve civilization.

Hence, what was the "right" outcome of dialogue must be judged by history, by the **metalogue**, the speech that comes afterwards ("meta" means, among other things, "afterwards" in Greek). In this sense, a dialogue is nothing but an event – however, an event turned inward towards its character as event; one talks about what one is talking about.

I do not mean to say that we shall abandon dialogues for these reasons. But we ought to acquire a more realistic view of them, because dialogues become extremely pragmatic phenomena from this perspective. They seem to happen because something else happens in another related, or bigger, dialogue. In other words: dialogues are strategic, and always terribly different in relation to context. But respect, or even reverence, make us dumb when the word is mentioned. To this must be added that dialogues are events, and hence their meaning and their significance remain open to the last day of history. The Principle of Translocutionarity is a principle of postponing. It invites us to wait for the last moment of this world, until it could be known for sure what was actually said. And yet everything that happens seems already dead and gone, seems done with for good, transformed into monument, unredeemable.

But this movement of deferring the final decision, consent, title, or name can also be seen as a way to conquer dialogues from the past, as well as to expropriate those of the future. The vivid reality of such urges meet us in law, be it in the frame of democracy, with its wealth of formalized ways to settle the demarcation of dialogues by selection (a "commission of inquiry" is the result of this even more, deciding the matter by a vote), or within the life of business, the contract. Everybody in our Western society feels the importance of stopping the permanent change from **dialogue** to **metalogue**, of blocking the constant oscillation between them: we feel at the same time the despair of the constant "re-negotiation" of meaning, and the inability to abolish the need of an open society as a warrant of an ever-open historical horizon.

Law represents a firm knowledge of the fact that one cannot rely on an inherent urge for universal justice within dialogue. The hurry to pin the principles down legally every time a sort of consent is reached, the rule of the precedent, attests to the contingency of the rationale of consensus? Power, price, and profit make any agreement unreliable. Even when people marry one might suspect that this ratification of a "dialogue-unit" for life – perhaps mingled with the voices of children, the whispers of family members, and the lightening of the burden of taxation – is a kind of security. A security not so much against disturbances to come from without, but definitely from within.

In sum, it seems as if the canonical metaphor of the dialogue, i.e., the untouched centre of sincerity from where a curative, creative, and culturally renewing movement, a powerful, centrifugal movement, shall be initiated again and again, has been shaken. However, there might be one exception: the most celebrated of all dialogue-units in Western culture, friendship, the phenomenon most obviously in opposition to the legal guarantees of the rules of balanced dialogue.

Aristotle's metaphors, in Book VIII and IX of the "Nicomachean Ethics", about friendship are important to us because they imply the concept of the centre, of the middle, and hence, of the common, social place in spite of the constant breaking of any natural demarcation of dialogical inertia. Symmetry is an important metaphor too, and of course reciprocity and mutuality (e.g. VIII,v,4). Figuratively these qualities are able to invoke the concepts of the centre, of the middle, too. One beautiful expression sounds like this:

"Friends have one soul between them" (mia psychē) (Book IX, viii, 2)

About the **habitus** of friendship Aristotle also says, stressing the reciprocity of the relation:

"for a friend is another self" (IX, iv, 5.)
"... very intense friendship resembles selfregard" (ibid, 6)

The symmetry in the dialogue-unit of friendship is based on the symmetry of genuine, moral self-reflection. This is the only place in the world where law is superfluous in reinforcing what passion, empathy, and reason, can create. Perhaps friendship could, and even ought to, be an ideal basis of managerial behaviour, and hence, a component of the virtues of leadership?

Now, what makes the dialogue so difficult to manage? Could it be due to the fact that it is a unique means of management in a democratic society pervaded by the four-dimensional grids of informatics, and by the filigree work of law?

Let us look at some relations of great importance to management that might be conceived of as dialogues with a symmetrical or balanced structure:

a. Consultancy: the rendezvous with the expert. Measures might be taken to evade too much asymmetry, but in the end it is the combination of interpretations of advice received, and their organizational implementations, which alone are able to settle this question (whether the dialogues between the CEOs and the consultants were actually symmetrical).
b. Negotiations between the CEOs and the shopfloor about salaries, work-hours, piecework contracts. Perhaps this could come very close to a symmetrical dialogue, because everybody knows from the beginning that this is definitely what it is not? The more irreplaceable and important the employees, the more the ideal of a balance could be approximated.
c. The settlement of "organizational learning". If the accentuation of group experiences is the goal, and no managers are present, the usual group dynamics will decide the matter. But if mid-level managers are present a **metalogue** has to be projected on the ongoing dialogue in order to create balance. Consultancy, i.e., some kind of "therapy through dialogue", is probably needed here. The existence of tacit knowledge among employees as the intangible target of managerial efforts shall make the construction of symmetrical processes very difficult.
d. The communication between the firm and the market can never be a dialogue. Advertising is genuinely strategic, even when it communicates at a meta-level, and signals (or in all its shrewdness feigns to signal) the limits of its own strategies – a phenomenon that is more and more the case with advertising today. (And so called "consumer guidance" might often look more like "seduction" in not yielding information as part of a balanced dialogue, but the results of public pressures, and, hence, self-defence on the side of management, being far more the effects of tactics than of an obliging posture).
e. The inner monologue created through managerial courses and "therapeutic" settings would rarely be a projecting of a genuine dialogue onto the mind of the manager. He is lured by his own voice into thinking something that transforms him into a purposeful machine and a short-term "winner". His inherent human nature would seldom be in balance with the needs of functional roles.

There is not much reciprocity, no real democracy of communication in the prototypical dialogues of business life. Instead we encounter strategies. The character of the pragmatic love between logic, psychology, the "mores", and profit, is – as often with arranged marriages – cold. Of course, CEOs might agree with the kind of passion procured by brandy behind club doors, and clandestine agreements might be intimate dialogues by nature, but we cannot hear them.

Let us return to philosophy.

To Plato, one might ask, this Socrates, does he not prove that it does not mean a thing what you say, even not, what you do, but only who you are? Why else, should it always be him that speaks when something said, really, essentially stated, told, even confessed, is expected? Does not Socrates, as a person, as a poetical device, as a rhetorical instrument, as the quintessence of the existence of dialogue, prove, that the dialogue does not exist? That there are only monologues, and dialogues with the voice built into them?

How on earth should we, in this life, be able to blow reality into a structure that only likes power and not voice, that only submits to the hidden voice of the Third? A structure that fears "the Fourth" as its own shadow?

7.6. Will and Desire: To Get in and out of the Dialogue, Safely

But we are speaking all the time in meetings, at lunch, in the bed, in the bathroom, on the roof, and in the basement. Those who seem to know, shall speak, and those who do not seem to know, shall speak too. And if you yell strongly enough in the light, or whisper intensely in the darkness, you might get the last word. Or get something even better: your will.

Because you only got the last word, because you got your will.

What does it mean to "get one's will"?

What is the **will**, anyhow?

Sometimes one might think that the will is something lying between the mind and the body. Or even a centre to which they both relate.

The Greeks did not have a word for the abstract will, nor did they know the concept of the "free will". Why do we want it?

Perhaps because it is a way to explain why something happened that we could not explain otherwise: "He got his will!", "It happened, because he would have it to happen!", "Mr. Churchill's iron will!"; "The will of the people!"; "Against one's will!"; "Two extraordinarily strong wills!"

The most important "will" in the history of Western culture is probably "The will of God". This important concept in Christian culture, and in everyday consciousness, puts a line of demarcation to knowledge. This just had to happen!

But does not this scope of signification still form the core of the concept of the will? "Somebody had enough will to make something happen." "Another person did not have enough strength of will." We operate with a kind of necessity here, when we speak about the will. But a necessity that cannot be analyzed through the canonical instruments of rationality.

Hence, the concept "free will" is a phantom: because the free will, i.e., the will that is strong enough to place the possibility of an alternative in front of itself, is not free at all.

Firstly it cannot explain this possibility/ability through itself.

Secondly it is only free, because it knows quite a lot of necessity – i.e., of the consequences of the act chosen.

But the will is at work, no doubt.

And the will belongs to dialogue. Here you can make things happen.

It is not the stubbornness, the persistency; not the seriousness, the stern frown; not the shouting; not the intonation, words harsh, words sweet; not the neglecting of your own fatigue; not the soft effort of empathy; not even the words chosen. What is it?

A sense of situation perhaps? A sense of the right moment, of – what the Greeks called **kairos**? Probably something like that. But there is still more to it.

You have to be at the right place at the right time. You have to have the ability of what one might call "eventuation". To have to be able not only to identify with the event, or to anticipate it, but you have to **be** the event.

The powerful will consists in the ability to **be** the event.

Eventum tantum! That, which happens only happens once!

Then it is up to you to transform the dialogue into the event that is you. The event that you **are**! Not more! Not less!

If you succeed, it shall be the triumph of **desire**. Plato called it "thymos" in "The Republic": the combination of will, vitality, desire, passion, aggressiveness, and meaning, and thought, and character.

A will with a thought inside it. A thought with a will inside it. A new concept of action, of **praxis**.

A new balance between speaking and doing?

But before we shall turn to this task of rethinking the concept of praxis from a normative perspective, we must proceed with the examination of the dialogue by looking at one of its most characteristic traits, **irony**.

7.7. Irony and Dialogue

Irony is a special transformation of will and desire into speech. But as a testimony of will and desire it is at the same time a denial of both this very will and this very desire.

It is a canonical, rhetorical instrument that when driven to its limit, seems to cancel the very concept of rhetoric.

Firstly, it exhibits both the will and desire, the very two phenomena that rhetorical techniques seek to hide because they use them all the time. The rhetorical gesture wants to influence them, to mold them in the hearer, to use them strategically. But to show their existence would be disastrous to the rhetorical goal.

Irony pushed to its utmost limit is the self-irony of Socrates, when he in the dialogue "Phaedrus" talks about a speech he is going to deliver. It is a speech that is intended to overrule a speech of a famous orator just repeated to him by Phaedrus, his young companion. This first speech was delivered by Lysias, much admired by Phaedrus. Now Socrates retorts:

Phaedrus asks: "... where have you heard anything better than this?"
    Socrates: "I cannot say, just at this moment; but I certainly must have heard

something, either from the lovely Sappho or the wise Anacreon, or perhaps from some prose writers. What ground have I for saying so? Why, my dear friend, I feel that my own bosom is full, and that I could make another speech, different from this and quite as good. Now I am conscious of my own ignorance, and I know very well that I have never invented these things myself, so the only alternative is, that I have been filled through the ears, like a pitcher, from the well springs of another; but, again because of my stupidity, I have forgotten how and from whom I heard it." (Phaedrus, 235C-D)

Here Socrates is obviously at the same time practising, and referring reflectively, but ironically, to The Principle of Translocutionarity. He will not claim to be the author of his own words.

In the beginning of the dialogue "Phaedo", when all the friends present in Socrates' jail cell, on his last day are mentioned, it is tersely, or en passant, remarked, "But Plato, I think, was ill." (Phaedo, 59B).

As Plato cannot be present in his own story, cannot be a witness, so Socrates cannot be the author of his own thoughts. There is a play with authenticity for the sake of authenticity.

There is always a "Third" one to whom the truth of the story and hence of the arguments, is referred. Phaedo telling about himself and Socrates in "Phaedo", but through the words of Plato, making Plato into the Third. And Plato telling about Phaedrus and Socrates in "Phaedrus", but as the invisible almighty, and omnipresent storyteller this time, not as the humble chronicle writer. Here, in this dialogue, Plato cannot restrain himself from letting Socrates devalue the phenomenon of writing in relation to speech, and hence Plato's whole project. It must not be forgotten that most of all Plato's dialogues reproduce Socrates' life and apparently his points of views. Bearing in mind that Socrates died in 399b.c., when Plato was approximately 28 years old, these dialogues must be seen as either works of memory, or works of imagination, or both. Thus "mnēmosynē", memory, is extremely important here. So when Socrates says in the "Phaedrus" about the technique of writing through the invention of the letters:

"For this invention will produce forgetfulness in the minds of those who learn to use it, because they will not practice their memory." (Phaedrus, 275A)

then he denounces his whole project which was to put dialogues into writing. Is Plato condemning himself when he a few lines later on says:

"He who thinks, then, that he has left behind him any art in writing, and he who receives it in the belief that anything in writing would be clear and certain, would be an utterly simple person, and in truth ignorant of the prophecy of Ammon, if he thinks written words are of any use except to remind him who knows the matter about which they are written." (275C-D)

Then, on the next page, Socrates seems to ameliorate his judgment of letters, when saying:

> "The word which is written with intelligence in the mind of the learner, which is able to defend itself and knows to whom it should speak, and before whom to be silent"

And Phaedrus finish the thought:

> "You mean the living and breathing word of him who knows, of which the written word may justly be called an image." (276A)

Here you are already presented with three levels of reality:

a. The eternal ideas beyond thoughts.
b. The eternal ideas as thoughts beyond their verbal dressing, beyond words.
c. Their verbal images in the philosopher's mind.

These levels can be differentiated further into:

d. Their verbal images in the mind of the sophist or the simply unknowing (not-yet-knowing/never-coming-to-know).
e. The written images of 3., (the verbal images in the philosophers mind, verbal images, which are true, right and beautiful).

The core of the problem relates, of course, to the authenticity of the thoughts presented. Hence, the problem concerns their authority.

This authenticity can only be established through the reference to an authoritative voice. This voice might be the voice of Socrates, but he denies this possibility, because "he knows nothing".

On the other hand, if it were the voice of Plato, we would only know it through two alternatives: the voice of Socrates, or through the whole choir of voices in each dialogue.

It is as if The Principle of Translocutionarity were all-dominating here, as if every dialogue sounded like:

"It is not me here who speaks who is actually speaking. My face which you see, my gesticulating body, is but a mask. Although the sound of the words comes from my mouth, I am not their real author."

This little word, "actually", is very important. Because it leads the sentence from a performative contradiction into something quite, else, and opens up the question who is really speaking?

Irony as a two-sided phenomenon makes this possible:

1. The authoritative person in the text does not invest himself in his wording. He speaks with the most persistent will, and with the most intense desire, however

understated, and he denounces this existential will and desire. The last words of Socrates on his deathbed in the dialogue "Phaedo" are: "Crito, we owe a cock to Aesculapius. Pay it and do not neglect it." (118A). And Aesculapius was the god of healing, so perhaps Socrates was hinting at the fact that death was the only healing process, or that he – a man without a voice – had been a living dead.

Not even the coming of death can make him reveal his true voice. Very symbolically he uncovers his face (which had been covered after he had been forced to lay down because of the effect of the poison which he was given) to say his last words. And one must ask "is there any voice at all?" Was it just borrowed? If so, from where?

2. The text itself is ironical in its form. Plato might not even believe in Socrates. Plato might speak through all those characters without knowing what he himself is saying. He might be committing the philosophical sin number one: to speak about a matter one does not know, as if one knew it. The sophists' and the rhetor's way.

But anyone who should be able to write a dialogue needs to have the qualities of the rhetor:

> "... he who is to be a rhetorician must know the various forms of soul", and he must know the "various classes of speeches, to one of each every speech belongs. So men of a certain sort are easily persuaded by speeches of a certain sort for a certain reason to actions or beliefs of a certain sort ..." so the rhetor "when he has acquired all this, and has added thereto a knowledge of the times for speaking and for keeping silence, and has also distinguished the favorable occasions for brief speech or pitiful speech or intensity and all the classes of speech which he has learned, then, and not till then, will his art be fully and completely finished; ... for, as we said in the beginning of this discussion, he who is to be a competent rhetorician, need have nothing at all to do, they say, with truth in considering things which are just and good ..." (Phaedrus, 271D-272D)

But Plato's dialogues seem to be practised rhetoric, constructed scenarios where voices mingle in accordance with this art. And this art is contrary to truth, not even a "bastard-thinking", but the thinking of "akolasia", of the attitude, that denounces the right, the beautiful and the true. So Socrates, the master of speech, has to say, of course:

> "at any rate, I possess no art of speaking."[19]

So the very form of the dialogue is ironical: it can never say what it says, because it says it in this way. Hence, there can neither be an authoritative nor an authentic voice.

---

19. "ou gar pou egōge technēs tinos tou legein metochos". Phaedrus, 262D. (Look at the front page of the present book).

Then the voice, which we want to hear, the voice of truth, is not present in the dialogues as a personal voice, subject to identification. It is not even present in the form. It only presents itself as an absence, as "The Fourth".

This absence as a possible presence is created through irony. But irony conceived of as a very broad phenomenon. Might one name it "metaphysical irony", because it questions the very framework of questioning and answering, of the canonical "dialectical method", not to speak of the "elenchus"?[20]

The one who obviously knows, denies to know. The one who writes, destroys his own message. But what kind of knowledge does he evoke then?

A philosopher very conscious of this function in the phenomenon of irony was Søren Kierkegaard. His answer to the question of what kind of knowledge Plato/Socrates might evoke, then, would be controlled by his fear of irony as a means to "the infinitely easy-going game with nothing", with absolute negativity instead of a "restrained irony" as a means to the "baptism of purification of the soul".[21]

Kierkegaard inscribes himself into the tradition of "negative theology", a tradition recently pursued by Jacques Derrida (and by the author of this book).

In an article, "Sauf le nom" (Derrida: 1993), Derrida relates to the Christian, mystical tradition, to which Plato, of course, has been extremely important – Plato speaks of four kind of "manias", or ecstasies, in the "Phaedrus". Derrida makes a distinction between, on the one side, a phrase from a mystical thinker or poet, when seen as a proposition, which can be understood properly, i.e., as referring to an experience, and, on the other hand, just approached as a string of words, a formula. As a proposition that can be understood properly, it evokes personal experience. As a formula it evokes an authoritative experience that a canonical person is supposed to have had once upon a time. The experience now survives within the formula, and by repeating it, and by developing its inherent, verbal logic, the present mystic tries to evoke this experience. This is also the problem of the Christian "kerygma": is "the word" a testimony of the experience of Christ and his followers, or is it a reliquae, and hence just a trace?

But these alternatives play in the whole opus of Plato. Firstly, of course, they appear in the standing quest for the authentic and authoritative voice. Secondly, they are explicitly treated within the dialogue "Cratylus", where Plato asks whether the words have an original meaning which can be sought by following their significance back into time. The Stoics thought so. But Plato, of course, will not answer. A word is a convention, and a word is the trace of the original experience. Irony also swells in this profound dialogue. Its answer seems to be, that there is no beginning for language. A theory of words shall not be able to tell us whence the voice comes.

---

20. The "elenchus" designates the method of getting to a provisional conception of truth by refuting the arguments of others. It was practiced in the early dialogues of Plato where Socrates is granted the honour of demonstrating it to us.

21. S. Kierkegaard's doctoral thesis "On the Concept of Irony", from 1841, which deals with Socrates.

There is no final voice, and there is no original face, for who should have been the one to hear it or to see it?[22]

We are now invested with enough tools to turn to the phenomenon of dialogue once more.

The Principle of Translocutionarity seemed to shake the fundament of social consciousness. A strong element of contingency is engraved onto speech. This opens the place of talking and listening to rhetoric, to the forces of will and desire. There is no criterion of truth, nor of beauty, nor of righteousness. There are only words, words not half as beautiful as bodies.

The beautiful lines from The Revelation to St John, 3.20, however, come to mind:

"Behold, I stand at the door and knock; if any one hears my voice and opens the door, I will come in to him and eat with him, and he with me."

We are still knocking, and the whole culture of the West was touched once and for all by this art of speaking that is no art, but just a gentle knocking; by these words, that are only words, repeating the voice that, because it did not have any author, could have been mine too. The voice to which a door might be opened.

But where the loss of the authoritative element of speech appears to be endurable, the loss of authenticity seems worse.

Not just conversation, but serious dialogue, becomes a game.

One might then ask, "what is authenticity, really?"

Perhaps it is not just the feeling of being-here, being real, of coming close to, of grasping, of really experiencing? Not the most obvious, Aristotle's "tode ti", or Heidegger's "Dasein"? But the very opposite? Perhaps authenticity consists of knowing that there is another kind of reality that calls upon us. The summoning to be "authentic" could mean: to be able to call. That we might be somebody some day who could speak with a voice, to which a door was opened, because we were the ones who were able to hear it, and to learn from it – that silent, first voice?

---

22. The beautiful expression of the opposite position by St. Augustine in his "Confessions" might be recalled: "Noli abscondere a me faciem tuam: moriar, ne moriar, ut eam videam" (Hide not thy face from me: let me die lest I die, that I may see it). St. Augustine (1919/1995): Confessions. The Loeb Edition. Transl. by W. Watts. Harvard University Press, Cambridge, London. Book I, V. However, Socrates uncovers his face to say his last words in the "Phaedo".

7.8. The High Hopes of Dialogue

What has been said about irony, it might be objected, could more correctly have been said about humour. But to me, irony is in its core metaphysical and revolutionary, whereas humour might be frequently too complacent. Irony dares the demonic dimension, the arena with the beasts, while humour chooses the safe seat far up in the spectators' enclosure. Irony does not take reconciliation for granted, while humour too easily makes itself the victim of a master plan to which nothing really matters, or in which any move is anticipated and controlled. Of course irony could be bitter, show ressentiment, be destructive, but humour could fall victim to that behaviour too. There is just as much bad humour as there is stupid irony.

Irony belongs to monotheism, humour belongs to polytheism. Irony makes the creator responsible for his work, and reacts with reciprocal irony, with a tremendous rage coiled into a quiet commentary, an almost detached objection against the "ironic and cruel blue sky", the face of the irony of fate.[23] Humour does not dare to, and might at times appear as a stance so well-educated for the happy ending, while irony might go the whole hog, exposing "an infinite and absolute negativity" – as Hegel reproached it in his "Aesthetics". Irony takes the evil seriously, humour shrugs it off, when it does not directly deny its existence. Irony takes the other person seriously, humour does not. That is why humour is allowed in dialogues, and even asked for, while irony is banished from the fine company of serious, goal-oriented conversation. Finally, irony tries to play with language as a phenomenon, identifying it as the battlefield of the Same and the Other, thus challenging it; humour accepts that language and uses it to play with the world.

Let us go on with the phenomenon of irony:

Irony does not go together with expertise.

"The Fourth" is the opposite of an expert.

Thus, irony challenges the information-society by claiming that there are no answers. It transforms the apparent rationality of this society into a horrifying aporia, because informations are answers that anticipate any question, by force, definite answers. Generally, the absence of authority proper to irony means the absence of expertise, and vice versa.

Irony is the opposite of power.

Can you imagine a potential manager answering a questionnaire from one of those hyper-modern pendants of the scavenger, the "Head-Hunter firm", the "employment-consultants", and giving an ironic answer?

Can you imagine one from a staff answering a worried employee in an ironic way?

Can you imagine the prime minister of country X, ironically stating his support of the politics of an allied country Y.

---

23. Charles Baudelaire: Les fleurs du mal. LXXXIX, Le cygne (the swan), (Baudelaire: 1964), noticed this aspect of irony, "la vorace Ironie" (the bitter irony), LXXXIII.

Can you imagine an ironic television reporter?

Irony does not seem to go hand in hand with public realities. Neither with the small ones, in firms, nor with the big ones in regions and countries, not to speak of "the world". "Mr. Clinton seriously regrets the sexual attitudes of the middle aged male!" "Mr. Hussein shall work on the task of getting this world thoroughly Christened!" "The chief of staff from now on promises to work at a negative profit!" "The French Government has agreed on enlarging the concept of 'sustainability', in order not to do any harm to pesticides!" "Your policy is perfect, just change all the staff, and fire yourself!", as the advice of a renowned management consultant to a CEO.

As soon as irony is let down from the heights of metaphysics into the valley of narrow, interpersonal relations it often gets impertinent. It mixes with the desire of the upstart, with the aggressiveness of the parvenu, it smells of bad company. Or it signals the reckless drive to power, it displays a will to power that does not even care to give its victims a chance of legitimizing their own oppression. But of course the irony of intimate relations might be gentle and even tender.

And yet, it might sometimes look as if irony was the original attitude towards speaking. Sincerity, then, would be a derivation because sincerity presupposes the possibility of dropping the face shield; it presupposes the presence of a person. But in irony nobody is speaking as nobody – a knowledge that saved Ulysses from the Cyclops. The contradiction of being, between the fact that essence is dependent on (constructed by) existence, by acting and speaking, and that these phenomena must manifest something behind/beyond them, if they shall be granted any meaning at all, is revealed through irony. Irony reveals a remnant in the way which language refers to the world. It points to the fact that the Order which philosophy, religion and science reveals might be pretended, and that even the essence might be a fake. It points to the logos of the Other.

The frontiers of advertising seems to have a hunch of this metaphysical urge of irony – even if they pervert it. As when a more than handsome young man on TV sprawled in an elegant chair complains about his longing for a woman who desires him, but does not need him; who wants his outward appearance, but not his soul – a desire, simply impossible to anybody, and yet perfectly rational insofar as the subject of desire has no soul. The sad truth of the narcissistic predicament of Generation X is overtly stated as the confession of an emotionally insoluble dilemma, the answer to which is a "Kevin Kline Perfume" for men called "Contradiction"!

The German soldiers in World War I getting up from the trenches, crying "Gott mit uns!" were confronted by the English soldiers, getting up too, but crying "Marmalade!" as an ironic commentary to both this impudent usurpation of a transcendent legitimacy, and to this making war into the business of God.

Is the last shout a presentiment of a very impending physical condition, or just simply the defiance of fate? If the last alternative is the right one, then irony might hide a kind of courage.

But we could also ask: what is the opposite of irony? Answers would probably be: sincerity, confessions, objectivity, tenderness (perhaps, but not necessarily, kindness), anger, passion, hate, impatience, irritation. However, they might all be the expressions of irony. Perhaps irony has not got any opposition?

Irony generally does not seem to match expressionism. But what about the dialogue, does it favour expressions?

In a way, irony tells us something extremely important about both what it means to speak and what a dialogue is.

Spontaneous expression does not appear to be that much subject to The Principle of Translocutionarity, because the meaning of the expression seems to be there already. The gestures of hatred, like the gestures of tenderness, often do not need to measure their own intensity and precision against anything else but the gesture itself, only sometimes on their effects on the other person. And we probably all agree that the dialogue must exist without them.

Irony controls emotion, because it controls will and desire. The dialogue ought, through its very definition, to do the same. "Dia-logos", through speech, and nothing else. Or, "dia-logos", beyond reason?

But then the difference between the ironic speech and the dialogue defined as being sincere must be found in their different ways to cope with **pathos**, passion. Or better, in the different ways in which they allow for the person to cope with passion.

Without doubt, irony cannot confess passion directly. The frameworks of intonation proper to irony must often be calm, but could possibly be harsh, or bitter, or cold, too. Irony goes with resentment. In the dialogue one has to state those emotions openly, to expose one's weak sides – or, in the more refined dialogue, to expose the phenomenon of exposing oneself. So, in the ideal dialogue you cannot allow the whole repertoire of expressions peculiar to irony.

Or put in another way: in irony you use The Principle of Translocutionarity through the way you control the musical possibilities of your voice and gestures. In dialogue you are fighting this principle. You are forced to watch and correct yourself all the time, to look for the genuine, serene, intonation and gesture. In irony you can feign a kind of "innocence of articulation". In the ideal dialogue you have to confess, that you – not yet – were the master of your own way of expressing yourself.

In irony you confirm the fact that you are a body speaking.

In the ideal dialogue you deny it. By the former, your bodily presence simultaneously cancels and reinforces your words by referring to the secret depths of the body, and by emphasizing them through its poise. By the latter, you are present as genuine spirit, and hence, as mere image, as person (persona = mask), as "a you" figuratively painted on your flesh, until your real "you" some day ...

Irony seems to address nobody, and at the same time it adresses especially you as nothing but body, as an object, as unlucky flesh, as the other, as the eternal stranger. Dialogue addresses a symbolic other, turned towards its own image, it confirms the fundamental identity of everybody, as fellow man, as citizen, allowing for small differences only – while it tacitly celebrates the insignia of knowledge, surplus of situational information, position, psychological skill, and sometimes, even wisdom.

But there is one more important difference between the two: irony cannot be controlled from outside. The dialogue can.

Irony never confesses. Irony never adheres to the canonical, right emotions, because irony never confesses to any emotions at all.

Dialogue confesses. In the ideal dialogue everybody examines their own emotions, their desires and their will, all the time.

And this is why people who try to live up to the standards of the ideal dialogue never know what they have said, until they have said it.

Then, we might say that irony is revolutionary, rebellious, and that the ideal dialogue is conservative, even conformist. Irony never gives anybody any opportunity to catch it in revealing the essences of meaning, emotion and will. Dialogue is ever feeling guilty, ever seeking a legitimate reason to feel what it feels, to mean what it means, and to want what it wants: an addiction to the truth.

Then, we might perhaps conclude in this way:

If Management Philosophy should be able to reflect the coming-to-be, reflect the otherness of any new market, any new employee, any new situation, then it ought to adhere to irony, not to the ideal dialogue.

Management Philosophy cannot develop a concept of the dialogue without relating to irony. But here we are met with a serious problem: the context in which management operates is framed by the computer; and the computer is an instrument of the ideal dialogue. It does not understand irony. However, it might be more than a media of the dialogue, supporting the constant shifting of roles between teacher and pupil, it might be the tacit demonstration of the secret of the very phenomenon of dialogue, a secret very far from the air through which any protagonist of the "dialogue-way" of life would pass it on to us: that the realized dialogue makes real understanding superfluous. Instead the computer introduces a series of knee-jerk reactions on the side of the user, anticipating and reinforcing a semantic familiarity with the peculiar world of informations bordering to a lack of consciousness, capturing the other in an obviousness with regard to the setting that transforms meaning into an effect of information processing as a cause concealing its own power. Their is no glance, no seeing that one is seen, no looking back, not even a smell as from roses watched, but only an observation almost identical to gazing, an eye looking at a painted eye. The light on/in the screen is a virtual blackout.

All communication in hyper-modern firms is built into the image of this ideal dialogue. Everything starts with this projection of an image of ideal communication existing in the body of the computer. Any manager has to know that the computer knows before he tries to know what it knows.

And should he try to question the "that" and even the "what", he cannot use irony, because the only dialogue mastered by a computer is the dialogue of the converted emperor. An emperor converted to the religion of a knowledge where power and sincerity, ignorance and innocence, are one.

However, as far as the dialogue can only function as a means to democratic interrelations when it is let into a democratic setting, how should it be able to produce this democratic setting?

Dialogues purge groups, they seem to function as mechanisms of the survival of the fittest. Dialogues prepare, create platforms, anticipate what is going to come. But dialogues are not what is going to come. There never was a permanent dialogue in the same way, as it might be claimed that there is an unending story. Only in dialogues, and in written poetry, is speech the real subject – this slowly rotating, self-mirroring galaxy of noise. It can be a temporary end, because dialogues, and poetry most often, are a means. Everywhere else speech is the humble servant. But when the talking has stopped, the real business may begin: to make money, to arrange for the next weekend, and book a room at the old people's home (not too expensive) for your father, to telephone your friend's mistress, to buy a puppy for your son, to fire the caretaker, to go to sleep, to caress an antique vase, to sell some shares, to eat a gastric ulcer pill, to kick the computer, to paint the summer house, to sit in the sun.

But the real business? The worship of silence?

Part III

The Virtues
of Leadership

CHAPTER 8

Praxis and Hexis

In the following chapters we shall try to get closer to the physiognomy of managerial virtues, and to their perfection through a conception of the virtues of leadership. But we have to begin with a rather thorough philosophical investigation in order to understand what a **virtue** actually is, and how it relates to human action, **praxis**, to moral character, **hexis**, and to the practicing of virtues, to wisdom, **phronēsis**. While I hope that the necessity of virtues in business life should have been argued sufficiently in the preceding chapters the philosophical content of the phenomenon of virtue still needs an elaboration.

The means to a "modest deduction" of the framework of virtues and of their possible content can only be Aristotle's "Nicomachean Ethics", because this book is still the most, not only authoritative, but also involved, elaboration of the epistemological conditions of speaking about "virtues".

What Aristotle actually does is to create the framework for deducing the concept of virtue from the general concept of human action, **praxis**, by way of a mediating concept, that of **hexis**, "habitus", "moral character". Virtue then, can be seen as a special case of human action.[1]

We shall try to reproduce this grandiose gesture of a thinking that transgresses both the canonical borders of modernism between epistemology, ontology, and moral philosophy, and that transgresses the feigned nihilism, the bewildered situationism, and the obsessive rationalism of the postmodern approach to ethics.

---

1. During the last ten years Aristotle's ethics has been viewed from a new angle; it has served as a foundation for rethinking ethics. Aristotle's ethics is presented as an ethics of the event, an ethics beyond maxims, beyond consequentialism, and even beyond moralism. It is seen as an ethics of wisdom, and, hence, both as a "third way" between approaches of utilitarianism and deontology. It is also seen as a radical programme of cognitivistic, moral philosophy. Inspirations here came not least from the book, "After Virtue. A Study in Moral Philosophy" by Alasdair MacIntyre in 1981. To phenomenological philosophy this new way of reading Aristotle creates an open space in which it is legitimate to demand an encore from the field of ethics. See for example, Paul Ricoeur, "Soi-même comme un autre" from 1990, translated into the English under the title "Oneself as another." (Ricoeur: 1994)

8.1. The Concept of Praxis

In the "Nicomachean Ethics", when dealing with the dianoetical virtues, Aristotle focuses on **proairesis**, which means the "choice founded by reflectivity/deliberation". The choice is, of course, essential to the possibility of ethics:

> "And then the object of choice is something within our power (tōn ef' hēmin) which after deliberation we desire. Choice (proairesis) will be a deliberate desire of things in our power; for we first deliberate, then select, and finally fix our desire according to the result of our deliberation" (Nicomachean Ethics, Ibid. III, iii, 19).

But choice alone cannot be the foundation of action, of **praxis**:

> "Whereas a thing done (to prakton) is an end in itself: since doing well (eupraxia) is the End, and it is at this that desire (orexis) aims.
>   Hence Choice (proairesis) may be called either thought related to desire (orektikos nous) or desire related to thought (orexis dianoētikē); and man as an originator of action, is a union of desire and intellect ("kai (hē) toiautē archē anthrōpos", which actually means "such a principle is only man", OFK)." [2]

Choice is only possible when desire and intellect unite. When thought feels passion, it is suffering (pathein); it is influenced externally, it is potentiality, **dynamis**, subject to **kinēsis**, causality, and not yet actualized, **energeia**. But when passion thinks, it is master in its own house. It is precisely **dynamis** and **energeia** that Aristotle contrasts in Book IX of his "Metaphysics". The person who on his own initiative, naturally does what is good, draws the passionate thought into the thinking passion, unites them in his "nature". Thus, **praxis** becomes **hexis**.[3]

It is **hexis** that it is all about: **moral character**.

For character is nothing but the will of deliberately nurtured desire, and the shape of the thinking of the will. This is **hexis**. When you have developed it in the right way, then many a dialogue shall belong to you. However, you might not find this kind of possession worthwhile!

In Book IX of the "Metaphysics", Aristotle distinguishes between two types of **praxis**: one that is limited by something other than itself, and thus is the means to an end over and above itself (examples are, "to construct", "to learn"); and one that

---

2. Nicomachean Ethics, op.cit. VI, ii, 5-6. The English translation here, as admitted by the translator, H. Rackham, is somewhat liberal.
3. The concept of **hexis** is much more familiar in its Latin translation by Cicero to **habitus**. However, the connotations of the latter concept are epistemologically all too narrow, and ontologically all too wide.

is unlimited in the sense of not delimited by anything but itself. This last type of **praxis** is called **energeia**, "full reality", "actualization", and it is the prototype of the concept of "action", its "regulatory idea". In Book IX of "Metaphysics" there would seem to be a normative attitude to the concept of action which is not that pronounced in the "Nicomachean Ethics", in relation to the concept of **praxis**, but probably in relation to the concept of **phronēsis**.[4]

But what kind of action, **praxis**, does Aristotle want to conceptualize in Book IX, vi, of the "Metaphysics"?

The following could be the answer, with every reservation for over-interpretation of these lines which are loaded with meaning and susceptible to many interpretations: there is a mode of action in which the contradiction between past, present, and future is dissolved, and where neither reflectivity nor the distinction between subject and object play an important role. The passages read:

> "Since no action which has a limit is an end, but only a means to the end, as, e.g., the process of thinning ...; it is the process which includes the end that is an action (praxis). E.g., at the same time we see and have seen, understand and have understood, think and have thought; but we cannot at the same time learn and have learnt, or become healthy and be healthy ...
>
> Now of these processes we should call the one type motions (kinēseis), and the other actualizations (energeias). Every motion is incomplete – the processes of thinning, learning, walking, building – these are motions, and incomplete at that. For it is not the same thing which at the same time is walking and has walked, or is building and has built, or is becoming and has become, or is being moved and has been moved, but two different things; ... But the same thing at the same time is seeing and has seen, is thinking and has thought. The latter kind of process, then, is what I mean by actualization, and the former what I mean by motion." (Metaphysics, IX, vi, 7-10)

Why is he who is learning not the same as he who learned? Why is he who is walking, and he who has walked, not the same? While, on the other hand, he who is seeing, and has seen, and is thinking, and has thought, is the same?

Why is learning not a simultaneous process, while living, thinking, and seeing possess simultaneity?

Because one cannot learn without knowing that one is learning something, or go in the direction of something without knowing that one is moving; while one

---

4. In the Nicomachean Ethics, I, ii, 1-2, the theme is merely touched on that there can be a goal for our actions (tōn praktōn) that we want for its own sake, and that this goal then will be the good, and that knowledge of this Good or Supreme Good (tagathon kai to ariston) must be the point of departure for ethics as a "science", because it must be the foundation of ethics as "praxis". The passage does not make a subject of the epistemological form and content of action.

can see, live, understand and think without knowing that one is doing so. Thus, one remains the same. One is one: reflectivity is superfluous, in being that in which the person is influenced by himself as if it were by someone else, the hexis of passivity (Metaphysics, IX, i, 5.). Passion has become totally social. The word has conquered the flesh.

> "To Carthage then I came
> Burning burning burning burning
> O Lord thou pluckest me out
> O Lord thou pluckest me out
> burning"

as T.S. Eliot, in "The Waste Land", succeeds in catching the still living meaning of the experience of St. Augustine.

What is crucial here, in Aristotle, is that thinking (noeō) is used as the recurrent example of the genuine action. Thus, there is a thinking that is both simultaneous with itself, and beyond reflection. The subject of such a process that makes past, present, and future the same by seeing, living and thinking, **is acting**, and hence, duration, time as a lasting moment. In this duration we are caught. It fills us up, and we are filled up by it. But time that does not appear as time, that does not take the shape of re-collection, not of remembering, that is neither a feeling of distance or dating, nor of longing, hope, not even knowledge, this is passion. Passion without object: pure emotion, mood. But a concept of mood extremely far from any subjective sensitivity in creating a room that transgresses what is outside and inside. A mood that comes from without as the moment of pure duration. St. Augustine called it "hodiernus dies", "the day of God", in his "Confessions". He says about the time of God:

> "And because thy years fail not, thy years are but this very day. And how many soever our days and our fathers days have been, they have all passed through this one day of thine (per hodiernum tuum transierunt): from that day have they received their measures and manners of being. But thou art the same still; and all to-morrows and so forward, and all yesterdays and so backward, thou shall make present in this day of thine: yea, and has made present." (Book I, VI)

The genuine action is timeless and without cause. Although this latter is, of course, a ideal of ethics, most often connected to Stoic wisdom, an ethical ideal of the wise man's independence of the situation, there is also both an important epistemological and ontological content. The genuine action cannot be explained by means of psychology or social psychology (as we would say); its point of departure is the norm (gnōmōn). Not "norm" in the sense of Kant, as a maxim, but rather norm as **pathos**, as **orexis**, as passion, but a passion that is cosmic, linked to the great logos and to the profound knowledge of God, to **gnōsis**.

This interpretation is supported by the passage in the "Nicomachean Ethics" already quoted at the beginning of this chapter, where, when dealing with the di-anoetical virtues, Aristotle speaks of **proairesis**. Here he defines it as the union of desire and intellect, as the articulation of desirering thought and thinking desire: you have brought yourself to a place where you cannot help to do the good, because you just and simply experience in this way. Almost a kind of "hard-won innocence", one might say.

Interpreting **orexis** as **passion** and not as desire, which is the usual translation, and which corresponds to the traditional meaning of the concept into which **orexis** is translated in Latin, **appetitus**, "appetite", may be justified through the passages about **orexis** in Aristotle's "De anima" (On the soul), Book III, ix-x (Aristotle: 1995).

Firstly, in Book III, ix, 432a, 31, of "De anima", **orexis** is defined as a mental char-acteristic, or state, that includes both the rational and irrational parts of conscious-ness. It is different from the Aristotelian concepts that designate desire, instinct, urge, will and passion, (namely **hormē, thymos, epithymos, boulēsis** and **pathos**). Will and desire (epithymia) are aspects of **orexis** (ibid. 433a 25).

Aristotle now examines **orexis** in connection with his attempt to answer the question of what makes a person carry out a movement (kinēsis): is it the whole of consciousness or a special part of it?

What is crucial is that **orexis** is the necessary condition for movement, but not the sufficient condition; thought (nous) is needed here.

The epistemological picture at the basis of Aristotle's thought is that there exists an idea, **phantasia**, that as an object of passion, in step with the thought making this object tangible by making it visible, draws the person to it. But thought can only do this by virtue of **orexis**, of passion, and passion alone can change thought to action (De anima, ibid., 432b).

Thus, the connection between passion, thought, idea, and action as a process looks like this:

"And every appetite (orexis, desire) is directed towards an end; for the thing at which appetite (desire) aims is the starting point of the practical mind (prakti-kou nou), and the last step of the practical mind is the beginning of the action (archē tēs praxeōs)." (Ibid. 433a 15)[5]

If one then regards "imagination as some sort of thinking process" (ibid. III, x, 11), **orexis** and **nous** are causes of movement, because the imagined object releases pas-sion through its tangibility by the consciousness through thought. But in what does this tangibility consist? Thinking is moved by virtue of the thought about "the prac-tical good", **prakton agathon** (ibid. 433a 30). Only this "mental object" is able to release both thought and passion at the same time – mental faculties during Mo-

---

5. I follow the choice of the translator, W.S. Hett, of rendering "orexis" with "appetite", but emphasize that "desire" is a better choice by placing it into brackets.

dernity most often in opposition to each other. But the realized practical good is the action itself. Thus the essence of **orexis** is movement in itself:

"The moving cause is of two kinds; one is unmoved and the other both moves and is moved. The former is the practical good (prakton agathon), while that which both moves and is moved, is the appetite (desire) (to orektikon) ..." (ibid. 433b, 15)

Passion changes into action for the sake of action, because action is a good thing in itself if, as a process in itself, it embodies the image it had of itself as the good action, the "object of passion", in the form of the passionate action.

In other words, **orexis** is what communicates between **dynamis** and **energeia** – and here a link is created to the thoughts expressed in the "Metaphysics" and in the "Nicomachean Ethics" – by being not merely the actualized (energeia) potentiality (dynamis) but the actualized movement, in the symbolic sense, between potentiality and reality.

Thus, on the basis of the "De anima" we can understand an action (praxis) as the movement (kinēsis) whose goal is itself, that is as a moving from **dynamis** to **energeia**.[6] But this movement is normative in essence; only the action that has as its goal (or objective idea) the practical good, is able to be the thinking passion or the passionate thought.

"Now mind (nous) is always right (orthos); but appetite (desire) (orexis) and imagination (phantasia) may be right or wrong. Thus the object of appetite (desire) always produces movement, but this may be either the real or the apparent good; and not every good can excite movement, but only practical good (prakton agathon)." (De anima, 433a, 27)

It then follows that only that movement is a movement, and thus only that action an action, through which, by actualization, the practical good in its procedural form **dynamis** (not in its result) is transformed into **energeia**. The essence of such movements or actions and their restraint in principle to the person, to ēthos (character) through ethos (habit), is **hexis**.

To sum up: the thoughts about **praxis** that have embodied time and reflectivity are assembled in the concept of **hexis**. It is the type of action that unites thought and passion by means of the spiral of "auto-learning".

The one, most important question behind the discussion of **praxis** and its relation to **hexis**, is the one posed by Plato in his dialogue "Protagoras": is it possible to learn virtue?

---

6. On this conception of **praxis**, see: Ricoeur: 1990.

An aspect of an answer to this old question might be the Socratic one: only **dialogue**, realizing the ideal of spiritual development, **paideia**, is able to give man the strength to build up the right **hexis**. But the answer is too overstated, however tempting, if it is interpreted to mean that character is "created" socially. Because, when one takes into consideration that the theoretical framework of learning here is Plato's idea of **anamnesis**, of knowledge as "recollecting", then the consequence is that you are only able to learn what you in some sense already know. Hence, dialogue is not to be conceived of as genuinely "productive" of ideas and attitudes – as Schopenhauer noticed in the quotation cited at the beginning of Part II of this book. But **paideia** is realized through the dialogue as a **maieutic** process, a process where your knowledge is released through talking with the right person, in the right way, and at the right time.

But nobody can claim that this has to be an élitarian perspective. It might rather be an acknowledgement of the contingency of the human condition which also means the contingency of organizational and managerial practices. However, need it be a concession to reflective thought and to reflective method? Might the concept of **maieutic** dialogue, the method of the philosophical midwife/counsellor, not reveal an insight into the importance of the unspoken, of that which we cannot know that we actually know? And could this insight not lead to a certain caution concerning the acquisition and the use of power?

8.2. Learning

In these thoughts we find a mutual play between three important concepts: **praxis**, **reflectivity**, and **learning**.

These three concepts are all of fundamental importance to the development of Management Philosophy as a discipline centred around the concept of managerial and leadership virtues. As a point of departure, the link between them may be illustrated on the basis of the concept of **learning**. The noun, "learning", expresses the substantive form of the Greek verb, **manthanein**, in the form of **mathēsis** (known to us in the variant "mathematics"). Already for the Pre-Socratics, this concept encompassed the unification of the acquisition of theoretical, practical and ethical knowledge.

In the dialogues "Phaedo" and "Phaedrus", Plato suggests the possible content of the concept of learning:

a. As consisting in the articulation of knowledge we already possess. This is the famous concept of **anamnēsis**, re-collection of knowledge from a previous existence. The argument of Socrates is here – among others – that this is the only way in which one can explain the ability to experience "abstract or absolute equality" (Phaedo, 75B). To acknowledge likeness presupposes the concept of likeness. This concept cannot be developed through experience without a circulus vitiosus, as Hume demonstrated in relation to the "principle of induction".

b. As consisting in the ability to receive learning from another, from a knowledge-able person. This is the so-called "maieutic" method of Socrates, and it can never be separated from the first type. Knowledge must be prepared in your experience, before you can receive it.
c. As consisting in the ability to learn from one's own experience, from one's praxis.

These three dimensions of learning, repeatedly found in different versions in the concept of consciousness during the whole of Modernity, could perhaps teach us something that transcends this culturally closed knowledge. Because to the Greeks it was crucial – which we can see in the further development of Plato's thinking by Aristotle and the Stoics – that in their essence all these three forms of learning are **ethical**.

It would, after all, be simple to interpret a as the expression of general knowledge of the human condition;[7] b as the educational acquisition of theoretical knowledge, both about the world and about the good; and c as the programme of pragmatics. But things are hardly so simple.[8]

What is important is that these three dimensions of learning, where a must be the prototype of learning, b the prototype of acquisition and mastery of reflective knowledge, and c the prototype of praxis, only give meaning to Greek thought because all three serve to build up the insight of the individual into the good.

Thus, in the context of this book the perspective must be that the relation between learning, reflectivity, and praxis is **normative**. This means that, fundamentally, business economics must be concerned with how we construct an organization and a managerial practice which in its essence is **normative**.

In order to maintain this, we must simply reject the modern idea of rationality.[9] We must simply say that the focus of modernity on human rights – being the result of the interpretation of "rationality" during the Enlightenment – is a minimum solution that is far too weak. What is decisive is a focus on human duties.

The concept of **duty**, which comes from the Stoic concept of **kathēkon** and was translated to **officium** in Roman times, expresses that learning is not merely a mat-

---

7. For the Stoic, Seneca, the whole of life was about learning to die: "tota vita discendum est mori" (De brev. vit. VIII, 3.) This dictum is also the programme of Heidegger's "Sein und Zeit" and thus of 20th century existentialism. It necessarily forms the horizon of any reflectivity ("Das Sein um dessen Sein es sich selbst geht" – as the reflective Being is defined in this masterpiece) (Heidegger: 1967).
8. This appears already as crossing the boundaries between the familiar tripartition: learning by example, learning by being told and learning by doing.
9. After all, Martin Heidegger pointed out that **ratio** as the Latin translation of Greek **logos** means a fundamental limitation, a distortion even, of this principle of being and reality to mean "that which can be counted" or "that which can be presented in such a manner that it can be manipulated" (Heidegger: 1957).

ter of acquiring neutral knowledge, of storing data, but deals with the relation of one individual to another, to society and to the cosmos, and that duty is never enough. Duty must become commitment. Learning is to perfect oneself as a human being, to attain what the Stoics called **katorthōma**, ultimate wisdom.

In modern times, the concept of duty became known first and foremost through the ethics of the German philosopher, Immanuel Kant. But in Kant's work the concept refers to a set of universal principles which the individual must learn to accept through the intellect. He espouses this position for the simple reason that not to accept them would imply performative contradictions. This disregards emotion. But emotion, desire, and passion, nevertheless appear even in Kant, because he admits that accepting the maxim as one's duty implies "good will", and that "good will" is inexplicable and incapable of manipulation. The movement from duty to commitment is transcendental (Kant: 1974a).

The point here is that, for the Greeks, passion is present when duty is dealt with. Thus the whole person is also involved. Reflectivity is not hollow intellectual acrobatics: praxis is connected with **pathos**.

What is crucial is, naturally, that today we simply can no longer construct organisations or prescribe management practice that does not in its essence unite thought and passion. The significance of this for business economics as theoretical praxis is: how can we construct strategies for organizational learning that are normative in essence while simultaneously being aimed at solving specific problems? And this is not about constructing casuistry, but rather about creating an open concept for normative learning, reflection and action.

In this respect the important dimension of learning is Plato's first, **anamnēsis**, the great metaphor for learning as "re-collection". "Re-collection" must here mean appropriation of one's own true nature.

Appropriating one's true nature means at one and the same time re-finding and creating one's true being, and this true being is first and foremost that which finds expression in being together with others and in relation to the community, to society. Today the company can no longer disclaim responsibility for the social dimension. It is thus obliged to be a forum for normative learning which includes reflection and praxis that acknowledges its own normative basis and sets itself its own characteristic normative goals.

The organization and the management practice necessary here on the eve of the new millennium is a practice that depends on learning that makes reflection about our true nature possible. The concept of **duty** returns to the centre here, because it indicates the maximum conditions for the possibility and capacity of the individual to function in a concrete social community. Here learning has to do with forming an identity.[10] But this process is simultaneously both re-collection and creation.

---

10. It is worth remembering that the former president of the BRD, Helmuth Schmidt, has proposed the idea of "Human duties" as a necessary supplement to Human rights.

In this respect we can learn from the concept of **hexis**. Hexis is the **habitus** of duty, but it is duty that has become passion.

8.3. Hexis

It is not without interest that Aristotle presents the concept of **hexis** as a concept that cannot be defined through reflection, but only through praxis:
    In Book V of "Metaphysics", Aristotle says:

"Having" means (a) In one sense an activity, as it were, of the haver and the thing had, as in the case of an action or motion; for when one thing makes and another is made, there is between them an act of making. In this way between the man who has a garment and the garment which is had, there is a 'having'. Clearly, then, it is impossible to **have** a 'having' in this sense; for there will be an infinite series if we can have the having of what we have. But (b) there is another sense of 'having' which means a disposition, in virtue of which the thing which is disposed is disposed well or badly, and either independently or in relation to something else. E.g., health is a state, since it is a disposition of the kind described." (Metaphysics, Book V, xx, 1022b)

We can think our thoughts; this is the nature of reflectivity.[11] Where Aristotle approaches a "cogito" with the concept "noēsis noēseōs", he excludes our being in the world, our reality of action, from the perfection of reflectivity with the concept of hexis. Hexis must begin with a fundamental choice, **proairesis**, and go on from deliberate choice to deliberate choice. But little by little a readiness, a habit (**ethos**) is prepared that establishes another type of "reflectivity", **practical reflectivity**, which is beyond the horizon of the concept, and which is only found as sensation, as "embodied knowledge", or what Aristotle calls **phronēsis**, "wisdom".[12]
    I think that it is vital to understand that what Aristotle undoubtedly means is

---

11. Aristotle often conceptualizes this both in the form of **noēsis noēseōs** (the thinking/thought of thinking) from the "De anima" and from the "Metaphysics", or in the equally famous formulation from the "Nicomachean Ethics" in Book IX where he speaks of "noōmen hoti nooumen": "we acknowledge in spirit that we acknowledge with the spirit", from this drawing the Cartesian conclusion, "hoti esmen": "that we hereby exist".
12. I have called this embodied knowledge the **body-mind**, and its relation to itself "practical reflectivity". I developed this special form of "reflectivity" in my doctoral dissertation (Kirkeby: 1994). In this dissertation I also developed the concept of "body-mind", which includes important aspects of the concept of hexis. An English introduction to my conceptual framework is found in (Kirkeby: 1998).

that while we can have (possess) ourselves in thought, at the same time it is his insight that we cannot have ourselves in our having ("ouk endechetai echein hexin"). This hexis is "dead time that lives", "being re-collected", to employ yet another Aristotelian formulation later taken over by Proust and Merleau-Ponty. On the one hand, it is our biological basis, our character, our temperament, the locus of our existence, our psycho-somatic necessity that is ēthos (with a long "e", "eta"). On the other hand it is simultaneously the totality of our ability in the capacity of what we find natural, ethos (with a short "e", "epsilon"), which means "habit". It is the natural and necessary in experience, what I have called selfcessity,[13] the presence of presence, and it is what Foucault in "Les mots et les choses" called "the unthought". It is, thus, the historically-socially given anonymity and blind spot that in the heart of our praxis we are to ourselves. Body-mind is a metaphor for this unresolved and processing secret: the singular's, the grammatical singular number's, the events', transformation into a unique, working re-collection.[14] Hexis embodies time and closes it to thought. It is the essence of knowledge that is always normatively informed tacit knowledge: anamnēsis, the re-collected, my re-collected. Hexis expresses that transformation of contingency to necessity inherent in the movement between proairesis, choice, and the creation of a characteristic, "somatic", basis of virtue (aretē), which might be conceived of as "an absorption of time into being".

Thus, Aristotle writes about the ideal for the relation between the good person and the good act:

"... on the other hand, it appears, there is a state of mind in which a man may do these various acts with the result that he really is a good man: I mean when he does them from choice (dia proairēsin), and for the sake of the acts themselves." (Nicomachean Ethics, VI, xii, 7-8)

Hexis is the character, the ēthos, which the individual forms on the basis of psychosomatic necessity through the potential of the consciously initiated habit, ethos.

---

13. For this key concept in my philosophical works, see first and foremost (Kirkeby: 1994), and "The Philosophy of Selfcessity" (Kirkeby: 1996).
14. Concerning the event, Heidegger says in his lecture, "Der Satz der Identität" "Das Wort Ereignis meint hier nicht mehr das, was wir sonst irgendein Geschehnis, ein Vorkommnis nennen. Das Wort ist jetzt als singulare tantum gebraucht. Was es nennt, ereignet sich nur in der Einzahl, nein, nicht einmal mehr in einer Zahl, sondern einzig." (Heidegger: 1957, p.25). "Singulare" is a grammatical term meaning "the singular (number)". "Tantum" is an intensifying adverb. That is: "the singular (number) to an intense degree". It is probably from this that Deleuze construes his term for the event in "Logique de sens", "eventum tantum" (Deleuze: 1990).

"We may then take it as established that virtue has to do with pleasure and pains, that the actions which produce it are those which increase it, and also, if differently performed, destroy it, and that the actions from which it was produced are also those in which it is exercised." (Ibid. II, iii, 11)

What is decisive in this regard is the difficult relationship between necessity, contingency, and freedom.

The first layer of necessity in human action is the hereditary aptitudes. They comprise a causal level, which the Stoics would later point out, placed every action in a causal chain. But in relation to the normative demand which is virtue and which is inherent in the ideal of the good life, of **eudaimonia**, the biological hardware is contingent. Freedom consists in **wanting** to conquer this contingency by intervening in the necessity which it veils.

This takes place by the individual slowly building up his or her ability to judge situations on the basis of the good, by doing what is good. There is an interaction here, a spiral of reinforcement. Because each time a human being has done what is good, he or she has become better at understanding what it consists of, specifically in the individual situation, and at the same time finds it easier to control the whole of his or her physical-psychological complex against the good act. It is precisely this self-made skill that lies in the dianoetical virtue, **phronēsis**, and its accompanying capacity for deliberation, **bouleusis**, and the choice of the right and the good, which is described in Book IV of the "Nicomachean Ethics". Phronēsis is the virtue of contingency, the virtue that maintains the good life as a goal in the midst of the changes and unpredictability that life brings. Aristotle remarks dryly about phronēsis:

"But no one deliberates (bouleuetai) about things that cannot vary ('mē endechomenōn'), nor about things not within his power to do." (The Nicomachean Ethics, VI, v, 3. 1140a)

But phronēsis is a special activity that belongs to the type of modus of action where unlike in **technē** action does not have a purpose extraneous to itself.

Phronēsis is not science (epistēmē)

"because matters of conduct admit of variation; and not Art (technē), because doing and making are generically different, since making aims at an end distinct from the act of making, whereas in doing the end cannot be other than the act itself; doing well is in itself the end." (Ibid. VI, v, 3)

As an ideal for action, phronēsis expresses both a spontaneity and what could be called "post-reflectivity", which can only be understood as the relation of **practical reflectivity** to itself. It is the interaction of hexis with hexis – for the sake of hexis.

An understanding of this statement about phronēsis would seem to imply that this naturalness in the "heart" of action, in its own relation to itself through space and time, must be understood as meaning that action as activity relates to itself. Thus, phronēsis realizes the inherent essence of action. It must imply that this "itself" is a non-reflective reason, that is, hexis. This is confirmed by what Aristotle says about phronēsis when the concept is first presented.

In the first place, he ties it to doxa, to experience and knowledge which are imperfect, which deal with the world of the senses, as it is later called (VI, viii, 9).

In the second place he says:

"But yet Prudence (phronēsis) is not a rational (logon) quality merely, as is shown by the fact that a purely rational faculty can be forgotten, whereas a failure in Prudence is not a mere lapse of memory." (Ibid. VI, v, 8)

In other words, phronēsis has grown into the landscape between soma and psyche. This is further confirmed when Aristotle pronounces his famous words about phronēsis, where he contrasts it with epistēmē as axiomatic activity:

"... while Prudence deals with the ultimate particular thing, which cannot be apprehended by Scientific Knowledge (epistēmē), but only by perception (aisthēsis): not the perception of the special senses, but the sort of intuition whereby we perceive that the ultimate figure in mathematics is a triangle; for there, too, there will be a stop. But the term perception applies in a fuller sense to mathematical intuition than to Prudence; the practical intuition of the latter belongs to a different species." (Ibid. VI, viii, 9)

The whole passage is to be interpreted as meaning that phronēsis is a mental skill that can perceive patterns in the sensed world that are more than both sensation and apophantic activity. Similarities with the Epicurean and Stoic concepts of epibolē and prolēpsis would seem to be clear here. Epibolē, which Wilhelm of Moerbeke translates as "intuitio" during The Middle Ages, means "instant insight", in contrast to discursively formed insight (diexodikos logos). And prolēpsis means "anticipatio". This originates in Epicurean philosophy where it denotes an experience-based visual image (eidōlon) which makes conception of new situations possible. But it is taken over by the Stoics and also means "pre-conceptual knowledge" – which characterizes the child – and thus an experience of the self through self-observation (synaisthēsis) that makes ethics possible (including the creation of the image of God). These concepts stress precisely the role played by re-collection in understanding new situations (we shall return to "intuition" and "anticipation" as two of our managerial virtues).

This stop involved in phronēsis (Prudence), "for there, too, there will be a stop", is actually the horizon of lived time that does not merely stop the reduction of concepts to axioms negatively by means of self-contradiction, but positively by means of certainty.

But let us return to this spiral of reinforcement between the choice of the good and habituation to experience through the spectacles of the good life. By this a level of causal framework conditions is constructed that makes freedom possible by confronting contingency, both the inner, physically and psychologically, and the outer, that of the situations and the others (Pohlenz: 1992, p.106).

Aristotle formulates it in this unsurpassed way in Book III of the "Nicomachean Ethics":

> "If then, as is said, our virtues are voluntary (hekousioi) (and in fact we are in a sense ourselves partly the cause of our moral dispositions (hexeōn), and it is our having a certain character that makes us set up an end of a certain kind), it follows that our vices are voluntary also; they are voluntary in the same manner as our virtues.
>
> We have now discussed in outline the virtues in general, having indicated their genus (namely, that it is a mean, and a disposition), and having shown that they render us apt to do the same actions as those by which they are produced, and to do them in the way in which right reason (orthos logos) may enjoin; and that they depend on ourselves (hoti ef' hēmin) and are voluntary (hekousioi).
>
> But our dispositions (hexeis) are not voluntary in the same way as are our actions (praxeis). Our actions we can control from beginning to end, and we are conscious of them at each stage. With our dispositions on the other hand, though we can control their beginnings, each separate addition to them is imperceptible, as is the case with the growth of a disease; though they are voluntary in that we were free to employ our capacities in the one way or the other." (III, v, 20-22)

Virtue is such a disposition.

According to Aristotle, we are free to create ourselves in the image of the good. We can teach ourselves commitment through reflective maintenance of the correct acts.

We were presented with an aporia of Western thought: that the person who does the good must act out of a disposition beyond reflective thought, and that this disposition must have been created by this very reflective thought through a reflective choice (proairesis). Although Aristotle elaborates **on the background of** this aporia, he does not try to solve it. Why should we?

We are now able to define the phenomenon of **virtue**:

A virtue is a form of human praxis actualized by hexis, "the good character", and using phronēsis, "wisdom", where acting has no subject outside the passion of acting itself, and where the essence of this acting is the absolute good.

Phrased with another central concept of this book: a virtue means in its essence an absolute relation to "The Fourth" in thought and action.

This is, of course, an ideal, a "regulative idea". It describes a continuum going from virtues of management where there still is a definite end of acting, to the virtues of leadership where the full realization occurs when the ultimate good action is done for its own sake only. But most virtues must, due to the nature of practical life, lay in the middle of this continuum, where one tries to find a balance between means and ends. The ideal of virtue shall shape this balance, and prevent that any end should be able to justify the means.

An action done only for its own sake shall often, in its relation to other persons, be identical to an example. When he depicts the life of Socrates, in his "Memorabilia", I, ii,3, Xenophon says:

"And yet not once did he profess to be a teacher of virtue; still, being so obviously virtuous himself, he made those who spent time with him hope that by acting like him they too would become virtuous."[15]

However, even though this distinction between universal virtues and special virtues is of great importance to Management Philosophy, it does not appear to present a type of problem that is able to find a solution. Management and leadership are ways to exist that shall forever comprise the dilemma between time and eternity, between the profane and the sacred space, between the duties to the world of means and ends, and the world of the absolute. Perhaps one could speak of a "trilemma" too, between the management of material processes, the leading of people, and the responsibility to oneself.

8.4. Universal versus Professional Virtues

First and foremost it seems almost impossible to communicate the concept of a set of universal virtues, e.g., the passion of duty, the uncompromising love of our neighbour, and hence to make this responsibility concrete, in a social setting where virtuous behaviour and devotion to duty are not the general norms – where these are totally lacking virtue might even entail tragedy.

Providing motivation for everyone to develop the normatively right hexis demands, in other words, a special kind of culture. But culture cannot be constructed, and can only be controlled with the price of its heart.

It is only against the background of a culture where the good manager is a good person as a matter of course, where it goes without saying that independent of pro-

---

15. Quoted from Nehamas: 1999, p.27.

fession and position the individual tries to perfect himself as a human being, that organizational structures and managerial practices can be developed in this direction. Here, the business community, the public, and the individual, must work towards the same goals.

Aristotle depicted his "dianoetical virtues" in the "Nicomachean Ethics": nous, epistēmē, technē, phronēsis and sophia. These virtues overrided the distinction between universal and professional virtues. The virtue of **technē** attests to that.

Plato's virtues were of a more universal kind, and The Stoic philosopher, Chrysippos (281/277-208/204), specified those classical four virtues, prudence (phronēsis), temperance (sōphrosynē), courage (andreia), and justice (dikaiosynē) – these also meant a lot to Aristotle – in the following way:

Prudence:	deliberation, being well-advised, presence of mind, practical intelligence, being focussed, skill in disclosing means.
Temperance:	love of order, decency, modesty.
Courage:	asceticism, perseverance in pursuing what one has acknowledged to be right, trustworthiness, magnanimity, fearlessness and vigour.
Justice:	gentleness, beneficence, piety towards the community and tolerance.

(Pohlenz: 1992, p.126).

Is this catalogue of social, and probably universal, virtues, able to express the special kind of normativity that has to be the objective of organizational development and managerial practice?

What could be the alternative? Are we able to give an alternative catalogue, that of the special virtues framed by the managerial **technē**?

Here it must be obvious from what was said already that the genuine virtues of leadership come very close to general virtues. However, they must have some characteristics of their own when they still should be virtues of leadership, not to mention management. So let us be humble and begin with the managerial virtues.

Now we must face the peculiar problem of whether there should be more, or even many, virtues, that cannot be seen as separated from the technē of management, but must be named "virtues" after all? "Punctuality", "boldness", "the inclination for compromise", "goal-directedness", even "severity" and "the ability to see through", seem to be able to serve as examples here, but this is mistaken. They are all too much bound to the managerial technē.

So we have to ask the following questions:

a.   Is it possible to ask for a definite technē of management?
b.   What are the virtues of this technē?
c.   Does this give us the right to talk about an area of philosophy with its own field
     of knowledge and with its own canons of action: Management Philosophy?

In the following exposition I shall generally abstract from types of firms as a factor
in the determination of the managerial technē. I do not develop systematically ana-
lytic distinctions of "managerial types" on the basis of concepts like "big company",
"medium-sized company", or "high-technology firm", but of course I refer to types
and sizes of firms when dealing with managerial problems. Nor do I apply types of
organizations as differing settings of the demands to managerial virtues. I simply
develop an ideal type of managerial virtues, the fulfillment of which are the virtues
of leadership, and claim its validity for any firm and any organization.

The technē of management can only be characterized in a critical way by Management Philosophy: as we noticed in Part I of this book the ideal type of management is in its essence strategic. So, the technē of management must be dissolved
into the hexis of leadership. However, the way in which the leader may react to the
demands of the production process, and hence, to the needs, to the weaknesses and
powers of other people, must definitely relate to a technē; primarily it must relate
to the technē of preserving the firm. A successful leader might thus be judged to
have acted merely strategically, even if he deliberately has tried to avoid strategy.

When the functional view of managerial roles is accepted uncritically, it is most
likely that the normative aspect will be placed "around" this core of functionality.
Normativity shall then be identical to narrow codices of morality. Normativity will
be about legitimate means to canonized ends – ends whose rationality are rarely
doubted; or normativity shall even be about following the book, and in the last instance, most often, the law. Legal demands, and hence, legitimizations, take the
place of the moral ones. However, this would destroy the Radical Normative perspective on management and leadership.

The problem is, of course, that a leader has to be a manager in relation to the
practical tasks. But he does not have to transform himself totally into the shape of
the manager, he just has to be a leader, and a manager too.

The crux of the matter is to be able to combine two perspectives that are never
able to form a unity. This means the ability **to exist** within a paradox. Neither to
forget the claims of efficiency, profits, development, and adaption, nor to forget to
pay attention to "The Fourth". This means first and foremost that normativity shall
never be a strategic project, as is sometimes rather obvious when people speak
about ethics in business.

Management Philosophy deals with the game between the strategic behaviour
and the challenge to abolish strategy which we called the movement between virtues of management and virtues of leadership. Management covers this interregnum as its field. It is an interregnum that is also an intermission, a non-existing

place (in Greek, **u-topia**), or phrased by the perhaps most apt metaphor, a movable place, a spotlight.

Management Philosophy relates to a field of social action that is shaped by the opposition between strategy, tactics, and moral or even ethical behaviour; it is the sphere of paradox. As long as societies exist that are based on individual rights and individual duties, based on the competition among autonomous economic units, on the network of antagonistic groups and their vested interests, and on an all-encompassing structure of mediation or even of reconciliation, this real paradox shall never be resolved. The gestures of extending the scope of signification inherent in concepts like "stakeholder", the gestures of making ethics more and more pragmatic, shall also make ethics more and more bureaucratic. Thus it might strengthen the aporia on the level of concrete and even delicate social actions, but most importantly, in the heart of the individual.

It is not the task of theory on the abstract level to abolish what appears as hard necessity in social reality. Rather, it is its task to insist on it.

CHAPTER 9

The Virtues of Management and Leadership

A leader is a person executing managerial functions, but who considers his identity as a human being far more important. However, this latter identity cannot be conceptualized through a reference to "social virtues" alone, as Francis Fukuyama believes:

> "The social virtues, including honesty, reliability, cooperativeness, and a sense of duty to others, are critical for incubating the individual ones, however, and have received considerable less attention in discussions of the subject" (Fukuyama: 1996, p.43).

Fukuyama is right, of course, in this observation of the reciprocal relation between social and individual virtues. However, the virtues mentioned are not all at the same level of epistemological and ethical discourse: virtues proper for employees and genuine managerial virtues mingle with virtues pointing towards leadership.

"Cooperativeness" is not the same as a virtue to the employee as it is to management; and the duties of relatively autonomous persons are not the same as the duties of the relatively heteronomous ones. Hence, "reliability", and even "honesty", are dependent on person, role, and situation. Fukuyama is right in observing the importance of the social virtues in creating the basis of "spontaneous sociability and organizational innovation" (ibid. p.48). So we cannot escape the acknowledgement that both the manager and the leader have to reflect the social virtues in their behaviour, though, at different levels.

Firms have long understood the importance of social virtues and of managerial virtues to the organization. Hewlett-Packard chooses potential top-managers through a catalogue of 26 criteria before they are sent to courses. The importance of potential leadership, however, is problematic.

Following Gary Yukl, it is not possible to distinguish an unambiguous set of "traits" characteristic to the good manager (Yukl: 1994, p.280). However, some salient characteristics indispensable to the effective manager might be emphasized, such as "self-assurance", "the power of speech", "the faculty of persuasiveness", "the ability to remember details", among others; but these traits are not virtues of leadership, even if they might be a function of leading. A virtue cannot be characterized functionally, even if virtuous behaviour is able to integrate functional aspects – which it is, of course. This should be clear if one remembers that virtues grow into personality forming a **hexis**, a partly self-created moral character.

Not least military historians such as Barnett (Barnett: 1963, p.10) have tried to show "the decisive effect of human character on history". But here we too often find rather shallow analytical distinctions from psychology. Dixon (Dixon: 1976), for example, tries to demonstrate that military fiascoes were bound to an "authoritarian personality", and no doubt, some distinctive traits recur in the actions of the leaders important to these events. This psychological typology, even if philosophers and sociologists such as Hannah Arendt, Herbert Marcuse, Th.W. Adorno, and Max Horkheimer seem to support it at certain levels, appears to me to have too much empirical inaccuracy and shallowness, to give the amount of information that Management Philosophy needs. On the contrary, the legacy of the Aristotelian ethics is to set the concept of character free of (everyday) psychology.

However, it is important that this mental complex, "character", cultivates an ability to watch every detail of one's own behaviour in order to be able to change it. Even if this mode of registration is emotional and not "just" a cognitive, intellectual capacity, it entails the problematic of **fulfilling** a virtue, and hence, the promises of one's character, or to betray them. The last item was phrased by R.L. Katz in 1955, in an article in **Harvard Business Review**, bearing the title "Skills of an effective administrator":

"Real skill in working with others must become a natural, continuous activity, since it involves sensitivity not only at times of decision making but also in the day-by-day behaviour of the individual ... Because everything a leader says and does (or leaves unsaid or undone) has an effect on his associates, his true self will, in time, show through. Thus, to be effective, his skill must be naturally developed and unconsciously, as well as consistently, demonstrated in the individual's very action."

The leader must be able to relate critically to his own role. He must be able to see through the strategic functionalism of managerial virtues.

To establish a catalogue of virtues oscillating between, and stimulating, the transformation from management to leadership might seem risky for many reasons. One important risk is to fall victim to historicism. This would mean that our choice of virtues on the one side had to be accidental, and on the other side too much of an extrapolation from earlier societies to the one we live in now. Both weaknesses might be due to philosophical sloppiness. The first one documents a lack of due methodological reflection. The other reveals gaps in hermeneutic competence. However, it might be possible to fall victim to the neglect of history too, just claiming some virtues to be eternally valid.

These three failures might be escaped by stating that the six virtues presented here are part of a socio-historically motivated utopia.

To catch ideas in the Greek store of concepts would seem more obvious when one reflects that our thinking is a product of those very concepts. Of course, this causal tie prevents us from returning to these concepts as something original – one cannot leap over one's own shadow – but it does not prevent us from using them to get far deeper into our own way of thinking, and perhaps even "feeling".

What we are able to escape by using Greek philosophical concepts is the immediate danger of "empiricism", of generalizing from socially salient attitudes, ideologies, manners, and from pragmatic and strategic positions, to categories of Management Philosophy. But we are also enriched in another peculiar way by this "regression to the future" by way of Greek concepts. The Greek society, by far an ideal society, exposed perspectives on the social nature of humans still out of reach because of our "scientific" optics. Body and mind melt together in this universe, and so do micro- and macro-cosmos; you shall find considerations of reason in all its aspects, not least a reason obedient and utterly sensitive to nature, both the outer and the inner as well. However, we do not have to skip rationality when we try to explain human behaviour. We just have to develop another kind of reason much more sensitive to time and place. Here we should be able to learn from Immanuel Kant, too, when he develops his theories of the beautiful. Because Kant does not betray reason, even if he abandons the intellect, and, hence, rationality, as the subject of experience. But he refines it, making reason delicate. Kant acknowledges that the very phenomenon of irrationalism only exposes the coarse mesh of reason, and that hence the irrational must be conceived of as the very result of a special reason and of its all too universal application.

In the period between 500 and 200 B.C., the Greeks had an opportunity to experience sides of the social, and to conceptualize them in a way that could provide guidance to our way of thinking about the relation between the individual and society. In the first place it forms an alternative to a thinking pervaded by the narrow rationality of technology and science. In the second place it can confront us with generations of intellectuals totally liberated from the need to work, and of any work ethic, too. The **technē** was conceptualized by people who did not often associate with artisans, but perhaps with a few artists.

The Greeks exemplified an ethos whose social pivotal point was a unique feeling of solidarity towards society. Identities were not created through work, and hardly through "private" occupation, but rather through the ways to act in public, be it as a philosopher, a politician, or an officer.

In the Greek fora an enviable communication took place, involving all of the free citizens. Not more than 100.000 people in the city-state of Athens, they were able to establish a rather high level of personal contacts. A working democracy, a direct democracy, abolishing – to a certain degree in the bloom of the Greek society – the differences based on ownership and income, yet, never the differences based on talent and education.

The "polis" was a society based on slavery and, for that reason, difficult to idealize. But this society might, like a lighthouse in the land of apparently lived through dreams, cast a lightening from behind, because the Greeks conceived of the state as an "ethical community" having the main purpose to realize virtues.[16] The state was

---

16. "The conception of the State as an ethical association for the attainment of virtue involves a conception of the relations of the State to the individual different from most which are current today" (Barker: 1970, p.7).

not seen as a necessary, but heavy, load on the individual, it was experienced as the genus of which the individual was the species. Solidarity with the public, a "secular piety", was the precondition for Greek thought. Individual responsibility towards the community, even care, was the axiom of social action – in the conceptual world of Socrates called "epimeleia". Greek political theory does not speak about rights, but about duties.

These duties were primarily within the aristocracy, but probably diffused into the whole martial society. They were exemplified as virtues – the already mentioned temperance, courage, wisdom, and justice. Their opposition is a passion that cannot be controlled, **epithymia**, in Latin **concuspiscentia**, licentiousness, specified through our seven deadly sins.

These virtues are aristocratic, they belong to a society in a permanent preparedness for war. However, to a certain degree Karl Marx's dictum that man's identity is created through his work might be challenged. This Greek society was able to support a vivid culture and a general education at a very high level lead by people to whom free time and a vivid sensation of the social bond were the pivot of identity, not the mutual experiences from conditions of work and the challenges of their peculiar technē.

These virtues are still relevant to any manager and to any leader because they are important to any human being. But they need a differentiation, and even more than was done in the last chapter. They need to be supplemented with virtues peculiar to the functions of managing and of leading in an industrial society shaped by information technology and a bureaucratic state apparatus.

The catalogue of virtues now presented shall not be conceived of as the minimum set of necessary managerial virtues, nor as the maximum set. Others might replace them, and more might be chosen.

In the preceding parts of this book these virtues have already been touched upon. I have tried to anticipate their necessity. They combine the managerial technē and absolute normativity. They bring these two different worlds into contact, but they do not pretend that their inherent opposition can be cancelled.

However, though convincing someone of the necessity of virtue per se to management and to leadership might be a surmountable task, deducing the indispensability of exactly six virtues, and the very six virtues now presented, seems to be a rather daring venture. The six virtues must be seen as a grand hypothesis, and as a suggestion of how to read one's experience.[17] To this must be added that these virtues do not enjoy the consistency, or coherency, established when concepts belong

---

17. A remark is appropriate here: the perspective of Radical Normativity makes it very difficult to exemplify the virtues by referring to dead or living managers or leaders. I do not find even a moderate use of such a procedure proper. However, a few examples will be given, but often from politics, or as prototypes, without names. However, this procedure does fit the image of the genuine leader suggested here: he/she is anonymous, a humble servant of his/her case.

to the same school of philosophy. They must create the picture of a consistency of their own produced by patterns in the field of knowledge itself: managerial and leadership practice subjected to the right of human integrity.

1. Euboulia

The first virtue is **euboulia**.

This concept denotes a complex virtue, and a complex of virtues, too. The Greek terminology is important here, because any single English concept would fail to convey this rich meaning, and because the Greek philosophical concepts open a horizon of possible significations to our mind that is most often inaccessible to everyday consciousness. The old word presents us to a new way of thinking. But the use of the word "new" is not meant to be a gesture of appeal to our weakness towards the brand new that nobody possessed before. On the contrary, it focuses the etymological connotation of "new", "nun" in the German, "nyn" in the Greek, namely, "now": that which is here forever.

The concept is one of Plato's, signifying the ability to deliberate in practical matters, both relating to one's own private life and to public life. It denotes the ability to get on in social reality. Thus, it comprehends speech and action. It is the quintessence of the social virtue, and as "epistēmē", eternal knowledge, it is placed in the top of the hierarchy of cognitive capacities. Plato presents us with the concept rather early in his opus, in the dialogue "Protagoras", where Socrates is confronted with the famous Sophist by the same name (Protagoras, 318 e 5-319 a 2).[18]

Plato talks about our relation to the state, to the "civitas" – as the Romans called it – but also to one's own management of one's house, called **oikonomia**, from **oikos** (house, household), and **nomos** (custom, rule, law). The concept shows us "economy" as a discourse on duty to oneself and to society, not as a "science". In the famous dialogue "The Republic", Plato emphasizes **euboulia** as a virtue proper to the philosophical élite in his ideal state, whose duty was to judge for the state as a whole, rather than simply to advice in particular political or legal matters.[19] For Plato euboulia must, as an epistēmē, be very close to the ideal form of knowledge about the eternal, **sophia**, and to practical wisdom, **phronēsis**, as well. Aristotle, on the contrary, does not estimate this virtue as being at that high level of insight, but conceives of it as a concept denoting the still unsatisfied search for knowledge (Nicomachean Ethics, op.cit. 1142, B,12).

However, the concept of euboulia could very well refer both to a virtue consist-

---

18. Plato (1956): Protagoras and Meno. translated by W.K.C. Gutrie. Penguin Classics, Harmondsworth.
19. Plato (1969): The Republic. The Loeb Edition. Transl. by P. Shorey. Heinemann, London. 428, b, 6, and d, 1.

ing in both the ability to think over totality, to deliberate upon the whole, and, hence, to deliberate on deliberation; and to deliberate upon the Socratic attitude towards knowledge as a process, as a search unable to be finished. Euboulia then, invokes the concept of **horizon**, of the limit, of distinction, and of definition – of the deferment of authoritative knowledge, but of the corroboration of its existence too.

But leadership can only provisionally deny authority. This is important. The appearance of truth in such and such a shape can be postponed, but not the exis-tence of truth as such. Euboulia is the virtue of wise postponement of the final judgment, and at the very same time a spectacular arranging of the discourses on the true and right action.

Then, euboulia is the most considerate arranging of the voices expressing devo-tion to the "mutual place", to society, and hence, articulating the content of duties which means to reveal both the just intentions and the strategic betrayals involved in pursuing them. The way to distinguish here must be acquired through having an eye to the future.

Euboulia displays the courage and the obligation to judge any intention and any opinion without knowing the authoritative truth. The humble will to be the au-thority oneself, that is, without being in possession of the promised certainty.

Euboulia contains the ability to view something against a new background, and the ability to see the incipient inside the old. In a way, it is an old man's virtue, but a lenient old man covering the righteous rage of youth. A gentle rebel. A mother, a nurse, a lioness. Anger on behalf of others. The leader testing his strength in this virtue is anything else but cool. He is passionate, but his passion is bright.

Euboulia applies reason, but it does not base itself on reason. It does not prac-tice any ideal of meta-reflection, no "planning of planning".[20] In other words, it can articulate what the Austrian author, Robert Musil, called "the sense of the possible" in his great, unfinished novel "Der Mann ohne Eigenschaften", published between 1952 and 1957.

For very good reasons it is not possible to construct an algorithm of the sense of the possible. In its essence it is the non-algorithmic per se. One could, of course, try to substantiate it with examples of people or situations manifesting such a faculty in order to build a prototype. But the sense of the possible abolishes strategies. It faces the leader, demanding him to pose himself the question about what the im-portant message sounded like, the message sent to him from his own experience by doing, a message about the possible – and hence, after all, about the real.

Like the other virtues, this one also demands a peculiar sensibility, a certain mood, a being "in tune", in a indefinable harmony with oneself.

Euboulia ought not to be identified with intuition, nor with expertise of any kind, even if it presupposes much experience. It is a far more complex attitude,

---

20. The program of the "planning of planning" was presented in Georg Steiner's book "Plan-ning. What Every Manager Must Know" from the end of the Seventies.

involving both devotion and distance from the matter and from oneself. It comprehends responsibility, and never innocence nor boldness. Euboulia centres around actions expressing a solidarity towards the community, placing public interests before one's own. This kind of commitment might be called a "secular piety". The Greeks named it "eusebeia" (or "epimeleia"): a feeling of piety towards the mutual, beyond any care of oneself.

From this detached passion spring the most thorough deliberations. The leader plays with his cards open. Hence, he is able to create new standards of leadership through his example. Such a new standard could be the denial to give in to any signals from the so-called "Financial Analysts". On behalf of the potential shareholders, the phantom-tribunal of gods for ever young, they manifest a comfortable "sense of reality". They expose a lack of every trait of normativity. They reinforce us to stick to a kind of "reality" of which only a few people can profit: a world in which capital is the actor, not people. At the same time, through their behaviour, they intensify the trends they only pretend to read. The real leader will not let himself be judged by the shareholders, not even by the board. He shall practice euboulia: the concern of the public, the employees, the consumers and the future. He shall not let himself be subject to an evaluation through figures; be it turnover, operating incomes, cash-flow, or stock returns. He shall defy the spreadsheet of evaluation built on a prognosis of turnover. He knows that a company first and foremost is a mutual space, something we own together, and which owes us something before it is free to grant any rights to private people and their interests.

In other words, at any time he must be able to put his position on the line.

2. Enthusiasm and Euphoria

The other virtue in our catalogue is the faculty of being able to commit oneself to, and to engage with, the ability of being intensely dedicated. Even if this virtue has been a part of everyday vocabulary for centuries, and has been the subject of an extensive interest on the side of practice and theory of management and organization, it has not become trivial. It is simply indispensable to management and to leadership.

The concept of **enthusiasm**, "placed in the heart of the deity", "admitted into" and, hence, "absorbed by the divine presence", was in the Greek tradition often relegated to the realm of poetry; the "enthusiastic" poet was the unconscious victim of the voice of the muse. Plato introduces us to the critique of this poetical trance – although he is also mentioned as the first one to put it into words. He emphasizes that the philosopher's enthusiasm is the only worthy one. Enthusiasm is in the dialogue, "Phaedrus", an aspect of "the fourth kind of madness", the madness of the true philosopher, like Socrates (Phaedrus, op.cit. 249D). He speaks through inspiration, like a poet, because the truth does not belong to him. But he is no prophet. He is too humble for that.

So enthusiasm refers to a commitment that definitely reduces the significance of one's own person, of one's own personality. The committed leader actually allows himself to be absorbed by the case, and through this identification, the case might happen to belong to him too. Like Nelson Mandela or Martin Luther King, he becomes the emblem of a project – to mention two of the most obvious cases.

When commitment becomes very intense devotion, it shall often display traits distinctive to another mental state described by the Greeks, **euphoria**. Whereas enthusiasm is at times very hard to feel, because the muse heaves and struggles with you, or because inspiration does not pay the wanted visit so you must get on by yourself, euphoria just carries you away. However, today's connotation of an uncontrolled excitement did not inhabit this concept during the period of Hellenism. To the Greek Stoics (there were Roman Stoics too) it used to denote the elegant movement of dancing, and in Chrysippos it referred to a human being's periods of increased productivity.

The original sense of the word "euphoria" was "to carry the unpleasant with an easy mind". This makes it possible to emphasize the power of our mind to transform reality, the will to re-create reality. This power is the core of a **poietical** sense.[21] Hence, let us conceive of euphoria as a concept that refers to a state of mind where your power of commitment is so great as to try to create reality. It is a peculiar sense of reality, a "reality-sense", because it moves our criteria of what the concept "reality" might actually mean.

Like the "possibility-sense", this "reality-sense" articulates the ability of being able to see otherness, the possible, and hence, to perceive the real in the actual, to read it from the letters of the hard facts.[22] But euphoria does not need to be identical to obsession. Even if it cannot be hard-headed, it could be sober-minded, "realistic" in a new sense: the unwillingness to accept brute facts as facts at any price.

---

21. The concept of **po-i-ēsis**, the basis of "poetics", is shaped in the "Poetics" of Aristotle. It refers to the ability of creating in the arts, but a creating without any authentic imitation as the ideal. Through **poiēsis** something new is introduced into the world, transforming reality. However, to the Greeks before Plato and Aristotle, the concept meant "acting" too, and was identified with the concept of **praxis**, while the two philosophers distinguish clearly between **poiēsis** and **praxis**. Where the subject of **praxis** is virtue (aretē), of **poiesis** it is artistic skill (**technē**). To the former, knowledge is the most important, to the latter practice. Praxis is valid due to the moral character of the one acting, **poiēsis** is valid through the qualities of the product. By the way, in postmodernism the two concepts are almost melting together: **praxis** is **poiēsis**, we create the world to which we relate as if it were real. Then let us create the world for real!

22. Micklethwait & Wooldridge, op.cit. say by the way:
    "In many of the best companies the chairman is responsible for creating a culture of obsession: an obsessive himself, he recruits other obsessives and encourages them to

Both enthusiasm and euphoria are contagious. First and foremost they are transmitted through example; as managerial virtues they deal with the ability to transmit. But this transmission must be able to be controlled. Where the manager uses organizational instruments to control commitment, the leader shall transmit a special kind of enthusiasm and euphoria that is thrown into relief by radical normativity. His enthusiasm and his euphoria shall release the sense of duty, while enforcing it.

But to release the sense of duty cannot mean a "duty" conceived of in a narrow sense. Hence, it is not any case that ought to be embraced by the concepts of enthusiasm or euphoria. Since euphoria must be seen as a function of enthusiasm, that enthusiasm should be able to call forth euphoria, rather than vice versa, let us concentrate on enthusiasm in this regard. Then it must be realized that to Management Philosophy, enthusiasm is a **transcendent** state of mind, i.e., it must always relate to something bigger than the group, the firm, the business, and even the nation, the people. Enthusiasm must be able to transgress the field of economic phenomena. It must be a virtue with a universal horizon related to mankind. It must relate to the future and to the past, not to momentary demands.

It must be obvious that the domain of problems touched on now are very difficult. Because it cannot be avoided that enthusiasm might be fooled, or put otherwise, enthusiasm cannot feign innocence. The only way in which enthusiasm can claim justification is through its relation to "The Fourth".

Both the manager and the leader can show enthusiasm in matters limited by short-term goals, but the real leader cannot withhold enthusiasm in matters characterized by any short-sighted strategy whatsoever. He is forced to seriously focus product quality, i.e., to answer for all the effects of a product in relation to the near as well as to the far future: how is it going to influence the development of markets as an end product or as an intermediary one as well; how is it going to influence nature, and the creation of customs concerning the care of nature; how is its production going to influence work-conditions, also in relation to the productions of the raw-materials used – to wit managers have increasingly refused to use products produced in totalitarian political systems, or by ecologically irresponsible conditions, as has been the case with the country Burma or with the company Shell.

But a leader has to reflect yet another limit to his enthusiasm here: he has to be

---

devote their lives to their products ... However an obsession without a target can end up as wasted energy. Hence the importance of vision ... Vision is the idea of how the market will look (or could be made to look) in the future which inspires and focuses workers." (Op.cit. p.150) The two authors quote Charles Handy for the following critique of the new tayloristic management strategy, "Re-engineering" (ibid. p.39): "blowing organisations apart is not conducive to a state of commitment and **euphoria** ... (emphasis mine. OFK)". The quotation is from "Charles Handy sees the future", FORTUNE, 31 October 1994.

conscious of the way a product will influence the construction of social reality. Any product is a building block, and hence, a unit of signs, through which the future essence of humanity is constructed; because we experience our essence and hence, our possibilities, through the horizon of our needs. But needs – within the very wide limits of an anthropologically given minimum – are shaped, refined, legitimized, and developed, through products and hence, through demands. The leader must be a pioneer, but not of any lucrative production, not of any beautiful design. Like Gailbraith argued many years ago, he must think in a radically different way in relation to mainstreams. He must be utterly suspicious of the surface logic of trends. He must not let rationality run away with him.

In a world where the firm increasingly is becoming the forum of socialization, becoming the centre of lifetime and hence, of the life-world, the leader must develop a clear vision of which kind of humanity he shall contribute to. He must take responsibility for the way in which future generations will be able to experience themselves, and conceive of a possible self. He must not think solely about his employees, about their skills, faculties, education, about organizational learning, and about corporate knowledge. He must reflect which kind of people the consumers of his products might come to be – and he must not be satisfied with the shallow talk of "life styles". In other words, he must learn to conceive of quite another content of "strategy", of a "counter-strategic" thinking that might very often be "counter-factual". He must reflect the concept of "stakeholder" in a radical normative way.

He must not even think "politically" in relation to his consumers, and try not to view them through the optics of power. Enthusiasm must first and foremost be solidarity with the social as such – the personal urge towards a new mutuality.

The **enthusiast** is an "idealist" in the old sense of the word that eliminates the fantastic, but emphasizes the matter-of-fact-attitude proper to the one who dares to see the possible beyond all the fair promises of fortunes and victories. Such an attitude might be extremely hard to bear, and it might easily destroy him, but after all it is the only attitude worthy of respect. Should he be able, then, to stay the course, it will earn him that respect which will create the real **enthusiasm** and the genuine **euphoria** among the co-directed.

3. Hypomonē

The third virtue is **hypomonē**. It reflects the leader's ability to be patient. But this is an active kind of patience, a kind of courage, stamina, endurance. Hypomonē also refers to the ability to influence other people to endure.

Aristotle introduces the concept when analyzing the properties of courage (andreia) in his "Nicomachean Ethics" (III, vi, ff). Hypomonē is indispensable to courage.

"We become temperate by abstaining from pleasures, and at the same time we are best able to abstain from pleasures when we have become temperate. And so with Courage: we become brave by training ourselves to despise and endure (hypomenein) terrors, and we shall be best able to endure terrors when we have become brave." (II, ii, 9)

Hypomonē is the opposite of opportunism. It goes well with cleverness and with prudence, but it does not use tactics for the sake of tactics. It is neither conservative, nor easy to get to promote any "just" case. It is neither grim, nor fanatic.

It is firm.

This virtue presupposes a mental detachment, a mental freedom, an attitude where the mind is self-contained. Hypomonē refers to a balance, even to a readiness for contemplation that does not stand in the way of perceiving the most delicate movements among the things and relations of the world. It is the virtue of waiting for the right insight and for the right options. But it is a virtue of tenderness, of nurturing, too. As such, it resembles the mode of the gardener.

Hypomonē belongs to courage because it does not place the personal happiness or success of the leader at the front. It is definitely a virtue of leadership, not of management. It denotes his ability to put himself at stake in the service of something higher.

Hypomonē must be the core of "self-management", and hence, of both directing oneself through temperance (sōphrosynē), and leading oneself towards the right end.

The German philosopher, Martin Heidegger, spoke about the attitude of "Gelassenheit". It means the receptiveness and sensitiveness coming from the lack of any trace of eagerness, even of expectation, the lack of any "intentionality" directed towards the world. "Der Gelassene" does not have any procedures ready at hand to decode reality. He does not anticipate his own motives, but waits for the thing to call on him. He does not decipher, he withholds interpretation. But first and foremost he does not conceptualize by way of pre-given categories and causal relations.

Pushed to extremes, this virtue implies that leadership is about more than managing somebody or something; it is about searching for the true cause. Thus, the leader does not hide his face behind doors and private secretaries, or behind experts or lawyers. He does not even hide behind the computer system, behind formalisms and procedures securing an awesome, if not menacing, anonymity.

He shall get out in the open, standing stright up, insistent and firm in the merciless spotlight.

4. Prolēpsis

The fourth virtue of our catalogue is **prolēpsis**, in Latin **anticipatio**, "anticipation". The core of this concept is epistemological in character, but it has an aspect of development psychology too: man perceives through linguistic concepts and prototypical conceptions that are innate, but have to be "filled up" with personal experience. These innate structures are able to "anticipate" concrete, situational experience. The word, and hence, the concept, as well as the plasticity of the common conception of "a thing", direct chaotic experience. The Stoics used this model to understand the development of the child's experience from a "tabula rasa" to a rich frame of knowledge into which the "logos" could eventually enter (Pohlenz: 1992, p.65ff). Introspection ("synaisthēsis") was seen as an important function of the development of prolēpsis so that the young person was able to unite with logos after the fourteenth year and create the basis of conscious use of concepts in order to search for truth.

As a virtue, prolēpsis reflects the ability to enrich common knowledge with the powers of personal experience. It denotes the play between individualism and universalism, aiming at new and important knowledge.

Prolēpsis has its origin in the philosophy of Epicurūs (341-270 B.C). It denotes the mutual reciprocity between the experience of many specimens of the same thing, or of the same situation, and a general conception of this thing, or of that situation. It is the ability to visualize. This visualizing must, of course, always take place on the basis of all too few experiences, so in a way, it has to be keen. The common conception is of some help here, but could also be a limit to insight.

If a manager must relate to the conceptual complex of "sustainability", he might visualize a bridge, but the richer his visions are, and the more concrete cases such prototypical visions are able to encompass, the better shall his capacities to take action be. However, if he is too much fixated on a few experiences with "sustainability", he shall probably not be able to acknowledge the real importance of the concept. Hence, prolēpsis is about breaking a wall between customary conceptions and too personal habits of perception. There is a critical force in this virtue, making faith in one's own experience possible.

The ability to judge situations, and hence, to create the event, is a function of prolēpsis, because you are at one and the same time forced to balance – more or less conservative – presumptions with radical hypotheses; a balance between talent and learning. In this connection we shall once more find Plato's question of whether virtue can be taught, and the related problem of the right managerial education. Here the metaphor of the balance must appear again, because practice seems indispensable to managerial skills, and must be integrated in any masters degree of management.

As a virtue, prolēpsis expresses the will to protect tradition, to adhere to the values which we have already created; to stick to social responsibility however much the fantasy might invoke new possibilities and radical interpretations of the bearings of situations.

But this virtue does indeed embrace solutions to very concrete problems of a technological and economical kind, too. It covers the concept of "inventiveness". It is obvious then, that prolēpsis also comes close to a **technē**. This aspect of anticipation as a visual projection is emphasized by Gary Hamel and C.K. Prahalad in their book "Competeting for the Future", when they try to diagnose the traits of successful firms, e.g., the ability of Motorola to visualize that possible world where the cellular telephone is taken for granted (Hamel, Prahalad: 1994).

However, it is of great importance that prolēpsis shall never be conceived of as only a technē. It must always be the result of a Radical Normativity, placing the needs of humans and the care for society as a precondition to any venture of inventiveness.

5. Epibolē

The fifth virtue of our catalogue is **epibolē**, in Latin "intuitio", i.e., intuition. The Epicureans spoke about **athroa epibolē**, "the insight in one blow", in opposition to the truth discovered in parts, little by little, **kata meros**.

Its opposition is discursive knowledge, **diexodikos logos**.

Intuition often appears in the light of this discursive reason where the intellect has left its unmistakable trace as something intangible, if not as a secret way of cognition beyond rationality. Intuition might appear as a postulate of the existence of an alternative way of acquiring knowledge.[23] However, intuition does not need to be unreasonable, imprudent or even irrational. Quite the opposite is the case. The French philosopher from the 17th century, Blaise Pascal, phrased the famous saying "The heart has got its reasons which reason does not know of." But this opposition between sense and sensibility, having such a long tradition in Western culture, is not without problems.

In the first place, there are quite a lot of ways to feel, and more than a few emotions which do not at all imply a carefulness towards their object. Often they involve quite the contrary. The extremes of emotions, desire, love, aggression, and hate, are very often appropriations of the object at a symbolic level. Hate probably wants to annihilate. Love probably wants to devour forever. Already Spinoza reminded us of the existence of three basic emotions: love, hate, and the instinct of

---

23. By the way: as we are often lacking proper words, it might be of interest that the English logician, J.H. Newman, in 1870 coined the neologism **illative sense** to describe intuitive logic. Of course, many writers have related to the concept of "intuition" recently, among others Bastick: 1982 – and many of the greatest philosophers of the past, among them Spinoza and Kant, but I shall not discuss them here.

self-preservation[24] – and this might be one reason why so many items in his famous "Ethica" remind us of Sigmund Freud. However, to Aristotle **orexis**, the instinct of self-preservation, contained dispositions like will, courage, and desire, it only combined with cognitive functions during the true way to act, and in hexis – as was shown in the preceding chapter. Perhaps then, intuition could be understood as an aspect of love, of **erōs**, not – as with later Darwinian and Marxist traditions – as a function of self-preservation through work and power. As a function of love, intuition relates to **pathos**, to the intense emotions arising between two people relating to each other. The eminent orator is able to rise emotions in the other(s) through which he shapes and directs their actions. **Pathos** is identical to a mood, and in the Greek tradition, often to the mood of weakness demonstrating the lack of ability to control your mind. Hence, it is placed in opposition to **ethos** and **ēthos**, to the habit of the strong personality and to the moral character. But **pathos** that relates to the body, both as a container of **erōs** and as a symbol of another "logos", might also be positive.

When one person in the dialogue shapes the other person's emotions he puts him into a certain "tune", this kind of mental "harmony", might release new insights because it changes attention. If we transfer the metaphor of dialogue to the working of the individual mind – as Plato did in the "Sophist" – then intuition could be conceived of as the way in which the mind "attunes" itself through the soul's dialogue with itself.

Concepts like "pathos", "the language of the heart", like "the will", "desire", "courage" and "love", are all concepts invoking "the body", and hence the conception of an individuality that is not accessible to discursive logic. Intuition often appears as an innate faculty, and, hence as the work of contingency. It cannot be taught, it is closely tied to a learning by doing.

Intuition seems to refer to a type of cognition beyond any rule-following, and thus beyond a direct control of the intellect. Of course, there are practices, mostly very personal, that can increase the possibility of the intuitive lightening. But intuition appears as "something that happens to one", and it is often ascribed to a special character of the left part of our brain, or to the psychology, and, hence, physiology, of women.

In intuition another kind of causality seems at play and hence, another kind of logic. Since Charles Sanders Peirce this logic has often been distinguished from "inductive" and "deductive" logic, and called "abduction". The logic of abduction has its parallel in Greek logic: Aristotle calls it "enthymēma", the core of rhetorical argumentation, the "rhetorical syllogism". It is concerned with

---

24. "Self-preservation", **conatus** in Latin, is the translation of the Greek concept of **hormē**, "instinct", "striving for something". The Greek concept of **orexis**, however, is the concept used by Aristotle to denote the principle of self-preservation. **Hormē** does not always have as good a sound, referring to lower instincts.

"endoxa", the ability to estimate, with a probabilistic and only possible, not a necessary truth.[25]

It is a kind of logic where one deduces from too few premisses.

Either the premiss is so well known that one feels it superfluous to mention it, or it cannot be stated as a proposition, or one does not know it (or know that one knows it). In the first case the "obviousness" of argumentation might very well cover strategic means.

Now, intuition might be a strictly deductive way to think where all the necessary premisses are present, but where we are too slow to recognize the process. Due to the speed of these processes "beneath the level of consciousness" we are able to be surprised by our own cognitive work – intuition is explained in this way by the Brazilian theorist of science, Mario Bunge (Bunge: 1962). But intuition might be the result of an alternative type of logic following Lukasiewics' polyvalent logic, and working with a much more rough concept of truth than the predicate calculus.

Following Peirce, an induction is a conclusion from the particular to the general, while a deduction is a conclusion from the general to the particular, but **abduction** is a conclusion from the effect to the cause. This cause can be particular or general. When Sherlock Holmes reaches the conclusion of how the murderer looks by observing the garden outside the house, he produces an **abduction** about a particular cause. When Kepler develops the hypothesis from Tycho Brahe's observation of the positions and movements of the planets that the shape of this movement must be elliptic, he produces an abduction to a general fact, to a law of nature.[26]

The crux here appears to be whether "abduction" testifies to a way of experiencing that constitutes rather firm knowledge without transforming it into propositions. This would give a special touch to the expression "where not all premisses are known", because it would mean that not all premisses could be known, and that they did not have to be knowable in the traditional sense, i.e., subject to discursive linguistic articulation.

However, what is important here is the fact that the "enthymēma", and "abduc-

---

25. Aristotle (1939/1994a): Art of Rhetoric, op.cit. I.i.11. In the "Topics" Aristotle defines "endoxa", "resting on opinion" in opposition to "epistēmē", the absolute truth, in the following way: "as "things generally admitted by all, or by most men, or by the wise, and by all or most of these, or by the most notable and esteemed" (Quoted by the translator, ibid, p.10). It ought to be mentioned that Peirce does not relate "abduction" to "enthymēmia", but to the concept of "apagōgē" in the Aristotelian logic, the last word being translated to "abductio" in Latin. Peirce's reasons might here have been that he wanted to evade the relation to rhetoric, and to stick to a firmer concept of logic.

26. I shall not address the whole discussion of the so-called "logic of scientific discovery" connected to the concept of **abduction**, and the implied criticism of Karl Popper's position. I have treated these problems extensively in other contexts. See: Peirce: 1931-35/1958; Fann: 1970; Habermas: 1968; Hanson: 1961; and Hesse: 1974.

tion", initiate a game about certainty. And as a virtue, intuition has to do with the faculty to create this certainty in oneself and in others too. Hence, intuition must also be close to courage, because it demands a kind of courage to believe in oneself – and sometimes to believe in others as well.

The secret of abduction has been sought within the ability to form analogies, and this might of course be the secret of intuition too (Miller: 1987; Hesse: 1966). But intuition and abduction both rest on opaque structures of the functioning of time within experience. However, what is of peculiar interest here, of course, is intuition apprehended as a virtue of management and even of leadership.

As a virtue, intuition has to do with the creation of solutions with a pronounced normative content to problems related to situations of great complexity, speed of processes, and with too many parameters to be accessible to reflective thought. Here the intuition of the manager has to be carried by trust on the side of the co-directed. Intuition has to convince, and it has to present itself with a certainty that is above any manipulation with assent. What is of decisive importance here is the fact that intuition relates to reality as the voice relates to the situation. The manager is a part of the situation. He is together with his "crew", and what matters is to be able to make everybody experience the situation in the same way. Intuition is the catalyst of the situation. It creates a point of condensation in the moment, in the intersection between the medians from an infinite space and an infinite time. This point is the event. Intuition anticipates the event, and must itself in a way be anticipated by it. Intuition gives the event a name, an identity without excluding the important parameters, and without cutting off the lines pointing into the future.

The real leader must be able to sense "what is going to happen". But he ought not use this ability as a sheer strategic means. He must not let himself be a victim of an opportunistic intuition, but always ask himself if he really wants what he feels so certain will occur to actually happen.

If epibolē is the art of the innovator, then it only pertains to innovations that possess a liberating power, which means a liberation from power and from ignorance.

6. Maieutic

The sixth virtue in our catalogue is **maieutikē technē**, the art of midwifery. As a virtue this art refers to Socrates' ability to stimulate another person to seek the truth, for the right and not for the wrong, for the good and not for the evil; his ability to stimulate the other person to feel an urge to find his own moral character, perhaps even his "self". The leader that practices **maieutikē technē** will stimulate a co-directed to find out for himself in which position, and through which tasks he can do his best. There should be no authoritative didactics here, but only questioning, and a healthy doubt towards the authority of the one who questions.

It was told that the father of Socrates was a sculptor, and his mother a midwife.

Both release. The former sets the form inherent in the stone free – as Rodin said. The latter delivers the baby from the woman in labour. Hence, the leader as a hodegēt must liberate the co-directed person.[27]

In Plato's dialogue, the "Theaetetus", Socrates says:

> "My art of midwifery is in general like theirs (the midwives. OFK); the only difference is that my patients are men, not women, and my concern is not with the body but with the soul that is in travail of birth. And the highest point of my art is the power to prove by every test whether the offspring of a young man's thought is a false phantom or instinct with life and truth. I am so far like the midwife, that I cannot myself give birth to wisdom; and the common reproach is true, that, though I question others, I can myself bring nothing to light because there is no wisdom in me. The reason is this: heaven constrains me to serve as a midwife, but has debarred me from giving birth. So of myself I have no sort of wisdom, nor has any discovery ever been born to me as the child of my soul. Those who frequent my company at first appear, some of them, quite unintelligent; but, as we go further with our discussions, all who are favoured by heaven make progress at a rate that seems surprising to others as well as to themselves, although it is clear that they have never learnt anything from me; the many admirable truths they bring to birth have been discovered by themselves from within. But the delivery is heaven's work and mine."[28]

Maieutic is the art of the real leader: his ability to give his co-directed the possibility to find, on their own, and in their own mind, the reason for what they do and are going to do. It is the ability to make it possible for the co-directed to choose whether to approve of, and to rally round, the program of the leader of their own free will, or to reject it.

It is a question of the co-directed's right to keep his own language, and, hence, to insist on the authority of his own cultural or even class background in spite of corporate culture; and it is the question of decent demands of uniformity regarding the articulation of individual experience. Translation of personal universes cannot be enforced, and ought not to be either. Taken seriously, maieutic will imply that the co-directed is granted the real – not just the formal – possibility to scrutinize his own mind. He is not only given the right of veto, he is given the duty to co-create corporate reality. And this must not conceal any "manipulative elegance", however tempting.

---

27. I shall recall the maning of "the hodegēt" as it was introduced in Part One: it means a leader that is able to be an example. He is simultaneously a gentle admonition and an enigma. The hodegēt relates to the Fourth. He shall always be a human being prior to being the man of society, the nation, the institution, or the firm.

28. Translated by Cornford, F.M. (1935/1970): Plato's Theory of Knowledge. Routledge, London. The dialogue "Theaetetus", 150 B-D. p.26.

In relation to "his" employees one ability first and foremost is essential to a leader: to be able to harmonize horizons of separate individual obligations.[29] This is a functioning catalyst, but of another kind than the one found by the virtue of epibolē: to be able to create an array of individual possibilities, of subjectively acceptable choices, through which the employee can pass from obligations to commitments. Maieutic might also be seen as a consequent form of "recognition".

The managerial virtue of harmonization, or even reconciliation, can only be maieutic, because this harmonization has to be experienced as the result of the effort of the employee himself. It is he who has to create it, as if from an inner urge. This can only be done through a reference to "The Fourth".

9.1. Katorthōma and Kathēkon

The virtues listed in the preceding chapter are not to be looked at as values. They are states of mind, emotional attitudes. As such they are strictly individual, and only partly accessible through language. They are "appropriated gifts", so to speak. Something that one must deserve, and never can deserve fully by one's own power. Only in this sense are values able to exist: as ideas incorporated in the form of attitudes into an individual's life.

Values must be lived, not analyzed.

Our six virtues all unite within the stoic cardinal virtue of **katorthōma**, the "wise person's ultimate good way of acting". It is a life in permanent relationship to "The Fourth". Katorthōma comprehends this strong ideal: to act on the basis of your proper (and to the Greeks divine) nature, to place the concern about others above the concern about oneself, never to accept any end but one that ultimately can be related to "The Fourth", to anticipate what will happen through the maintaining of what is of essential value to our culture.

However, this could be phrased in the following way too: the real leader must never, by as much as a grain, differ from the good person.

The good leader attends to his office – the word "office" originating in the Latin "officium", itself a translation from the concept of stoic philosophy, **kathēkon**, "duty", by Cicero. Within the attitude of kathēkon, person and role become fused. However, kathēkon might refer to an obligation constituted by the state – or the firm – and not by the universal community. Pragmatic acts, acts being in agreement with the principles of nature, like keeping one's health, or supporting the state,

---

29. To borrow an expression from Gerd Althoff, where he in his book "Spielregeln, der Politik im Mittelalter. Kommunikation in Frieden und Fehde" deals with the different obligations constituted by the bonds of kinship, of friendship-communities, and of domination, in which obligations have to be reconciled (Althoff: 1997).

articulate the virtue of kathēkon, but they do not automatically express ways of acting aimed at the optimum good, at katorthōma. To the stoic philosopher, Zenon from Citium (333-262 B.C.), who introduced this concept, it is secondary to katorthōma, to the optimum good action of the wise person. His duty is to the universal order, to the great logos, and to his own soul; society comes on the second place here. From this it should be clear that to a leader the concern about economical or technical parameters should never be primary to the concern about the other person. The concept of "social" referring to a community finds its true meaning here where "strategy" finds its boundary.

It must be added now that the six virtues mentioned, as well as kathēkon and katorthōma, of course shall relate to the employees too, to the co-directed. In Part I the importance of the **symmetrical relation** inherent in real leadership was emphasized. It was generalized to involve all stakeholders, but the closest and most important aspect of this symmetrical relation is, no doubt, the one between the manager and his employees.

It is of great importance that the employee himself also relates to "The Fourth". This relation has always, from Hellenism through all of Modernity, been named by the word "duty". Here we stand at the crossroads of genuine manipulation versus almost saintly lack of suspicion, bordering on self-sacrifice by the leader. In a way, the employee shares this destiny. This is inherent in the concept of "duty", and it is of great significance to understanding the concept of "the social". The concept of "duty" has a Janus face: at one and the same time it restricts and liberates the individual's domain of action. You might even object that "duty" is the hexis of the dominated. But employee-virtues such as commitment and cooperativeness do not exclude managerial virtues like recognition and patience; and it must be obvious that the idea of a managerial relation characterized by symmetry must imply the idea of virtue as a reciprocal relation if it has to result in "leadership". It is evident that any co-directed has to aim at virtues like prolēpsis and epibolē, at fantasy and intuition as the basis of innovative performances. After all, how should the co-directed be able to appreciate the example of the leader if they do not have the possibilities of developing the virtues themselves?

The important identity of the real leader as an example presupposes that the virtues of leadership can be inherited down through the organization. After all, these six virtues, and especially the kathēkon and the katorthōma, are virtues of "self-leadership", and the ability to lead oneself goes for the man on the floor, as well. At the same time, one must not forget that these virtues are the best means to protect the co-directed, both when they are present in the leader, and when they are nurtured in their own minds.

Part IV

Space and Time
in Management

CHAPTER 10

The Space of Management and Leadership

From the platform of Management Philosophy we shall now try to develop a conceptional framework based on Radical Normativity, on the first hand of space and place, and on the other hand of time in management.[1]

Space and place in management refer to such different phenomena as the shop-floor, the corporation, the market, the internet and its virtual spaces. We shall seek a mutual core of all these localities and non-localities, spaces and places that are filled with artifacts, but often artifacts themselves too.

It is of extremely importance today to acknowledge the possibilities to management and leadership of spaces and of places. We are able to to use them, but must accept to be used by them too, in order to create them, and to be victim of them. Because all the time new spaces are ventured, and old places changed.

If all these places shall not be conceived of as operational spaces to management, as a strategically circumscribed domain of future victories, but as something else, far from the martial metaphors, what could they be, then? Then, we must leave the way of looking at the firm as an inner market place, as the forum of transactions and negotiations, and of the implementation of legal obligations. When the space of management becomes the universe, but also the universes created by technologies, e.g., the hyper/cyber-space, what then might its place be? Is there a region proper to management with its material as well as moral borders, and is that region the genuine object of planners and politicians and their visions? Or must any region be the subject of its own process of coming to be – so to speak. After all, a place is noting but a living space, and hence a living-place, with its fundamental preconditions in history, geography, in patterns of languages, in its "ethnos" and in its "genos", in its mores and in its "life-world". When technical designers in Germany or Australia compete on the computer in the CAD of the most surface-rational solution to often non-existing problems, then extremely important national and ethnic places get lost, and quasi-communities are created which enclose potentials, not for mutual creativity, but for conflict. But how are we to conceive of a region, where a politician and a planner serve, and even pay homage to, existing and potential realities, without trying to play the "demiurge" of technical and economical progress? Would it be a region where management is acting out of quite a new kind of concern? A region that as a place opens up a space without funda-

---

1. An article, containing some of the passages about "chōra", was delivered to the Project "Invoking a Region" treating the possibilities of the new "Öresunds-region" after the arrival of the bridge between Sweden and Denmark. "Chōra" is also treated extensively in my book "Secunda philosophia", published August 1999, but in Danish.

mental conflicts? This region must be a mutual space encircling a mutual place. What is a mutual place? What might its body be? Or is it already loosened from the human body invading immaterial networks and virtual sites?

The concepts of **space** and **place** must be reflected through their historically first and still probably most important theoretical manifestation in the dialogue "Timaeus", written by Plato rather late in his life. This is a key concept philosophically, and it reveals the need already existing at that time to make an epistemologically and ontologically sound analysis of the concepts of "place" and "space" – I shall not elaborate on the distinction between these concepts until later. This analysis must transgress the prevailing everyday notions, but also the philosophical framework of the "politeia" (city-state), and the concepts of the "ethnos" and "genos" (people, gender), and of "Gaia" (the earth as a living organism) herself, and even the "Cosmos", too. But it should be stated that in Plato one does not find any concept of a transnational, universal community. This "feeling" does not arise until two hundred years later, when Alexander the Great has destroyed the autonomy of the city-state, and the Romans, through the building of their Empire, are beginning to fulfill this process. The idea of a universal community, also including the "Barbarians", belongs to Hellenism, and hence to the Stoic concept of **logos**, as well as to the Gnostic movements preparing the Christian concept of the other person.

In the "Timaeus" the passages from 48-53 on the concept of **chōra** are the place where the pre-conceptual framework of "place/space" is discussed. These passages have been interpreted and re-interpreted vehemently for fifteen hundred years. From a philosophical point of view, probably Jacques Derrida has done so most recently (Derrida: 1993).

Chōra differs from **topos** in a complicated way in Plato's text, but we can state: "topos" sometimes means "place" at the time-space coordinate, i.e., its meaning converges more to the concept of "point" (in the modern sense), and hence chōra contains the "topos".[2]

The very first question, then, that I have to answer is: "what is a mutual place?" My answer shall look something like this:

1. a "mutual place" is a place where you can forget who you **were**, but not lose your past.
2. a "mutual place" is a place where you can remember who you **are**, but not lose your future.
3. a "mutual place" is a place that constitutes a centre that is everywhere ("ubicumque" in Latin, "everywhere" because it is here).
4. a "mutual place" is a place that is invisible, impervious to manipulation and indestructible. It always bears the same name.
5. a "mutual place" is a place that receives and transforms every individual initiative into a common point of view.

---

2. Of reasons that eventually should emerge, I do not say the chōra, but always only chōra, as if it were a proper name – and perhaps – a "she", if not even a lady.

6. a "mutual place" is a place where you at one and the same time live the social binding and are able to reflect it.
7. a "mutual place" is the place where we all can develop a mutual **hexis**.
8. a "mutual place" is a common power-stuff, a working dream.[3]
9. a "mutual place" is a place in time, a place giving content to temporality, a permanent network of events, a hyper-event.[4]
10. a "mutual place" is not only a part of our thinking, but it dwells in our body, hence, it contains a "choreography" of forces, or perhaps a situated and incorporated dynamics.
11. a mutual place is the quintessence of a centre, a middle, and as a centre it moves in order to stabilize and strengthen itself as something enclosed within its own horizon.

There exists a concept that meets all these parameters, the concept of chōra.

10.1. Chōra

In "The Republic", Plato outlines utopia with many qualities, but one important one is that there is no ownership. Plato repeats this idea in the introductory parts of his dialogue "Timaeus" as an overture to the concept of chōra.

In perhaps the most important place in the "Timaeus" where chōra is presented, Plato says about the building blocks of reality:

> "and a third Kind is ever-existing Place (tēs chōras, aei,), which admits not of destruction, and provides room for all things that have birth, itself being apprehensible by a kind of bastard reasoning (logismō tini nothō) by the aid of non-sensation, barely an object of belief (piston); for when we regard this we dimply dream (oneiropoloumen blepontes) and affirm that it is somehow necessary that all that exists should exist **in** some spot (en tini topō) and occupying some **place** (katechon chōran tina), and that that which is neither on earth nor anywhere in the Heaven is nothing."[5]

---

3. I shall not discuss the many attempts at interpreting chōra as a "stuff", as the "platonic matter", and hence as a conceptual preparation for the Aristotelian distinction between form and matter ("morfē/hylē"). Nor will I – although I am tempted – address Shakespeare's possible allusion to chōra in "The Tempest": "We are such stuff as dreams are made of, and our little life is rounded with a sleep."
4. I have chosen not to develop the relation between chōra and the concept of "network".
5. The First genus is the eternal "ideas". The second genus is the existing phenomena. Plato (1929/1966): Timaeus. The Loeb Classical Library. Transl. by R.G. Bury. William Heinemann, London. 52A-B.

The focus here should be on the expression "occupying some place", "katechon chōran". Because "katechon", as a verbal form here expresses the fact that chōra is a place where everything has to be, if it has to exist at all. The verb "kat-echō" has got quite a lot of different senses, but to us the important ones are "to keep", "to acquire", "to seize on", "to stand", as well as the intransitive forms of "to finish", "to be found (to be)", "to stay", "to carry on", "to be the case", "to happen". All those senses have a distinct relation to the concept of "place". They expose "movement" (dynamis/kinēsis) and "rest" (stasis); they expose the shifting of powers (dynamei), the losing of position (stereō), and – most importantly – the meaning of "kat-echō" is obviously temporarily coined, it denotes action, happening, process, **event**.

Even if there is no etymological connection between "kat-echō" and "kathēkon", it ought to be mentioned that the latter concept, "kathēkon", was later to become the core concept of Stoic ethics, and Cicero translated it into "officium" (as mentioned in the last chapter) from whence a host of senses were transferred to our modern world. Most important perhaps was the translation of "kathēkon/officium" into the middle-high-German word "Pflicht" (duty, obligation), which served as the place of departure in the ethics of Immanuel Kant and formed the common ground of an occupational ethics in the bureaucratic layers of the emerging European state; hence, it stands as an important brick in constructing the state as an autonomous place, (sic!)

Let me go straight to the point: the expression "katechon chōran" might be interpreted to mean that the place that is opened to everything is the **social place**. This means that chōra might be understood as the sum total and the quintessence of the event, because the event is what the place is in the social dimension: "The Battle of Waterloo", "The last meeting of the parliament", "The negotiations in Plaza Hotel", "The sales on the markets of Estonia", "The transport through East-Africa".

That this interpretation makes sense could be argued in the following way:

Chōra might be conceived of as a complementary concept in relation to another concept presented in the beginning of the dialogue, "Timaeus", "anaplēroō", "to fill (a place)". A place is filled up when something happens there. But it is not every happening that is able to fill up a place. To Plato it is only the eternal game between truth and falsehood, between the eternal ideas (Being) and their pale and unstable images, the earthly phenomena (Becoming). It is the game of – what later was to become an important philosophical concept – "the chorism", the sharp distinction between the eternal realm of truth and the earthly realm of shadows, of phantasms ("Phantasm", I might add, is now a fashionable postmodern concept).

In the very first lines of the dialogue (as I addressed the subject in Chapter 1 of this book) Socrates asks the three other characters (Timaeus, Hermocratēs and Critias) for the fourth guest. This question shall never find an answer. The fourth person stays unknown. Even if it is he who creates the link to the dialogue of yesterday, which might have been the dialogue, "The Republic". Instead it is the task of the present three persons, besides Socrates, to fill the place.

Here you find a whole dialogue about space (the universe) and place (the polis), which should have been told by a person who is absent ("apontos"), i.e., the dialogue is spoken in his place, a dialogue about place. But the absent one might not be Plato himself as has been suggested – and not even chōra ("herself"), as Derrida proposes – but you and me. We, the listeners, and after all, the readers, have to fill the place of the one who is missing, where he ought to deliver the speech on the concept of place.

A few pages inside the dialogue Socrates touches upon the subject that might have been spoken on by the absent one, namely the creation of the perfect state. From this we might imagine, that this dissertation of place should have been on the proper place of place, i.e., the social place, the community, the new ēthos, because one of the senses of ēthos is "home-place".

This interpretation of the dialogue "Timaeus", as a dialogue on the sense and signification of the social place, might also be reinforced by the following – epistemologically strange – passages that underline the fact that inside the phrasing "katechon chōran" there is also implied the notion of "the right social and cosmic order". This meaning was also acquired by kathēkon in Stoic philosophy together with the complicated concept of "oikeiosis".

That chōra is the space of the ordered place, is expressed by the mentioned strange passages (51C-E), where Plato argues for the distinction between the eternal ideas and the earthly phenomena – the so-called "chorism" – by referring to two distinct ways of knowing. The two ways are the nous, "mind", "thought", "intellect", and the doxa alēthēs, "the true everyday knowledge". The "nous" makes it possible to realize that there must exist an eternal realm of ideas (which can never be known per se). The "doxa alēthēs" makes it possible to operate in the "earthly sphere" – by way of the feeble and often faulty knowledge of the senses and of language. We can be sure of the existence of those two ways of practising knowledge, Plato says, because we are "taught" (dia didachēs) the first one (and here Plato implies "by the philosophers", without bothering to mention it). And because the other one is acquired through persuasion (hypo peithous) (and here Plato implies "through the Sophists", and again he does not mention it).

Now the argument goes that as far as these two distinct ways of knowing exist, the first one reflecting the true use of thought (alēthous logou), the other reflecting the false use (alogon), then their object, the two cosmological or ontological realms must also exist.

Here Plato resumes his treatment of the distinction between the Philosophers and the Sophists – a distinction pertinent to almost all his work, and especially, of course, to the dialogue the "Sophist", which we shall quote later on.

What might Plato mean by doing this?

Apart from the almost obvious "constructionist" perspective here – which we of course cannot accept from the point of view of his whole opus, and because of trying to evade evident anachronisms – the implication might simply be that the social place is the place, where we are given the possibility of distinguishing between the true and the false.

But when he described chōra in the first of our quotations Plato mentioned – with an odd expression – that to realize chōra, you had to employ a kind of "bastard thinking" (logismō tini nothō), a way of thinking that is neither genuine reflection by thought nor perception. Because Plato does not say: "Not by perception either", but he says "by the aid of non-sensation" (anaisthēsias) he evokes the concept of an unspecified mental act called "non-sensation". This could be both an imaginative act without mental pictures, or denote imaginative processes including dreaming, i.e., every act of perception not due to the immediate or direct activities of the senses. In Danish the word "anelse", in German "Ahnung", (suspicion, feeling) (concepts commonly used during the Romantic Movement) might capture this, but also, of course, "invocation": to (re-) produce the image of the New Jerusalem. And he follows up on this phrasing by saying:

> "So because of all these and other kindred notions, we are unable also on waking up to distinguish clearly the unsleeping and truly subsisting substance, owing to our dreamy condition, or to state the truth, ..."

Plato shows, in other words, that we acknowledge chōra through a kind of mental operation closely related to a dream, "we dimly dream and affirm that it is somehow necessary that all that exists should exist in some spot and occupying some place", as was stated above. The social place is a place of dreams. We are in a way, negatively and positively, dreaming the social reality. We might also say, that when you are dreaming, neither using discursive thought, nor our "outer" senses, we apprehend through emotion, through **pathos**. We **anticipate**. To anticipate is als to use often – what you might call – "un-reflected", and perhaps "not-at-all-reflectible", points of views to project a course of events.

Here we are close the world of magic, to the concept of invocation or even conjuration, because they are practices related to dreamy conditions, to virtual realities.

This is the first way to catch a conceptual glimpse of chōra: it is the place that gives place to the distinction between truth and falsehood, right and wrong. In that capacity it is an eternal event, the permanent happening of the game of truth.

But how are we able to experience chōra, if this is a possibility at all?

Plato mentions four more facts about chōra:

a. chōra is "the receptacle, and as it were the nurse, of all Becoming" (49A-B).

"Receptacle", in Greek "hypodochēn" from the verb "hypodochai", which means "reception", "to receive as a guest", and "conception". "The nurse of all Becoming", chōra is all-receptive (pandeches, 51A). Those phrases might express the ability of chōra to receive everything in a impassive, but also motherly, i.e., care-taking way. Hence the virtue of patience is called upon here.

What is it that chōra here receives?

Might it not be the story itself, the narrative in the dialogue? And might it not even be the way in which Plato – and we, much later – try to conceptualize or put words onto chōra? We are the guests of chōra, when we try to talk about her.

That means that we are always in chōra even when we try to make her into an object. She shall never be an object, but always a subject. She is a state. Not of mind, however, but among people and their actions. As soon as such a state has been given expression, it is an event.

But Plato also mentions that chōra is (51A)

b.   invisible (anoraton)
c.   without any form (amorfon)

Of course chōra is invisible, because a place is neither identical with any of the concrete phenomena which dwell in it; nor is it given beforehand, finished, but it is always in a flux, ready to be recreated, and itself creating.

Now we lack only one important mode of existing of/in chōra.

In 50D Plato says that chōra "must be called always by the same name" (tauton autēn aei prosrhēteon).

This can be conceived of as another way of expressing the fact that chōra is "the centre." This is due to the fact that a centre or a middle must always be perceived in an identical way from any point on the periphery.[6] Pascal baptized the social middle "milieu" – a concept haunting the last 70 years of psychology, sociology and their derivations.

Another expression of this might also be to talk about a "centre that moves". It moves towards the right place within an area in order to stabilize and strengthen it, i.e., to shape it into its very own place, into a region. Perhaps "the spotlight" might again be the proper metaphor here?

From the point of view of management theory, or even Management Philosophy, the focus must be on the movement that has the power to change, to turn the possible into a state as close to reality as we could imagine – and here I have not forgotten that reality is not at all real. That means: reality is not an object, and dynamics are no force in the physical sense, but there is a complicated reciprocity between an invisible subject and an invisible object, an inertia leaving its trace as what Mar-

---

6.   The centre or the middle is in Greek called "messothen" or "meson". Plato speaks of the famous metaphor of Parmenides ("messothen") in his dialogue "The Sophist", 244-245. Parmenides compares the universe to a sphere. Plato quotes two lines from the poem of Parmenides:
"On all sides like the mass of a well-rounded sphere, equally weighted in every direction from the middle ("messothen"); for neither greater nor less must needs be on this or that" (The Loeb Edition, op.cit.).

tin Fuglsang called "network-ing". As a never-ending process of coming to be ("genesis" in the Greek vocabulary).[7]

Of course chōra would enclose dynamics within it as the place of the powerful possibilities. This is almost so obvious that it is menacingly close to bad rhetoric. So perhaps we had better say that chōra is the only place where the possible can be real – perhaps because chōra respects or even nurses the real, sets it free? Hence chōra could also offer the **temporal** metaphor, or the metaphorically articulated temporality, of opportunity as an ontological fact, or – using the Greeks' word for it – **kairos**, the right moment.

Then **dynamics** as a concept might express this very fact about chōra, that she is the place that gives place to the transformation of Possibility into Reality.

The all-receptiveness of chōra defines a space of unlimited freedom: freedom to act, to think, to be.

Concerning the space outside factories, buildings, tunnels, rooms, this might allude to a place in the open, to an infinite and, hence, unbounded liberty of action. It might be a vision of a country with room and possibilities to everybody – like the dream of the American West. But it might contain the dream of the conquerors too, the dream of the New World. The metaphor of "unshaped" applied to chōra seems proper here, because the invaders and immigrants actually shape the shapeless, new land. Little by little they turn the space into a place, they make the invisible visible. They fill the void. Then they shall commit an offence against chōra. They transform what could have been a moveable feast into a settled session; they change borderlines, only felt as unmarked features of the landscape, into frontiers; they transform the earth, the land, into regions. All this fastens chōra to time. A time made visible and tangible through buildings that survive generations as false birthmarks or tattoos on chōra's soft skin.

Through these processes a necessity of arranging originates in the open space, closing it slowly, constructing connections suitable to the drawing of maps. A destruction of randomness, of the contingency implied in the concept of "home", which gives birth to planning, to the domesticated, to the downtrodden, to the suppressed place. This closing of horizons annihilates chōra as the place of places.

But the freedom inherent in the concept of chōra, that it is invisible, unshaped, all-receptive, and that it will not give place to anything but bastard thinking, certainly does not mean that chōra should be thought of as the market-place, as the "open space" of "free" markets. Freedom does not entail liberalism.

Neither does it mean that a space could be constituted by changeable artifacts, nor by some kind of "dynamic" artifacts. The mutual place can never be a market-

---

7. I am aware, that this way of thinking – without a subject and an object, i.e. thinking the process as mere "ginnesthai", as mere "coming to be", "das Werden" in the German, "vorden" in the Danish – opens up the metaphors of systems science, especially to the conceptual world of post-Hegelian Hegelianism, as in Niklas Luhmann. But I shall leave this thread of Ariadne to my colleagues.

place. It is a place where bodies meet, mingle and touch, as with the transient traces of chains of dancers, or choirs moving, song-lines. Or the most impressive metaphor perhaps: an enormous crowd walking very slowly or standing still, as far as the eye can reach, hand in hand, without a single voice rising, or even a whisper somewhere in the calm, soft darkness of bodies. Chōra only allows flesh to fill her emptiness.

All over the space that we have transformed into a place called "world", where places combat just as nations combat, and nationalities try to usurp the universal place, voices silenced long ago, and bodies absent for so long, haunt the holes in a time made more and more coherent and massive. The worlds of yesterday haunt us. But they cannot be recreated through any technological gesture in which the lost worlds are invoked as virtual realities.

You might earn a fortune by selling ventures or futures through the internet, or save time by ordering your goods. You can acquire "The Nicomachean Ethics" through the internet and read it from the screen, and you could meet your future wife. The internet, this real quasi-world, is the world of postponement, of a deferment of redemption only payable in the cash of flesh. A formidably structured absence that can only be abolished through presence. But presence is body. The only criteria of distance are time, memories and the void between bodies.

So the mark of chōra is left by homes, memories and bodies. It is hard to overcome this condition of life.

The leader has to know that. If he does not, he will try to construct chōra by an all too strong belief in technology and planning. Or he will try to anticipate the spirit of chōra and invoke a crude or negligent liberality. But to mistake what is natural for an artifact might be fatal. He must be able to diagnose it when it appears as the dilemma between a product bearing the marks of national "life styles" selling well on the home-market, and this very same product's possibilities on the international markets. The combat of life styles is a combat on chōra, now transformed into a field, and about the attempts to win her favour by sticking colours into her soft body. The essence of reality is social. Reality is a mutual place, and a mutual place is far, far more than any life style. It is a form of life. Where a life style is hermetic a form of life is opened beneath, as a house without a floor, it is standing in chōra.[8]

The person who wants to be a leader must be able to visualize the points of contacts of bodies and places. He must build on an empathy that overcomes the real and fictive distances of the awe-inspiring, but artificial new space, the internet. He

---

8. This important concept, "a form of life" was developed, however rudimentary, in the posthumous works of Ludwig Wittgenstein, primarily in the "Philosophical Investigations". Wittgenstein emphasizes the indefinite or transcendental character of this concept too: it cannot be defined, cannot be transformed into an object of conceptualization, because we shall always be a part of it, and, hence, it is a part of our mental sight – like the event.

must be ready to win back this space to chōra, to use the instrument to abolish the "instrumentalization" of communication. He must be able to recreate the mutual space. A space between the forced and faked community constructed by the state mechanisms, and the strategic social places constructed by corporate cultures, corporate images, corporate "values", and corporate alliances and connections.

The potential leader has to think in this way because the construction of this huge, pseudo-public space, the internet, makes it impossible to hide. Buyers and investors like "Good Money", and "green pages" are already informing the public through the internet about firms that honestly try to answer to social and ecological demands. In Denmark several banks already exist that arrange loans to social purposes only, at a very low interest rate. New organizations transgress the existing labour markets bringing volunteers and unemployed in contact with social projects; these projects try to combine the principle of capitalist enterprise with the social responsibility of the state. And new organizations work on reestablishing local communities, on strengthening and renewing old places in the new space. Initiatives spring from non-profit motives and communitarianism, but they want to legitimize themselves through the capitalist ideals of economic autonomy and self-financing. Examples of this are already flourishing.

Inside the corporate space a proper interpretation of the presence of chōra shall involve the three "maxims of the human mind" outlined by Immanuel Kant in his Aesthetics ("Kritik der Urteilskraft"), Paragraph 40, already mentioned in previous parts of this book:

> 1. Autonomous thinking
> 2. Empathy: to be able to think as if you were any other person.
> 3. At any time to be able to think in harmony with yourself: "self-management" on the basis of self-insight.

A free space involves a place where you have time to contemplate, because this shall increase your efforts, and anticipate the shapes of social community among employees. Time to think also means time to think about doing things better, and about who your fellow workers are. Free time opens a new space where the other person is able to matter.

A free space also means broad definitions of jobs, small units, and few hierarchies, because the fewer the formal roles, the easier it shall be to approach the other person when you are sincere. Combined with free time to get ideas and to talk together informally, this open space of communication shall enrich work conditions and increase innovation rates.

The last maxim is placed as the most important, being the precondition of the first two. The virtues of leadership shall create the conditions of its realization in giving everybody the possibility "to become who he is" (to quote Friedrich Nietzsche).

The manager must open his place to a new social space. He must create a mutual place, i.e., a place open to people without work, people without education, people without the means of subsistence. He must create a space that is a social space in the truest sense: everybody's space. He must help people to help themselves, and not primarily as a means to increase his firm's profits. In other words, he must practice the **kathēkon,** the duty to the mutual place.

CHAPTER 11

The Time of Management and Leadership

The time of management and leadership is centred around the **event**. In that it does not differ from the experience of time in everyday life.

Before our first attempts at analyzing it, we have to ask the question: what is an event?

The simplest answer is probably that it is such a kind of an object "in which" something has taken place. This "something" is action, and the concept of "action" covers almost everything a human being is able to do, including thinking and feeling. This action, however, must be something that has already been, is going to be, or is happening just now. So we could state that an event is an action primarily characterized by its position in time, and hence, through its position in relation to somebody, because time is always an experience of one mind and of one body, no matter how much this experience is shared by others. The identity of an event is dependent on perspective, whether it is emotional or "paradigmatic", or both.

An event could be easy to recognize, or it could be secret, and merely the construction of conjecture. Millions of people could be presented in it, as at the New Year's speech of the Pope, or only one, as with a suicide. It could cover centuries, as with the rise and fall of the Roman Empire, or last only one second, as when somebody shuts off the radio in anger. It could involve beetles eating a dead rat, or two prime ministers dining.

Normally one would tie the existence of an event to some notion of "objective existence", to some being "outside our mind". But I think it safe to claim that an event does, however, exist in a restricted sense, even if it is imagined in the mind only, and that the event, then, consists in more than this very process of imagination, because it normally can be communicated. Even if communication is not a quality of any event, it must be realized that most events contain speech from the very beginning, so even if an event cannot be classified as an action always containing speech, it could be said to be its prototypical appearance (we shall return to this).

Most events are presented as rather short, not longer than "episodes", even if it could be reasonable to say that they last much longer through their degrees of diffusion into the contextual network.

Most events can be divided into parts, but the minimum size of those shall generally be the "lens of the word", even if we might feel that much smaller occasions exist at some "social micro-level".

Most events are connected to other events. Through causal links, appearing to be determined, but also through mechanisms and patterns hard to reveal, even, perhaps, through something akin yo "fate".

Some events seem to belong exclusively to only this particular person, others seem to belong to anyone.

Some events present themselves as the obvious starting point of some decisive process, as the story of the first little remark that began to shake the confidence in a manager; others are mere hypothetical deductions, as pinpointing the first second that the first cell mutated on its way to cancer. But there shall always exist another story of the real beginning, and there will always exist at least one more event than the one who claims to be the last one: "Well, he got the golden handshake, and everybody thought that this story was all over, but ..." Or "The public access to the archives has shown that "X", contrary to everyone's belief, had been a double agent."

Events are wrapped into each other, as when the reporter on location tells us, the television viewers, about what we are seeing and not seeing happen.

In the information society the majority of events dealt with are "indirect" events, events which answer to no individual's personal experience. Their authenticity depends on another person whom we have never met, or is "guaranteed" by a media, by printing, "documentaries", or by the omnipresent lenses of cameras.

Most events seem to have at least one event to which they bear some resemblance, if not the marks of identity. But sometimes we imagine that an event can be unique. In Latin, the word for event is "eventum", and you can express this particularity and singularity of the event through the grammatical form of "singulare tantum" – as was already mentioned above. However, events are created, which means that one always must be in one event in order to create a new one. The event, that the Stoics named "tynchanon", was in Plato and Aristotle called by two names, "pragma" and "ergon" (two forms of the same verb). The first concept denotes the as yet unfinished happening, the other one denotes the finished actions, having a name, a physiognomy, and an unshakable identity already. Hence, the recognition of the identity of both the event in becoming and the event fixed and their mutual interplay, is the precondition of goal-directed action. The place in time where the **embedded** event, the event to come, intersects the "mother-event", is often called "timing", or in Greek, **kairos**, the right moment.

A colonel in the army of a rather conservative, central European country is asked for a conversation by his very best captain a week before the company is sent into Bosnia on their first real mission. The colonel knows that the captain is going to tell him what he himself has figured out long ago but chosen not to relate, namely that he, the captain, is a homosexual living in a "marriage" with another man for some years now.[9] The captain wants both to ease his own inner pressures, but also to invoke acceptance of his peculiar way of existing. He is a determined man.

The colonel knows very well that to tell the soldiers about this fact right now would abolish the authority of the captain, however able and brave he might be, and hence, endanger the course of the dangerous action. Yet, to postpone the infor-

---

9. A story close to the following was actually reported in "Die Zeit" during early spring 1999.

mation might lead to even greater difficulties in case of emergency, because the captain's partner is going to join the company as a computer specialist. The captain is strictly irreplaceable if the company shall be able to carry out its mission. The situation is not made easier by the fact that the colonel respects the captain highly as a soldier and as a person, and that he is a man with very few prejudices.

During their conversation it becomes clear that the captain would never agree to conceal this delicate fact about his personal existence much longer, and his offer of resignation cannot, under any circumstances, be met by the colonel. However, the captain is absolutely loyal to his company, so it is possible that he will not resign, even if the colonel manages that his partner not take a part in the campaign. But such pulling strings behind doors is not the colonel's style, and after all the performance of the captain would very probably be affected by it.

This event of the conversation is, of course, embedded within the more comprehensive event of the conflict in Bosnia, and the more durable events of the love-life of the captain, and the building of the company. And within this event of conversation the possibilities of the future campaign as an event are embedded too, this event covering many possible events.

It is obvious that the colonel's possibilities of controlling, or at least influencing, the future, depends just as much on when he shall choose, as on what he shall choose.

The colonel remembers the beginning of the Iliad where the death of Achilles' lover cost the brave Hector his life and Troy its sovereignty, and he decides to tell the men himself.

11.1. The Concept of Influence

The time of management and leadership has three dimensions in response to the existential conditions laid down by the future, the past and the present:

- To the future the response is planning, of course, but also a more imaginative and spell-binding kind of prediction, the vision, and, hence, storytelling.
- To the past the response is deliberation, explanation, understanding, mutual agreement on "what happened", the attempt at finding the meaning behind the experience and, once more, storytelling; but this time the narrative might dispense with authenticity, as long as it appears to be true.
- To the present the response lays in the attempts of closing in on the event, or even coming to grips with it.

We shall relate to the challenges of the future and the past as narrative structures involved in management and leadership in chapter 13 and 14; here we have to concentrate on the event.

To understand the phenomenon of the **event** we have to begin with two important analytical distinctions, distinctions to a certain degree common to both everyday existence and to managerial and leadership functions. But as we continue the development of a grid of delicate, analytical distinctions, we shall move away more and more from this likeness.

The first distinction drawn concerns your ability to influence an event at all.

The second one relates to your being inside or outside an event.

The combinations of these two issues form the scenario where you are able to influence the event, be it from the inside or from the outside, or both.

Concepts like "to influence", "being inside", and "being outside" are complicated, however simple they might seem to be.

"Influence" might often be a very obvious concept with its prototypical cases, as when you start a firm, or sign a contract of cooperation with another firm, or sell a quantity of goods, or install a new machine, or buy the majority of shares in a company, or give a grant to an NGO focussing on a peculiar issue. To whom the influence belongs is rather evident here, which goes for material, causal influences, and limits of acting, too: a stricter governmental control of firms' pollution effects, more refined techniques of sewage, and a sudden rise in demand, seem an obvious explanation of rising employment rates among involved firms. However, the overwhelming number of borderline cases cannot help to complicate this concept, and hence, the understanding of how to conceive of an event.

Do you have "influence" on the company board if you are strong enough to get your man to be taken into consideration as a candidate, but not strong enough to obtain his appointment?

Do you have influence on the sudden rise to zenith of the value of the shares in USA's number one war equipment company – number one out of three existing – when your broker buys on behalf of you as the 1,235th shareholder? And could you then be held morally responsible for the development of quite new methods of war through the R&D engagement funded by that capital, and held responsible, to casual deaths in Bosnia during NATO's bombing raids, or even to future deaths in future arenas of war?

Obviously influence is about power and responsibility, and mainly about persons, even if companies and institutions, as well as other events, might also be seen as influential agent. However, we still conceive of an event as the result of people's actions, even if we often speak about influences as if they were made by agents other than humans, and perhaps especially within the areas of economics and business science: the rising interest rate forced the firm to reduce employment; structural changes within the Educational System made it more difficult to comply with the needs of generalists' qualifications; VW's takeover of both Bentley, Bughatti, Lamborghini and Rolls Royce seems to create more difficulties with an overall plan of marketing than expected.

But the more we want to write influence off – a very important factor too – the more we perceive occurrences as "accidents" or even "catastrophes", as events beyond our control, and hence beyond our responsibility, we baptize them with names of places, like "Sevezo", "Chernobyl", or even "Hiroshima". We silently construct a semisphere within social reality where humans do not seem to have any influence. "Competition forced the firm to use these dubious materials", and so on. "At that time the German people could not do anything else but follow Hitler." G.W.F. Hegel baptized this "the cunning of History", hinting at forces of social and cultural development which the agents could not see through, and, hence, dispensing with the ultimate demand to responsibility, because of the cognitive impenetrability of the event. Power could always be vindicated through the reference to the opaque character of the event concealing real influence, and this influence might then be identified with the blessings of what seemed to have happened, i.e., be identified with the victorious status quo. But almost every event has its losers, and, hence an alternative rationality would appear nurturing another, and beautiful, possible world. Because of his belief in the power of self-conscious thought to defeat all loose ends and all goals contrary to reason, conquering this "cunning" at the end seemed to him to imply the reconciliation of reason with itself.

Influence as overt and even rude power might easily be legitimized through referring to the phenomenon that J.P. Sartre called "contra-finality" in his "Dialectics of Critical Reason". "Contra-finality" refers to the fact that provisions made on the firm ground of technical reason might end up with producing quite the opposite result. A dam might increase the flood both because of its preventing the land to absorb the water, and because of the new and worse effects produced by the eroding banks from where the soil to the dam came. But this is Nature, of course, who plays a trick on us, stamping her very own logic in front of our faces. Contra-finality is at work within the social domain too: when government pulls taxes in order to create new public employment the unintended increase in the demand of labour might raise salaries and effect lay offs. It is the well-known vicious circle of Keynesianism – might it be diagnosed sufficiently through this simple causality, or not.

From Stalin, Hitler, and Mao, one lesson can be learnt: events under very little influence are easy prey. "Neutral" or balanced social events are rare unless they are constructed through institutions, sanctioned, guaranteed and preserved by power, or else they are just opportunities. Opportunities to be grasped to acquire and enhance influence. Opportunities to get inside the event as if you stood outside it pulling the strings.

In short, influence is a very complicated phenomenon, and so is the event: the man who unwillingly is present at a murder attempt, and thus prevents it by doing nothing but being a witness, he cannot be said to have "influence" on the event in the full meaning of the word unless he chooses to testify. Because "influence", after all, seems to presuppose intention, and hence some pre-knowledge of the event.

But of course you might have influence on an event if you really do not want it to happen, and are able to prevent it from happening, like grass-roots preventing the building of a nuclear power station by activating public opinion and political decision making; or like an "emergency manager" bringing an end to a very near suspension of payments at a certain firm.

To conceptualize the event, then, demands analysis on many levels of contextual settings and circumstances, involving complicated patterns of historical and geographical causalities. It seems to demand a merging of time and space into forces and places.

11.2. What It Means to Be Inside or Outside an Event

The metaphor of containment is an important element of the figures of thought through which the event present itself. The point of intersection between the coordinates of space and time constituting the event is, indeed, contained: "it happened in Copenhagen."

The reporter standing **on** location, **in** the middle of happenings, addressing us immediately and directly **in** our homes, is inventing a **"para-event"** that is **embedded** within the "mother event". This para-event is a parasite on a reality most often developed outside, or without any knowledge of its future transformation into such an event inside the television boxes, an artificial embeddedness.

What we are interested in here is a peculiar concept of the event, a kind of permanent happening with a firm centre of signification which very often would be the space appearing as a place. From this perspective we might ask: why is the event happening exactly here?

But this question belongs to the problem of the very relation between the centre and the periphery. How do you, in space and time, delimit the place in its incorporatedness as a container of an event? Why is it called "The meeting in Paris", and not "The meeting at Hotel Ritz"? But "The concert in St. Paul's Cathedral" and not "The concert in London"? Sometimes the processes of naming seems almost arbitrary.

Of course the answer would very often legitimize itself by referring to history, to some principle of continuity, or to the "logic" of metonymy; to geography, politics and planning and to ethnos and genos if possible. But there is an important fact here which is – if I may express myself that paradoxically – the "embeddedness of the event".

This embeddedness is the quintessence of the place, of **chōra,** as though there were a necessity working secretly here, demanding that the event should be given the name of one place only. The relation between place, event and circumstances,[10]

---

10. By the way: the concept of "circumstance" comes from the Latin "circumstantia", which is a translation of the Greek word "peristasis", "peri" (around) the "stasis", (that which stands still), i.e., the centre, the middle. But "stasis" also means "the getting-up", "the insurrection", "the rebellion", "the struggle", which could mean that the centre is not always what it has been enforced into being; behind its immobility something prepares itself.

then, appears to be a relation mise en scène by something close to "fate". As if events on the verge of happening were longing for their proper place to such a degree as to "make themselves happen in it".

However, something that does not happen, but obviously might have happened, must at least have existed in some way. It "is inside" a mind, and we appear to agree on the notion that a real event must be "outside" the mind in order to exist. But when we are talking – an "outside activity", because speech is "physical" – of a common idea of an event "inside" our heads, then this conversation is an event "in" which there is a notion of a future event. Then, this virtual event is the subject of a "real event", but itself not real until ... This "until" depends on the character of this virtual event. If it happens to consist in the dream scenario where you and I really reach each other, then the conversation about the possibility of this event might be the very realization of it. But this obviously does not work for the general staff's discussion of tomorrow's attack. Here the two events can be said to be both mutually inside and outside each other.

The problem might be that we seem to know what it means that an event is "real", but that it is extremely hard to define if this definition shall cover all possible instances.

The expression "being in a market" implies the container metaphor both in relation to space and to time, but so does the expression "being in trouble". However, the market seems to be a place, but only "as long as" ... there is demand, i.e., needs, information, interest, in relation to a certain good. The market is constituted by processes of time taking place in a place, e.g., Estonia. These processes of time seem to have their very own space when looked at as logistic trajectories forming a web, inscribing themselves on the surface of the earth, and involving thousands of people making them act in totally new ways along the lines drawn by the dots of computers or cars as commodities. But they might only be lines in a manager's mind, or an issue on the agenda of the board, or existing as still unsettled negotiations. The question is: when does an event begin to exist?

This is of crucial importance, both to the problem of how to influence it, that means, **when to**; and to the knowledge of how and when you are outside or inside it.

But both these issues seem to result in one and only one ability – that of being able to identify positions in time and space in which it becomes advantageous to take action. There seems to be a metaphor of "gliding" here, of getting slowly close to something, of grasping the influence, or of getting into the centre of the event. But the metaphor also works in the opposite direction. It evokes connotations of escaping, of stopping in due time. All these movements of the mind in relation to the event might be called **timing**.

Timing seems to presuppose anticipation, and hence, an ability to "read" the texture of happening. This does not mean that there has to be an alphabet of events within the events, but perhaps something is present, though there is scarcely a trace and more like a fragrant nuance, not open to anyone's eye. A world of micro-occasions accessible only as a clandestine dynamic not so far from this knowledge ascribed to old country people about the weather next summer, a knowledge that appears to be far superior to the forecasts of meteorology with its chaos mathematics, millions of parameters, and mega-computers. But waiting at the other side of time for **its** moment: the ultimate micro-event of the "winking of an eye".

But how small, then, can an event possibly be? And, of course, how big, too? The giga-event of the evolution of life, or of the, so-called, Western Civilization – the civilization that Ghandi could not spot.

Dylan Thomas writes

"The hand that signed the paper felled a city;
Five sovereign fingers taxed the breath,
Doubled the globe of dead and halved a country;
These five fingers did a king to death."[11]

This signature is very small in size and short in duration in opposition to its importance. It is a kind of finishing event, a gesture, tiny only because of this symbolic value worked up through years of struggle. But what about the apparently insignificant events, the event without names in our language – called "nōnymon" by the Greek philosopher, Democrit? Like pouring half the content of a good bottle of wine into the sink, or of two allies exchanging glances at exactly the wrong moment before signing the contract? Or of choosing the wrong face to a television commercial? Or do we need to go "deeper", to a level where mimics, or gestures scarcely identifiable through slow-motion, play the important part? Are we victims of events at such a micro-level? Or are we victims of such micro-occasions being the result of coincidences in which they unite through a mixture of necessity and mere chance?

---

11. From Thomas, D.(1963): Miscellany. J.M. Dent & Sons Ltd., London. p.25. The rest of the poem goes:

The mighty hand leads to a sloping shoulder,
The fingers joints are cramped with chalk;
A goose's quill has put an end to murder
That put an end to talk.

The hand that signed the treaty bred a fever,
And famine grew, and locusts came,
Great is the hand that holds dominion over
Man by a scribbled name.

The five kings count the dead but do not soften
The crusted wound nor stroke the brow;
A hand rules pity as a hand rules heaven;
Hands have no tears to flow.

Nonetheless, it seems that the event most often is something to be addressed by words. Not just because words are the micro-lenses of experience, but because they constitute the texture of action. Eighty percent of the time we shall find managers reading something. Even if important events, often catastrophic, shall happen because of some kind of reinforcing dynamic at the level of micro-events physically seen, as when a chemical factory explodes, or a harvest fails, then, even crashes of the stock exchange, and the slow growing of the national debt, are the results of words, on the level of words.

But is an event a word, "an utterance", something implied within a proposition?

11.3. The Problem of the Ontology of the Event

When we look at the event as bound to the word, to the denotation through a proposition, we must be ready to face a number of problems.

The first one would be: does the event exist outside language? Does it exist when nobody has uttered anything about it?

Of course events exist outside their "wording". We do not have to invoke happenings in the early history of the earth, occurrences at a very large scale like the ocean being everywhere for millions of years, like floods, and the birth of mountains. It will be sufficient to recall the carnal pleasures of sleeping, eating and of making love, as well as their opposites, injuries, wounds and death, to speak of realities beyond language. However, the meaning, the significance of an event, must be a social fact, a fact if not conceived, then at least born by language.

Here we must realize that perhaps it is not possible to draw the very strict lines of demarcation proper to both epistemology and ontology when we are speaking about the relation between the event as a linguistic phenomenon and the event as the result of a process beyond this level.

Perhaps we ought to speak about a "social ontology" here, or even better, about an "ontological social being": because the event seems only to exist "to us", and its elements only to be of importance to us, as far as "they" can be expressed through words.

A meeting between stakeholders about a certain, perhaps rather delicate issue, is managed through the agenda, i.e., through some keywords and their phrasing by somebody into descriptions of "a situation" and into possible arrangements. This "situation" can, of course, never be the very same as the "situation" called "the meeting". The "situation" might be the possibility of the firm to move to the Far East in order to reduce labour costs.

This possibility of moving is the event that it is all about, but it is still uncertain. Perhaps then, it would be reasonable to name it "situation" until the moment when its physiognomy is rather definite. By now people would argue about issues like: should the whole firm be moved? What about social responsibility? Which amount of compensation to what kind of employee? Is it possible to sell the existing plant at a price acceptable to shareholders? What about product quality? What about the political system in the new country ... and so on.

This situation is very complex, and in it are involved human beings, machines, buildings, stocks, information and information systems, a lot of formal and informal relations, skills, know-how, routines, expectations in the surrounding community, traditions, national and corporate symbols, and much more ... of which quite a lot shall disappear forever. In this situation a few elements or relational structures might be present to which language gives us no access. But these elements to which access through words are given seem overwhelming.

The agenda at the meeting, as well as the carefully prepared speeches by the chairman, as well as by the local politicians, the representatives of the grass-roots and of the small shareholders, and not to forget the shop stewards and other representatives of worker's interests. They are all attempts at transforming this chaotic situation into an event.

But they all want to transform it on their premises.

Now, this transformation of the situation into an event is itself a situation, a situation that must be an event too. So, the meeting as an event will decide what kind of event the situation of the removal of the firm is.

It must be clear that this process involves struggle, because it involves power. It is about the dividing of both responsibility and advantage onto groups, and it implies gains as well as losses, rewards, and perhaps even punishment.

A rather complicated pattern of causal interconnections shall emerge here.

Normally much will already have been decided at the level constituting the first situation: the provisional removal of the firm. As a virtual event it has been carefully prepared by its promoters. Relations of power and practical possibilities have long been investigated. On this background the phrasing of the whole venture has been chosen by the promoters, even if there does not exist any agreement among CEOs and between them and the board. So, at this virtual level the situation has already been transformed into an event, and this is not the world of castles in the air. It is kept firmly on the ground by the weight of forces, knowledge, and pressures.

Now from the perspective of this virtual event the other situation/event, i.e., the meeting where everything is finally decided, is an important side of the **context** or some crucial **circumstance**. It has to be managed. To the meeting as a situation/ event however, this virtual event is **the** context. If the removal is decided, the meeting will emerge to be a less important event, but of course, rather instructive to a few of the stakeholders. Should it after all succeed in preventing the removal of the firm it could, as an event, be the cause both of the continuation of the firm, or, eventually, of its going bankrupt. But it might in any case change into a prototypical event too, into an event that forms precedence and hence, introduces new possibilities of contents and courses to situations and to events.

I shall no longer dwell on these problems of reciprocal causation at different levels here. Instead I will add a few words on the distinction between the event and its contexts.

The same event might have more contexts, and the same context might have different events.

However, the problem of what exactly can be meant by "the same" – the central problem of the two dialogues of Plato, "Parmenides" and "The Sophist" – cannot be attacked sufficiently here. We must be content with some – clearly insufficient – notion defining "the same" in this connection as the situation in which a third part would experience a context or an event as "identical".

That different contexts relate to the same event is a well-known problem of politics and of the business world, because it is **the** strategic device. This goes for all the kinds of lobbying, and all the well-known ways to present a situation as a virtual event from the perspective of the one to whom one is speaking at this moment. The reduction of the working day from eighteen to twelve, then to ten hours, during the second half of the last century is from the context of labour power an amelioration of the conditions of life, but was felt by some as a restriction in their ability to increase earnings as well. The prohibition against child labour especially was felt as a restriction in the possibilities of earning family income. From the perspective of the bourgeois this was presented as a victory of humanitarianism, but it was also a technical means to enhance the productivity of labour, and a political means to reduce national pressures. Like the educational programmes following in the wake of these laws, they might very well be conceived of as ways to create a national identity and hence, resources on which imperialist politics might draw.

Here we see the problem already so often touched upon in this book that an action done on a basis of what the actors felt to be genuine value-oriented might prove itself to be strategically beneficial – a fact that makes the concept of "strategic thinking" most complicated. Not just love, but even charity, could serve the augmentation of power and money.

Very often the same context might involve more than one event, which also could be expressed as the fact that the same event has many identities.[12] When I return from a discussion I often ask myself what I actually said or did. And often I shall never get the answer, because asking one of the persons present might not bring me any farther, because I have to interpret it. Probably most of the time I shall forget about it.

---

12. If we choose this formulation we have to rely on a strictly "physical" definition of "the same event", and hence we have to dispense with any subjective perspective, i.e., there could be no observer then. By saying that the same context might have more events we allow for a wider span of occurrences within what was experienced as the same context. The concept of "context" is from the beginning such an indefinite quantity that we do not have to bother much about what it means that it is "the same".

When two or more persons refer to some incident, they generally shall refer very differently. That is why it is often so difficult for the police to get reliable testimony.

This casts a light on the problem of **interpretation**, as one of the great problems in relation to events. It covers the question: "What actually happened?" And it involves the reconstruction of the event. The historian shall use various sources, and here and there fantasy. The manager might use the narrative. We shall return to that in chapter 14.[13]

This problem seems to attest to the fact that the event exists outside language. The historian reconstructs causal occurrences that often are not documented through anything written (or depicted). Perhaps the manager creates a history of the company that was never introduced within its walls as any kind of vision or mission. He invents an understanding of which he could say "that it must have been there since they acted as they did ..." We get close to the figures of thought of psychoanalysis here. And like the psychoanalyst we have to feel our way towards a reality that seems to consist of words, but where it sooner or later is necessary to **choose** only one entrance, because there are so many doors, and because so much matters. Sometimes the hermeneutical process might remind one of the old enigmas where two monsters guard two doors, of which one leads to survival, the other to destruction. Here one monster always gives false answers and the other only right ones, and you only have one question.

Perhaps the right way to know about the event actually consists in asking what it is not? However, this might be a rather extensive procedure.

---

13. A rather suggestive explanation of the importance of the narrative to business economics today, and more specifically to the theory of organizations, is put forward by Dian-Marie Hosking and Ian E. Corley in their book a "Social Psychology of Organizing" (Hosking, Morley: 1991). They suggest that the narrative might be the means to keep to the historical basis of negotiations, so far as the metaphor of contracting is still binding for business science, and hence, negotiations. Let us quote them: "We take the view that each negotiation may be regarded as an historical narrative to be decomposed into open-ended stages. The historical narrative comes in because, when people make commitments, they look for a clear rationale, linking what is happening now to what has happened in the past, and to what needs to happen in the future." Insofar as tacit knowledge and very hard to describe tasks eventually come to dominate the high-technology firm, negotiations move into never-ending spirals that demands the creation of some rationale in order to be managed at all. The narrative might function like that within the organization.

11.4. Kairos

To identify and control the event very often consists in choosing an angle that is most likely too loose in the contest of interpretations. After all, common sense is a bad compass in matters of history, however reliable it might seem, but real, moral sense is not. There seems to be an inner connection between a pronounced sense of historical significance and this moral sense. However, moral sense has to be nurtured, **hexis** has to be developed from decision to decision, until a kind of spontaneous level of interpretation or diagnosis is reached where you perceive the problem in such a way that the action taken is obvious. Then choice will be carried by the fusion of desire (being an outward directed type of emotion) and thought. Let me repeat this passage from "The Nicomachean Ethics", op.cit. VI, ii, 5:

> "Hence Choice (proairesis) may be called either thought related to desire or desire related to thought; and man as an originator of action, is a union of desire and intellect."

In the sentences before that, Aristotle defined the genuine action, both as different in relation to the art of making (poiēsis), and to actions viewed only as a means to something:

> "Whereas a thing done is an end in itself; since doing well (welfare: eupraxia) is the End, and it is at this that desire aims."

The real leader attempts to do well, acting in a way that makes action itself into the end, i.e., into an example. As the utmost consequence of a life led by the virtues he cannot help but to do so. What does that tell us about his relation to the event?

In order to answer this question we have to change the angle of looking at the event, because up till now we have conceived of it mainly from the perspective of the future and the past. We have treated the event as an occurrence in which prospects of the future always projected from the past were transformed from possibility to reality. Now we have to conceive of the event as **the moment**. The Danish philosopher, Søren Kierkegaard, made "the moment" viewed as "the moment of decision", "the **crucial moment**", a main subject of his thinking.

In the crucial moment something very important is at stake, determining the what and the when of the decision by submitting them to the why, and hence, deciding the identity of the event.

The crucial moment is irreversible because, while choosing to choose, you create the what and the when of your choice. To Kierkegaard this crucial moment of choice could be said to be "situated outside time", because in choosing to choose you negate any determination of your choice, you act in an "unconditioned" way.

Kierkegaard's perspective is religious, but we are able to learn from it, even for our more profane problems. Because the leader also has his crucial moment.

In the language of Plato, from the dialogue "Parmenides", there is a moment "inside" time, **to nyn**, the passage leading from the past to the future, that abolishes itself in the service of this movement, "for it always is now whenever it is" (152E). And there is the moment "outside" time called "the sudden", (156E) **to exaiphnēs**, from which time can be experienced as time, i.e., the process in which reality is created by your own imagination.[14]

It is probably this last concept that inspires Kierkegaard to conceptualize his "crucial moment"!

The crucial moment was acknowledged by Greek philosophy, and named "**kairos**", "the right moment". Kairos was depicted as a god, often standing at the entrance to the Olympic Stadium. However, "Kairos" also covered a concept of instrumental time, originating in the "kairologic" of Aristotle in his "Metaphysics", the legacy of which were the theories of probability developed by Leibniz, modern analytical philosophy, and, finally, the "logic of time" constructed by Cognitive Science and Artificial Intelligence.

A phenomenology of the event can show that there are events with an absolute negative content, yielding absolutely no happiness and not even experiences worthy to be called "human", as is seen during wars and terror. On the other hand there are also utterly happy events that appear to grant "welfare" to anybody involved. But most events shall probably constitute a mixture.

The real leader will try to transform the mixed events into the events with the most "welfare" to everybody, the first exception from this rule being himself. But even if this seems utopian, it is a powerful regulative idea.

However the crucial moment can be analyzed through five dimensions where the criterion of "crucial" relate to

- the leader himself
- the other, or the group
- the institution, company, society
- the nation, and the state
- the unconditioned (The Fourth)

Every one of these dimensions gives a platform to Kairos, to the right moment, meaning more than "timing", because the criterion can never be only technical or economical, but must always relate to the action as an end in itself.[15]

---

14. Plato (1926/1996): Parmenides. Transl. by H.N. Fowler. The Loeb Classical Library. Harvard University Press, Cambridge, London.

15. Here the book by Joseph L. Badaracco, Jr. (1997): Defining Moments: When Managers must Choose between Right and Right. Harvard Business School Press, Boston, ought to be mentioned. Badaracco creates the concept of "defining moments". These are moments in which character is formed through choices between ideals in which we honestly believe. Badaracco also distinguishes between such "defining moments" crucial to per-

Only one example is used here to make the point clearer, because it must be emphasized that all the five dimensions necessarily would be present at the same time as perspectives on every example. To construct an example to illustrate every dimension would be too artificial. So it is a question of the ability to isolate one and only one dimension at a time.

Pertaining primarily to the leader's own consciousness the crucial moment can be illustrated through the following story:

A mediumsized Danish firm, producing advanced software and information systems solutions for government and industry faces a major crisis with overhanging reductions at all levels, when a subcontractor to the American military industry delivers a very comprehensive order for a software component. This component is meant to be a part of the control system in a new type of missile that will be able to select its own target, and only that: flesh that has been into contact with all kinds of firearms within the last twenty four hours. The company has a very fine position as the potential contractor, because of certain patented and extremely advanced know-how. However the deal is top secret, so only the vice president knows about it. The usual public debate has not arisen yet, and the character of the software makes it easy to conceal its real purpose. Thus the discussions about the function of the weapon, attack, defense, and the whole political setting are not involved yet. As an intermediary principle solving rather general problems of control, the real purpose of the software does not even need to be revealed to the people who are going to develop it. Not even the board or the CEOs are informed yet.

Being one of the few devoted Protestants left, the vice president finds himself caught up within a painful predicament.

If he makes the contract now he will save the company and he might even have a chance to invoke an innocence on behalf of the company, if, and when, matters become public. The subcontractor fills his ears with the blessings of this new weapon as a vehicle to defend world peace and to prevent terror. It seems to be the best weapon ever to stop the terrorism of small militant groups. If he delays the decision, stakeholders, public and politicians might make the legitimization of action much easier, but the bargain might be lost.

Actually, he is in a very complicated situation of which at least the following options are obvious:

---

sonal identity, to group identity, and finally to the identity of the company. I think this book is an important contribution to Business Ethics even if it might sometimes, in describing the context and the outcome of choice, make a too strategic bias for my taste. For reasons easy to understand but not easy to accept, one criterion is never questioned in his discourse: winning, the all-American metaphor of victory which conceals the fear of real change conceived of as disintegration.

a. he can make the contract now, save the firm, and take the responsibility.
b. he can refuse, satisfy his own conscience, and let the refusal take the strategic form of a technically substantiated delay.
c. he can inform the board and let them decide.
d. he can resign silently and let the board and another CEO take over.
e. he can resign in public and influence the whole project through world opinion.

This "pentalemma", aggravated by the ten years used by this vice president to build the firm, reveals all the mentioned dimensions and options of the crucial moment:

a. the leader's possibility of being "one mind with himself", i.e., searching for his mind, for the "key" in which desire and thought are united in harmony.[16] The ten commandments might be this key.
b. the responsibility to the threatened groups of employees within the firm, meaning not just employment, but employment waged against their right to know what they actually are producing, i.e., their right to moral choice too.
c. the consequences to the firm, its public image, be it as a morally integrated organization, or as rather shady company.
d. the consideration of the nation. As a member of NATO and as a society not that accessible to terrorism, Denmark must show concern about the countries that are. It must not betray its picture as a protagonists of democratic humanism, of conflict-solutions through dialogue and consensus, not through force.
e. the duty to the unconditioned, to the "irrational rationality" of the gospel: love your neighbor as yourself.

The brute fact is that any choice involves the creation of one very particular event, and any sanctioning of this event would involve the offending, if not the violation, of most of the other criteria involved in the remaining options. However the leader has the possibility to create a new type of event through his choice, an event that reveals the moral impact of the development of weapons even meant to defend peace and prevent terrorism.

So, our leader choose the following solution: he convenes a meeting with the board, the CEOs, the representatives of employees at all levels, the major subcontractors and customers, and informs them calmly, with gentle authority, about all the options, stating that he himself shall not accept the order. Thus, by violating the principle of business secrecy, and hence, seriously damaging his own reputation, he creates a new kind of event.

This vice president had to resign, of course, and he did resign at that very meeting. His choice might have had a moral impact on the people present, an impact

---

16. Kierkegaard named Aristotle's concept of "desire" (orexis), so pertinent to choice and character, "passion".

spreading in the shape of new initiatives, new alliances, new visions, and perhaps new enterprises, new firms, so that the shareholders did not lose their money after all. As to what became of him, it is of less interest.

This example, however, ought not to be interpreted as an indirect adherence to the idea that there are rational solutions to almost all these kind of "lemmas", hence, that it is possible to cut the Gordian knot, or that "the event shall find its own way". Lemmas express bounded rationality built into an unbounded field of circumstances, of which our souls are a pertinent part. There is "a language of the heart" involved in choosing, especially when the choice does not constitute a level of conflicting criteria, but prepares the field for a **poetic** activity, where the choice also creates the one who chooses. No secret, benevolent technical or economical imagination can be found here, but also drama, and often, as in classical drama, tragedy.

Zooming in on the unconditioned, on what in this book has hitherto been addressed as "The Fourth", will most typically reveal the "Trap of Antigone"[17] – the condition of being caught between social aims, norms and obligations on the one side, and the demands of nature, of universal values, and the commitment to "the absolute", on the other. But this opposition does not reject the social dimension as such, it is anything but hostile towards the community. What it really does is juxtapose another kind of social tie, imitating – what might be called – a "choreography of centripetality": drawing the lights of rights and duties into the circle of the self. Thus, recreating **chōra** as the place of being in harmony with oneself, as a threshold of a new solidarity. But the sway of this harmony and hence, to stick to the metaphor, its inherited inertia of "concerted" action, presupposes the lack of harmony, presupposes misgiving, conflict and the whole classical repertoire of violent emotions too, of hate, despair, avarice, obstinate craving for wealth, and the permanently seething lust for power.

What might be called the "fear of tragedy", pervading most American contributions to business economics, often shall prevent the "scientist" to realize the "Trap of Antigone". The unquestioned, tacit metaphors of war and sport running underneath these discourses not only block realism, but construct a pseudo-reality with an irresistibly suggestive power: victory, unity, esprit de corps, forming a type of commitment where individual responsibility is allowed for only within narrow strategic frames.

We must dare change this attitude at its root, and confront these delicate matters, confront the deeds subject to court-martial. They are vague and often utterly subjective phenomena like "cowardice", "desertion", "insubordination" leading to "retreat", and even to "defeat", and to "dissolution" of units and spirits. But they might very well be an expression of "the prerogative of the master to give names",

---

17. In the tragedy of Sophocles, Antigone and the ruler, Creon, come into confrontation when she insists on burying her dead brother in spite of the despot's orders.

as Nietzsche spoke about in "Zur Genealogie der Moral". These pejorative labels of attitudes stamped on bodies disobedient to the rationality of masters. These martial concepts that so "naturally" are translated into the vocabulary of business economics under labels as "lacks of commitment", of solidarity, of cooperation, of responsibility, of social virtue, generally. This self-established right of power to baptize is first and foremost the right to baptize the event – so tragi-comically demonstrated by the most meticulous care with which totalitarianism in the East and West try to anticipate, and, hence, to settle, the experience of any event. But what is judged as "treason" to the principles of private interests could be understood as duty to the public or to a person's own conscience. One must not forget that so-called "industrial espionage" still, in many nations of the West, is sentenced much harder than child pornography, even if it could be motivated by a clear will of an individual to sacrifice himself to the interests of nature and people.

After all, **kairos** might be the crucial moment where an alternative timing is made real, a timing adjusted to the time of a real humanist culture.

Perhaps one could find, inside the public versions of events, consented upon and authorized as History, a fragile but revolutionary momentum, manifesting itself at the level of individual predicament, and hence, in the eternal play between the person as a manager and as a leader? A conflict so inaccessible to strategic, and even to pragmatic, solutions that it could carry the message of a healthy dissolution of invested structures of power and wealth?

11.5. Kairology

In his "Nicomachean Ethics" Aristotle claims that "the whole theory of conduct is bound to be an outline only and not an exact system" and a little further on he adds "and matters of conduct and expediency have nothing fixed or invariable about them". He concludes:

> "And if this is true of the general theory of ethics, still less is exact precision possible in dealing with particular cases of conduct; for these come under no science or professional tradition, but the agents themselves have to consider what is suited to the circumstances on each occasion" (Op.cit. II, ii, 3-4).

The word "Kairos" comprehends "what is suited to the circumstances on each occasion".

Aristotle thus refuses to grant any "scientific status" to practical philosophy in the sense of what we use to understand as "the social sciences" – but he grants to the good person the possibility of acquiring and using absolute knowledge (epistēmē). Thus, we can conclude that Aristotle does not identify exact knowledge with real knowledge, as we do in the concept of "science".[18] However, of importance here is the fact that Aristotle does not think that a discipline could exist in which future events were predicted with certainty, or in which the consequences of actions relative to a more precise scale of time could be assessed with certainty. The methods used by such a "discipline of kairos", or what I should term, **kairologic**, comes very close to guessing, or to a rather unreliable calculation of probability. The mental capacities constituting an approach to the evaluation of the right moment must be found in cognitive faculties manifested through the virtues of "epibolē" and "prolēpsis", in intuition and fantasy.

An approach that does not elevate itself to a scientific discipline, not even to a technē, I shall call **Kairology**. Kairology is in opposition to any "kairologic" that pretends to predict the future by way of logic or mathematical means.

It is, of course, possible to try to imagine what will happen in the future, as well as trying to figure out what did happen in the past, but this is not the subject of a science. Why should not the network of conditions and implications of human action be far more complicated than the weather, and the weather can still not be forecasted with any tolerable precision for more than a few days, even though super-computers get more and more powerful every day. If the setting of social relations, the "weather of actions", should be more simple and its "rainy days" and "hurricanes" should be predictable here, then the only reasons could be that we act through words, and that words are rather few and rather simple, or that we deliberately try to fulfill our own prophecies. But the meaning of acting through words and acting deliberately must then come very close to each other, and it should be possible to neglect that, in trying to fulfill prophecies, these very prophecies might be made even more complicated, instead of coming true.

But perhaps the use of words in propositions shall appear to be even more complicated than the accessible parameters of the weather?

Something points to the fact that the tempting metaphors from mathematics and natural science of "chaos" and "turbulence" do not work any longer as conceptualizations of cumulative processes that cannot be predicted. Something more is demanded to catch the force of social change and its uncertainty.[19]

---

18. The matter is complicated by the fact that "epistēmē", "real knowledge", "knowledge of the essences of things", normally is translated into "science" by Western scholars. And the concept of "phronēsis", "practical wisdom", does cover far more than a concept of "exact knowledge", because it presupposes the right way to generalize about experience, a way anticipated by the right hexis, and hence, by virtue (aretē).

19. It is interesting that so influential a theorist of business science as Peter Drucker calls his last book, from 1996, "Managing in a Time of Great Change", while in 1980 he published a book with the title "Managing in Turbulent Times". Post-modernism destroys the obviousness that metaphors of natural science used to have to thought processes within the philosophy and the social sciences. Perhaps one of the last bestsellers building on mathematical metaphors was Tom Peters' "Thriving on Chaos" from 1989?

The new concept is the post-modern **contingency**, and it has to be shaped in relation to the event.[20] It covers the fact that even if we do not have any possibility to know the decisive parameters generating an event, nor the array of important trends emerging from it, we act as if we do. Because at the same time we have this hunch of a play of necessities, necessities probably inaccessible to thought, but not to another sense, the sixth sense, the **koinē aisthēsis**, to which answers a language of an inherent social sensibility, a language of the heart – quite unlike the game between chaos and turbulence and the instruments permanently developed to defeat it.[21]

This means that "contingency" in a way presents itself as the brute fact, as "haecceitas", that which **is**, and that proves itself to be necessary, just because it is – the right English word for "haecceitas" is probably facticity. Hence "contingency" expresses a way in which randomness hides itself within necessity.

Something comes to be. It happens in a place, and it happens to place; it presupposes circumstances, and it creates circumstance. "Circumstatio", "peristasis", "surrounding" as a state of affairs, surrounding a "stasis", ("standing", "stand-still", "position", "place", "attitude"), that perhaps seem stable, in spite of being a centre that transforms or is itself subject to transformation.

So this contingency is really what matters when we are speaking of a place as an event, where dynamics and speech (invocation) unfold themselves. We have to seek the secret of contingency, and it shall reveal itself as the secret of the many still-remembered places. But it will also hide itself to thought.

---

20. The concept of "contingency" referred to here must not be confused with the concept of "contingency theory", according to which the important parameters of action can be known. Contingency theory, "which suggests that all organizations have a limited number of contingent factors to deal with, and that it is how they deal with them that structures the organizations. Amongst these contingencies are: the environment, as more or less turbulent; the size of the organization, as comprising more or fewer employees; the technology of the organization, as more or less routine or search-oriented in its functioning; and the culture of the host country in which the organization is located. Implicitly, the argument goes, successful managers have to identify correctly the contingencies that they are dealing with; having done that they can adopt the organization design that best fits these contingencies, according to contingency theory research." (Clegg, Palmer: 1996, p.12-13).

21. Let me restate the definition of "contingency" in Chapter One: it originates in a Latin word "contingere", that means something like "eventually touching" – perhaps the metaphor refers to the links in a chain chosen rather arbitrarily, as a child chooses shells or small stones with a hole in them to put on a string. But "contingere" is a translation by the early Christian philosopher, Boëthius, of two concepts from Aristotle: "endechetai" and "symbainein". The first concept expresses "the possible, that might be necessary, but does not have to be". The second means "it happens". Thus "contingency" actually means "that which has happened, but of which we cannot tell (yet/ever) if it necessarily had to happen, and which we then have to treat as if we had wanted it to be".

Our culture is pervaded with great events concealed in the names of places: Bethlehem, Golgatha, Jerusalem, ... Hastings, Waterloo, Stalingrad, Jalta, ... the Kölner Dome, The Berlin Wall, ...

The names of churches, of central stations and of airports, the names of sport centres, cinemas, and shopping centres, the destination of calculated as well as almost innocent pilgrimages to sanctuaries of small and unknown deities. As if a place could warrant the necessity of what happens, and in itself contain the common denominator of inexhaustible and inscrutable experiences through the crossing, in transit, of infinite individual fates.

And often a personal name achieves almost the same significance, Churchill, Russell, Gorbachev, carnal places figuring as wandering events.[22]

When managerial efforts through the creation of public relations, and management literature in their wake, try to exploit these phenomena by creating destinies of new places and entrepreneurs they shall often fail. **Chōra** is not that easy to usurp or to domesticate. The so-called "management of processes", and the new discipline "management of events", frequently carry with them the mistakes of "symbolic management": the notion that culture can be artificially created. Often they shall give away their badly disguised attempts at dominating chōra through the production of flat events or even worse, through economic disaster.

There seems to be a broad gap between the carefully planned project and the event. The conceptional figure inherent in the notion of "project" belongs to operational analysis: a subject with a plan confronting a dynamic world that can be manipulated through knowledge of its fundamental parameters. Even if reservations are made in relation to the perfection of this knowledge, the model still presupposes that the event can be an object, a thing outside the planners mind and context. Perhaps the trait of Japanese management that a plan is never conceived of through algorithmic procedures, is a more important secret of the Japanese success than the celebrated concepts of "lean production" and "just-in-time". In opposition to the ideal of the algorithmic procedure in which a future is anticipated in every detail, and the steps leading to its implementation are fixed, Japanese managers see a plan as a much looser framework organized around visions and notions about the mission of the firm. The Japanese system, with its life-long employment and a democratic concept of management that weighs the integration of employees in decisional procedures and focusses on consensus, is favorable to long-time planning, because the employees are involved actively in its implementation. The role of the manager can be more passive, the more the process functions easily and the more it "organizes itself" (Ohmae: 1982; Ohmae: 1985). By all means, this idealistic picture of Japanese management could still be accepted during the Eighties. But even this softer version of strategic thinking is instrumental, after all, and it demands a

---

22. Novelists and biographers have always known the fact that series of events, even stories, could be caught symbolically within the name of a place: "Le Coté de Guermantes", "Berlin Alexanderplatz", "Der Tod in Venedig".

thorough change in the whole concept to adjust it to the realities of the event.[23] However, the real acknowledgement of the character of the event forces us to move the centre of the happening out into the world.

The event "hides itself" inside a reality, in the small, hardly perceptible preparations of something going to happen, and in overhanging trends of necessity ready to seize at us, with all the force of the sudden. What has become known as "language creating behaviour" might seem not to function at all.

In a way, the real problem does not consist in creating meaning through constructing "a language", or more modest, through some apt propositions, but to escape the force of the obvious meaning. "Occurrences" might be seen as "events" with such an evident meaning that they can be identified with their names. However, such evidence can only be created through social dominance of some kind, a dominance that transforms such events into occurrences within a story constructed, ratified and protected by power.

If the board and the CEO have chosen to introduce a new technology in spite of extensive protests at the lower level of management and among workers, one shall often find that this event is interpreted as a success in the annual reports in the years following, even if from the shopfloor level it appeared to destroy established ways of cooperation, and hence, innovative efforts. The board and the CEO will focus on its cost-reducing effects, relating to cuts in material waste and in man-hours. But the story might be told from another angle, as the story about reduction of product quality, and the story about an increase in pressures inside the labour process, and hence as an intensification of stress, and an increase in the turnover of labour. For a few years the event might still be seen as this unambiguous occurrence, increasing profits through the increase in turnover of products, until the market begins to fail due to lower product quality (and, of course, increased competition, too), and the work force begins to be extremely unreliable due to the injuries to informal cooperation from organizational changes in the wake of the new technology. Then the story has to be changed, and with it the understanding of the event, and of its heroes and villains. This description might relate rather closely to the American car industry in the Seventies.

The real leader shall keep the event open to interpretation.

He does not fix the **continuity**, as if the event were a centre with concentric circles surrounding it, all subject to observation and hence potentially known to him.

To him the event is **unique**, i.e., a fact that can never be fully comprehended, nor totally explained, but which always gives ways to the new angles of acknowledgment to come in the future through the very consequences of the event itself. In this sense, the meaning of an event is always **transcendental**, related to the secrets of

---

23. Professor Henrik Herlau at the Copenhagen Business School, in his so-called KUBUS Model, has with a great deal of success tried to re-shape the concept of the project, exploiting group dynamics, tacit knowledge and other non-discursive principles of inventive inertia in order to stimulate innovative processes.

"The Fourth". The event is never over and done with. The game between **situation** and **event**, already touched upon, reveals this. The situation could be described through a metaphor which might remind of one of these astronomical models constructed during the Baroque: the earth at the centre is surrounded by circles of metal, in a great many angles, somehow intersecting each other, and each ring at each angle being a system of concentric circles constituting an event.

The leader must control this game of truth[24] between the situation and the event through **euboulia**, through the sense of the possible.

The leader must wage war not only against the trivial interpretations, but even more against the necessary and forceful ones. He must always be sensitive to "the event of meaning", always far more than to the "meaning of the event",. He must be ready to overrule and redeem any identity that seems proper to the event.

Cooper and Burrell are well aware of this characteristic of post-modern managerial experience:

"Organizations do not first pre-exist and then create their relationships; they **occur** in existential gaps which lie beyond knowledgeable discourse. These gaps are the loci of operation of **mise-en-scenes** and strategies which focus their attentions on, and emerge out of, the unprogrammable and non-discursive." (Cooper, Burrell: 1988, p. 108)

The virtues of the manager and, most important, of the leader have to compensate for that. They are, through their inherent moral, and, hence, historical sensitivity, allied with the events to come. One might say that the leader as an example is the anticipation of the phenomenology of the event as a **social** happening, as a happening **in** chōra, because the way in which he creates significance through his actions never can be grasped analytically. There is an aura of the living "totem" about both the event and the person here.

The virtues of management and of leadership not only compensate for this lack of conventional rationality, they use it as a clue to the secret forces of what happens. The leader must be utterly sensitive to traces, not of changing surface trends, but of a hidden necessity – the only name of which through centuries has been "fate".

This competence of the manager and the leader is not identical to a spontaneous creativity, nor, of course, to demagogy. On the contrary, it must be called a "poetical" competence at the level of Greek drama where the plot is subject to laws existing somewhere between necessity and fiction. Are we able to speak about "the fiction of necessity"?

A metaphor to understand the fact that the event cannot be artificially created – unless the social setting is totalitarian – and hence, to understand its inherent and clandestine relation to place, might be "the puzzle".

---

24. The concept is used by Michel Foucault, "jeux de verité" in the French.

The puzzle involves a process. It is actually about the process of accomplishing, and not that much about the accomplishment. The puzzle I have in mind is an "evil" one, where you do not know the motive. The most evil one would be a puzzle where the bricks were all the same colour. You have to work only from the form; the motif would then be on the other side. But I think that our puzzle has its motives, however complicated they might be. E.g., it is not so much the puzzle about why you exactly had to meet your wife in Stockholm, of all places, as about the enigma why you did meet her that day in that month of that year.

Where, on what, are we laying the bricks down? In **chōra**?

Is it she who is receiving them? Is she the patient board with the box-like edges, demarcation lines of a world? Or is chōra the hidden motive? So, if you for some reason should be able to anticipate the place of what is going to happen, you could anticipate the event?

I hope that this is not the explanation for why managers move their firms to the Far East; or begin sales campaigns in Russia; or never move to the outskirts of London, as was expected; or why they place all available capital in Silicon Valley. However, chōra could never be caught by the constructing of buildings in European metropolises with walls of glass inviting the gaze, but which one, however, cannot look through. When our gaze is confronted with the reflection of the buildings and the sky on the other side of the street which – if they are of glass too – will reflect the reflecting facade and its sky, this simulated void cannot grasp chōra. This is an all too tempting post-modern metaphor: that nothing is in itself, it is only what the other is – and the other is not what it is, but what it is not. Through these reciprocal reflections the two fronts will close the view, they will make a prisoner of the crucial aspect of time and place, the **horizon**. In Greek this word, "horizō", means "to delimit", "to draw boundaries", "to border on", "to consecrate" and "to delimit by hand of words, i.e. to define". But there is no horizon without chōra.

The horizon of a region might tell us something about its hidden centres and, hence, of the position of the firm; as well as about the feebleness and the strength of words (because they reveal the horizon). But the horizon means both what we might see from the places of the place; and what we cannot see because of it, meaning the "overt and the hidden contextual circumstances".

It might be nearly obvious to define an event as the place from where horizons move themselves. The never-ending, unfinished character of the event, where a possible new event is able to change the meaning of every past event, is grasped by the metaphor of the horizon. So long as a horizon is the essence of dreams, visions, hopes, and longings to a firm, it is the task of the leader to build it into his gestures, and to keep it open.

Perhaps the most striking way to refer to the concept of horizon is through the Greek amphitheatre, where the upper edges of this opposite, hollow cone delimit the sky, and hence the real world. Placing a world within the world, such as the firm very often wants to position itself: a microcosm imitating reality in the hope of being able to cast its very image back in order to control it.

CHAPTER 12

The Drama of Decisions.
The Theatre as a Metaphor of the Union
of Time and Place: The Play of Fate

Choosing the right man at the wrong time, or the wrong man at the right time, not only appears to be the fault of emperors, prime ministers and managers, but seems to be the principles of fate, if we listen to Greek tragedy. Fate manifest itself in what Aristotle names "reversal" ("peripeteia") in the expected run of events in the plot:

> "Reversal ("peripeteia") is a change to the opposite direction of events, as already stated, and one in accord, as we insist, with probability ("eikos") or necessity ("anankaion"): as when in the **Oedipus** the person who comes to bring Oedipus happiness, and intends to rid him of his fear about his mother, effects the opposite by revealing Oedipus' true identity."[25]

Here **myth** (mythos) manifests itself as a correction of the plot as the possible product of organized, social action. A force manifests itself, enforcing another order on the network of human action and negating the expectations and predictions of the common horizon of rationality.

This lesson, no matter how its metaphysical or cosmological roots might have presented itself to the Greek mind, can still be learnt by modern management as the persistent message ("hermēneia")[26] from this powerful tradition: events cannot be controlled by creating stories at the level of deliberate decisions, however carefully planned and shaped through vision. Events follow another logic, another "logos".

It is this "logic" that the theatre is able to reveal to us, and hence, to the manager and the leader, if they choose to listen with sufficient sensitivity.

However, this does not imply that there is a clandestine level of events, meaning a "deeper" level, an essential structure emerging at the surface exactly at the intersection of time and space on the stage as the one and only line. There is no "one and only line", but only authors' attempts at phrasing what, due to its very mode of ex-

---

25. Aristotle (1995a): Poetics. The Loeb Edition. Transl. by S. Halliwell. Harvard University Press, Cambridge (Mass.) London. XI, 1452a.

26. "Hermenēia", "speech", or "interpretation of speech", is the core of the word "hermeneutics", the discipline of the "hermēneus" or the "hermēneutēs", the one who deciphers messages, messages often brought by the god Hermes from the realm beyond to the mortal ones. By the way, Hermes is also the god of merchants, and, not least, the god of thieves.

istence, cannot be phrased sufficiently. This postmodern insight, however, must not be transformed into the seemingly obvious and widespread dogma that "meaning" is something that can be created, or even "constructed". Meaning is the phenomenon that can never be created, not even under totalitarianism, and not even nurtured in young and feeble souls during education, without a heavy price, if it has to be for real. "Meaning" is, at one and the same time, a phenomenon surrounding itself with the air of ontology and transcendence, and at the very same time only existing at the surface. As such, it is an aporia, and deserves a name that answers this condition: meaning is **epiphany**.

This word, which was used about the coming of the Magi to do homage to the Baby Jesus at Bethlehem, and hence, to the coming of Christ into this world (its Latin translation is "adventus"), exhibits a paradox which Kierkegaard named "The God inside time". It is a Greek term reinforcing the signification of "phainō": to bring to daylight, appear, make visible, make audible, make acknowledgeable; but it also means: to shine, and to happen, to call on, to be present. The word "phainō" is the core in the word "phainomenon": "phenomenon".

Meaning breaks on us. This is the insight transferred by this many-sided word that invokes all senses, just like the happenings on the stage do, but primarily sight and hearing. A word that fuses all its facets into one centre of signification: contingency.

Meaning as epiphany is simultaneously something thrown at us from the flow of time, and something summoning us on behalf of a necessity which only draws on a legitimacy that comes from the very fact that it exists. Thus it contains, contemporaneously, the possibilities of holiness and deceit.

The theatre not only demonstrates this, it is also its inherent force and the clue to its power over us. On the stage a myth is staged that is the product of a mortal human being, it is man's accomplishment but also something far more than that. But not just insofar as it seizes us, because this seizing cannot be arbitrary. As Aristotle states in his "Poetics", this seizing must be seen as the result of "anagnōrisis", of "recognition".

The concept of "recognition" invokes the notion of a more fundamental knowledge.

> "Recognition, as the very name indicates, is a change from ignorance to knowledge, leading to friendship or to enmity, and involving matters which bear on prosperity or adversity. The finest recognition is that which occurs simultaneously with reversal, ..." (Poetics, XI, 1452a)

The theatre, then, imitates "recognition" through an event incorporating "reversal". But the means of the theatre is **repetition**.[27]

---

27. It is almost impossible to escape the conceptual world of Kierkegaard and Nietzsche here, and hence, what was borrowed from them: the concept of "repetition"; in the former it

The gesture of repetition challenges the unique as an event, at the same time imitating it and cancelling it. As an image of **chōra**, the stage is a false place, a non-place. As an image of time, of the event, it is a simulacra, an artificially nurtured contingency. But as the negation of "the negative" it exhibits the possibility of the real.

What can the manager and the leader learn from this?

First and foremost that recognition cannot be the result of invention. They must invent what is already there. That means: they must get into touch with the myth, with the "alphabet of existence", with the "grammar of speculation". These concepts refer to the idea that ontology can be developed by epistemological deliberations upon lingustic forms. The grammatical figures such as the noun or the verb, reveal the content of human knowledge by simultaneously pointing at its limits.[28]

But they must also recognize the importance of "reversal" which means that they must find the right moment to communicate "recognition". This right moment, **Kairos**, depicts an action that is able to form a genuine example. Through such a prototypical, or even "archetypical", event they must be able to exhibit a necessity that reaches us at the surface level, as an opportunity.

I think that this is the first, important lesson that managers and leaders can learn from the Greek theatre: meaning must be discovered, never invented. The good person, the true hexis, can never be invented. Virtues are articulated, and exhibited as "human nature" – no matter how hard the labour had been that let to their acquisition.

Hence, consensus is anticipated, and the illusions of the concept of consensus is abandoned, because at another level passion and thought ("orexis" and "nous") have already been reconciled as the will to will.

From this point of view the metaphor of "negotiation" is out of place as an approach to understand how the employees relate to the plot, whether they are conceived of as listeners, audience, readers on the one side, or as authors, instructors and actors on the other. The concept of "negotiation", apparently an increasingly suggestive metaphor when the seizing power of the "winning stories" of organizations shall be explained, does not capture the interplay of deceit and holiness, of the way fiction is overruled by the necessity inherent in contingency, in "the factual". Instead it places insight at the level of the voluntary, and hence, as a function of consensus. The danger is, that the world of manipulative rhetoric shall come to dominate on behalf of poetic (poiētic), if the widespread concept of "choosing meaning" is maintained, as in the following phrasing by J.A. Conger: "It is important that business leaders see their role as 'meaning makers.' They must pick and

---

points to the possibility of a final release through mercy, in the latter it points to the cruel game of fate with man. Postmodernism draws heavily on this notion (Deleuze: 1994).

28. "Grammar of speculation" was the name used about this way of thinking by the followers of Duns Scotus during the Middle Ages, founding the whole tradition of looking at thinking, acting and feeling as bound to language games, or "existentialiae".

choose from the rough materials of reality to construct pictures of great possibilities" (Conger: 1991). It must be realized that "the rough materials of reality" are already there as the mythical structure rendered to us, and they can neither be dispensed with nor voluntarily chosen from. They compel.

The other important lesson granted to us by the Greek theatre is the knowledge that decisions are bound to fate. They are determined by character viewed as a "metaphysical role", and by a necessity that always escapes human knowledge in its proper principles of continuity and coherence. The good person can only save his soul, not secure his existence against the evil play of fortune.

Perhaps this naturalistic concept of fate does not appeal to a modern mind, but after all, it also stresses the fact that socio-historical processes generally, and hence, the environment of the firm, cannot be controlled. And this view of fate meshes closely an experience with the slogan of postmodernism.

Postmodernism generally counters this condition with recourse to constructivism, emphasizing that the person must "construct" himself through his decisions. Such a well-known business scientist and psychologist as Weick phrases this in the following way:

> "Choice imposes value on information or, said differently, values are created by our choices. We do not choose an antecedent good, but make something good by choosing it. The key point is that each individual chooses himself or herself. Who we are emerges from our decisions, and if we make no decisions, then we are left only the vaguest sense of who we are as persons. In the beginning each of us exists as a field of possibilities. As we project ourselves into some of these possibilities, and reject other ones, we begin to determine who we are and who we will be ... Those binding decisions are the ones that define us."[29]

At first glance this agrees very well with Aristotle's description of the process through which the right hexis is acquired, but this remains a superficial likeness. In the first place, persons do not create themselves by choosing deliberately. Sartre had to admit to that late in his life, agreeing with his former friend, Maurice Merleau-Ponty, on his insight that we are far more the products of small and large histories, far more the products of the circumstances and contextual settings than reflective reason could imagine. In the second place, we certainly do not "make" the good, we find it. First and foremost because we are created by the event, secondly by our ability to "use" it in the formation of our identity. How could it be otherwise as long as we are tied to a biological material that grows extremely slowly, caught in a cultural setting that does not allow for much experimenting with "values"? Of course we do not create values, values arise, just like myths and stories arise. Nobody was ever

---

29. (Weick: 1979). See also Weick's recent book: Weick, K.E. (1995): Sensemaking in Organizations. Sage Publications, Thousand Oaks.

free to choose himself from scratch, but only to try to navigate within a situation – which, of course, does not exclude walking against the tide.

This is exactly what the theatre shows us.

When drama concentrates on choices, carefully constructing situations of decisions from Sophocles to Ibsen, from Tennessee Williams to Albee, from Strindberg to Norén, the result seems to be that decisions are surface-illusions accompanying acts obeying another "logic":

Firstly, clear-cut situations of decisions are subject to suspicion; they seldom release or accomplish the expected result. It is as if they conceal processes of quite another kind that are displaced, following paths in their violent movements just underneath the surface of the events of the plot. We seem to be able to catch a glimpse of them, to get a hold on them, but ultimately they escape us. And this tension between the plot with its overt dilemmas, reinforced situations, distinct characters, and prototypical dialogues, and the overwhelming otherness that they invoke creates the nerve of the drama. This is, of course, why the great drama not only invites us to interpret, but forces us to. Here one can find the reason why genuine fiction is never fictitious, but creates a new level of the factual: because it invokes the otherness of language games, of the games of truth. Secondly, the drama mocks us. By apparently imitating the ways in which we are acting as if the stage were reality itself, the play accomplishes a second-order imitation, imitating our way of imitating a time in which decisions and choices seem to depend on us. In concentrating on dialogues and solutions to dilemmas of cognition, the drama mocks the role of dialogue in our lives by exhibiting it to us as a game of emotion and will. Dialogues are exhibited as phenomena that always succeed too well. They always come out that right or that wrong, with the result that their fooling of both the intellect and the emotion reveals itself; they function too well as answers, anticipating the questions and hence annihilating them. Dialogues are developed to such a degree of brilliance that we acknowledge their real character as games.

The theatre erases the distinction between faction and fiction by showing us that the factual is a mode of being tied to repetition where the difference to otherness is abandoned.

Nurturing the metaphor of the theatre in relation to management leaves us with a lot of questions.

The first one is how to interpret all the functions of the theatre in relation to the firm, its management, and its environment.

The concept of "role" has had a tremendous influence on managerial and organizational theories through its development within psychology and sociology from the Sixties and far into the Eighties. However, this concept is complicated, and cannot be understood properly, unless we relate it to the other crucial functions of the stage. It must cover both a person-side: the author, the director, the prompter, the actors, and the audience. As well as a material-side: the play, the production, the setting, the piece of scenery. And finally, an immaterial-side: the plot, the myth, the events, the dialogues. However, the theatre might be viewed as a corporate firm itself, the product of which is "cultural experiences" and with the increasing "immaterial" character of products and the weight on services, the analogy becomes more and more important, as documented by the recent work of Pierre Guillet de Monthoux.[30]

It is not that simple to decide how to develop the analogy. Shall the manager be thought of as the author, the producer (to make him the manager of the theatre would destroy the analogy), or as a principal actor – probably not as the rather anonymous prompter. And where shall we place the employees? As actors, or as audience? Finally, what are the plot and the myth? Are they parts in the combined, or perhaps conflicting, stories about the organization and its management? And does this story have to be overt and mutual in the forum of the firm, or can it belong to only a few, or even be clandestine, if not transcendent? Which events can be classified as acts and episodes in the drama of the firm?

To this comes the problem of the genre: is the drama of the firm a tragedy or a comedy? Is it earnest or satiric? Or does it belong to the new kind of plays involving the audience as parts of the play, even as co-authors – like the play Tamara-land (Boje: 1995; Lund: 1999)?

From the perspective of strategic management, the analogy would probably place the manager as the author of the play, and in its modifications through symbolic management he would be the director or the set designer. The last function is emphasized when the artifacts of corporate reality are the subject of organizational theory and research, as in the inspiring work of P. Gagliardi (Gagliardi: 1990). In postmodernism the manager might fill the function of a prompter ensuring that some lines are said in the right way. However, in the wake of postmodernism, and with the emphasis on the leader's virtues and on the integrity of his character, the leader could be thought of as a hero in a play from classicism, by Schiller, or even Goethe. To me, this leader appears as Faust, standing between two worlds: the material world of success, pleasures, power, strategic knowledge and technical expertise, on the one side, and the world of the absolute, on the other.

However, the drama of the firm ought not to distribute the roles to the environment and on the employees in such a way as to sustain a manichean view of the world, appointing the good and the bad guys, the winners and the losers, the ones lost and the ones saved. Even if this is a crucial feature of the myth, not only the ones that appear almost "universal", but national, institutional, group-related or personal myths too.

Now, it must not be forgotten that the theatre has made the movie possible, wintering inside this technique, and hence, that the marvellous distance to the conventional cosmology found in the Greek theatre often has been lost. The result has

---

30. Pierre Guillet de Monthoux has recently made a comprehensive analysis of the theatre as a subject of business economics, mixing philosophy, aesthetic theory, and business economics in a very suggestive, postmodern style (Monthoux: 1998).

been the victory of brute contrasts, and of crude characters, blowing life into metaphors from war, tribe- and family-bonds, patterns of sexual relations, but without the moral perspective from tragedies like "Macbeth", "Romeo and Juliet", or "King Lear". Here the ability to look destruction right in the eyes without any compromise, or any trace of a happy ending, repeats the distance produced in the Greek theatre in relation to the myth it works on.

It would, of course, be very difficult to ask the leader to promote this attitude of great tragedy, and even absurd to ask for the far more obvious play of the distance between the story and its staging in comedy. However, the audience demands authenticity from the play, and the actors must at least understand it, if they should be able to convince. Thus, it is not that easy to make the play cooperate on the coordination of patterns of events that seem to wait for a story to give them their "real" meaning. This is primarily due to the fact that the plot must be anticipated through the way in which the future is buried and generated in the past, and in which it shapes the past by being its horizon, i.e., through **memory**. We must not forget the emphasis which Aristotle gave to "recognition", to remembering. This demands a continuity from the story, or the plot, that makes up the play, based on both the individual and the collective experiences of the actors/employees. However, the articulation of these experiences have very narrow bonds: they have to anticipate stories of success. This makes the "general story" of the firm rather tedious, or irrelevant, just like it makes so many movies unimportant to the heart of experience, because of the dogma of the happy ending.

The question left now is the following: what story distinguishes itself so much as to be an example of the myth? We cannot accept pure formal criteria here; the imagery of voluntarism must be rejected. There has to be a line of demarcation.

CHAPTER 13

The Myth and the Saga

In dealing with the narrative in relation to the firm it is rather obvious to adhere to the metaphor of the theatre. The reciting poet, the commenting know-it-all are characters of the theatre. The firm is no literary salon.

The narrative is the game of memory. But memories appear to be easily captured by "constructions" of memories. However, this is not so. Personal memory is indebted to myth, and vice versa. So from personal memory the criteria must be able to be fetched through which the myth is distinguished as a myth, so that the questions can be met properly: is "Julius Caesar" by Shakespeare a myth? Is "Per Gynt" by Henrik Ibsen a myth? Is "Doctor Zhivago" by Boris Pasternak a myth? Is "Look back in Anger" by John Osborne a myth? Are "Who is Afraid of Virginia Wolf" by Edward Albee, or "The Old Man and the Sea" by Ernest Hemingway, myths? If age should be a criterion of myth, the answer would be easy. But this is not so. Instead some shall try to reduce the stories to basic patterns of stories, then named "myths". But this procedure presupposes rather dubious interpretations. "Per Gynt" and "Doctor Zhivago" as versions of Ulysses, but Ulysses as a version of ...? And "The old man and the sea" (with/without Spencer Tracy) as a version of Noah, or even of Prometheus. And Prometheus as a version of ...? "Julius Caesar" as a version of "Cain and Abel", and "Cain and Abel" as a version of ...? Is the answer "mathematical structures"? If it were, it would be an enigma how such structures could found patterns of meaning. When their symbols triumph in being empty.

So, a myth is something that does not yield to solutions containing notions from Lévi-Straussian structuralism like "opposite couples", or any other concepts. It is something that does not allow for any meta-language relative to its very own level of experience. Where the transference between expressions by hand of analogy seems to work for a while, it does not appear to yield any theoretical sufficiency. The question is persistent still: what is a myth?

To Aristotle **mimēsis** is the core concept of art. But mimēsis understood as a creative process of imitation. Mimēsis is a way in which to approach reality by presenting us to the otherness of this reality; by preparing us for another reality, perhaps not "behind" or "beyond" the one familiar to us, but "inside" it. The myth strikes this doubleness, this borderline.

Let me repeat once more: what is a myth?

The answer is that a myth is an event.

But what kind of event?

An event in which a voice summons us. But a voice inside every human voice, a first voice. Because this first voice exists inside the voice that tells the story, or secondarily, inside the writing, it is possible to preserve it through repetition. This first voice, this "archē-voice", can never be heard except in the voices that unfold it, as if it were their very own. This first and clandestine voice is identical to the phenomenon called "die Sage" by Martin Heidegger in his fabulous collection of essays "Unterwegs zur Sprache".[31]

Then, the only criterion of the "truth" of the myth is that it seizes upon us in a **sudden** movement ("to exaiphnēs" in the words of Plato). It is the product of the moment, filling the moment as its very content. Through this gesture of the first and concealed voice it is drawing us into an epic movement, into a rhythm of eternal repetition, into the myth as the subject that is able to transform our lives by making any event a part of a saga. A saga, a concept originating in old Icelandic society, is a myth told through contingent events. So the saga does not exhibit the myth through prototypical events, where every event contains the myth wrapped up, and concentrated, as with a holographic image (to use, for once, the metaphors of mathematics). The saga conceals the myth by letting us long for it. The saga installs a borderline between contingency and a transcendent core, and through this very gesture it invites us to try to cross it.

The criterion of truth here must be twofold:

Firstly it consists in a revealing of something that, however, does not show itself completely. Martin Heidegger used the common Greek word for truth here, **alētheia,** but tried to release it from the worlds of Plato and Aristotle, tying it to an earlier Greek philosopher to Parmenides. For him truth meant "that which shows itself to us through the gesture by which it hides itself" (Heidegger: 1954). Heidegger's point is that truth cannot be a subjective phenomenon, it cannot be bound to certainty, and hence, never to consensus, and it cannot be bound to any criterion of correspondence, either – in this connection, where we are dealing with art, the latter seems obvious.

The myth shows itself to us through the saga, through the story about us, and it conceals itself in every and each event that carries it. But at the same the saga also conceals the event by transforming every event into a means to its own end, by wrapping every event in its unique continuity and coherence, in its peculiar time, and hence, by always deferring the answer to the question: "What was the meaning of that which happened?"

By "getting on the train" of the saga we travel back into our own memory, transforming it through the poetic effort of the myth, watching it with the eyes of the myth, and trying to sense the criterion of certainty peculiar to it. But perhaps the myth is nothing more than the fragment of a melody, a feeling of a tune, a feeble sense of a beautiful harmony. And "beautiful" indeed, because – in spite of all

---

31. To translate "die Sage" is very difficult, because so many significations are involved: "the trans-subjective form of the utterance", "the content of the utterance as a message beyond human communication", "the utterance as a trace of something left by the very sound of it", "the event of uttering", and "the saga" (Heidegger: 1959).

cruelty – the myth watches us through the veil of beauty: the breathtaking beauty of that which had to happen.

Thus, we cannot use a criterion of truth originating in rhetoric. We cannot refer to the pathos which the story shall arise in us through the spoken words that carry it. We cannot refer to any "validity" of the saga, to any "narrative probability or fidelity", because we are not the subjects of this process, as Weick and Browning seems to think in relation to the story of the organization (Weick, Browning: 1986).

Secondly it consists in, what Aristotle in his Poetics called, **katharsis**. This complicated and richly interpreted concept that Aristotle never defines, does not relate to a subjective feeling of release, but to a moment of a deep feeling of belonging to the myth. A belonging that opens up to the transgression of the personal. Here one certainly does not "negotiate" the meaning of the play, truth seizes upon us, and in this eruptive gesture it draws us with it into the realm of another passion, the passion of the wonder, the promises of the miracle. It is the world of epiphany. Thus tragedy can be defined by Aristotle in the following way:

> "Tragedy, then, is mimesis of an action which is elevated, complete, and of magnitude; in language embellished by distinct forms in its sections; employing the mode of enactment, not narrative; and through pity ("eleou") and fear accomplishing the catharsis of such emotions." (Poetics, Op.cit. VI, 1449b)

The theatre demonstrates that the spoken word is the true media of myth. It shows us that we have to deserve the ability to get near to the myth. Aristotle emphasizes this: the spectator must be a co-actor in the play; he must join the saga, he must approach the myth through co-suffering, and besides suffering is reversal and recognition, the third component of the plot.

> "... the structure of the finest tragedy should be complex not simple as well as representing fearful and pitiable events (for this is the special feature of such mimesis)." (Poetics, Op.cit. XIII, 1452b)

The real tragedy shall arouse "fellow-feeling" (philantrŏpon) (ibid), or pity, or fear. This is done through exposing "suffering" (pathos), "and suffering is a destructive or painful action, such as public deaths, physical agony, woundings, etc." (ibid, XI).

The indispensable element of the story is **fellow-feeling**. This is what any leader ought to know who tries to discover a story about his firm. A fellow-feeling in relation to all stakeholders of the company, but also in relation to the environment. While the manager might still allow himself to operate with images of an enemy, the leader has to be very careful here. It is his task to dissolve concepts of an enemy, not to nurture them. If he appears to be a hero, it is of the war against war. If he stands forward as a person who gives freedom, what he sets free is the event. The real leader shall liberate the event from any strategic and pragmatic purpose. So it is the task of the leader to liberate the event from the story in which it is caught. Just as it is his task to liberate normativity from the talk of "values". Or as it is phrased so beautifully by Gilles Deleuze in "The Logic of Sense":

"Either ethics makes no sense at all, or this is what it means and has nothing else to say: not to be unworthy of what happens to us ... What is really immoral is the use of moral notions like just or unjust, merit or fault. What does it mean then to will the event? ... If willing the event is, primarily, to release its eternal truth, like the fire on which it is fed, this will would reach the point at which war is waged against war, the wound would be the living trace and the scar of all wounds, and death turned on itself would be willed against all deaths ... The splendor and the magnificence of the event is sense. The event is not what occurs (an accident), it is rather inside what occurs, the purely expressed." (Deleuze: 1990, p. 149)

CHAPTER 14

The Narrative: The Theatre of Memory and the Aesthetic Energy of Management and Leadership

How does the leader set the event free? And how does this match the overall need of a strategic approach to the narrative, and hence, to the attempts at exploiting the event both as an incident that gives the opportunity to tell an appropriate story, and as the unit which carries the symbolic content of the story, strengthening it through its readiness for repeated interpretation?

Often one shall find that the incident or occurrence are anticipated by their transformation into an event, and the event itself is anticipated by some "program", or "strategic intention", waiting for the shape of a story. It would be wrong to see a real causal relation between occurrence, event, and story, however. An example of taking such an "inherent causal" relation for granted could be the story of the "open lab stock" in Hewlett-Packard, described by Peters and Watermann in "In Search of Excellence" incorporating the program of this firm to stimulate invention, and hence, innovation among employees through trust, confidence, and indirect methods of encouraging.

> "Legend has it that Bill (Hewlett. OFK) visited a plant on a Saturday and found the lab stock area locked. He immediately went down to maintenance, grabbed a bolt cutter, and proceeded to cut the padlock off the lab stock door. He left a note that was found on Monday morning: 'Don't ever lock this door again. Thanks, Bill.'" (op.cit., p.245)

Here a manager and entrepreneur breaks into his own property in order to abolish the sacred walls of the firm, especially the symbolic walls which secure know-how and technology. This incident is about stimulating solidarity towards the firm by presupposing it. This is the attitude found among members of a family, or a community tied together by strong traditional demands on the individual. But the content of the transformation of the occurrence into an event is not unambiguous, because it could also be interpreted as an expression of a severe pressure on the individual to use all his efforts, all his spare time, even all his life time, in the service of the firm. The force of trust might appear to be of quite another kind: the demand to speed up innovation rates, and to reduce the interval of time between innovation and marketing.

However, this occurrence was anticipated by the concept of a **seminal event**, an event that confirms the truth of the story in which it is wrapped. This relation between event and story can often be said to have a tautological character, a shape of reciprocal confirmation. However, this is not unproblematic to the validity of the particular narrative.

First and foremost, competing narratives might arise, meaning that two or more levels of narration could be found in the organization, constituting a "formal" and an "informal" level of stories.[32] Today, the formal story is nurtured intensively in public relations and in advertising, strengthened by the logo, by carefully scrutinized symbols of honesty and responsibility, and – paradoxically, but not unexpectedly – by multi-levelled references to more or less sophisticated pleasures of mind and flesh.

Informal stories, however, are able to challenge power, reflecting the saying of Nietzsche from "The Genealogy of Morals" that "it is the prerogative of the master to give names." These informal stories might very well be the more "real" stories, because they arise outside the chronicles of the ruling classes, taking the shape of anecdotes, adventures, fables, and allegories. One shall often find the shape of the song too, being the antidotes to the poisonous experience of domination, in invoking a "we" of quite another kind than the pluralis majestatis of kings, generals, mayors, managers, brutal sergeants, cruel teachers, and obsessively obedient supervisors. The problem of the relation between formal and informal stories covers the problem of who it is that has the right to represent the concealed voice of the true story. We approach the contradictions inherent in the concept of "reason" itself, so brilliantly analyzed in the opus of Michel Foucault. Perhaps we should be able to view this contradiction as one between two forms of "poietics", the theatre and the epic? About the last form Aristotle says:

> "In tragedy one needs to create a sense of awe, but epic has more scope for the irrational (the chief cause of awe), because we do not actually see the agent." (Poetics, op.cit. XXIV, 1460a)

Epic is powerful because we are allowed to use our imagination to such a high degree, even if we usually have a very fine sense of the prohibitions to change anything in the story, and, of course, because it does not need any notion of an author. Anecdotes emerge overnight, and the following day nobody can tell who made them up. Stories arise, develop and even reproduce themselves, or are multiplied in many directions, forming reality as the media of remembering. **Mimēsis** as the way in which the poet relates to the world, whether it is a Racine composing classical drama, or the washerwoman slightly transforming a trivial song through a mixture of bad memory, melancholy, and the remnants of a worn desire, is phrased by Aristotle in his peculiar, terse and minimalist style:

---

32. See the excellent Ph.D. dissertation by Søren Nymark (Nymark: 1999, p.121).

"Since the poet, like a painter or any other image-maker, is a mimetic artist, he must represent, in any instance, one of three objects: the kind of things which were or are the case; the kinds of things that people say and think; the kind of things that ought to be the case." (Poetics, op.cit. XXV, 1460b)

The opposites between which **mimēsis** oscillates are, on the one hand, historical fact and brute fact, the former and present product of sense experience (Aristotle is no constructivist), and on the other hand, the "ought", the realm of real knowledge, of ethics and of political utopias. Between them one finds "the kinds of things that people say and think" (phasin kai dokei), "doxeō", denotes common sense, the **doxa**.

On the stage this "doxeō" exists as **dianoia**, the "thoughts" expressed by the actors through **lexis**, the "style". The style is subordinated the **ēthos**, the "character", itself once more subordinate to **mythos**, to the plot as a borderline between the bond of events woven by the action and the Otherness of our truth- and language-games.

However, the leader can never be satisfied with common sense, he must walk on the borderline, a genuine Nietzschean tightrope walker, and as an image-maker his real media of images are the words.

The most important factors of tragedy are the events as the way in which individual character, through action, confronts fate, and the "immanent transcendent" "logic" of the **myth**. The actors do not present themselves; tragedy is no "individual study of character", but it is the presentation of the power of events, and the pains of action taken, as a surface underneath which the myth, the real reality, is taking place:

"Plot ("mythos"), then, is the first principle and, as it were, soul of tragedy while character is secondary ... Tragedy is mimesis of action ("mimēsis praxeōs"), and it is chiefly for the sake of the action that it represents the agents." (Poetics, op.cit. VI, 1450a-1450b)

Men manifest and betray themselves through speech and action, through **dianoia** and **praxis**. "Dianoia" covers "the parts in which, through speech, they demonstrate something or declare their views" (Poetics, op.cit. VI, 1450a).

The theatre makes it clear to us that speech and action are able both to strengthen, and to suspend or invalidate each other. What is said has to be interpreted in relation to what is done. The event folds around this peculiar mixture, giving it its space of possibility. Who is saying what, and who is not saying it, or saying something that might be expected, or not expected, are of great importance to the plot. Probably, alas, many informal stories will concentrate pejoratively on the character, distributing blame far more than merit, firing shots at random, fabricating sequences with bad logic described in the following way by Aristotle:

"It is above all Homer who has taught other poets the right way to purvey false-hoods: that is, by false inference. When the existence or the occurrence of **b** follows from that of **a**, people suppose that, if **b** is the case, **a** too must exist or be occurrent; but this is false." (Poetics, op.cit. XXIV, 1460a)

This has to be the false inference which managers so often use too, when they feel obliged to attribute the cause of an unsuccessful event to another event which usually means: to another person. Instead, they ought to follow another path. As Aristotle continues:

"So, if the antecedent is false, but were it true some further fact would necessarily exist or occur, the poet should supply the latter; ..."

If the implementation of an innovation is belated beyond reasonable expectations, the manager ought not to be satisfied by blaming the team, he has to find out why; and as a genuine poet he might even "discover" a new parameter crucial to the easy flow from invention to marketing. This parameter could emerge if he were capable of seeing the relevant plot behind the swarm of stories, if he is able to escape the search for the obvious; the starting point should be what he himself could do to improve the processes, not what they did wrong – to phrase the matter with inevitable banality.

From the perspective of Management Philosophy, dealing with the narrative within business economics very often appears naive, if not shallow: as if the multitude of levels presented in the event by the event were not acknowledged at all, from where it could be possible to realize that the concept of "narration" seems far more complicated and ambiguous. The "ratios" of stories compete, discourses clash; the fabricated stories transform values into objects, and take problematic values as given. The most important stories might not be heard at all, or even untold: because the most important story is the plot, and the plot is the subject of events, not a nice and clear structure that can be presented at will in a transparent fable. On the contrary, the fable is demonic, and the concept of the "demonic" was defined by Søren Kierkegaard in the masterpiece "The Concept of Angst" as the inability to transform one's inner life into speech, the simmering silence. The physiognomy of events might be buried inside the plot, and the plot is only presented through characters, through their speech and action, the whole setting, once more, being the products of the events.

"the plot (mythos) is the mimesis of the action – for I use "plot" to denote the construction of events." (Poetics, op.cit. VI, 1450a)

So, events are constructed by a plot in the mode of a "transcendent immanence": the myth escapes us exactly when we pronounce what we think is the essential plot. The way in which the theatre relates to us, through the possibility of recognition on our part, i.e., through the revitalizing of our memory, might be a fraud. The only witness eavesdropping behind the curtain, our only hope of authenticity, the sacred Third, was pierced by our own sword. Then, even tragedy is a fraud, and becomes comedy. In the words of Gilles Deleuze: "... humour is the co-extensiveness of sense with nonsense" (Deleuze: 1990, p.141). Is the myth behind the plot actually an Otherness that comes close to nonsense? An Otherness that through the alienation in the heart of action, the strangeness in the soul of the plot, comes close to a per- formance of an irony, and, hence, close to the essence of **mimēsis** which is in the last instance, itself a grand metaphysical piece of irony?

Aristotle's elaboration of the concept of **recognition** matches this phenomenology of – what could be named – the **theatre of memory**. It might also, more cynically, be named "the human comedy of wasted aesthetic energy", to supplement Balzac – energy wasted at efforts of controlling a plot, through the fabrication of stories, that can never be the subject of control. Then, managerial and organizational projects of story-telling verge on the absurd, transforming "corporate poetics" into a trav- esty, themselves an object of an unacknowledged irony.

Following Aristotle, there are five types of recognition:

a. recognition "through tokens"
b. recognition through artificial contrivances – they do not work well
c. recognition "through memory"
d. recognition "by reasoning"
e. recognition "ensuing from the events themselves" – the best form, according to Aristotle (Poetics, op.cit. 1455a, XVIff).

We are here presented with the prototypical phenomena through which the narra- tive works, and we are presented with all the constellations of narrative roles as well.

Recognition through tokens, of course, covers the logo, the public and private symbols of the firm as a means to invoke sides of memory favorable for its prod- ucts: high quality, reliable service, environmental responsibility, "green conscious- ness", social and moral consciousness, moderate eagerness for profits, a high degree of self-financing, confidence in employees, trust between management and labour, security to employees, and a sound attitude towards shareholders.

A fine use of tokens can be attributed to the Danish shipping company and multinational firm, Maersk. Its houseflag with a star on a blue ground refers to the story told by the founder of the firm, who one stormy night on his ship was pray- ing for his sick wife, asking God for a sign. The dark sky then suddenly opened up into a clear blue, and a bright star was seen. The wife recovered, and the firm had its logo. The obvious power of this story lies, of course, in its proximity to myth; in its ability to refer with naive sincerity to the bright side of the lot of man, not stra- tegically to business.

Recognition through artificial contrivances might cover the corporate over- eagerness for sustainability and social virtues. One might be suspicious about a little bit too much ado over the sponsoring of morally laudable projects, like hospitals in countries of the Third World. This also goes for a little bit too much emphasis on the concern for children, like the McDonald's clown and a little bit too much demonstrative interest in the independence of small coffee farmers in Latin America. Sometimes the stories surrounding these symbolic acts appear almost too praiseworthy, and are unable to create trustworthiness in rendering the good intent. Aesthetics contradicts ethics, deconstructing at the level of expression that which was meant, through its interpretation, to be experienced as the genuine good will.

Recognition through memory, however, is far more important than emphasized by Aristotle, if we conceive of memory as both the individual and collective paths of remembering. And this type of recognition melts into recognition by reasoning, because reasoning takes its instruments from memory too – no matter how much it might use the whole arsenal of logic.

The story, if it is a really good story, fuses the levels of individual and collective memory into one another, in the shape of a memory that gives place to a peculiar kind of reason. This "invested" reason is, like the myth, "transcendentally immanent", it is for ever hidden to us. We are enigmas to ourselves, and only provisional stories can present us to images of the self that are able to claim a certain level of authenticity, because they grant us a clue to a few events in which we were able to prove ourselves worthy of what happened to us.

"The Principle of Translocutionarity" presented earlier in this book suggests the narrative as a solution to the epistemological dilemma of personal identity: that we do not know what we actually mean, until we have put it into words inside an event. We are forced to stage our inner life. So, the story not only gives us the clue to our mental space of virtual meaning, it also opens the possibility of personal identity. Through telling stories we "accomplish" an image of ourselves. We are told in telling, even if we have no chance of coming to know whom the author is.

But not every story is authentic, meaning something true in relation to my life. If the Principle of Translocutionarity seems to imply that we "persuade ourselves" by telling, it also has to imply a concept of conviction. It has to invoke a notion of certainty. But this certainty cannot belong to me.

Certainty is the core of recognition. Certainty mixes "is" and "ought", the brute fact with belief, naturalism with faith. It cannot help but do this, because almost any fact is the effect of a belief – as Wittgenstein showed in his last work, "On Certainty". Certainty is an aporia: you have to believe in the subject of it, and then it cannot reflect a knowledge that is beyond doubt.

But "certainty" is a feeling, or an attitude that has survived all versions of modernism and postmodernism, because the medium of certainty is passion. However, certainty might deceive, and certainty has certainly fooled so many people during this century that we must be careful about it.

The leader has to sail in these waters, not just looking for an invisible, equatorial line between the continents of the "is" and the "ought", but trying to find the line between the false and the genuine certainty. In doing this he has to be certain. He is never allowed to feign.

"So far as possible, one should also work out the plot in gestures, since a natural affinity makes those in the grip of emotions the most convincing, and the truest distress or anger is conveyed by one who actually feels these things." (Poetics, op.cit. XVII, 1455a)

The dimension of certainty is passion. But certainty cannot be a state of mind, a "stasis", it has to be an attitude, a gesture towards something. This gesture must be certain, desire for truth must not be feigned, but the content of certainty shall always be questioned. This is the desire for "The Fourth". And this is what makes the whole project so difficult.

However, we are trying to pin down the passion of the good human being, and hence, a certainty relative to "The Fourth". This leads to the question: what shall the real leader do when it appears, as so often in this life, that his case is not just, and when he is not directly responsible for the state of this case, himself?

Let us take an example. A man is made the manager of a medium-sized firm in the chemical sector. The firm is half a century old. It produces fertilizers for agriculture in many countries, not least its own, as well as technology for the processing of certain, very common, ecological dairy products especially enjoyed by children. It is by now famous for its research into the reduction of food additives.

Our manager is expected to increase the development in food processing, and to change the production of fertilizers to alternative, "green" products, which would make possible the processing of the soil on a more and more natural basis.

Now, just after his accession it becomes known that the firm during the Sixties was a subcontractor to companies abroad, producing dioxin for the US Army during the war in Vietnam. It has also become known that the firm far into the Seventies, through a daughter company in the Far East, produced extremely dangerous fertilizers sold under rather misleading trade-descriptions in Latin America.

The manager is dismayed but chooses to stay, and attend to the task charged by the board: to tell a story that is able to legitimize the firm to the public, and to weld the organization together by reconciling it with its past.

The pivot of the whole task is **recognition**. Recognition through memory and reasoning which means the necessity to relate to the memory of every individual inside the firm, and – potentially – of every individual stakeholder and the public, and to their moral reasoning. To this must be added the need to address the phantom called the "collective memory" of the firm, and the "collective memory" of the environment.

Both philosophy and psychology have theorized extensively about the essence and functioning of memory through Modernity, based on the thoughts of Plato and Aristotle. Memory appears to be the key to an understanding of time, but the phenomenon of memory seems extremely hard to grasp, just like the phenomenon of time. I shall not relate to this overwhelming material here, but only mention two concepts, "the present of the past", and "the past of the present" (Kirkeby: 1994).

The "present of the past" is a presence of the past in the moment as if it were able to rule over "direct experience". The past calls on us through passion, controlling the way we interpret events, but through reasoning too, transforming the complex patterns of stored experiences into generalizations about the real, and the unreal. The problem is, that in the moment we do not experience this intentionality, there has to elapse a second before we are able to realize that we already have sensed something in a peculiar way. Meaning assails us as if from outside, even if we contribute to it ourselves. The present of the past is this permanent transformation of memory into reality. The power of the present of the past is hard to break.

The manager has to find a clue to the present of the past of all these memories – huge landscapes under the surface of the earth where layers are constantly displaced, where new mountains are born any minute, where smoke rises from craters, and the falling stones never reach the bottoms of ravines. He has to locate the small group of persons wandering under the swollen porphyry heavens from the smoldering darkness up towards the weak light coming from the crack in the ground. The manager has to choose whether he shall ever let them through, or banish them eternally to a life in this underworld dungeon, the subjects of curious, scornful, and revengeful observation. The manager must be able to accomplish to the great work of collective as well as individual reconciliation with the past.

The manager has to grasp the past of the present as well. He has to exhibit it so plastically as to appeal to reconciliation, forcing the eye to look at it from new angles, calling forth compassion, even fellowfeeling. The past of the present allows for no empty passages, no holes in the eternal bond, no blind spots, no silence. It is an underworld metropolis in the centre of which stands a cathedral. There is light everywhere, life, movements, smells, sounds of all kinds, but first and foremost voices.

The manager can try to fabricate a story where the basically good intentions of the founders of the firm are emphasized: their sympathy with the American case, their attempts to help the underdeveloped Latin American agriculture without causing (further) tensions between labour and capital. He can present the CEOs from this sensitive period of the firms history as "John Wayne types", or as misinformed advocates of conservative standards, or as victims of a natural science that pretended to know enough. He can choose to seek villains on the political scene, giving the public to understand that there were certain political pressures.

But he can also choose to write off the past of the firm, ignoring the shareholders and even the board, and underlining the fact that the firm definitely is not the same any longer. He can emphasize the transformation, the return of the lost son, the morally elevating story of conversion to sustainability and to social and even ethical accounting – regardless of whether the legislation appears to make this conversion rather rational.

However, the firm has a fine relation to the agricultural organisations, to local government, to local politicians, and even to grass-roots, and its research and development are highly esteemed internationally. Our manager cannot beat his own breast too vehemently, he owes solidarity to his allies and sponsors, to all the groups and persons with symbolic and vested interests in the firm. It seems not to be the right time for castigation, neither of the firm's past, nor of its present.

Of course, he could pass the buck to all the other companies with the same past, but perhaps not with the same present now beyond reproach. But that would be bad strategies, even if a journalist on a renowned and independent, critical newspaper launched it on his behalf. But he shall probably choose to emphasize with the utmost care how the firm now uses the best of science, even perhaps alternative science to make the best product for the children who eventually shall populate the brave new world. He might even emphasize that his firm was among the first to do this. He shall arrange TV-interviews, some whole-page portraits in newspapers and magazines, and sponsor a documentary of the situation of this type of firm during that period. He shall probably also choose to visit the countries to which the firm was accused of exporting the dangerous fertilizers, and stand among blossoming fields with healthy farmers and workers who are the descendants of the supposed victims.

He shall calm the employees, perhaps by telling them that the doors to the past are shut forever, or by urging them to understand the necessity of the unhappy occurrences, or by ridiculing legislation. He might through suspicion on parts of the public and the politicians regarding their motives; or he might just work up enthusiasm about what the firm is doing now. Whether our manager chooses to cleanse the firm, selecting his traitors carefully, or if he chooses to confess, but appeal to an understanding of motives, circumstances, contexts of values and information, he shall betray the past, and hence, betray the event. He plays with memory, mocking the wanderers in despair through the underworld darkness, laughing at the sincere ringing from the cathedral. He exploits the delicate and generous hand of reasoning offered to him.

Most stories betray the event only through the way in which they are told. Is it actually Liporello that tells the story of Don Juan, and Sancho Panza the adventures of Don Quixote, and is this the reason why the first one appears as a bastard, the second one as a fool? Whose voice sounds in the choir of Greek tragedy? Who is, actually, Socrates? Who is the author of the Saga of Gunlaug Omrstunge, and why is it told, and to whom? Who wrote the Gospels? Did St. Paul exist? Was he only one person? Why is it necessary that the event is wrapped in all these images, and in the writing? Why must it be concealed by murmur, by this aggressive silence, by textures with indistinct impressions, by sheets covered with figures of ink from a long forgotten alphabet, or with the scorn of a candid printing, a structure of palimpsests, of words grown into each other, of paper dissolved upon each other, like amalgamated corpses, victims of a violent intercourse, impossible to separate, why all this noise from dumb objects, when the only thing we need is the voice, clear and concise?

Here we meet the final form of recognition, the one ensuing from the event itself. The event that longs to shake off the fetters of the story. Here, we also meet the final test of the real leader: his ability to protect and secure the event, against the stories, against memories, and against his own subjective certainty.

Could one not imagine an event without a grain of a story? An event totally liberated from any trace of the myth? An event that is nothing else but that it is. It would be untouchable, a sculpture, not something in time, not a "time-thing", but a "thing-time" that dwells in an infinite multitude of dimensions.

In this event, every gesture would be a genuine gesture, and any virtue so fully present that we would be able to be the ones we are.

But this event would be the moment.

"Lo! I tell you a mystery. We shall not all sleep, but we shall all be changed; in a moment, in the twinkling of an eye, at the last trumpet."

Bibliography

A

Ackoff, R.L. (1970): A Concept of Corporate Planning. Wiley, New York.

Ackoff, R.L. (1985): "Where do you intend to go now?" In: Johnsen, E. (Ed): Trends and Megatrends in the Theory of Management. Brett International, Copenhagen.

Althoff, G. (1997): Spielregeln der Politik im Mittelalter. Kommunikation in Frieden und Fehde. Wissenschaftliche Buchgesellschaft, Darmstadt.

Alverez, J.L. (1997): The Production and Diffusion of Business Knowledge in Europe. Macmillan, London.

Alvesson, M., Berg, P.O. (1992): Corporate Culture and Organizational Symbolism. An Overview. Walter de Gruyter, Berlin New York.

Argyris, C., Schön,D. (1978): Organizational Learning: A Theory of Action Perspective. Addison-Wesley, Reading Mass.

Aristotle (1926/1994): Nicomachean Ethics. The Loeb Edition. Transl. by H. Rackham. Harvard University Press, Cambridge Mass. London.

Aristotle (1936/1995): On the Soul (de anima), parva naturalia and On Breath. The Loeb Edition. Transl. by W.S. Hett. Harvard University Press, Cambridge Mass. London.

Aristotle (1933/1996): The Metaphysics. The Loeb Edition. Transl. by H. Tredennick. Harvard University Press, Cambridge Mass. London.

Aristotle (1926/1994a): Art of Rhetoric. The Loeb Edition. Transl. by R.H. Freese. Harvard University Press, Cambridge Mass. London.

Aristotle (1995a): Poetics. The Loeb Edition. Transl. by S. Halliwell. Harvard University Press, Cambridge Mass. London.

Augustin, St. (1919/1995): Confessions. The Loeb Edition. Transl. by W. Watts. Harvard University Press, Cambridge Mass. London.

Austin, J.L. (1962): How to Do Things with Words. Oxford.

B

Badaracco, J.L. Jr. (1996): "Knowledge Links". In: Myers, P.S. (Ed.): Knowledge Management and Organizational Design. Boston, Butterworth-Heinemann.

Badaracco, J.L. Jr. (1997): Defining Moments: When Managers must Choose between Right and Right. Harvard Business School Press, Boston.

Barker, E. (1970): Greek Political Theory. Methuen & Co Ltd., London.

Barnett, C. (1963): The Swordbearers: Studies in Supreme Command in the First World War. Eyre and Spottiswoode, London.

Bastick, T. (1982): Intuition. How we think and act. John Wiley and Sons, Chichester.

Baudelaire, C. (1964): Les fleurs du mal et autres poémes. Garnier-Flammarion, Paris.

Bennis, W. (1989): On Becoming a Leader. Hutchinsons, London.

Bennis, W.J., Parikh, J., Lessem, R. (1994): Beyond Leadership. Blackwell, Oxford Cambridge.

Berg, P.O. (1989): "Postmodern Management? From Facts to Fiction in Theory and Practice". Scandinavian Journal of Management 5 III, pp. 201-217.

Bernstein, B. (1971): Class, Codes and Control. Routledge & Kegan Paul, London.

Beyme, K. von (1977): Ökonomie und Politik im Sozialismus. Ein Vergleich der Entwicklung in den sozialistischen Ländern. Piper & Co. Verlag, München.

Blanchot, M. (1997): Friendship. Transl. by E. Rottenberg. Stanford University Press, Stanford California.

Bloc, M. (1962): Feudal Society. Routledge and Kegan Paul, London.

Boje, D.M. (1995): "Stories of the storytelling organization: a postmodern analysis of Disney as 'Tamara-land'". Academy of Management Journal Vol. 38, No.4, pp.997-1035.

Borum, F. (1990): Technological Innovation and Organizational Change – Danish patterns of Knowledge, Networks and Culture. Nyt fra Samfundsvidenskaberne, Copenhagen.

Bravermann, H. (1974): Labor and Monopoly Capital. Monthly Review Press, New York London

Buber, M. (1932/1983): Ich und Du. Verlag Lambert Schneider, Heidelberg.

Bunge, M. (1962): Intuition and Science. Prentice-Hall, Englewood Cliffs, New Jersey.

Burrell, G. (1997): Pandemonium – Towards a Retro-Organization Theory. Sage, London.

Burrell, G., Morgan, G. (1979): Sociological Paradigms and Organizational Analysis. Heinemann, London.

Byrn, J. (1993): The Whiz Kids. Ten Founding Fathers of American Business – and the Legacy they Left Us. Currency Doubleday, New York.

C

Casey, E.S. (1997): The Fate of Place. A Philosophical History. University of California Press, Los Angeles.

Cassirer, E. (1994): Philosophie der symbolischen Formen. Erster Teil. Die Sprache. Einleitung und Problemstellung. Wissenschaftliche Buchgesellschaft, Darmstadt.

Chandler, A.D. (1990): Scale and Scope. The Dynamics of Industrial Capitalism. The Belknap Press of Harvard University Press, Cambridge Mass. New York.

Charniawska, B. (1997): Narrating the Organization. Dramas of Institutional Identity. Chicago University Press, Chicago.

Cicero (1989): Cicero. In Twenty Eight Volumes. The Loeb Edition. Harvard University Press, London.

Clegg, S.R, Palmer,G. (1996): The Politics of Management Knowledge. Sage Publications, London.

Conger, J.A. (1991):"Inspiring others": The language of management. Academy of Management Executive Vol. V, No.1, pp.31-45.

Cooper, R., Burrell, G. (1988): "Modernism, Postmodernism and Organizational Analysis: An Introduction". Organizational Studies 9 (1), pp. 91-112.

Cornford, F.M. (1970): Plato's Theory of Kowledge. Routledge, London.

Cressey, P., Macinnes,J. (1980): "Voting for Ford: Industrial Democracy and the Control of Labour". Capital and Class 11, pp.5-34.

D

Davis, S.M., Lawrence, P.R. (1977): Matrix. Addison-Wesley, Reading Mass.

Deuleuze, G. (1969/1990): The Logic of Sense. Transl. by M. Lester. Columbia University Press, New York.

Deuleuze, G. (1994): Difference and Repetition. Transl. by P. Patton. The Athlone Press, London.

Denna, E. (Ed.)(1993): Event-driven Business Solutions – Todays Revolution in Business and Information Technology. Irwin, Homewood Ill.

Derrida, J. (1971): "La mythologie blanche". In: Rhétorique et philosophie. Poétique 5. Éditions du Seuil, Paris.

Derrida, J. (1987): "Chōra". In: Poikilia: Etudes offertes à Jean-Pierre Vernant. Ecole des Hautes Etudes en Sciences Sociales, Paris.

Derrida, J. (1993): Sauf le nom. Editions Gallilee, Paris.

Deuleuze, G., Guattari, F. (1972/1983): L'Anti-Oedipe. Les Editions de Minuit. Eng. transl. by R. Hurley et al.: Anti-Oedipus. Capitalism and Schizophrenia. The Athlone Press, London.

Diogenes Laertius (1995): Lives of Eminent Philosophers. The Loeb Edition. Transl. by R.D. Hicks. Harvard University Press, Cambridge Mass. London.

Dixon, N.F. (1976): On the Psychology of Military Incompetence. Jonathan Cape, London.

Dobb, M. (1963): Studies in the Development of Capitalism. Routledge and Kegan Paul Ltd, London.

Drucker, P.F. (1980): Managing in Turbulent Times. Butterworth-Heinemann, London.

Drucker, P.F. (1985): Innovation and Entrepreneurship. Butterworth-Heinemann, Oxford.

Drucker, P.F. (1996): Managing in a Time of Great Change. Truman Talley, New York.

Dubois, P. (1979): Sabotage in Industry. Penguin, London.

E

Edwards, R. (1979): Contested Terrain. The Transformation of the Workplace in the Twentieth Century. Basic Books, New York.

Eliot, T.S (1936): Collected Poems 1909-1935. Faber & Faber, London.

Engels, F. (1972): On Marx's Capital. Progess Publisher, Moscow.

Evans,R., Pruzan,P., Zadek,S. (Eds.)(1997): Building Corporate Accountability: Emerging Practices of Social and Ethical Accounting, Auditing and Reporting. Earthscan, London.

F

Fann, K.T. (1970): Peirce's Theory of Abduction. Martinus Nijhoff, The Hague.

Fikes, R.E. (1982): "A commitment-based framwork for describing informal cooperative work". Cognitive Science 6, pp.331-47.

Forschner, M. (1995): Die stoische Ethik. Über die Zusammenhang von Natur-,

Sprach- und Moralphilosophie im altstoischen System. Wissenschaftliche Buchgesellschaft, Darmstadt.

Foucault, M. (1975): Survellir et Punir; Naissance de la prison. Editions Gallimard, Paris.

Freeman, R.E. (1991): Business Ethics – the State of the Art. Oxford University Press, New York.

Fuglsang, M. (1998): At være på grænsen. En moderne fænomenologisk bevægelse. ("Being on the Border. A Modern, Phenomenological Movement"). CBS, Copenhagen.

Fukuyama, F. (1996): Trust. The Social Virtues and the Creation of Prosperities. Free Press Paperbacks, New York.

G

Gagliardi, P. (1986): "The creation and change of organizational cultures – a conceptual framework". Organization Studies 2, Vol. 7.

Gagliardi, P. (1990): "Artifacts as Pathways and Remains of Organizational Life", in Gagliardi, P. (ed.): Symbols and Artifacts: Views of the Corporate Landscape. De Gruyter, Berlin.

Goldblatt, J.J. (1997): Special Events. Best Practices in Modern Event Management. Van Nostrand Reinhold, New York.

Goodman, N. (1976): Languages of Art. An Approach to a Theory of Symbols. Hackett Publ. Comp. Inc., Indianapolis Cambridge.

Graham, P. (Ed.)(1995): Mary Parker Follett: Prophet of Management. Harvard Business School Press, Boston.

Grant, M.G. (1996): "Towards a Knowledge-based Theory of the Firm". Strategic Management Journal 17 (Winter Special Issue) pp.93-122.

H

Habermas, J. (1968): Erkenntnis und Interesse. Suhrkamp Verlag, Frankf.a.M.

Habermas, J. (1981): Theorie des kommunikativen Handelns. Suhrkamp Verlag, Frankf. a.M.

Hamel, G., Prahalad, C.K. (1994): Competeting for the Future. Harvard Business School Press, Boston.

Handy, C. (1995): Beyond Certainty. The Changing Worlds of Organizations. Hutchinson, London.

Hanson, R.N. (1961): Patterns of Discovery. An Inquiry into the Conceptual Foundations of Science. Cambridge University Press, Cambridge.

Hegel, G.W.F. (1952): Phänomenologie des Geistes. Nach dem texte des Originalausgabe herausgeg. von Johannes Hoffmeister. Verlag Felix Meiner, Hamburg.

Heidegger, M (1927/1967): Sein und Zeit. Max Niemeyer Verlag, Tübingen.

Heidegger, M. (1950/1963): "Die Zeit des Weltbildes". In: Holzwege. Vittorio Klostermann, Frankf. a.M.

Heidegger, M. (1954): Vom Wesen der Wahrheit. Vittorio Klostermann, Frankf. a.M.

Heidegger, M. (1954a): Vorträge und Aufsätze. Neske, Pfullingen.
Heidegger, M. (1957): Der Satz vom Grund. Neske, Pfullingen.
Heidegger, M. (1959): Unterwegs zur Sprache. Neske, Pfullingen.
Heidegger, M. (1961): Nietzsche. Vol. I-II. Neske, Pfullingen.
Hesse, M. (1966): Models and Analogies in Science. University of Notre Dame Press, Indiana.
Hesse, M. (1974): The Structure of Scientific Inference. Los Angeles.
Historische Wörterbuch der Philosophie (1971-). Herausgegeben von J. Ritter und K. Gründer. 10-. Vols. Wissenschaftliche Buchgesellschaft, Darmstadt.
Hofstede, G. (1991): Cultures and Organizations. McGraw Hill, Maidenhead.
Hosking, D-M., Morley, I.E. (1991): A Social Psychology of Organizing. People, Processes and Contexts. Harvester Wheatsheaf, New York.
Husserl, E. (1980): Logische Untersuchungen. Max Niemeyer Verlag, Tübingen.
Husserl, E. (1987): Cartesianische Meditationen. Eine Einleitung in die Phänomenologie. Herausgegeben von E. Ströker. Felix Meiner Verlag, Hamburg.

J

Janis, I. (1972): Victims of Groupthink. Houghton Mifflin, Boston.
Johnsen, E. (1968): Studies in Multiobjective Decision Models. Studentlitteratur, Lund.

K

Kant, I. (1974): Kritik der Urteilskraft. Herausgegeben von W. Weischedel. Suhrkamp Verlag, Frankf.a.M.
Kant, I. (1974a): Kritik der praktischen Vernunft. Grundlegung zur Metaphysik der Sitten. Herausgegeben von W. Weischedel. Suhrkamp Verlag, Frankf.a.M.
Kanter, R.M. (1983): The Change Masters: Innovation and Entrepreneurship in the American Cooperation. Simon and Schuster, New York.
Kanter, R.M. (1996): "When a Thousands Flowers Bloom". In: Paul S. Myers (Ed.): Knowledge Management and Organizational design. Butterworth-Heinemann, Boston. pp.93-131.
Kierkegaard, S. (1963): Samlede Værker. Gyldendal, København.
Kirkeby, O.F. (1993): "Cognitive Science". The Encyclopedia of Language and Linguistics. Pergamon Press, Edinburgh.
Kirkeby, O.F. (1994): Event and Body-Mind. A Phenomenological-Hermeneutic Analysis. (Published in Danish). CBS Publishers, Copenhagen.
Kirkeby , O.F. (1995): World, Word and Thought. Philosophy of Language and Phenomenology. (Published in Danish). CBS Publishers, Copenhagen.
Kirkeby, O.F. (1996): The Philosophy of Selfcessity. (Published in Danish). Modtryk, Aarhus.
Kirkeby, O.F. (1996): The Seasons' of Words. Fragments of a Meticulous Philosophy. (Published in Danish). The Little Publishing Company, Copenhagen.
Kirkeby, O.F. (1998): Of Significance. Tetragrammatonical Reflections. (Published in Danish). CBS Publishers, Copenhagen.

Kirkeby, O.F. (1997): "Event and Body-Mind. An Outline of a Post-postmodern Approach to Phenomenology". Cybernetics & Human Knowing Vol. 4 No 2-3. pp.1-31.

Kirkeby , O.F. (1999): Secunda Philosophia. (Published in Danish). Samfundslitteratur, Copenhagen.

Kotter, J.P. (1982): The General Managers. The Free Press, New York.

Kotter, J.P. (1996): Leading Change. Harvard Business School Press, Boston.

Krogh, G.F. von, Ross, J. (1995): Orgnizational epistemology. McMillan, Oxford.

L

Langefors, B. (1986): "Information and Management Systems". In: Johnsen, E. (Ed.): Trends and Megatrends in the Theory of Management. Bratt International.

Leonard-Barton, D. (1995): Wellsprings of Knowledge: Building and Sustaining the Sources of Innovation. Harvard Business School Press, Boston.

Lévinas, E. (1961): Totalité et Infini: Essai sur l'Extériorité. Phaenomenologica Vol. 8. Nijhoff, The Hague.

Lipps, H. (1958): Die Verbindlichkeit der Sprache. Vittorio Klostermann, Frankf. a.M.

Lipps, H. (1938/1976): Untersuchungen zu einer hermeneutischen Logik. Vittorio Klostermann, Frankf.a.M.

Ljungstrøm, A.C. (1997): "The silent voice of law: Legal philosophy as legal thinking". Law and Critique Vol. III, No.1.

Ljungstrøm, A.C. (1998): Rettens Alkymi. Om venskab, retfærdighed og pathos. Samleren, København.

Luhmann, N. (1985): Soziale Systeme. Grundriss einer allgemeinen Theorie.

Lund, A.G. (1999): Creative Leadership – The Theater and the Poetics as Organizational Opportunity-experience. Ph.D. Dissertation. Aalborg, Denmark.

Lyotard, J.-F. (1997): Postmodern Fables. English translation by G.van den Abbeele. University of Minnesota Press, Minneapolis London.

M

MacIntyre, A. (1981): After Virtue. A Study in Moral Philosophy. University of Notre Dame Press, Notre Dame, Ind.

MacPherson, C.B. (1970): The Political Theory of Possesive Individualism. Hobbes to Locke. Oxford Paperbacks, London.

Mann, M. (Ed.)(1965): Das Thomas Mann-Buch. Eine innere Biographie in Selbstzeugnissen. Fischer Bücherei Frankf.a.M. Hamburg.

Mantoux, P. (1973): La révolution industrielle au xviii'e. siècle. Essai sur les commencements de la grande industrie moderne en Angleterre. Éditions Genin, Paris.

March, J. (1988): Decisions and Organizations. Basil Blackwell, Oxford.

Margalit, A. (1997): Politik der Würde. Über Achtung und Missachtung. Alexander Fest Verlag, Berlin.

Marx, K. (1969): Das Kapital. Vol. I. Dietz Verlag, Berlin.

Marx, K. (1970): Einleitung zur Kritik der politischen Ökonomie. In: Zur Kritik der politischen Ökonomie. Erstes Heft. Dietz Verlag, Berlin.

McCloskey, D.N. (1990): If you're so Smart: the Narrative of Economic Expertice. The University of Chicago Press, Chicago & London.

McCloskey, D.N. (1994): Knowledge and Persuasion in Economics. Cambridge University Press, Cambridge.

McCloskey, D.N. (1996): The Vices of Economists – the Virtues of the Bourgeois. Amsterdam University Press, Amsterdam.

McGregor, D. (1960): The Human Side of the Enterprise. McGraw Hill, New York.

McKendrick, N. (1971): "Josiah Wedgewood and factory discipline". In: David S. Landes (Ed.): The Rise of Capitalism. MacMillan, New York.

Merleau-Ponty, M. (1945): Phénoménologie de la perception. Gallimard, Paris.

Merleau-Ponty, M. (1960): Signes. Gallimard, Paris.

Mickletwait, J., Wooldridge, A. (1997): The Witch Doctors. What the management gurus are saying, why it matters and how to make sense of it. Heinemann, London.

Miller, I. (1987): Imagery in Scientific Thought Creating 20th-Century Physics. The MIT Press, London, Englewood Cliffs.

Mintzberg, H. (1973): The Nature of Managerial Work. Harper & Row, New York.

Mintzberg, H. (1979): Structuring of Organizations. Prentice-Hall, Englewood Cliffs.

Mintzberg, H. (1989): Mintzberg on Management. The Free Press, New York.

Mintzberg, H., Quinn, J.B. (1992): The Strategy Process. Prentice-Hall, New Jersey.

Mintzberg, H. (1994): The Rise and Fall of Strategic Planning. Prentice-Hall, New Jersey.

Mohan, M.L. (1993): Organizational Communication and Cultural Vision. State of New York Press, New York.

Monthoux, P.G. de (1998): Konstföretaget. Mellan spektakelkultur och kulturspektakel. Bokförlaget Korpen, Göteborg.

Morgan, G. (1986): Images of Organization. Sage, London.

Morgan, G. (1988): Riding the Waves of Change. Developing Managerial Competencies for a Turbulent World. Jossey-Bass, San Francisco.

Morgan, G. (1993): Imaginization. The Art of Creative Management. Sage, London.

Morris, C. (1964): Signification and Significance. The MIT Press, Cambridge Mass.

N

Die Nachsokratiker (1923). Deutsch im Auswahl mit Einleitungen von W. Nestle. Vols. I-II. Eugen Diederich, Jena.

Nehamas, A. (1999): Virtues of Authenticity. Essays on Plato and Socrates. Princeton University Press, Princeton New Jersey.

Nietzsche, F. (1955): Zur Genealogie der Moral. In: Werke in drei Bänden. Herausgegeben von K. Schlechta. Vol. II. Karl Hanser Verlag, München.

Nohria, N., Eccles, R.G. (1992): Networks and Organizations. Structure, Form and Action. Harvard Business Sholl Press, Boston.

Nonoka, I. (1995): The Knowledge-Creating Company. Oxford University Press, Oxford.

Normann, R. (1977): Management of Growth. Wiley, New York.

Nymark, S. (1999): A Discourse on Organizational Storytelling: Creating Enduring Values in a High-tech Company by Storytelling. Dept. of Business Studies, Aalborg University, Aalborg.

O

Ohmae, K. (1982): The Mind of the Strategist. Penguin, Harmondsworth.

Ohmae, K. (1985): Triad Power. The Free Press, New York.

Olins, W. (1978): The Corporate Personality: An Inquiry into the Nature of Corporate Identity. Design Counsul, London.

P

Peirce, C.S. (1931-35/1958): Collected Papers. Hartshorne, C., Weiss,P., Burks, A.W. (Eds.). Vols. 1-6. Harvard University Press, Cambridge Mass.

Peirce, C.S. (1955): Philosophical Writings of Peirce. Selected and Edited with an Introduction by Justus Buchler. Dover Publications, New York.

Peters, T.,Waterman, R.H. (1982): In Search of Excellence: Lessons from America's Best-Run Companies. Warner, New York.

Pfeffer, J. (1992): Managing with Power. Politics and Influence in Organizations. Harvard University School Press, Boston.

Pirenne, H. (1965): Economic and Social History of Medieval Europe. Routledge & Kegan Paul, London

Plato (1956): Protagoras and Meno. translated by W.K.C. Gutrie. Penguin Classics, Harmondsworth.

Plato (1995): Euthyphro, Apology, Crito, Phaedo and Phaedrus. The Loeb Edition. Transl. by H.N. Fowler. Harvard University Press, Cambridge Mass. London.

Plato (1921/1996): Theaetetus and Sophist. The Loeb Edition. Transl. by H.N. Fowler. Harvard University Press, Cambridge Mass. London.

Plato (1926/1996a): Cratylus, Parmenides, Greater Hippias and Lesser Hippias. The Loeb Edition. Transl. by H.N. Fowler. Harvard University Press, Cambridge Mass. London.

Plato (1930/1969): The Republic. The Loeb Edition. Vols. I-II. Transl. by P. Shorey. Heinemann, London.

Plato (1929/1966): Timaeus, Critias, Cleitophon, Menexenus and Epistles. The Loeb Edition. Transl. by R.G. Bury. William Heinemann, London.

Pohlenz, M. (1992): Die Stoa. Geschichte einer geistigen Bewegung. 7. Auflage. Vandenhoeck & Ruprecht, Göttingen.

Pollard, S. (1965): The Genesis of Modern Management. A Study of the Industrial Revolution of Great Britain. Cambridge Mass.

Poras, J., Collins, J. (1995): Built to Last: Successful Habits of Visionary Companies. Harper Business, New York.

Porter, M. (1980): Competetive Strategy. The Free Press, New York.

Porter, M. (1985): Competetive Advantage. The Free Press, New York.

Prahalad, C.K., Hamel, G. (1990): "The core competencies of the corporation". In: Harvard Business Review Vol. 68, pp.79-91.

R

Ricoeur, P. (1990/1994): Oneself as Another. Transl. by K. Blamey. The University of Chicago Press, Chicago London.

Rifkin, J. (1995): The End of Work: The Decline of the Global Labour and the Dawn of the Post-Market Era. Putnam, New York.

S

Sartre, J.-P. (1943): L'être et le néant. Gallimard, Paris.

Sartre, J.-P. (1976): Critique of Dialectical Reason. Vol. I. New Left Books, London.

Schaeffler, R. (1989): "Heidegger und die Theologie". In: Gethmann-Siefert, A., Pöggeler, O. (Eds.): Heidegger und die praktische Philosophie. Suhrkamp Verlag, Frankf.a.M.

Schein, E. (1985): Organizational Culture and Leadership. Jossey-Bass, London.

Schopenhauer, A. (1913): Sämtliche Werke. Edited by Paul Deussen. R. Piper & Co. Verlag, München.

Searle, J. (1974): Speech Acts. An Essay in the Philosophy of Language. Cambridge University Press, London.

Seneca (1986): Moral Essays. Ed. Basore, J.W. I-III. The Loeb Edition. Harvard University Press, London.

Senge, P. (1990): The Fifth Discipline. The Art and Practice of the Learning Organization. Doubleday, New York.

Sextus Empiricus (1993): Outlines of Pyrrhonism. Transl. by R.G. Bury. Harvard University Press, Cambridge Mass. London.

Simmel, G. (1930): Philosophie des Geldes. Verlag Drucker & Humblot, München Leipzig.

Simon, H. (1957): Administrative Behaviour: A Study of Decision Making Processes in Administrative Organization. (2nd edn). Collier/Macmillan New York.

Sjöstrand, S-E. (1997): The Two Faces of Management. The Janus Factor. International Thomson Business Press, London.

Sraffa, P. (1960): Production of Commodities by Means of Commodities. Cambridge University Press, Cambridge.

Stogdill's Handbook of Leadership. A Survey of Theory and Research. (1981) Revised and Expanded Edition by B.M. Bass. The Free Press, New York.

Stone, K. (1975): "The Origin of Job-Structures in the Steel Industry". In: Edwards, R.C., et al. (Eds.): Labor Market Segmentation. D.C. Heath, Lexington, Mass.

Suarez, F. (1857-58): Opus tripartitum de gratia. Opera. Herausgeg. A.D.M. André, Paris.

T

Tampoe, M. (1996): "Motivating Knowledge Workers – The Challenge for the 1990s". In: Myers, P.S. (Ed.): Knowledge Management and Organizational design. Butterworth-Heinemann, Boston. p.179-189.

Taylor, F.W. (1947): Scientific Management. Harper, London New York.
Thomas, D. (1963): Miscellany. J.M. Dent & Sons Ltd., London.
Thrift, N. (1996): Spatial Formations. Sage, London.
Thyssen, O. (1994): Kommunikation, kultur og etik. CBS Publishers, Copenhagen.
Trentin, B. (1978): Arbeiterdemokratie. VSA-Verlag, Hamburg.

V

Vries, Josef de (1983): Grundbegriffe der Scholastik. Wissenschaftliche Buchgesellschaft, Darmstadt.

W

Waterman, R. (1995): Frontiers of Excellence. Learning From Companies That Put
People First. Nicholas Brealey, London.
Weick, K.E. (1979): The Social Psychology of Organizing. Oxford University Press,
Oxford.
Weick, K.E., Browning, L.D. (1986): "Argument and narration in organizational
communication". Journal of Management Vol. 12, No.2. pp.243-259.
Weick, K.E. (1995): Sensemaking in Organizations. Sage Publications, Thousand
Oaks.
Williamson, O. (1979): "Transaction Cost Economics: The Governance of Contrac-
tual Relations". Journal of Law and Economics 22, pp.233-61.
Williamson, O. (1975): Markets and Hierarchies. The Free Press, New York.
Williamson, O. (1985): The Economic Institutions of Capitalism. The Free Press,
New York.
Wilson, D.D. (1996): Managing Knowledge. Butterworth-Heinemann, Oxford.
Wittgenstein, L. (1989): Philosophische Untersuchungen". Werkausgabe, Band I.
Suhrkamp Verlag, Frankf. a.M.
Wittgenstein, L. (1974): Philosophical Investigations. Blackwell, Oxford.
Woodward, W.H. (1913): Cesare Borgia. A Biography. Chapman and Hall, Ltd.,
London.
Wright, S. (1994): Antropology of Organizations. Routledge, London.

Y

Yates, F. (1994): The Art of Memory. Pimlico, London
Yukl, G. (1994): Leadership in Organizations. Englewood Cliffs, New Jersey.

Z

Zaleznik, A. (1992): "Managers and Leaders: Are They Different?" In: Harvard Busi-
ness Review March-April, pp.126-135.
Zimbalist, A. (1979): Case Studies on the Labor Process. Monthly Review Press,
New York London.
Zukin, S. (1995): Landscapes of Power. From Detroit to Disney World. University
of California, Berkeley.

Index

A

abduction, **194**.
Ackoff, R.L., 57.
aesthetic management, 251f.
anamnēsis, 169-71, 173.
Althoff, G., 198.
anagnōrisis(recognition), 240f, 255f.
anticipation, 192f.
Aristotle, 14, 27, 50, 106, 118, 228, 247.
    -Nicomachean Ethics, 147f., 165f.,
     173f., 185, 190f.
    -Metaphysics, 164f., 172f.
    -De Anima, 129f., 167f.-
    -Art of Rhetoric, 21, 73.
    -Poetics, 239f, 249, 252-60.
Artificial Intelligence, 102.
Augustine, St., 155, 166.

B

Badaracco, J.L.Jr., 111, **228**.
Barker, E., 183.
Barnett, C., 181f.
Baudelaire, C., 156.
Beauty, 21.
Bennis, W., 37.
Blanchot, M., 50.
Bloc, M., 83.
Bravermann, H., 86.
Buber, M., 47.
Bunge, M., 195.
Burrell, G., 13, 32, 105.
Business Ethics, 57f.

C

capitalist production process, 79f.
certainty, 256f.
Chandler, A.D., 93, 94.
chōra, 23, 27, 204-213, 220, 231, 237-38.
chorism, 27, 29, 30, 48.
Chrysippos, 178-188.
circumstance, 220.

Clegg, Palmer, 234.
coach, 117.
co-conductor, 48f.
co-directed, 44f., 47f., 116, 119, 199.
Conger, J.A. 241.
conscience, **67**.
consensus, 50f., 57.
contingency, 10f., 14f., 27, 174, 234, 240.
control, 82f.
Cooper, R., 32.
Cooper, Burrell, 237.
cooperation, 79.
    -and innovation, 87f.
    -formal, 88f.
    -ideal, 96f.
    -indirect, 86, 87, 88f.
    -informal, 88f.
    -organic, 82f.
coordination of work, 83f.
Corporate Symbolism, 99f.
Cressey, Macinnes, 91.
CSCW, 102.
Cusa, Nicolaus of, 70.

D

Davis, Lawrence, 100.
Deleuze, G., 10, 173, 241, 250.
Deleuze, Guattari, 20, 75.
denotation, 19.
Derrida, J., 7, 154, 204, 207.
Descartes, 141.
dialogue, 123f., 145f.
dianoetical virtues, 106.
discipline, 82.
discursive ethics, 133.
division of labour, 80f.
Dixon, 182.
Drucker, P.F., 25-26, 33, 93, 233.
duty, 170f., 198-99.

E

Empowerment, 92.
energeia, 164-65.
Engels, F., 80-84, 87.
enthusiasm, 187-90.
enthymēm, 194f.
epibolē, 175, 193-96.
epiphany, 241.
epistēmē, 106f., 110, 117.
erōs, 194.
ethics, 27f., 170.
ethos, 168, 172, 173.
ēthos, 29, 127, 168, 173, 207.
euboulia, 104, 118-19, 185-87, 237,
eudaimonia, 174.
euphoria, 187-90.
event, 44-45, 73, 206f., **215**, 215-38.
    -embeddedness of, 216.
    -influence on, 217-20.
    -ontology of, 215-226.
    -seminal, 251f.
    -to be inside an, 220f.
    -to be outside an, 220f.
exchange-value, 61f.

F

fate, 10f., 239f., 242.
fellow-feeling, 249.
friendship, 50, 147f.
Foucault, M., 33, 41, 85, 173, 237, 252.
The Fourth, 28-30, 66, 68f., 76, 176,
    189, 198, 199, 237, 257.
Fuglsang, M., 58, 111, 210.
Fukuyama, F., 49, 181.

G

Gagliardi, P., 89.
Gelassenheit, 191.

H

Habermas, J., 54, 136.
Hamel, Pralahad, 193.
Handy, C., 32.
Hegel, G.W.F., 39, 48, 67, 74, 156, 219.
Heidegger, M., 12f., 19-21, 44, 69, 75,

138f., 141, 170, 173, 191, 248.
heimarmenē, 10.
hexis, 14, 106, 163f., 168, 172-77, 181,
hodegēt, 75f., 197.
Hosking, Corley, 226.
HRM, 62f.
Humanism, 12.
hypomonē, 190-91.

I

inscription, 17.
innovation, 86f., 93f.
intuition, 193f.
invention, 88, 89.
invocation, 104.
irony, 150f., 156f.

J

Janis, I., 89.
Japan, 97f., 235.

K

kairologic, 75f., 233f.
kairology, **233**, 232-38,
kairos, 94, 104, 150, 210, 216f., 227-38,
    241.
Kant, I., 45, 68, 90, 140f., 171, 183.
kategēt, 76f.
Kanter, R.M., 90, 95, 100f.
kathēkon, 170, 198-99.
katorthōma, 171, 198-99.
Katz, R.L., 182.
Kierkegaard, S., 15, 154, 227, 240.
knowledge, 106f.
knowledge management, 107f.
koinē aisthēsis, 234.

L

Langefors, B., 47.
language of the heart, 55, 234.
leader,
    -the good, 36f.
    -ideal type of, 36f., 37f., 44f., 48f.,
    95, 103f., 116.
leadership, 35f., 71.

leading, the concept of, 71f.
learning, 169-172.
Lévinas, E., 69.
Lipps, H., 14, 138, 140.
Ljungstrøm, A.C., 50.
Luhmann, N., 140.

M

MacIntyre, A., 165.
MacPherson, C.B., 84.
magic, 52.
maieutic, **110**, 119, 169, 170, 196-98.
management, 6f., 13f.
   -ideal type of, 33, 37f., 39f., 95, 96, 103f.
   -of place, 203f.
   -of space, 203f.
   -of time, 216f.
   -phenomenon of, 34f.
   -science of, 6f.
Management Philosophy, 3-8, 25, 36, 106, 109f., 116, 159, 169, 179f., 189, 203, 209.
managerial predicament, 52f.
manufacture, 80, 85.
Margalit, A., 87.
Marx, K., 61f., 63f., 80f., 81-84, 87, 89, 92.
memory, 247-60.
   -theatre of, 255f.
mentor, 117.
Merleau-Ponty, M., 102, 138, 140, 242.
metalogue, 146f.
metaphor, 20f., 27.
Micklethwait, Wooldridge, 4, 32, 111, 188-89.
mid-level manager, 99f.
mimēsis, 247f., 252f., 255.
Mintzberg, H., 34, 99.
moment, 74, 227-38.
mood, 73f.
Monthoux, P.G. de, 244.
Morgan, G., 13.
movement, 71f.
Musil, R., 186.

mutual place, 204f.
Münchhausen trilemma, 27.
myth, 239f., 247-60.

N

negative theology, 154f.
negotiation, 241f.
Nehamas, A., 177.
network, 110f.
network-ing, 58f., 210.
Newmann, J.H., 193.
Nietzsche, F., 12, 17, 128, 240, 252.
Nohria, Eccles, 111.
normativity,
   -hidden, 7.
   -radical, 5f., 27f., 29, 36, 48, 66, 68f., 109f., 170f., 173, 179, 189, 203.
Nymark, S., 252.

O

off-scription, 18f.
Ohmae, K., 235.
operations research, 57.
orexis, 164f., 167f.
organizational learning, 100.
The Other, 69f.
out-scription, 17f.

P

paideia, 169.
Pascal, B., 193.
passion, 50, 55, 115, 158, 166, 230.
pathos, 73f., 127f., 158, 166, 171, 194, 208.
Peirce, C.S., 194f.
Peters, Watermann, 33, 101, 251.
Phenomenology, 9f.
phenomenological paradigm, 9f.
phronēsis, 118, 163f., 172f., 174-75.
Pirenne, H., 179.
Plato, 14, 27, 28, 29, 31, 39, 69, 94, 106, 118, 148f., 168, 169, 187.
   -Phaedo, 151f., 169f.
   -Theatetus, 197.
   -Phaedrus, 21-23, 29, 150f., 169f., 187.

-Protagoras, 185.
-Cratylus, 14, 130, 140f., 154.
-Parmenides, 69, 228f.
-Sophist, 209.
-Timaeus, 20f., 22, 27f., 204-10.
Pohlenz, 192.
poiēsis, 188.
post-modern phenomenology, 12.
practical reflectivity, 172, 174.
praxis, 163-68.
proairesis, 165f.
prolēpsis, 118, 175, 192-93.

Q

Quine, W. van O., 42.

R

Radical Phenomenology, 13f.
recognition, 39, 49.
re-engineering, 99f.
repetition, 240f., 247f.
representation, 19.
respect, 50.
Ricoeur, P., 19, 50, 165, 168.

S

saga, 247-250.
Sartre, J.-P., 242.
Schein, E., 88.
Schopenhauer, A., 45.
scientific thinking, principles of, 11.
selfcessity, 173.
self-leadership, 199.
self-management, 90, 191.
Seneca, 170.
sincerity, 49f.
Smith, A. 80.
social place, 207f.
Spinoza, B. de, 193.
Sraffa, P., 11.
stakeholder-model, 57f.
Stogdill's Handbook of Leadership, 103.
Stoicism, 170f., 178, 188, 198, 204.
subcontract, 58f., 111f.

subcontracting, 58f., 80f., 110f., 115f.
Symbolic Management, 42.
symptomatic, 128f.
synkinaesthesia, 20.

T

tacit knowledge, 91.
Tampoe, M. 108.
taylorism, 42, 84, 86.
technology of knowledge, 106f.
theatre, 239-250.
The Third,
timing, 216f., 221.
TQM, 42, 62, 91, 97, 98.
transaction-cost theory, 40f., 59f., 112.
transcendent immanence, 25-27.
Translocutionarity, Principle of, **132**,
      133-45, 151f., 155, 158, 256.
trust, 49f.

V

virtues, 50, 77, 93, 163f., 173, 176f.
      -leader, 93f., 116f., 179f., 181-99.
      -managerial, 93f., 103, 110, 116f.,
      178f., 181-99.
      -social, 49, 181.
      -universal versus professional, 177-
      80.

W

Wedgewood, J., 82-83.
Weick, K.E., 142, 242.
Weick, Browning, 249.
the will, 44f., 149f.
Williamson, O., 40, 59, 107, 112.
Wittgenstein, L., 138, 211, 256.

Y

Yukl, G., 181.

Z

Zenon of Citium, 199.

Druck: Strauss Offsetdruck, Mörlenbach
Verarbeitung: Schäffer, Grünstadt